UNIVERSITY FINANCES

UNIVERSITY FINANCES

Accounting and Budgeting Principles
for Higher Education

DEAN O. SMITH

 Johns Hopkins University Press, Baltimore

© 2019 Johns Hopkins University Press
All rights reserved. Published 2019
Printed in the United States of America on acid-free paper
9 8 7 6 5 4 3 2 1

Johns Hopkins University Press
2715 North Charles Street
Baltimore, Maryland 21218-4363
www.press.jhu.edu

Library of Congress Cataloging-in-Publication Data

Names: Smith, Dean O., 1944– author.
Title: University finances : accounting and budgeting
   principles for higher education / Dean O. Smith.
Description: Baltimore, Maryland : Johns Hopkins
   University Press, 2019. | Includes bibliographical
   references and index.
Identifiers: LCCN 2018018038 | ISBN 9781421427256
   (hardcover : acid-free paper) | ISBN 1421427257
   (hardcover : acid-free paper) | ISBN 9781421427263
   (electronic) | ISBN 1421427265 (electronic)
Subjects: LCSH: Universities and colleges—United
   States—Finance. | Universities and colleges—United
   States—Accounting. | Education, Higher—United
   States—Administration. | Education, Higher—
   Management.
Classification: LCC LB2342 .D553 2019 | DDC
   378.3/8—dc23
LC record available at https://lccn.loc.gov/2018018038

A catalog record for this book is available from the British
Library.

*Special discounts are available for bulk purchases of this
book. For more information, please contact Special Sales at
410-516-6936 or specialsales@press.jhu.edu.*

Johns Hopkins University Press uses environmentally
friendly book materials, including recycled text paper that
is composed of at least 30 percent post-consumer waste,
whenever possible.

CONTENTS

When I was a university executive officer responsible for generating sufficient revenue and managing expenditures to support the university's mission, I wrestled with finances on a daily basis. This entailed regular conversations with university fiscal officers, governing board members, state legislators, auditors, and accountants. Through this on-the-job experience, I developed a profound interest in university finances.

Ex officio, I was usually the one who had to explain the university's financial condition to faculty members, deans, and various other campus constituencies. These explanations were not always easy, especially during times of budgetary stress. Occasionally, I encountered rumors about troves of money horded by the administration. The rumors were partly true; the university did have sizable restricted fund balances. Understandably, frustrated colleagues questioned why these funds could not be used to alleviate financial hardship in the operating budget. As former Stanford University president Donald Kennedy noted, "If we're so rich, why do we feel so poor?" The explanations sometimes involved financial reporting methods that were familiar to professional accountants but were unfamiliar to most college and university faculty and staff members. Or to many others who worked directly or indirectly with colleges and universities. This unfamiliarity was unfortunate because it bred confusion and misunderstanding about the university's financial condition. And that weakened university governance.

To ease this confusion, I decided to write this book, explaining basic accounting procedures, budgets, and financial statements for the extended academic community. My goal has been to clarify topics that I encountered routinely and that often frustrated my colleagues. Throughout, various aspects of university finances are explained in the context of fundamental accounting principles, usually with rigorous, illustrative calculations. This includes explanations of standard financial topics, such as budgets, debt financing, and financial statements. In addition, less ordinary (but certainly important) financial topics are explained in depth, such as methods for calculating fringe benefit rates, refunding bonds, and allocating indirect costs. Some of these explanations are simply unavailable in print or online to anybody but a handful of professional accountants. In that sense, these explanations are a unique resource.

This book is intended to be a reference for faculty members, staff, administrators, governing board members, and anybody else who deals with university finances. The broader audience also includes potential donors, investors in university-issued debt, and state and federal officials overseeing government appropriations, grants, and contracts. To broaden its usefulness, financial statements and related data are presented for both public and private universities. Moreover, financial calculations are presented for both large and small institutions whenever size makes a difference.

Professional accountants who are unfamiliar with institutions of higher education constitute a secondary audience. By presenting fundamental accounting principles in an academic context, it provides a sound introduction to unique aspects of financial management of colleges and universities. As an example, an accounting firm hired to audit a university's financial statements might find this book particularly useful as an introduction to unfamiliar features of academic finances and culture.

For students of higher education, this book could serve as a core textbook for courses and seminar series on higher education finance. It could also serve as a supplementary textbook for introductory courses on higher education administration and management. Furthermore, this book would most probably interest students taking specialized training courses in higher education finance. Indeed, it is ideally suited for workshops on university finances such as those offered periodically by universities and various trade organizations

Pedagogically, each chapter is introduced by one key question about university finances. "Who controls the money?" "How is the money counted?" And so forth. The goal of the chapter is to answer that question in depth. While developing the answer, fundamental accounting principles are introduced and interpreted in an academic context.

Initially, two introductory chapters provide the background necessary to appreciate and understand accounting principles for colleges and universities. The first chapter explains the hierarchy of authority to administer university finances. Special attention focuses on the labyrinthine fiscal structure for spending money based on the segregation of duties. The second chapter introduces the principles and routine practices of accounting. The main objective is to familiarize the reader with basic concepts and terms used by bookkeepers and accountants. Importantly, this is an introduction for newcomers to the topic, written from the perspective of a nonaccountant.

With this background, the following three chapters examine income, expenses, and capital assets. Chapter 3 defines income from an accounting point of reference and then analyzes various sources, such as tuition and fees, state appropriations, federal grants, and endowments. Similarly, chapter 4 defines expenses from an accounting point of reference and then analyzes important categories: salaries and wages, fringe benefits, supplies and services, and scholarships. And in chapter 5, capital assets, such as buildings and major equipment, are discussed. They are expensive, so the main question is: How are they paid for? This leads to a discussion of depreciation and debt financing through bond issues. The chapter concludes with an analysis of the tax implications of using capital assets for activities unrelated to the university's primary mission.

The following two chapters examine the core financial documents, specifically the budget and the financial statements. In chapter 6, budgets and budgetary accounting are introduced, followed by an analysis of budgetary allocation models. Particular attention focuses on revenue-based models, such as responsibility center management. Chapter 7 describes the three main financial statements, the balance sheet, the income statement, and the statement of cash flows, and their accompanying notes. Basic procedures for analyzing and interpreting the financial data in these statements are then presented.

Chapters 8 and 9 address topics related primarily to the university's research mission. Chapter 8 focuses on grants and contracts: what are the federal cost principles, how are they audited, and how does the university get the award money? Also, it explains how federal formula funds are allocated. Then, chapter 9 explains how indirect costs are allocated and reimbursed by the federal government to the university. Standard calculation algorithms as well as simplified procedures for smaller institutions are explained.

The final chapter, chapter 10, looks at institutional strategies for managing finances, with an eye on the potential return on investments and on financial strategies for increasing a university's resources: How does the university stretch its money? Examples include self-insurance, faculty salaries, and indirect cost allocation policies.

Throughout the book, sample calculations illustrate the principles of financial accounting in a university context. Data used in these examples were derived mainly from the published financial reports of the University of Alabama in Huntsville, Montana State University, the University of Wisconsin–Madison, the University of California, Berkeley, The Colorado College, Harvard University, and Stanford University. The format for a fictional private college was adopted from John H. McCarthy et al., *Understanding Financial Statements: A Strategic Guide for Independent College and University Boards*, published by the Association of Governing Boards of Universities and Colleges (1997). The financial data from all of these sources were melded into composite, hypothetical examples for a public and a private university. In this general context, I wish to thank Erin Daly (National Institute of Food and Agriculture), Stacy Lutz Davidson (The Colorado College), and Gloria Greene (University of Alabama in Huntsville) for clarifying various aspects of their institution's financial reports for use in illustrative tables.

Naturally, I wish to thank all of my colleagues who have contributed helpful comments about various aspects of this project. The list of names is long and illustrious. Special thanks go to Kathleen Cutshaw (University of Hawaii), Ray Pinner (University of Alabama in Huntsville), and Yaa-Yin Fong (University of Texas at Arlington) for continually providing guidance on various technical aspects of financial administration. Foremost, I thank Dr. Karlene Hoo (Montana State University), who read preliminary drafts of the manuscript critically and provided invaluable comments along the way. She gave me the extra encouragement needed every now and then.

A	administration
AAU	Association of American Universities
ACH	Automated Clearing House
AHDR	Animal Health and Disease Research
AICPA	American Institute of Certified Public Accountants
ANSF	assignable net square feet
APLU	Association of Public and Land-Grant Universities
AREERA	Agricultural Research, Extension, and Education Reform Act
ASAP	Automated Standard Application for Payments
BP	British Petroleum
CASE	Council for Advancement and Support of Education
CDHP	consumer-directed health plan
CEFA	California Educational Facilities Authority
CFO	chief financial officer
COBRA	Consolidated Omnibus Budget Reconciliation Act
COGR	Council on Government Relations
COP	certificate of participation
CPA	certified public accountant
CUPA-HR	College and University Professional Association for Human Resources
DA	departmental administration
DCE	direct charge equivalent
DFAS	Defense Finance and Accounting Service
DHHS	Department of Health and Human Services
DOD	Department of Defense
DOE	Department of Energy
DSU	Dickenson State University
DUNS	Data Universal Numbering System

EIN	employer identification number
EMMA	Electronic Municipal Market Access
EPSCoR	Experimental Program to Stimulate Competitive Research
ERISA	Employee Retirement Income Security Act
ETOB	every tub on its own bottom
F	Facilities
F&A	facilities and administration
FAC	Federal Audit Clearinghouse
FAF	Financial Accounting Foundation
FAR	Federal Acquisitions Regulation
FARM	Financial Accounting and Reporting Manual for Higher Education
FASB	Financial Accounting Standards Board
FDP	Federal Demonstration Partnership
FFR	Federal Financial Report
FICA	Federal Insurance Contributions Act
FLSA	Fair Labor Standards Act
FSA	flexible spending arrangements
FSR	Financial Status Report
FTE	full-time equivalent
FUTA	Federal Unemployment Tax Act
FV	forward value
FY	fiscal year
G&A	general and administrative
GA	general administration
GAAP	generally accepted accounting principles
GAGAS	generally accepted government auditing standards
GAO	Government Accountability Office
GASB	Governmental Accounting Standards Board
HSA	health savings account
HIPAA	Health Insurance Portability and Accountability Act
HMO	health maintenance organization
HVAC	heating, ventilation, and air conditioning
IBS	institutional base salary
IDeA	Institutional Development Awards
INBRE	IDeA Networks of Biomedical Research Excellence
IRA	individual retirement arrangement
IRS	Internal Revenue Service
JV	journal voucher
MIT	Massachusetts Institute of Technology
MSRB	Municipal Securities Rulemaking Board

MTC	modified total costs
MTDC	modified total direct costs
NACUBO	National Association of College and University Business Officers
NASA	National Aeronautics and Space Administration
NAV	net asset value
NIFA	National Institute for Food and Agriculture
NIH	National Institutes of Health
NoA	Notice of Grant Award
NOW	negotiable order of withdrawal
NPV	net present value
NSF	National Science Foundation
O&M	operations and maintenance
OIA	other institutional activities
OMB	Office of Management and Budget
ONR	Office of Naval Research
PAF	personnel action form
PBU	private business use
PI	principal investigator
PMS	Payment Management System
PV	present value
R&D	research and development
RCM	responsibility center management
REUI	relative energy utilization index
ROI	return on investment
S&W	salaries and wages
SAS	student administration and services
SBIR	Small Business Innovation Research
SEC	Securities and Exchange Commission
SPA	sponsored projects administration
SUTA	state unemployment tax acts
UBIT	unrelated business income tax
UCA	utility cost adjustment
UPMIFA	Uniform Prudent Management of Institutional Funds Act
USDA	United States Department of Agriculture
WAWF	Wide Area Workflow

UNIVERSITY FINANCES

Chapter 1
University Financial Management

The University as a Business

A university is a business. As a business, a university provides goods and services, such as instruction, research, student housing, dining halls, and athletic programs. Like most businesses, it must concern itself with the demand for its goods and services. This requires marketing strategies to price them competitively, identify market niches, develop a brand name, and so forth. And, as a business, a university must bring in money to pay salaries, provide financial aid, buy course supplies, pay for utilities, construct and equip classrooms and laboratories, et cetera. In this latter context, a university must adhere to certain financial standards. For example, because it accepts money from external sources such as donors, foundations, state and federal governments, and investors, a university must provide accurate information about its financial condition: Is it generating sufficient revenue to pay its bills, to repay its debt?

These business activities must conform to a university's fundamental mission of creating and imparting knowledge and to the traditional ethical standards inherent in the academic community. On top of that, the management of these activities may be under intense scrutiny by members of the faculty, who, by their nature and training, often second-guess managerial decisions. Indeed, the conjunction of business and academe can be turbulent at times, especially when budgets are being cut. The turbulence is amplified by misunderstandings among administrators and faculty members of accounting principles, spending restrictions, financial reporting requirements, and the university's overall financial condition.

To calm the turbulent waters, so to speak, this book seeks to shed light on the fundamental principles of university finances. It addresses simple questions like "Who has the money? How is it spent? Why can't I have some of it?" as well as more nuanced questions such as "How are indirect cost rates and federal formula funds calculated?" Throughout, to simplify wording, all institutions of higher education, ranging from community colleges to large research universities, are referred to as "universities." Major differences between private and public institutions are pointed out in context. Furthermore, the term "private" refers to private nonprofit institutions, unless for-profit status is mentioned explicitly. Except for some aspects of financial reporting, most of the accounting principles apply to for-profit as well as nonprofit universities.

Authority to Spend Money

To understand university finances, an important first question requiring an answer is: "Who has the ultimate authority over the institution's financial matters?" That is, who *really* controls how the money is spent? Obviously, not just any employee can spend university money on just anything. Somebody must be in control. Who?

A priori, the answer is simple: *the governing board has the ultimate authority over the institutional finances.*[1] The board's authority is stated clearly in the founding documents of all institutions, whether public or private. Accordingly, the governing board controls the money and determines who can spend it on what.

But this authority is usually delegated to the administration, starting with the chief executive officer—that is, the president, the chancellor, the rector, or whatever title the chief executive officer has. For simplicity, the title "president" will be used here. For example, at Stanford University, this delegation to the president is quite explicit: "[The president] shall be responsible for the management of the University and all its departments, including the operation of the physical plant and the administration of the University's business activities."[2] Importantly, however, the governing board always has the power to rescind or modify the delegation of authority over all aspects of university financing.[3] Except in highly unusual situations, such as pending bankruptcy or fraudulent mismanagement, governing boards do not exercise this ultimate authority. Thus, the president has de facto control over the university's money.

Significantly, the board may place limits on the delegated financial authority. For example, at the University of Hawaii, the president has full authority to execute financial agreements on behalf of the university and may delegate this authority to other university officials. However, there is a caveat: "Should it be determined, in consultation with the board, that a contract or settlement is anticipated to have a significant impact on policies, programs, or operations; or result in potential institutional liability the prior approval of the board shall be required regardless of amount and source of funding." Furthermore, the board's approval is required for any construction contract, consulting agreement, legal settlement, or procurement exceeding, respectively, $5 million, $1 million, $500,000, and $5 million.[4] Limitations like these are not uncommon in academia.

The president, usually with the approval of the governing board, further delegates authority for managing university finances to the chief financial officer (CFO), who has the title "vice president for finance" or something similar. Regardless of the exact title, the CFO is responsible for managing all institutional financial activities. The duties include financial planning, monitoring cash flow, analyzing the university's financial strengths and weaknesses, overseeing the accounting and finance departments, and ensuring that the university's financial reports are accurate and completed on time. The extent of these duties is exemplified by the University of California system: "The CFO division has oversight of financial and capital project management at the campuses, academic medical centers and Lawrence Berkeley National Laboratory. Areas of responsibility include budget analysis and planning, accounting and financial controls, risk management, capital markets financing, capital resource management, strategic sourcing, and external relationships with rating agencies, investment houses, banks, financial auditors and financial regulators."[5] The list is long. Because of the importance of these responsibilities to the overall institutional operations, the CFO often ranks just below the president, along with the provost, in the organizational administrative hierarchy. These reporting relationships are illustrated in a generic organization chart, shown in figure 1.1.

Under the direction of the CFO, the financial administration has four core officers: controller, treasurer, budget officer, and investment officer. Their primary responsibilities are illustrated in figure 1.2. Understandably, the exact titles and job descriptions vary between institutions. But these four officers are present in one manifestation or another. Generally, the *controller* (also called the comptroller) manages the accounting department. In that role, this person is responsible for all transactions, controls within the accounting department, and financial statements and other financial

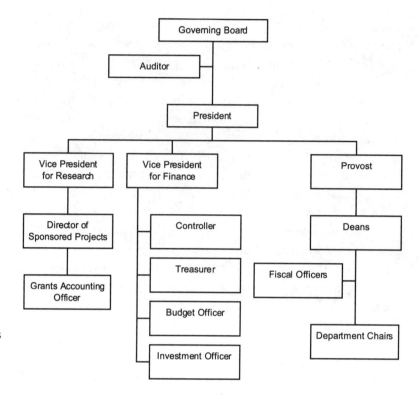

Figure 1.1. Core offices in the financial administration: the overall university

reports. In some institutions, one person may serve a dual role as both the CFO and the controller. The *treasurer* manages the receipt and disbursement of money. As an accounts manager, the treasurer is in charge of collecting money owed to the institution and paying its bills. Accordingly, the treasurer approves procurement requests and cash disbursements. As the title implies, the *budget officer* manages the institution's budget. In conjunction with the provost and other senior administrators, this person prepares the budget and monitors adherence to it. Significantly, at some universities, such as Yale, the provost is considered the chief budget officer who is assisted by the budget officer in the financial administration.[6] The *investment officer* develops and maintains an investment portfolio where the institution's excess cash is invested.

Many organizations also may have a separate internal audit group that reviews the work of the financial administration. Because internal auditors are reporting on the effectiveness and integrity of other units within the organization, they usually report directly to the governing board.

The president, via the CFO, delegates limited financial authority and, therefore responsibility, farther down into the organization's

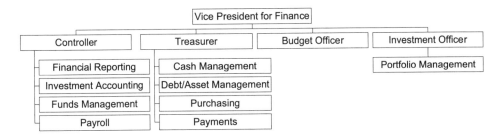

Figure 1.2. Core offices in the financial administration: the vice president for finance

hierarchy to the level of the deans, directors, department chairs, and principal investigators. They oversee university finances for their specific unit or program, such as a college, school, center, institute, department, or research grant, usually with support provided by trained fiscal officers. As an example, Stanford University's decentralized policy states that authority to sign expenditure documents for the purchase of services and materials on a project, task, or award may be delegated by a university official, such as a CFO, and "the University official may authorize the person to whom authority is delegated to further delegate signature authority."[7] Thus, the CFO may delegate authority to a dean, who may further delegate authority to department chairs, directors, and principal investigators, enabling them to expend funds to accomplish their assigned responsibilities without always obtaining higher-level approval. Therefore, these individuals may decide how money is spent in support of their unit or program—what to buy, whom to hire, et cetera. They have general authority to decide how funds in their budgets will be spent.

But that does not necessarily mean that these individuals have the authority to sign purchase orders, pay bills using university money, or make any other financial commitments on behalf of the university. That is, they may have general authority to decide how money is to be spent, but they don't have the authority to approve a specific transaction. That authority to approve transactions is delegated only to trained fiscal officers, whose role is to ensure that any expenditure conforms to institutional policies—including those imposed by granting agencies, donors, state governments, and so forth. For example, at the University of Hawaii, "Vice Presidents and Chancellors and their designees are delegated authority to execute contractual documents for procuring goods, services, and construction in amounts less than $25,000. Such authority may be delegated to fiscal administrators of departmental units under their direction and jurisdiction."[8] Moreover, the authority to submit a purchase order to a vendor may reside in another fiscal officer, and the authority to pay the vendor's invoice may reside in another fiscal officer. The authority to receive delivery of the ordered item may reside in yet another individual.

Commonly, the CFO must approve these delegations of authority to fiscal administrators. In some public universities, a state procurement office must approve the delegations. Private institutions delegate financial authority in much the same way. At the University of Southern California, for example, "only those employees given explicit written authority by the President or his designee (e.g., senior vice presidents) may execute procurement agreements. (Procurement agreements are written contracts that bind the university and a supplier to a purchasing obligation.). . . . Very few individuals have been delegated signature authority."[9] Therefore, although the governing board delegates responsibility to individual university officers to make decisions about how funds in their accounts are to be spent, the specific authority to make the corresponding financial commitments, such as issuing a purchase order, paying an invoice, or signing a contract for services, is most commonly delegated only to very senior administrators and specially trained fiscal officers.

Parenthetically, as noted above, the source of the delegated authority—the governing board, the president, the CFO, and so on—always retains the ultimate responsibility and authority. As stated in *Understanding Authority in Higher Education*, "as a fundamental rule, the governing board may delegate authority, but it always retains the ultimate control. In other words, its principal authority always takes precedence over any delegated authority."[10] Therefore, from a practical perspective, CFOs may delegate signature authority to a fiscal officer, but they retain the authority to overrule a fiscal officer's decision.

Deans and department chairs may hire trained fiscal officers to serve their units. However, the fiscal officers' signing authority and responsibility for overseeing financial transactions derives from the CFO. Consequently, they are de facto agents of the CFO, although there is no formal reporting line in the organization chart (figure 1.1). Because of this relationship, the CFO serves a protective role, shielding fiscal officers from pressures to approve inappropriate purchases. This protection may seem superfluous since neither fiscal officers nor their bosses (such as a department chair) may flout institutional fiscal policies, but it provides a clear reminder of that limitation.[11] Therefore, a chair may decide what to spend department money on, but the fiscal officer controls whether it will be spent. And that depends on whether the expenditure complies with policies and regulations.

Purchasing cards (p-cards) enable department chairs, principal investigators, and other faculty-level employees to commit university money directly without the immediate involvement of a fiscal officer. These individuals may be required to attend training sessions covering institutional fiscal policies before receiving the authority to use a purchasing card. This authority is usually limited to a fairly low dollar value, for example, less than $2,500 per purchase. And it may exclude certain items such as meals, travel expenses, and so forth. Regardless, purchasing card expenditures are not immune from fiscal officer oversight. Ultimately, a fiscal officer reviews the expenditures monthly. The purchaser must reimburse any inappropriate expenditures to the university. Thus, despite their convenience, purchasing cards do not provide a conduit for by-passing the scrutiny of the CFO.

Segregation of Duties

Within the framework of this extensive delegation of financial authority, a frequent question in academic institutions is "Why are so many people involved in making a purchase?" As one frustrated colleague said, "It seems to take an entire village to buy a pencil. Isn't the university just making a simple thing complicated?" With the extensive delegation of financial authority down into the hierarchy, this is a reasonable question to ask.

The answer is that academic institutions, like all businesses, follow the fundamental accounting principle known as "segregation of duties." The goal is to separate the major responsibilities of any transaction to deter fraud. By breaking tasks that may reasonably be completed by a single individual into multiple tasks to be completed by more than one individual, no single person is solely in control, thus reducing the risk of error and fraud. As Yale University's finance department puts it, "Segregation of duties is critical to effective internal control; it reduces the risk of both erroneous and inappropriate actions. In general, the approval function, the accounting/reconciling function, and the asset custody function should be separated among employees. . . . Segregation of duties is a deterrent to fraud because it requires collusion with another person to perpetrate a fraudulent act."[12] Accordingly, Yale stipulates that no single person should have the authority to:

- initiate a transaction
- approve a transaction
- record a transaction

- reconcile account balances
- handle assets
- review reports

This principle is seen routinely at any business establishment: a cash register clerk accepts payment for goods bought, but a second clerk collects and counts the money for deposit in the bank. A third individual, usually at the managerial level, reconciles deposits with account balances. Although one individual, such as the cash register clerk, could perform all three tasks, accepting, depositing, and reconciling payments, the tasks are segregated to three different individuals. No single individual has authority to perform all three tasks. In a university setting, the same principles of cash receipt apply. The person who opens the mail and prepares a listing of checks received should not be the person who makes the deposit or the person who maintains records of the accounts receivable. This segregation of duties is best practice in both business and academic settings. It is akin to the separation of powers in the three branches of government.

The segregation of duties occurs throughout a university's purchasing process. The person who requisitions the purchase of goods or services is not the person who approves the purchase. For example, a faculty member may order supplies, but a fiscal officer must approve the purchase. This approval process may not be clearly visible in an environment of electronic purchasing systems and purchasing cards. But it is there. In electronic purchasing systems, software "edits" prevent inappropriate purchase orders. And fiscal officers routinely examine purchasing card receipts for propriety. Furthermore, the person who approves the purchase of goods or services and, therefore, payment of an invoice should not be the person who signs checks for paying invoices. An "accounts payable" officer in the treasurer's office has that responsibility. With the advent of electronic payment systems, this step, too, may seem "invisible," as software controls match purchase orders with receipts (such as packing slips). But the duties are segregated nonetheless; no single individual has the authority to complete all of the tasks involved in purchasing.

Although it improves security, breaking tasks into separate components reduces efficiency and increases staffing requirements. For that reason, institutions may segregate duties only in the tasks that are most vulnerable to error and fraud or those that exceed a tolerable risk threshold. Money is the common element of those tasks.

When these functions cannot be separated because of staff limitations or organization complexity, a compensating control activity must be in place. According to the University System of Georgia:[13]

> We should always strive for the optimum degree of segregation of duties. However, due to limited staff sizes at some schools, optimum separation of duties cannot be achieved. In those circumstances you should at least strive for an acceptable (minimal) level of segregation of duties which when combined with compensating controls will minimize the impact of control deficiencies and exposure to errors or irregularities. A minimal level of segregation of duties could possibly be achieved by verifying that no one employee performs more than two of the "incompatible duties." For example, an employee might perform the authorization and verification/reconciliation functions but they should not record the transaction or maintain custody of assets. A compensating control would be managerial review.

Compensating control activity usually involves a supervisory review of related business activities such as transactions involving the purchase of goods and the approval of the purchase. And all transactions must be transparent. For example, within a small department with limited staff, the same person who requests a purchase (that is, prepares the requisition) may also approve the requisition and place the order. In that case, the supervisor (department chair) must review all purchases for compliance with relevant rules and regulations. This review by the boss is the compensating control activity. Another example: the person making the requisition and the person approving the purchase both report to the same boss. At least in this situation, the duties are segregated; two individuals are involved, reducing the risk of fraud. But there is still the risk that the boss may intervene and require both individuals to make an improper purchase. Thus, to minimize risk, a higher-level supervisor may review purchase orders issued by the department—at least those above a certain threshold (such as $500). The University System of Georgia provides useful suggestions for compensatory controls in various other situations.[14]

How can fraud occur when duties are not segregated properly? Joseph Wells provides numerous interesting examples in *Fraud Casebook*.[15] In a case involving academia (and fictitious names), Laurence Fairbanks, the assistant vice chancellor for communications at Aesop University, was allowed to make purchases for under $2,500 without external approval. An art lover, sometimes he bought things for himself, such as expensive antiques, art objects, and so forth. He did this by replacing the vendor invoices for these personal items with fake invoices that he created. These fake invoices had items that more closely resembled those that were expected to be purchased by a communications department. He submitted the fake invoices to the accounting department for their records and to the disbursing department for payment. How could he get away with this? The university had not properly segregated related purchasing activities. One person, namely Laurence Fairbanks, was ordering items and receiving the items and the invoices. Thus, he had control over the documents used to account for the purchases and, therefore, was able to substitute fake invoices. Segregation of duties is designed to avert cases like this.

Affiliated Foundations

Although the governing board has full authority over the university's money, it may not have immediate control over monies donated to either the university as a whole or to one of its components. Instead, donations are received and administered by an affiliated nonprofit foundation. Examples include foundations serving the university as a whole, the athletic department or even single sports teams, individual fraternities and sororities, art museums, the alumni association, and so forth. In addition, some foundations administer grant and contract awards from both federal and private sponsors. Affiliation agreements between universities and supporting foundations vary greatly from state to state and from institution to institution. There can be a great deal of control by the university administration, including a majority presence on the foundation board, or there can be a high level of independence for a foundation board to authorize and process transactions. Notably, some universities do not have foundations, preferring to receive gifts directly, while others prefer to receive gifts through a foundation but don't refuse gifts specifically designated to go directly to the university.

Irrespective of their financial arrangements with the university, all of these foundations are separate legal entities, although senior members of the university administration, such as the president or CFO, may serve ex officio on the foundation's governing board. Accordingly, the foundations maintain their own, independent financial records and file their own tax return with the Internal Revenue Service (IRS). Symbolic of this independence, foundations usually have office space off campus.

Despite their legal independence, these affiliated foundations have a fiduciary responsibility to serve only their designated purpose, which is to provide benefit to the university or its component programs. Thus, the foundation cannot enter into unrelated business ventures or support activities unrelated to its primary purpose. Occasionally, the foundation and the university may disagree on what is truly "related," but these disagreements generally resolve themselves amicably.

Because they perform "governmental functions," foundations affiliated with public universities may be subject to state policies applicable to all state agencies. For example, in response to a reporter's request, the Dickenson State University (DSU) Foundation refused to release internal correspondence about its real-estate investments, claiming that the foundation was a private corporation not covered by North Dakota's public-records law. However, North Dakota's attorney general ruled that university foundations must respond to requests to inspect and copy their records, just like the universities they sustain: "The DSU Foundation exists solely to support and aid DSU. Any activities that the DSU Foundation performs on DSU's behalf, such as aiding or supporting DSU, are 'governmental functions' subject to the open records act."[16] Likewise, at least 12 states have declared explicitly that the records of public universities' foundations are open for public inspection. In general, "when journalists seek access to the financial records of university foundations, they usually succeed. While some states protect the names of donors by statute, records reflecting how donors' money is invested and spent are far more likely to be available."[17]

How does a foundation pay for university-related expenses? There is no straightforward global answer to this question because of the variability in affiliation agreements. Typically, however, funds received by a foundation may be spent directly by the foundation. Although university spending guidelines do not apply legally to foundation funds, most foundations adopt guidelines more or less similar to those imposed by the university. Of course, there may be notable exceptions, such as allowable alcohol expenditures. And, as private entities, foundations are not subject to state personnel hiring and procurement guidelines. Freedom from these restrictions is a raison d'être for many university foundations. Alternatively, a foundation may transfer a majority of its funds to the university before they are spent. In these cases, the funds become part of the university's budget, subject to the same rules that apply to expenditures of its other funds. And, in some cases, there may be hybrid arrangements. The University of Hawaii Foundation, for example, cannot legally pay university salaries. So, that money is transferred to the university via the office of sponsored projects. However, the foundation can pay all other operating costs. Although foundation fiscal officers may process these expenditures, to simplify bookkeeping, university fiscal officers also have the authority to manage foundation accounts. Either method works as long as the foundation and the university have a good working relationship. The important thing is to have sound internal control on both sides.

Tax Status

As businesses, both public and nonprofit private universities benefit financially because of favorable tax treatment. Because they are instrumentalities of the state, public universities are exempt from paying federal or state taxes, and they can finance capital assets by issuing tax-exempt bonds. Likewise, nonprofit private universities organized under section 501(c)(3) of the IRS tax code do not have to pay federal income taxes, and they, too, can finance capital assets with tax-exempt bonds. These tax benefits are predicated on the institutions' educational mission, which the federal government considers critical to the wellbeing of a democratic society. Because of their tax exemption, universities are able to use more resources that would otherwise be unavailable to fund their overall academic operations. In contrast, private for-profit universities must pay corporate taxes; they are not exempt.

Although public and private nonprofit colleges and universities are tax-exempt organizations because of their educational mission, they are subject to tax on any income earned from some activity that is not substantially related to this mission.[18] That is, they must pay tax on any unrelated business income. Appropriately, this tax is called the unrelated business income tax. In practice, most universities conduct unrelated business activities of one kind or another that are not part of their educational mission. Examples include:

- alumni use of golf courses, recreation centers, etc.
- sale of routine analytical services to nonuniversity users
- rental of laboratory facilities to nonuniversity users
- sale of advertising space in periodicals such as alumni magazines
- sale of child care services to nonuniversity users
- affinity credit card or long-distance service sales participation
- cafeteria/restaurant service to nonuniversity users
- rental of athletic facilities to local independent school districts

For these and myriad other possible unrelated business activities, the unrelated business income tax applies only to business activities that are carried on regularly and are not sporadic or infrequent. So, activities that occur over a period of only a few weeks are not "regular" for an exempt organization if the activities are of a kind normally conducted by a nonexempt business on a year-round basis. However, year-round activities are regular even if they are conducted only one day a week, and seasonal activities may be regular even though they are conducted only for a short period each year.

Royalties from university intellectual property licensed to private companies that have nothing to do with the university's mission constitute unrelated business income. However, royalties are excluded from unrelated business income tax.[19] That is because the IRS defines royalties as a tax paid to owners of a patent, copyright, or other property right for the use of it or the right to exploit it. This royalty exclusion includes all licensing fees from intellectual property assigned to the university by the inventors. However, the university must play a passive role in the licensing arrangement; if the university plays an active role in the management of the intellectual property, the IRS will not characterize the payment as a royalty excluded from the unrelated business income tax. For example, if the university provides endorsements or services that are important to the success of the arrangement, the IRS views the royalty payment as consideration for services performed and not a royalty.

In general, there are many nuances to the unrelated business income tax code. The IRS provides broad guidelines for a general audience.[20] More explicit and helpful guidelines for universities can be found online, such as the Texas A&M University website, for example.[21]

Summary

Within the university, the governing board has the ultimate authority over all institutional finances. But this authority is usually delegated to the administration, starting with the president (or chancellor). With the approval of the governing board, the president further delegates authority for managing university finances to the chief financial officer, who has the title "vice president for finance" or something similar. The chief financial officer delegates limited financial authority and, therefore responsibility, farther down into the organization's hierarchy to the level of the deans, directors, department chairs, and principal investigators. They oversee university finances for their specific unit or program, such as a college, school, center, institute, department, or research grant. However, the authority to approve transactions is delegated by the chief financial officer only to trained fiscal officers, whose role is to ensure that any expenditure conforms to institutional policies. According to the principle of segregation of duties, accounting tasks that might reasonably be completed by a single individual are broken into multiple tasks to be completed by more than one individual. Thus, no single person is solely in control of a complete transaction. Commonly, universities do not have direct control over all monies donated either to the university as a whole or to one of its components. Instead, donations are received and administered by an affiliated nonprofit foundation. Both public and nonprofit private universities benefit financially because of favorable tax treatment. As instrumentalities of the state, public universities are exempt from paying federal or state taxes, and they can finance capital assets by issuing tax-exempt bonds. Likewise, nonprofit private universities organized under section 501(c)(3) of the IRS tax code do not have to pay federal income taxes, and they, too, can finance capital assets with tax-exempt bonds.

Notes

1. Dean O. Smith, *Understanding Authority in Higher Education* (Lanham, MD: Rowman and Littlefield, 2015), 7–9.

2. Stanford University, "The President Powers and Duties," https://adminguide.stanford.edu/chapter-1/subchapter-2/policy-1-2-1 (accessed December 14, 2015).

3. Smith, *Understanding Authority in Higher Education*, 9–10.

4. University of Hawaii, "Board of Regents Policy," http://hawaii.edu/policy/?action=viewPolicy&policySection=rp&policyChapter=8&policyNumber=201&menuView=open (accessed December 16, 2015).

5. University of California, "Office of the Chief Financial Officer," http://www.ucop.edu/finance-office/index.html (accessed December 10, 2015).

6. Yale University, "§1101.3 Budgetary Oversight," http://policy.yale.edu/policy/1101-guiding-principles-business-and-financial-administration (accessed December 11, 2015).

7. Stanford University, "Delegation of Authority," https://adminguide.stanford.edu/chapter-3/subchapter-2/policy-3-2-1 (accessed February 2, 2016).

8. University of Hawaii, "Delegation of Authority to Execute Contracts Goods, Services, and Construction Less Than $25,000," https://www.hawaii.edu/policy/?action=viewPolicy&policySection=ep&policyChapter=8&policyNumber=107&menuView=open (accessed December 21, 2015).

9. University of Southern California, "Purchasing and Signature Authority," https://policy.usc.edu/purchasing-and-signature-authority/ (accessed December 21, 2015).

10. Smith, *Understanding Authority in Higher Education*, 7.

11. Smith, *Understanding Authority in Higher Education*, 84–85.

12. Yale University, "Segregation of Duties," http://www.yale.edu/auditing /balancing/segregation_duties.html (accessed February 17, 2016).

13. University System of Georgia, "Separation of Duties Matrix," www.busfin .uga.edu/controller/Segregation_of_duties_matrix.xls (accessed February 19, 2016).

14. University System of Georgia, "Separation of Duties Matrix."

15. Joseph T. Wells, *Fraud Casebook: Lessons from the Bad Side of Business* (Hoboken, NJ: John Wiley and Sons, Inc., 2007), 3–15.

16. Wayne Stenehem, North Dakota Attorney General, "Open Records and Meeting Opinion 2014-O-04" (2014), https://attorneygeneral.nd.gov/sites/ag/files /Legal-Opinions/2005-L-05.pdf (accessed May 4, 2017).

17. Student Press Law Center, "It's Foundational: Ruling Reaffirms That How Universities Invest Donors' Money Is the Public's Business," http://www.splc.org /blog/splc/2014/04/its-foundational-ruling-reaffirms-that-how-universities -invest-donors-money-is-the-publics-business (accessed May 4, 2017).

18. Internal Revenue Service, "Publication 598 Tax on Unrelated Business Income of Exempt Organizations" (2017), https://www.irs.gov/pub/irs-pdf/p598 .pdf (accessed March 24, 2017).

19. 26 U.S.C. § 512 (b)(2).

20. Internal Revenue Service, "Publication 598 Tax on Unrelated Business Income of Exempt Organizations."

21. Texas A&M University System, "Unrelated Business Income Tax," https:// www.tamus.edu/business/budgets-and-accounting/tax-services/tax-manual/10 -0-unrelated-business-income-tax/ (accessed March 31, 2017).

Chapter 2
Principles of Accounting

Accounting

To understand university finances, an important question requiring an answer is: "How does the university account for its money?" That is, how does it keep a record of its resources? The answer to this question requires a rudimentary understanding of accounting in a university context. The goal of this chapter is to provide sufficient information to understand university financial reports and, perhaps more important, the financial management vernacular—what the financial officer is talking about. The goal is not to teach the practice of accounting. That kind of detail is available in accounting textbooks and online tutorials.[1]

By definition, accounting refers to "the process or work of keeping financial accounts," and accounts refer to "record[s] or statement[s] of financial expenditure and receipts relating to a particular period or purpose."[2] In everyday jargon, accounting involves keeping the books: how much money was brought in, and how much money was spent. Thus, accounting provides an answer to the question: How much money does the university have?

Within these broad definitions, there are two further distinct categories of "accounting," *management accounting* and *financial accounting*. These two terms are distinguished by the intended audience: internal or external to the institution, respectively. Incidentally, the CFO is primarily responsible for both management and financial accounting functions.

Management Accounting

Stated formally, management accounting refers to the provision of financial data and advice to an organization for use in the development of its activities. In that context, management accounting aids decision making. The intended audience is internal to an organization, such as the governing board, senior-level executive officers, and department heads. Accordingly, management accounting generates reports with information required by administrators and managers to make not only long-term but also short-term and even day-to-day decisions about various aspects of the university. There are no formal guidelines for the content or format of these reports; they contain whatever information the institution requires for effective management. Within a university, these reports typically show the amount of available cash; revenue generated or expected to be generated through tuition and fees, grants, contracts, endowment, and auxiliary services; outstanding obligations; budget balances; reserve amounts; and other data as needed. Often, these reports include analyses of spending trends; spending rates (sometimes called the burn-rate); anticipated investments, expenditures, and revenue; financial modeling based on "what-if" propositions; and other statistics useful for managing the organization. Management accounting reports may document nonmonetary statistics, such as course enrollments, teaching loads, student-to-faculty ratios, and so forth. But, ultimately, these statistics are used to make monetary decisions.

Two major elements of managerial accounting warrant particular attention.

Budget. One of the most important elements of management accounting is the budget. By definition, the budget is "an estimate of income and expenditure for a set period of time."[3] Realistically, a department's budget is the amount of money allotted to it for a specific period of time (usually a year) and guidelines for how it will be spent. Symbolically, the budget means much more than conveyed by this simple definition. It represents in financial terms the institution's plans for "a set period of time," which may be one year (the annual budget) or many years (the long-range budget). In that context, it aligns the institutional strategic plans with expenditures. This alignment helps guide managerial decisions. Because of their importance, budgets are the subject of an entire chapter (chapter 6) in this book.

Cost accounting. Another important element of management accounting is cost accounting. As the term implies, this type of accounting addresses the costs of delivering a service (such as instruction), running an office, making a product, et cetera. In other words, it seeks to answer the question "How much does it cost to do this?"

How much something costs depends on the object of the costs, known as the *cost objective*. This is an important concept because it identifies what the money is spent on. In government accounting terms, "*cost objective* means a function, organizational subdivision, contract, or other work unit for which cost data are desired and for which provision is made to accumulate and measure the cost of processes, products, jobs, capitalized projects, etc."[4] In academic parlance, cost objectives refer to specific university activities such as instruction, sponsored research, public service, or auxiliary enterprises (housing, dining halls, etc.). On a more detailed level, cost objectives may refer to a particular degree program, academic unit, research activity, or responsibility center. In addition, they may refer more specifically to individual sponsored research projects funded by a federal grant or contract. In these examples, expenses are incurred in the performance of these cost objectives.

For each cost objective, the costs are grouped together into so-called *cost pools*. For example, if the cost objective—the focal point of the costs—is a degree program, then the associated costs of operating the degree program (for example, faculty and staff salaries, supplies, utilities, and so forth) become a cost pool. Or, if the cost objective is the library, then its costs (for example, staff, journal subscriptions, book purchases, air conditioning, and building depreciation) become a cost pool. The goal of cost accounting thus becomes a matter of tracing the costs to the institution's cost objectives. Specific aspects of cost accounting will be examined in context in chapters 8 and 9.

Financial Accounting

In contrast to management accounting, financial accounting refers to a field of accounting that treats money as a means of measuring an organization's economic performance. It encompasses the entire system of monitoring money as it flows in and out of an organization as assets and liabilities and as revenues and expenses. Financial accounting generates reports summarizing an organization's finances: the balance sheet, financial activities, and cash flow. Usually, external auditors examine these statements for accuracy and completeness. The intended audience is the governing board and individuals external to the organization, such as legislators and government officials. In the business world, this audience includes current and potential investors.

Financial account records are organized into specific time periods. The basic period, the accounting time period, is the *fiscal year*, often abbreviated as FY. This may be the calendar year or some other one-year period. For example, the federal government's fiscal year is from October 1 through September 30. Many universities' fiscal year is from July 1 through June 30. *Note on terminology:* Fiscal years are denoted by their end date. So, if the fiscal year is the calendar year, FY 2018 runs from January 1, 2018, through December 31, 2018. For the federal government, FY 2018 runs from October 1, 2017, through September 30, 2018.

Within the university community, both managerial and financial accounting reports contain useful information about the institution's finances. However, because the managerial reports are generally forward-looking, they do not necessarily provide a comprehensive, accurate picture of the institution's financial activities. The financial statements produced by financial accounting are based on past, audited data, however. Thus, they generally contain more factual information about the organization's financial activities. Indeed, individuals familiar with financial statements can derive a sound understanding of an institution's financial health. Accordingly, financial statements are the subject of an entire chapter (chapter 7) in this book.

Generally Accepted Accounting Principles

Because financial accounting intends to enable anyone to appraise the institution's current financial position with reasonable accuracy, guidelines have been developed to ensure that the financial reports present a "true and fair view" of the financial affairs. These guidelines, which specify the type and the format of financial information made available to an external audience, are known as generally accepted accounting principles (GAAP).

GAAP is a common set of accounting principles, standards, and procedures that organizations (including private companies) use to compile their financial statements. These principles are a combination of authoritative standards set by policy boards and commonly accepted ways in the profession of recording and reporting accounting information, covering such things as revenue recognition, balance sheet item classification, and other accounting practices. Auditors look for institutional adherence to GAAP. According to the National Association of College and University Business Officers (NACUBO), "In order for an AICPA [American Institute of Certified Public Accountants] member to express an unqualified (clean) opinion on an entity's financial statements, those financial statements must not contain a departure from GAAP that has a material effect on the statements taken as a whole, unless that member can demonstrate that adherence to GAAP would result in misleading information."[5]

Historically, Congress designated the Securities and Exchange Commission (SEC) to specify GAAP for profit-oriented companies that traded their stock publicly. In 1972, the SEC commissioned a nonprofit group, the Financial Accounting Foundation (FAF), to oversee the development and promulgation of GAAP.[6] A year later, the FAF appointed the Financial Accounting Standards Board (FASB) to set accounting standards for businesses and all nongovernment organizations.[7] Then, in 1979, this responsibility was expanded to include nonprofit institutions, including private universities. Thus, the FASB establishes accounting and financial reporting standards for all private-sector commercial and nonprofit entities. Over the years, the AICPA has built on the standards set by the FASB and interpreted them for the nonprofit sector. Many of those interpretations now have been incorporated into the FASB guidelines. The Governmental Accounting Standards Board (GASB) was created in 1984 by the FAF to establish GAAP for state and local governments and their component units, which include government-controlled organizations such as public colleges and universities.[8] Consequently, the GASB establishes accounting and financial reporting standards for all state and local governmental entities including governmentally controlled nonprofit organizations. *In summary:* The FASB—private universities; the GASB—public universities. Because of their different constituencies, the two different boards sometimes issue different standards.

As a result of these differences, soon after the GASB was established, a potentially divisive issue arose: Which board should set uniform standards for colleges and universities? On the one hand, there are few operational differences between public and private institutions that warrant two different accounting standards. On the other hand, government hospitals and universities differ fundamentally from their nonprofit counterparts because they have different rights, responsibilities, and obligations. For example, they are accountable to the state legislature as well as a governing board of trustees. And then there was the issue of sovereignty. Some private universities claimed that they had little in common with a state university and did not want to fall under the authority of the GASB. Likewise, government officials refused to yield authority to the FASB because of its main concern with the for-profit private sector. Ultimately, in 1989, the FAF, the FASB, and the

GASB agreed to maintain status quo; the FASB has authority over private institutions and the GASB has authority over public institutions.

Fortunately, at least for university faculty members trying to understand their university's financing, in 1999 the GASB modified its guidelines for public universities, allowing them to follow the guidance for "special purpose governments [either] engaged only in business-type activities, engaged only in governmental activities, or engaged in both governmental and business-type activities" in their financial reports.[9] Most chose business-type activities, those that are financed in whole or in part by fees such as tuition charged to external parties (for example, students) for goods or services (for example, instruction). By allowing public universities to follow the guidance for special purpose governments engaged "only in business-type activities," the GASB brought its financial reports more in line with the FASB guidelines for private universities. Although there are still technical differences, the financial reports of public and private universities are now quite similar—but not identical—in format and content.[10] More details about the two accounting boards and the differences in their reporting guidelines are documented in the *Financial Accounting and Reporting Manual for Higher Education* (nicknamed the FARM) published by the NACUBO.[11]

Basic Financial Elements

Several basic elements of financial accounting appear over and over again, often as pairs: assets and liabilities; revenue and expenses; deferred inflows of resources and deferred outflows of resources. Like Yin and Yang, these paired terms may seem to contrast, but, in fact, they complement each other. Their meanings are about the same as in everyday parlance. However, various technicalities in the financial-accounting context warrant attention.

Assets and Liabilities

Simplistically, these two words mean "what you own" and "what you owe," respectively. In the more nuanced accounting lexicon, "an asset is an item of economic value that is expected to yield a benefit to the owning entity in future periods."[12] In the public realm, the GASB's definition is even further nuanced: "an asset is a resource that a government controls at present that can be used to provide services."[13] Noticeably, the GASB emphasizes that an asset is controlled at present.

An asset can be either short-term or long-term. On the one hand, a short-term asset lasts less than one accounting period, which is typically one year. Tuition is an example of a short-term asset. It is spent within a fiscal year. On the other hand, a long-term asset lasts more than one accounting period. Office buildings and machinery are examples of long-term assets.

In the accounting lexicon, "a liability is a legally binding obligation payable to another entity."[14] Liabilities are incurred to pay for the ongoing activities of the university. Again, the GASB rephrases the definition: "A liability is a requirement to give up resources that a government generally cannot avoid."[15] Examples of liabilities are accounts payable, accrued expenses, wages payable, and taxes. These obligations are eventually settled by a university through the transfer of cash or other assets to some other party, such as a vendor or an employee.

Like assets, liabilities can be either short-term or long-term. Liabilities expected to be settled within one year, such as a credit card accounts payable, are short-term; they are called current liabilities. All other liabilities, such as bank loans, are classified as long-term liabilities, and they are usually paid off over multiple accounting periods.

Revenues and Expenses

In colloquial jargon, these terms refer simply to money taken in and money paid out. More formally, revenue is an increase in assets—usually cash—or a decrease in liabilities consequent to the provision of services or products to other individuals. Conversely, expenses represent resources leaving the institution during the fiscal year, usually through a cash payment or promise to pay or by being used up like inventory. Stated differently, revenues are inflows, and expenses are outflows of resources within a fiscal year.

The term "expenditures" also is used in financial accounting. Although closely related, it has a meaning slightly different from "expenses." On the one hand, expenditures represent an outflow of money for the purpose of making various payments; it is a disbursement. On the other hand, expenses may involve a disbursement—but not always. They also may represent the consumption, the "using up," of an asset. For example, payment of cash to purchase a piece of equipment constitutes an expenditure; depreciation of the equipment, which does not involve a disbursement, constitutes an expense. In that sense, expenditures are a logical subset of expenses.

Deferred Inflows and Outflows

In public-university accounting, another complementary pair of terms arises: "deferred inflows of resources" and "deferred outflows of resources."[16] Like revenues and expenses, these deferrals represent flows of resources into and out of the institution. However, as the GASB accentuates, "unlike revenues and expenses, which are inflows and outflows of resources *related to the period in which they occur,* deferrals are *related to future periods.*"[17] For example, if a university receives a grant in FY 2018 and can start spending the money in that year, the grant is recorded as an asset. However, if the money cannot be spent until FY 2019 (a future period), the grant is recorded as a deferred inflow of resources. The GASB specifies only a limited number of items that should be reported as a deferred inflow or outflow, and only a few of them apply to universities. Common deferrals involve pensions, and they will be discussed in context in chapter 3.

Of course, these same deferred inflows and outflows occur in private universities as well. However, they are reported as either assets or liabilities; they are not reported separately. Incidentally, before FY 2015, public universities also reported deferred inflows and outflows as either assets or liabilities. The GASB introduced the terminology changes on the premise that they add greater clarity to the financial reports by indicating when the inflow or outflow occurs.

Accounts

Accounts are another basic element of accounting. Indeed, they are the elementary unit of a financial system. By definition, an account is "a record or statement of financial expenditure and receipts relating to a particular period or purpose."[18] Stated differently, an account is simply a record of all changes to a specific asset or liability. In everyday experience, an individual might have several accounts, such as a checking account, a savings account, and a credit card account. Each of these accounts records information about a specific purpose.

Most institutions group their accounts into five basic account types:

- asset
- liability
- net assets
- revenue
- expense

Within each type, there are many different accounts. For example, asset accounts include accounts receivable, bank accounts, and other accounts representing things owned by the university that have monetary value. Liability accounts include accounts payable, bank loans, credit card accounts, and other accounts representing money owed by the university. And so forth for the other three types.

Because of their myriad activities, universities usually have many accounts. Furthermore, an account may have numerous sub-accounts, depending on the information desired. For example, a university might break down an equipment account into more specific sub-accounts, such as centrifuges, X-ray equipment, microscopes, and so forth, depending on the resolution needed. In addition, every grant and contract from an external sponsor is usually assigned a unique account number. From that perspective, it is easy to comprehend that universities may have a large number of accounts, often numbering in the thousands.

Events that cause a change in the assets, liabilities, or net assets of an account are called transactions. They usually involve money taken in or paid out of the account. To keep track of these transactions, they must be recorded somehow. And that is the responsibility of bookkeepers.

There are also temporary accounts, known as clearing accounts, where transactions are entered for a short time until they are transferred to a permanent account. This may be as simple as entering cash received in a clearing account until the money is verified and deposited in the bank. Or, a clearing account may be used for accounts receivable until the actual payment arrives. Ultimately, clearing account balances must be zero: what comes in must go out. Indeed, standard accounting practices call for "zeroing out" clearing accounts periodically by moving everything to other accounts, leaving a zero balance. Functionally, clearing accounts may be used to segregate duties. For example, one fiscal officer will receive all cash from tuition payments. These deposits are entered as cash received, with the money going to the clearing account. A second fiscal officer then transfers the deposits from the clearing account to a permanent tuition account.

Accounting Basis

The accounting basis refers to the time when revenues, expenses, and their associated assets and liabilities are entered into the account records. Stated differently, the accounting basis refers to the methodology of recognizing (that is, recording) revenues and expenses in the financial records. There are three primary methodologies: cash basis, accrual basis, and modified accrual basis.

Under the *cash basis*, the institution recognizes revenue when cash is received and expenses when bills are paid. Thus, cash accounting is based on the underlying cash inflows or outflows; revenues and expenses are recognized only when cash is received or paid, irrespective of the timing of actual services, sales, or purchases. This is an easy approach to recording transactions and is widely used due to its simplicity. But it can be misleading, for it fails to record revenue for a service rendered if cash payment has not yet been received. Consequently, the cash accounting basis does not comply with GAAP.

Alternatively, under the *accrual basis*, the institution recognizes revenue when it is earned and expenses when they are incurred, whether or not any cash is received or paid. Revenue is often earned before payment is received, and expenses are often incurred in a period different from when the payment is made. In that sense, the accrual basis of accounting provides a better picture of an institution's finances during an accounting period. It reports all of the revenues actually earned during the period and all of the expenses incurred in order to earn the revenues, thus matching revenues and expenses. This conforms to the so-called matching principle: expenses and liabilities should be recorded and reported when the institution incurs them, not when the institution pays them.

FASB guidelines require use of the accrual basis of accounting in university financial management. The GASB requires use of the accrual basis of accounting for public universities opting to report their financial activities as a government agency engaged in business-type activities. Nearly all public universities choose this method for their financial reports. Consequently, both private and public university financial reports adhere to the accrual basis of accounting.

The GASB requires government agencies, but not public universities, to use a third accounting methodology for government funds (but not proprietary funds), the *modified accrual basis*.[19] This is a combination of accrual and cash basis accounting. It differs from the accrual basis mainly in the recognition of revenues. Revenues are recorded when they become "measurable" and "available." In this context, revenues are considered "measurable" if a reasonable estimate of the amount can be provided; they are "available" if they are collectible within the current accounting period or soon enough afterward to be used to pay liabilities of the current period. The requirement that revenues be "available" distinguishes modified accrual revenue recognition from that of the accrual basis. In the modified accrual basis, expenditures are recorded using the full accrual basis. There are no exact specifications for what is allowed under the modified accrual basis since it has developed through common usage; there is no accounting standard that has imposed any rules on its usage.

Technically, under the modified accrual basis of accounting, government funds incur expenditures rather than expenses. Under the full accrual basis, all expenditures are called expenses. Regardless of technical differences in the terms, they both refer to decreases in net financial resources.

FASB guidelines do not permit use of the modified accrual accounting basis. GASB guidelines require use of the modified accrual basis of accounting by governmental agencies if they opt to report their financial activities as a government agency engaged in governmental business. Few public institutions choose this reporting option, as mentioned above. Regardless, some states (such as Texas) require their public universities to report their financial activities to the state controller using the modified accrual basis. In those cases, the universities must prepare two sets of financial reports, one using the accrual basis and the other using the modified accrual basis of accounting.

Like the modified accrual method, the *modified cash basis* also combines elements of the cash and the accrual methods. It uses the accrual basis for long-term balance sheet elements and the cash basis for short-term ones. Because both the cash and the accrual accounting methods have inherent limitations, an organization may use a modified cash method if it presents a more accurate picture of its finances. While the modified cash method may be used for internal purposes, this method does not comply with GAAP, which universities must follow when preparing their financial statements.

Grants and contracts pose special questions. As sources of revenue, they are recorded using the accrual basis. But federal grants are usually on a reimbursement basis. Grant expenditures are paid by the university, and the government reimburses the university. Stated differently, reimbursement of universities for grant expenditures is conditioned on the university incurring qualifying costs. So, when should revenue and expenses be recognized: when the award is received, or when the costs are reimbursed by the granting agency? In a nutshell, grant revenue is recognized only as the university incurs qualifying costs. According to the FASB, grants are a form of contribution and should be accounted in that way: "Conditional promises to give, whether received or made, are recognized when they become unconditional, that is, when the conditions are substantially met."[20] The GASB has a similar statement: "revenues should be recognized when all applicable eligibility requirements are met *and* the resources are available."[21] Thus, if a university receives a $300,000 3-year grant from the federal government for $100,000 per year (covering direct and indirect costs), the university may recognize no more than $100,000 in expenses as they are incurred and revenues as they are reimbursed in that accounting year.

The Accounting Equation

Against this backdrop, the theoretical foundation for all accounting systems will now be introduced: the accounting equation, also called the basic accounting equation. According to this simple equation, an organization's assets equal its liabilities and equity:

assets = liabilities + equity

In this context, the term "equity" refers to the difference between assets and liabilities. But it has slightly different meanings, depending on the nature of the organization. In the for-profit sector, equity means the owner's equity; a positive value represents a profit and a negative value represents a loss. In the nonprofit sector, which does not have owners per se, all of the equity must be reinvested in the institution. Consequently, the term "equity" has a slightly different meaning for universities. In fact, the term "equity" is replaced with two more appropriate terms for private and public universities, "net assets" and "net position," respectively.

To clarify the financial reports of nonprofit institutions, in 1993, the FASB imposed guidelines requiring use of the term "net assets" instead of "equity" in reports intended for external audiences.[22] Thus, for private universities, the accounting equation becomes:

assets = liabilities + net assets

The GASB imposed similar guidelines, changing the term "equity" to "net assets." But, they were modified several years later.[23] In 2012, the GASB added two additional elements to the financial statements of public universities: *deferred inflows of resources* and *deferred outflows of resources* to account for changes in net assets—either consumption or acquisition—that are expected to occur in a future accounting period.[24] The addition of these new elements changed the number of terms but not the nature of the accounting equation. With the new terms added, the GASB version of the accounting equation became:

$$assets + deferred\ outflows = liabilities + deferred\ inflows$$
$$+ (net\ assets + deferred\ outflows)$$

According to the GASB's logic, deferred outflows and inflows technically are not considered to be assets or liabilities because they do not occur in the current accounting period. Therefore, the difference between assets and liabilities no longer equals net assets.

To simplify all of this, the GASB adopted the term "net position" for the difference between assets plus deferred outflows and liabilities plus deferred inflows. Arithmetically, it equals net assets plus deferred outflows. In other words:

$$assets + deferred\ outflows = liabilities + deferred\ inflows$$
$$+ net\ position$$

Accordingly, any reference to net assets in a GASB-formatted financial statement was changed to net position. And that is how it stands today. The basic premise of the accounting equation remains the same for both the FASB and the GASB, but the GASB version has an additional term on each side.

Regardless of how many terms are in the accounting equation, the left-hand side must equal the right-hand side. So, any addition or subtraction to the left-hand side must be accompanied either by an equal subtraction or addition, respectively, on the same side or by an equal addition or subtraction, respectively, on the right-hand side. As this statement implies, the balancing additions and subtractions may be on the same side of the equation. For example, in the FASB format, an increase in assets (for example, inventory) must be accompanied by a corresponding decrease in another asset (for example, cash) on the same side of the equation or by an equal increase in liability, net assets, or a combination of both (for example, accounts payable) on the opposite side of the equation. The equality of the left- and right-hand sides of the accounting equation is the foundation of modern bookkeeping systems and financial reporting.

Double-Entry Accounting

In accordance with the accounting equation, every financial transaction affects at least two different accounts. For example, when a company takes out a loan from a bank, it receives a cash asset from the loan and also creates a liability that it must repay in the future. This single transaction—taking out a loan—affects both asset accounts and liabilities accounts, maintaining the equality of the accounting equation.

To record the two entries resulting from this transaction, standard bookkeeping practices worldwide use what is known as "double-entry accounting," where each transaction entails entries in at least two different accounts, thus maintaining the equality expressed in the accounting equation.

T-Account

As a training tool for visualizing double-entry accounting practice, the bookkeeping profession has adopted a recording method to separate the two entries for a single transaction. It is known as the *T-account* because it resembles the letter T. A T-account formats transactions in two columns, with a heading that displays the name and number of the account. A vertical line separates the two columns, forming the stem of the T, and the heading across the top "crosses" the T. Each transaction will involve at least two T-accounts.

By convention, the left side of the T-account is known as the *debit* side; the right side of the T-account is known as the *credit* side. Thus, making an entry on the left and the right sides is called debiting and crediting the account, respectively. Notably, the T-account format enters only positive numbers. The "plus and minus" aspect of any transaction is preserved in the two-column, debit-credit method. Mathematically, a debit adds to an account, while a credit subtracts from an account. Stated differently, debit entries increase asset or expense accounts and decrease liability, net assets (net position), or revenue accounts. Credits do the opposite: decrease asset and expense accounts and increase liability, net assets, and revenue accounts. Indeed, debits and credits are mirror images of each other. These debit-credit relationships are summarized in table 2.1.

In double-entry accounting, every debit that is recorded must be matched with a credit. Actually, more than two accounts can be used if the transaction is spread among them, just as long as the sum of debits for the transaction equals the sum of credits for it. In other words, total debits and credits must be equal in every accounting transaction. Conceptually, this makes sense, considering that assets are necessarily paid for by liabilities and/or revenue. Therefore, a transaction that increases assets (that is, debits the asset account) also increases liability and revenue (that is, credits the liability or revenue accounts). That is,

transaction debits = transaction credits

Table 2.1. Debit-credit relationships and normal balances for different account types

Debits	Credits
Assets and liabilities	
Increase assets	Decrease assets
Decrease liabilities	Increase liabilities
Decrease net assets	Increase net assets
Revenues and expenses	
Decrease revenues	Increase revenues
Increase expenses	Decrease expenses

Account type	Normal balances
Assets	Debit
Liabilities	Credit
Net assets	Credit
Revenues	Credit
Expenses	Debit

Although debits must equal credits for every transaction, the sum of all debits need not be equal to the sum of all credits for every individual account. Because the debits or credits for a transaction may be spread among several accounts, some accounts may receive more debits (or credits) than others. Indeed, each account will generally have either a debit balance or a credit balance, depending on the account type. The normally occurring account balances are shown in table 2.1 (*lower panel*). Importantly, however, when adding up the total debits and credits for *all* accounts in a fund, the total debits must equal the total credits. Otherwise, there must be some mistake in the bookkeeping.

The principle of double-entry accounting is illustrated in table 2.2 by four T-accounts recording the purchase of supplies and payment of the vendor's invoice. In this example, on August 1, 2016, the university ordered $1,000 in supplies, charging them to its account with the vendor; the "supplies" account (an asset account) was debited $1,000, and the "accounts payable" account (a liability account) was credited $1,000 (*upper panels*). One month later (September 1, 2016), upon receipt of the vendor's invoice, the university paid the invoice for the supplies; the "accounts payable" account (a liability account) was debited $1,000, and the "cash" account (an asset account) was credited $1,000 (*lower panels*). At the end, "supplies" (an asset account) had a debit balance of $1,000, and "cash" (also an asset account) had a credit balance of $1,000. The "accounts payable" credit and debit balances canceled each other.

Table 2.2. T-accounts

Purchase supplies

Supplies				Accounts payable			
Debit		Credit		Debit		Credit	
Date	Amount	Date	Amount	Date	Amount	Date	Amount
8/1/2016	1,000.00					8/1/2016	1,000.00
Balance	1,000.00			Balance			1,000.00

Pay invoice

Accounts payable				Cash			
Debit		Credit		Debit		Credit	
Date	Amount	Date	Amount	Date	Amount	Date	Amount
9/1/2016	1,000.00					9/1/2016	1,000.00
Balance	1,000.00			Balance			1,000.00

Note: Four T-accounts are shown for the purchase of supplies (upper panels) and the payment of the invoice one month later (lower panels).

Technical note on numerical table entries: In the tables, numbers represent US dollars unless some other unit is stated explicitly. Also, the value zero is represented by a blank entry.

Although T-accounts provide a straightforward way of visualizing double-entry accounting for each transaction, modern accounting software sidesteps them when recording transactions through so-called journal entries.

Journal Entries

Journal entries record transactions chronologically in two sequential steps. The first step is a simple list: transactions are recorded sequentially in a journal. Money taken in or paid out is designated by either a debit or a credit, respectively, unlike positive or negative entries of a checking account. Thus, every economic transaction involving an account is recorded chronologically in a journal. These entries, called vouchers, are accompanied by supporting records that note the details of a transaction for record keeping and auditing purposes. Journal vouchers include the names of accounts affected, the date of the transaction, a description of the transaction, signatures of authorizing parties, and other details critical to proper accounting procedures.

Only individuals certified by the CFO, such as fiscal officers, have the authority to make these entries. Because this is the first record of an account transaction, the journal is the so-called book of original entry.

Ledger Posting

At the journal-entry stage, the transaction has not been assigned to a particular account. That assignment occurs when journal entries are transferred—"posted" in bookkeeping terms—into a ledger, which organizes the transactions into the appropriate account. The ledger is known appropriately as the "book of second entry." The journal and the ledger can be visualized as two notebooks, with the transactions arranged according to either the time when they occurred (the journal) or the account to which they apply (the ledger). Most accounting software programs post journal entries to the ledger automatically.

The main ledger, known as the *general ledger*, is the official record of the university's financial transactions. It includes all revenue and expense transactions, as well as balance sheets, for every account. Accordingly, financial accounting reports are derived from information in the general ledger. Some institutions also maintain subsidiary ledgers for specific aspects of the university's operations, such as grants and contracts and auxiliary services (for example, athletics and dining halls). These subsidiary ledgers usually contain more detail than the general ledger but fewer transactions. Importantly, information in these subsidiary ledgers feeds into the general ledger.

If a voucher was entered incorrectly for some reason, it can be adjusted using a journal voucher. For example, a voucher has been entered using account 123. However, it was discovered later that the expense should have used account 456. To make the necessary correction, a journal voucher is entered and posted that reverses the amount posted to account 123 and adds that amount to account 456. Colloquially, journal vouchers, called JVs, refer to these corrective journal entries.

Fund Accounting

A cardinal feature of university accounting is fund accounting, which sorts the university's money into specific pools called funds. To understand fund accounting, it helps first to understand the meaning of the word "fund." As a verb, it means providing money for a particular purpose: "We will fund your project." As a plural noun, it simply means money: "We don't have enough funds for this project." As a singular noun, it refers to a sum of money made available for a particular purpose: "We set up a fund to support graduate-student research in the economics department." The term "fund accounting" derives from this third meaning: "The economics department graduate-student research fund has $3 million available for distribution this year."

The concept of fund accounting comes from the many different sources of money received by the university—donors, government agencies, grants and contracts, and so forth. Each source may stipulate specific restrictions or limitations on the use of its money. Therefore, universities must somehow keep tabs on how revenue from these various sources is managed. They must focus on accountability. Is the money being spent according to the stipulations of donors, foundations, or the federal and state government?

To accomplish this, universities classify their accounts into so-called funds according to the specific stipulations placed on their use by the resource providers. For example, a federal grant to study autism and a gift to support undergraduate study abroad will have very different spending guidelines. Therefore, they are placed in two separate funds. And, within each fund, there will be a series of accounts. According to the GASB, a fund is "a fiscal and accounting entity with a self-balancing set of accounts recording cash and other financial resources, together with all related liabilities and residual equity or balances, and changes therein, which are segregated for the purpose of carrying on specific activities or attaining certain objectives in accordance with special regulations, restrictions or limitations."[25] Restated differently, each fund is a separate accounting entity, with its own revenue, expenditure, transfer, asset, and liability accounts, to ensure compliance with limitations and restrictions placed on the use of its resources. As Stanford University puts it in its Administrative Guide, "The University maintains its accounts in accordance with the principles of fund accounting. Because the University receives funding from a variety of sources, with different types of terms and restrictions, each source must be tracked as a separate accounting entity in a unique fund."[26]

To help with this accounting, income and expenditure transactions are assigned to codes, usually called object codes, as they are recorded in each account within a fund. Generally speaking, an object code is a generic description of the transaction. An object code may be used across many or all funds and accounts, but most accounting systems are capable of restricting the use of an object code by fund or by specific account through a system of programmable internal checks, usually called edits. In this way, the university can establish an automated control system within its financial accounting system to help ensure that restrictions imposed by the source of funds will be carried out. The internal control system of a university will be a complex combination of policies, procedures, automated and manual reports, audits, and so forth. The university accounting system, including accounting manuals and accounting policies, is one component of an internal control system.

An institution may have hundreds or thousands of different funds, depending on its size and complexity. For example, at Harvard University, the endowment alone is composed of more than 12,000 funds; the 2 largest categories of funds support faculty and students, including professorships and financial aid for undergraduates, graduate fellowships, and student life and activities.[27] The University of California, Berkeley, has nearly 22,000 funds. And these two universities are not unique.

Money can be transferred from one fund to another under limited circumstances. For example, a donor lifts restrictions or some milestone is reached that lifts restrictions, allowing the transfer of assets from a restricted to an unrestricted fund. Usually, a fund may go into deficit at any time during a fiscal year, but by the end of the fiscal year, any fund with a deficit must be made whole by transferring money into it from some other appropriate funding source. However, as separate entities, funds cannot be commingled; that is, they cannot be merged.

Following the delegation of financial authority, the individual responsible for managing a particular fund is called the fund owner. This may be a faculty member or principal investigator, a department head, a university officer, or the university as a whole. The owner of the fund has the fiduciary responsibility for prudent management of fund resources, in accordance with any spending restrictions and institutional policies.

Fund Classifications

For accounting and reporting simplicity, most universities classify funds with similar characteristics into so-called fund groups. The fund groups usually encountered in an educational institution are summarized in table 2.3. They are organized as current, noncurrent, and agency funds.

Current Funds

Current funds are used for the ongoing operations during the current fiscal year that are directly related to the university's mission. They are divided into "unrestricted" and "restricted" categories.

Table 2.3. Typical university fund groups

Fund group	Characteristics	Examples of funding sources
Current		
Unrestricted	Current unrestricted funds can be spent in the current operating cycle. No outside person or agency has specified how the funds are to be spent.	Tuition and fees State appropriations for instruction and departmental research F&A cost reimbursement Interest on cash investments Sales of goods and services
Restricted	Current restricted funds can also be spent in the current operating cycle. An outside person or agency has specified how the funds are to be spent.	Gifts for current or continuing use Distributions from the endowment State appropriations for specific purposes Grants and contracts for research
Noncurrent		
Endowment	Endowment funds may not be spent and are invested "in perpetuity."	Endowment principal
Loan	Loan funds are distributed to students.	Gifts and federal funds to provide loans to students
Plant	Plant funds are associated with purchasing and maintaining the university's physical plant and equipment.	State appropriations for buildings and equipment Money borrowed for construction (for example, bond issues)
Agency	Agency funds are held by the university as a fiscal agent for an organization or other entity.	Student organizations Alumni associations Some federal student loans

By definition, current *unrestricted* funds have no restrictions imposed on them by entities outside the university. Often called general funds, they can be used for any legal and reasonable institutional purpose designated by the governing board in carrying out the mission of the institution: instruction, research, and public service. Understandably, from the university's perspective, including the CFO and all faculty members, the most useful money is unrestricted. Salaries, supplies, travel, and most other operational expenses are paid from the general fund. Common sources are tuition and fees, state appropriations, patent-generated revenue, clinical income, and interest earned on various components of the university's budget (such as tuition).

In reality, these funds are not truly free of restrictions, for they are still subject to university and perhaps state spending regulations. For example, alcohol may be bought only in certain circumstances; preferred contract vendors, including travel agencies, must be used; and three bids may be required for purchases exceeding a threshold amount. Moreover, the governing board may specify (designate) the use of some current unrestricted funds for student scholarships. For example, the governing board may designate many of the unrestricted gifts received by the university. However, since these designations are not legal commitments, the university can reverse the designation without legal ramifications.

In contrast, current *restricted* funds have explicit restrictions imposed by an external entity, such as a federal agency or a private donor. They must be spent only for the purpose intended by the outside entity that established the restriction. As a steward of these funds, the university has a legal obligation to abide by fund restrictions. Therefore, it is important for the university to be aware of the restrictions and monitor the funds for appropriate use.

The primary sources of restricted funds are sponsored projects (such as grants and contracts) and gifts that must be spent in support of a funded project. Thus, at the University of Hawaii, all grants and contracts accounts are assigned to a single fund within the fund group "Current Funds Restricted." Each project (grant or contract) is assigned an account number, and the account number has an attribute to identify the sub-fund group—federal or nonfederal funds—for that project account. Likewise, a donor (for example, Smith) may earmark a gift to support a named professorship in cell biology, and it goes into the Smith Professorship fund. In these cases, the money cannot be used for any other purposes.

Noncurrent Funds

Noncurrent funds have a longer timeframe than current funds. Typically, they are not spent in the current fiscal year but may be held for many years. Endowment funds are a good example. They are derived from gifts or bequests with donor-imposed stipulations that the principal must remain inviolate and that only the income may be expended. The expendable endowment income is transferred from the endowment fund to the current fund (usually restricted). In some cases, a donor does not instruct explicitly that it be used as either a current gift or an endowment. At their own discretion, universities can deposit these donations into a fund that functions as an endowment.

Noncurrent *loan* funds include funds administered by the university that are available for loans to students as financial aid, faculty members for housing, and students and employees for emergencies. For example, as discussed in chapter 3, federal Perkins Loans are awarded to the university, which then disburses them to students, who repay the loans to the university. Money is lent, collected, and lent again. Accordingly, loan funds are not reported as revenue or expenses.

Noncurrent *plant* funds are used for the university's capitalized assets. They pay for accumulated costs of capitalized assets such as new buildings or equipment during the timeframe that they are being constructed or acquired. Similarly, they pay for remodeling, renovation, or replacement of fixed assets. These funds are used usually for departmental equipment reserves as well. Plant expenditures also include money used to pay back long-term debt that the university incurred to finance plant facilities. Often this is in the form of bond issues. In that context, bond proceeds must be spent on the project specified in the bond issue. That is, the expenditures must be traceable to specific capital projects. This is known as "specific tracing."

Agency Funds

Agency funds come from nonuniversity sources. The university serves as a custodian of these funds. Accordingly, the funds "flow through" the university, with the sources that provide the funds having the sole discretion over expenditures. Agency funds are not reported as university income and expenditures, as these sources are not considered official units of the university. Many agency funds held by a university are owned by various student clubs and other organizations affiliated with the university. Further examples of agency funds are scholarship funds provided by an organization that retains the right to choose the scholarship recipients, fees charged for meetings to cover incidental costs of the particular event, and federal student loans that are serviced by an outside vendor.

In addition to these basic fund groups, there are several other types of funds that warrant mentioning.

Proprietary funds. In academia, two kinds of proprietary funds are sometimes used: *enterprise funds* and *internal service funds.* Enterprise funds are used to account for any activity that charges a fee to external users for goods or services. User charges are expected to cover operating expenses. These are common for auxiliary services. Internal service funds are used to account for the financing of goods or services provided by one department to other departments on a cost reimbursement basis.

Discretionary funds. Although not a specific fund type, discretionary funds are given to the university for use at the discretion of a president, dean, or other university official. They are generally used to support special departmental needs, as the administrator determines appropriate, within the limits of reasonableness, legality, and university policy. They are not personal funds, so when the administrator vacates the position, the funds fall under the stewardship of the succeeding administrator. These funds may be current-use gifts restricted for use by the specific administrator, or they may be unrestricted gifts that have been internally designated as discretionary by the governing board. Importantly, discretionary funds are usually the only funds that can be used to purchase alcohol.

Revolving funds. This commonly used term refers to funds that are continuously replenished as withdrawals are made. They are intended to be self-supporting, with no institutional support. Generally, they do not have any time limitations. Money comes in, goes out to finance operations, and comes in again. At the University of Hawaii, facilities and administration (F&A) indirect costs reimbursement goes into a revolving fund; expenditures from the fund are continuously replenished by further F&A reimbursement. Similarly, loan funds are typically revolving funds. Other examples include commercial enterprises, student health center, and conference center funds.

Fund Balances

Each fund is characterized by its assets and liabilities. Remember: according to the accounting equation, the arithmetic difference between assets and liabilities is called net assets in nonprofit financial accounting. However, this difference is called the *fund balance* in fund accounting; essentially, it is the bottom line for each fund. *Note:* The only dissimilarity between the terms "net assets" and "fund balance" is the context since they both equal the difference between assets and liabilities.

Thus, in fund accounting, the fundamental equation for accounting is reworded:

assets = liabilities + fund balance

Or, upon algebraic rearrangement,

fund balance = assets − liabilities

A positive fund balance would be "profit" in the business lexicon but is "excess revenues over expenses" in the nonprofit lexicon. Similarly, a negative fund balance would be "loss" in the business lexicon but is "excess expenses over revenues" in the nonprofit lexicon. These wordy terms were chosen to avoid any confusion between for-profit and nonprofit organizations.

A priori, an individual might conclude how much money a university has for discretionary use by adding up the fund balances of all funds. After all, that is how most individuals would probably determine their net discretionary wealth: add up all of the liquid assets (bank account balances, stocks, and so forth) and subtract all of the liabilities (credit card bills, mortgages, car loans, and so forth).

But the sum of all fund balances does not give a true measure of how much discretionary money a university has at its disposal because some of the fund balances are restricted or flow through agency funds. So, in that sense, the fund balance can be quite misleading, for an individual cannot easily tell from the financial documents which funds are restricted and which ones are unrestricted and whether they are being spent properly.

To provide some clarity, according to the GASB, fund balances must be reported in two components—reserved and unreserved.[28] When a fund balance is reserved, it means either that the resources are in a form that cannot be appropriated and spent (such as inventory) or that the resources are legally limited to being used for a particular purpose. For instance, grant monies from the federal government that may be used only for building roads would be reported as a reserved fund balance in the general fund or a broad capital projects fund. Universities also tend to report the nonexpendable portion of their endowment funds—the resources that can be invested but not spent—as a reserved fund balance.

The portion of fund balance that is not reserved is fittingly called an unreserved fund balance. It represents resources that can be used for any purpose of the fund they are reported in. Unreserved fund balances in a debt service fund can be used to repay any outstanding debt. Unreserved fund balances in the general fund can be used for any purpose at all. So, a sleuth looking for "hoarded" money should look first at unreserved fund balances.

But beware: universities may or may not report designations of their unreserved fund balance. Although an unreserved fund balance is not legally limited to any specific purpose, a university may designate some unreserved fund balance to express its intention to use available resources in a particular manner. A designation is not legally binding but does convey an institution's plans for using its available resources. Universities are not obligated to report fund-balance designations.

A cautionary note for public universities: failure to report major internal designations of unrestricted funds can cause trouble. In recent years, several state legislatures reduced state appropriations to universities reporting sizable unrestricted fund balances, on the assumption that the unrestricted funds could be used to offset these reductions. Understandably, the universities responded defensively by emphasizing their various commitments for the use of unrestricted fund balances. For example, the University of California, Merced, issued an explanation that "substantially all of these [unrestricted] net assets have been committed internally to specific programs and to meet a wide range of needs, such as supporting academic programs and services on a multiple-year basis, research initiatives, approved capital projects, funds already committed ('liened') for authorized equipment purchases and services that have not yet been expended by the end of the fiscal year, or other purposes."[29] Likewise, in response to a legislative call for the University of Wisconsin–Madison to tap its unrestricted fund balances to offset severe cuts in the state appropriation, Chancellor Rebecca Blank stated that most of the university's unrestricted fund balances "are already fully committed to approved programs, but just haven't been spent yet, so we have little that can be labeled as true reserves. . . . That means that we cannot continue to fill budget gaps with fund balances, and it means that the university has very few discretionary dollars available to meet needs that might arise on campus this year."[30] To emphasize the point, the university then itemized several intended uses of its unrestricted fund balances. These two examples illustrate the wisdom of reporting more rather than less information about a university's unrestricted fund balances, especially when state budgets are tight.

Encumbrance Accounting

Encumbrance accounting is an important aspect of management accounting in a university setting. By definition, an encumbrance is "a contingent liability, contract, purchase order, payroll commitment, tax payable, or legal penalty that is chargeable to an account. It ceases to be an encumbrance when paid-out or when the actual liability amount is determined and recorded as an expense."[31] Stated differently, an encumbrance is the name given to funds that have been reserved to cover the cost of a purchase or payroll commitment.

When these commitments are made (for example, a purchase requisition is processed), funds are set aside to pay for that transaction when the invoice arrives. Those funds are no longer available for use in other transactions. Accordingly, when the encumbered expenditure is posted in the ledger, the amount of money required to fund the item is set aside and is accounted for as an obligation.

Liquidation refers to the paying of an encumbrance. When the vendor or employee is paid, the encumbrance is reversed—liquidated, in bookkeeping terms—and the funds are recorded as an expense, thus reducing the fund balance. Occasionally, the amount billed differs from the amount encumbered, due to unanticipated changes in price, tax, or freight charges. In those cases, the encumbrance must be corrected to account for the changes.

The purpose of encumbrance accounting is to avoid overspending. Thus, outstanding (unliquidated) encumbrances are always subtracted from the actual fund balance to get a true picture of the funds available for future use. By recording the estimated cost of purchase orders and contracts as encumbrances, managers are aware of the future impact of previous financial decisions. In practice, encumbrance accounting is invaluable for fund management.

Chart of Accounts

To keep track of the myriad accounts and funds, an identifying number is assigned to each transaction as it is entered into the financial system. Information about the transaction is encoded in this number. At minimum, this number encodes basic account and fund information, such as:

- fund group
- function code (encoding the cost objective, such as instruction, research, or public service)
- funding source code
- department
- project indicator (usually a sponsored project identification number)
- account code (asset type)
- budget period

In a large university, these identifiers consist of about 10 or 11 digits, with each digit encoding some aspect of the transaction.

The key to this code is the so-called *chart of accounts*. The chart of accounts is a list of every account and fund in the accounting system along with their identifying numbers. Thus, when entering a

Table 2.4. Examples of accounts and information recorded in a chart of accounts

Account number	Account title
Assets	
101	Cash
112	Accounts receivable
126	Supplies
130	Prepaid insurance
157	Equipment
158	Equipment depreciation
Liabilities	
200	Accounts payable
212	Salaries and wages payable
230	Interest payable
240	Taxes
Net assets	
301	Reserves
Revenues	
400	Tuition
401	Student fees
410	Research grants
420	Endowment income
430	Patent income
Expenses	
501	Salaries and wages
510	Supplies
560	Rent
570	Utilities
576	Telephone
Other	
632	Depreciation
650	Interest

transaction, a fiscal officer can look up the appropriate identifier in the chart of accounts. As the source of financial information that flows through the financial system into the general ledger, the chart of accounts is the organizing framework for all university financial transactions. As the University of Minnesota notes, the code numbers in the chart of accounts are the "*language* of the financial system."[32] They "allow for accurate and consistent communication, structure, and parameters across all financial system users." An example is shown in table 2.4.

Most institutions use a chart of accounts numbering system based on the five account types. Typically, all asset accounts have a prefix of 1 while liability accounts might have a prefix of 2, and so on. The numbering system looks like this, where the "x"s are digits encoding other specific information:

- Assets: 1-xxxxxxxxxx
- Liabilities: 2-xxxxxxxxxx
- Net assets: 3-xxxxxxxxxx
- Revenues: 4-xxxxxxxxxx
- Expenses: 5-xxxxxxxxxx
- Other: 6-xxxxxxxxxx

This numbering system helps bookkeepers and accountants keep track of accounts along with what category they belong to. For instance, if an account's name or description is ambiguous, the bookkeeper can simply look at the prefix to know exactly what type it is. The bookkeeper would be able to tell the difference by the account number. An asset would have the prefix of 1 and an expense would have a prefix of 5. This structure can avoid confusion in the bookkeeping process and ensure the proper account is selected when recording transactions.

The Time Value of Money

As an addendum to the topic of accounting, a fundamental principle of finance should be introduced: the time value of money. If money can earn interest, any amount of money is worth more the sooner it is received. That is, money available at the present time is worth more than the same amount in the future due to its potential capacity to earn interest over time. The interest represents an investment gain that increases with time. In its simplest form,

$$i = P \times r \times t,$$

where interest (i) is the amount earned in one time (t) period (for example, one year) and principal (P) is the original amount invested at a periodic interest rate (r). So, in this simple case, \$100 (P) invested at an annual rate of 5 percent (r) will earn \$5 interest (i) in 1 year (t), \$10 in 2 years, \$15 in 3 years, and so on. After 20 years, this investment would earn \$100 in interest. This simple form assumes that the interest is withdrawn as soon as it is earned. Thus, the principal stays the same throughout the time period.

The investment becomes more lucrative when the interest is added to the principal rather than withdrawn. Consequently, the principal keeps getting larger, and the larger principal will earn more interest in the next year, and so on. The interest is compounded. Algebraically, when interest is compounded, the total interest earned over n years is:

$$i = P \times (1 + r)^n - P$$

Thus, if 5 percent interest is paid once per year (r), after 20 years (n) the $100 investment ($P$) would earn $165.33 in interest ($i$), which is significantly more than the $100 earned when the interest is not compounded. If interest were paid more frequently, the investment would grow even more with time. In this example, if the interest were paid quarterly instead of annually, the total earned after 20 years would be $170.15.

Rearranging the formula, the total amount accumulated, principal plus interest, is:

$$P + i = P \times (1 + r)^n$$

So, after 20 years at 5 percent interest paid annually, the $100 investment would yield $265.33 (principal plus interest). The accumulated principal plus interest ($P + i$) paid over the n years is called the *forward value* (FV) of the investment. Accordingly, in the equation above, $FV = (P + i)$, and in the example, the forward value of the $100 investment is $265.33. Using the data from this example, the effect of compounding is illustrated graphically in figure 2.1.

The current value of the investment is called the *present value* (*PV*), corresponding to the principal, P, at the time of the initial investment. Conceptually, the present value refers most commonly to the amount of money that must be invested now to earn some future amount. Drawing from the example above, how much money should be invested today at 5 percent interest paid annually to accumulate $265.33 (the FV) in 20 years? The answer is $100, the PV. Rewriting the equation in these terms,

$$FV = PV \times (1 + r)^n$$

and rearranging,

$$PV = \frac{FV}{(1 + r)^n}$$

Accountants, by the way, have shortcuts to determine the time required for an investment to double its value via compound interest. The most commonly used is the so-called rule of 72. Simply divide the number 72 by the annual interest rate; the answer is the number of years needed to double the FV at that interest rate. For example, in figure 2.1, the initial principal ($100) plus interest (5 percent annually) doubled in $72/5 = 14.4$ years.

Present value calculations are extremely important in many financial contexts. Indeed, these are the core calculations of bond

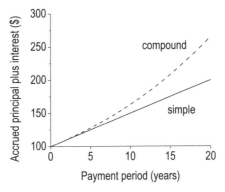

Figure 2.1. Accrued interest plus principal when simple or compound interest is calculated

yields and pension obligations. They answer questions such as "How much money must the university set aside today to meet pension obligations 20 years from now?"

Incidentally, a related concept used to calculate the profitability of a project, such as building a new football stadium, is the *net present value* (*NPV*). This refers to the present value of a project minus the present value of income or costs incurred by the project. Stated differently, NPV is the present value of the cash flows of the project compared to the initial investment. NPV calculations are commonplace tools in the for-profit business world, but they are used much less frequently in a university context.

Summary

Universities keep records of their resources by monitoring assets, liabilities, and money flowing as revenues and expenses. To ensure that these records present a "true and fair view," universities follow guidelines known as GAAP. Simplistically, assets and liabilities refer to "what you own" and "what you owe," respectively, and revenue and expenses refer to "what comes in" and "what goes out," respectively. Records of all changes to a specific asset or liability are organized into an account, the elementary unit of a financial system. The accounting basis refers to when revenues, expenses, and their associated assets and liabilities are entered into the account. Universities use the accrual accounting basis, which means that they record revenue when it is earned and expenses when they are incurred, regardless of whether cash is received or paid. The foundation of all accounting systems is the accounting equation: assets = liabilities + net assets. Accordingly, every financial transaction affects at least two different accounts. Transactions are recorded chronologically in a journal and then transferred into a master ledger that organizes the transactions into the appropriate accounts. Universities receive money from many different sources, and each source may stipulate how the money can be used. To keep tabs on these stipulations, accounts are organized into specific funds; each fund is a separate accounting entity, with its own revenue, expense, asset, and liability accounts, to ensure compliance with restrictions placed on the use of its resources. This is known as fund accounting. For each fund, the fund balance equals the difference between the fund's assets and liabilities. To keep track of the myriad accounts and funds, an identifying number is assigned to each transaction as it is entered into the financial system. These numbers are encoded in a so-called chart of accounts. Invested money increases with time as it earns interest.

Notes

1. For example, "My Accounting Course," http://www.myaccountingcourse.com/ (accessed March 3, 2016).

2. Oxford University Press, "Oxford Dictionaries," http://www.oxforddictionaries.com/?gclid=CMa5maK2p8kCFU1cfgodiXoNoA (accessed November 23, 2015).

3. Oxford University Press, "Oxford Dictionaries."

4. *Federal Acquisition Regulation*, 48 C.F.R. § 9905.502.30.

5. National Association of College and University Business Officers, "Financial Accounting and Reporting Manual for Higher Education" (2016), http://efarm.nacubo.org/farm (accessed February 29, 2016). ¶107.2.

6. Financial Accounting Foundation, "FAF," http://www.accountingfoundation.org/home (accessed January 21, 2016).

7. Financial Accounting Standards Board, "FASB," http://www.fasb.org/home (accessed January 21, 2016).

8. Governmental Accounting Standards Board, "GASB," http://www.gasb.org/ (accessed January 21, 2016).

9. "Statement No. 35: Basic Financial Statements—and Management's Discussion and Analysis—for Public Colleges and Universities: An Amendment of GASB Statement No. 34" (1999), http://www.gasb.org/cs/ContentServer?site=GASB&c=Document_C&pagename=GASB%2FDocument_C%2FGASBDocumentPage&cid=1176160029094 (accessed January 27, 2016); "Statement No. 34: Basic Financial Statements—and Management's Discussion and Analysis—for State and Local Governments" (1999), https://www.google.com/search?q=gasb+statement+34&ie=utf-8&oe=utf-8 (accessed January 27, 2016).

10. Larry Goldstein and Sue Menditto, "GASB and FASB," *Business Officer*, January 2005, http://www.nacubo.org/Business_Officer_Magazine/Magazine_Archives/January_2005/GASB_and_FASB.htm (accessed January 27, 2016); National Center for Education Statistics, "IPEDS Finance Data FASB and GASB—What's the Difference? A Guide for Data Users," https://nces.ed.gov/ipeds/factsheets/fct_ipeds_finance_1.asp (accessed January 27, 2016).

11. National Association of College and University Business Officers, "Financial Accounting and Reporting Manual for Higher Education."

12. Accounting Tools, "Asset," http://www.accountingtools.com/definition -asset (accessed September 15, 2016).

13. Governmental Accounting Standards Board, "The User's Perpsective: A Plain-English Guide to Deferrals," http://gasb.org/cs/ContentServer?c=GASBCo ntent_C&pagename=GASB%2FGASBContent_C%2FUsersArticlePage&cid=11 76163674320 (accessed September 15, 2016).

14. Accounting Tools, "Liability," http://www.accountingtools.com/definition -liability (accessed September 15, 2016).

15. Governmental Accounting Standards Board, "The User's Perpsective: A Plain-English Guide to Deferrals."

16. "Statement No. 68: Accounting and Financial Reporting for Pensions— an Amendment of GASB Statement No. 27," http://www.gasb.org/jsp/GASB/ Pronouncement_C/GASBSummaryPage&cid=1176160219492 (accessed July 20, 2016).

17. "The User's Perpsective: A Plain-English Guide to Deferrals."

18. Oxford University Press, "Oxford Dictionaries."

19. Governmental Accounting Standards Board, "Statement No. 34: Basic Financial Statements—and Management's Discussion and Analysis—for State and Local Governments."

20. Financial Accounting Standards Board, "Statement of Financial Accounting Standards No. 116: Accounting for Contributions Received and Contributions Made," http://www.fasb.org/summary/stsum116.shtml (accessed May 18, 2016).

21. Governmental Accounting Standards Board, "Statement No. 33 of the Governmental Accounting Standards Board: Accounting and Financial Reporting for Nonexchange Transactions," www.gasb.org/st/summary/gstsm33.html (accessed May 18, 2016).

22. Financial Accounting Standards Board, "Statement of Financial Accounting Standards No. 117: Financial Statements of Not-for Profit Organizations" (1993), http://www.fasb.org/summary/stsum117.shtml (accessed February 19, 2016).

23. Governmental Accounting Standards Board, "Statement No. 34: Basic Financial Statements—and Management's Discussion and Analysis—for State and Local Governments."

24. "Statement No. 68: Accounting and Financial Reporting for Pensions—an Amendment of GASB Statement No. 27."

25. GASB Codification section 1300.

26. Stanford University, "Fund Accounting," https://adminguide.stanford.edu /chapter-3/subchapter-1/policy-3-1-2 (accessed January 28, 2016).

27. Harvard University, "Endowment," http://www.harvard.edu/about-harvard /harvard-glance/endowment (accessed February 3, 2016).

28. Governmental Accounting Standards Board, "Fund Balance: It May Not Be What You Think It Is," http://www.gasb.org/cs/ContentServer?pagename=G ASB%2FGASBContent_C%2FUsersArticlePage&cid=1176156737123 (accessed December 28, 2016).

29. University of California, Merced, "Profile of UC Unrestricted Net Assets: Myths and Facts," http://senate.ucmerced.edu/news/profile-uc-unrestricted-net -assets-myths-and-facts (accessed February 22, 2016).

30. Greg Bump, "UW—Madison Tuition Balance Drops by 41 Percent, UW System Reports," University of Wisconsin–Madison, http://news.wisc.edu/uw -madison-tuition-balance-drops-by-41-percent-uw-system-reports/ (accessed February 22, 2016).

31. BusinessDictionary.com, http://www.businessdictionary.com/ (accessed March 17, 2016).

32. University of Minnesota, "Chart of Accounts Manual," http://www.finsys .umn.edu/coa/coa_b_intro.html (accessed March 4, 2016).

Chapter 3
Income

Income Defined

Universities bring in money. Even if they're bankrupt, they bring in money—just not enough of it. Where does this money come from? The answer to that question raises the topic of income.

According to the *Oxford Dictionary*, income is "money received, especially on a regular basis, for work or through investments."[1] In a university setting, instruction constitutes work, so tuition and fees constitute income. Similarly, investment gains (dividends, etc.) generated by an endowment also constitute income. In contrast, borrowed money is not considered income because it is not earned through work or investment activities.

The two sources of income implied in the definition are referred to as "revenue" and "gain." Revenue is income earned through regular business activities; in a university, they comprise primarily teaching and research. Gain refers mainly to investment returns and donations. The sum of all revenue and gain is called total income. When the costs of generating income (for example, faculty and staff salaries) are deducted, the resulting sum is called net income. That is, net income refers to the amount of money left over after paying expenses. In business terms, net income means profit. If any revenue had to be returned for some reason (for example, tuition refunds), the remaining revenue is called net revenue.

Note on terminology: Although revenue and income differ by definition, the two terms often are used synonymously in the accounting lexicon. Indeed, in financial records, revenues usually include income gained from investments and interest.

Sources of Income

Brushing aside definitional pedantry, the original question—
where does the money come from?—may be rephrased: where do
the revenue and gains come from? In reply, they come from seven
specific sources and one miscellaneous "catch all," simply called
other sources:

- revenue
    tuition and fees
    state and local government appropriations, grants, and contracts
    federal grants and contracts
    educational activities
    auxiliary enterprises
- gains
    private gifts and grants
    investment returns
- other sources

The percentage of income from each of these sources for all US
degree-granting institutions of higher education that have received
federal funding is tabulated annually by the National Center for
Education Statistics.[2] Complete sets of data are available for each
individual institution as well as national averages. The average percentages in FY 2015 for all two-year and four-year institutions are
shown in figure 3.1. Clearly, the percentages depend on the university type: public, private nonprofit, or private for-profit. For example,
private for-profit institutions rely on tuition and fees for 90 percent
of their income, whereas private nonprofit and public institutions
rely on tuition and fees for only 35 and 21 percent of their income,
respectively.

Because few public institutions have significant unrestricted income from gifts and endowments to support instruction, some
data sources refer to "total educational revenue": the sum of state
appropriations and net tuition revenue, excluding any tuition revenue used for capital and debt service.[3] It measures the amount of
revenue available to public institutions to support instruction (not
counting medical students). Since total educational revenue does
not include all sources of income, no matter how small, the percentages for state appropriations and tuition and fees go up relative
to comparable data calculated using total income as the denominator (for example, figure 3.1), which will be a larger number. There-

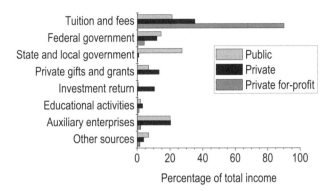

Figure 3.1. Revenue sources, expressed as average percentage of total income for all US degree-granting institutions of higher education for FY 2015

fore, data based on total educational revenue will always yield higher percentages.

Now, the most important sources of income will be looked at in further detail.

Tuition and Fees

Although they are technically separate sources of revenue, tuition and fees generally are reported as a single revenue source in most university financial reports. For accounting purposes, the gross revenue from tuition and required fees equals the published tuition rates plus required fees times the number of full-time students (expressed as full-time equivalents, or FTEs). That is,

gross revenue from tuition and required fees =
   (published tuition rates + required fees) × number
   of FTE students

However, the actual revenue from tuition and fees depends on the amount of scholarship allowances offered by the university. A scholarship allowance is defined by the NACUBO as "the difference between the stated charge for goods and services [such as instruction] provided by the institution and the amount that is billed to the student and/or third parties making payments on behalf of the student."[4] More simply, a scholarship allowance is the difference between the published tuition and required fees (the "sticker price") and the amount actually charged to the student. In essence, it constitutes a grant of financial aid. Most often, scholarship allowances are offered to needy students as financial aid. However, they may also be offered to attract students with particular attributes, such as athletes and under-represented minorities.

The scholarship allowance may be accounted for in two possible ways. On the one hand, if the institution provides students with institutional resources (for example, a check) that they use to pay part or all of their tuition, fees, or other expenses, the full tuition and fees (the gross revenue) are recorded as revenue, and the scholarship allowances are recorded as expenditures. On the other hand, if the institution simply discounts the tuition and fees (that is, reduces the rates), the waived tuition and fees are subtracted directly from the gross revenue that might have been received in the absence of any discount; the scholarship allowance is "forgone revenue," which is not reported as an expenditure. Stated colloquially, tuition discounting occurs when the institution charges a student less than its "sticker price." Either way, the net tuition and fees received by the university is the full (gross) tuition and fees less the scholarship allowance.

The overall discount rate is the ratio of total institutional tuition and fees discounted as grant aid relative to gross tuition and fees revenues at an institution:

$$tuition\ and\ fees\ discount\ rate =$$
$$= \frac{total\ tuition\ and\ fees\ discounted\ as\ grant\ aid}{total\ gross\ tuition\ and\ fees\ revenue}$$
$$= \frac{total\ tuition\ and\ fees\ discounted\ as\ grant\ aid}{(published\ tuition\ price + fees) \times number\ of\ FTE\ students}$$

According to Moody's Investor Service, which surveys about 250 colleges and universities every year, in 2015 the median tuition and fees discount rates for all undergraduate students at private and public colleges and universities were 35.5 percent and 31.3 percent, respectively.[5] The rates are about 5 percent higher for incoming freshmen.[6] These rates tend to increase every year, as do tuition and required fees. In essence, as universities increase the cost of attendance to match increased costs of operation, they must increase financial aid. For some institutions, this can become a potentially ruinous cycle.

Specific attributes of tuition and fees now will be considered separately.

Tuition

At any institution of higher education, tuition constitutes a major source of revenue. For some private institutions, tuition may be the only significant source of operating revenue. For public institutions, it may not be the largest source, but it is certainly an important source. And, for most public universities, its importance is increasing as state support is decreasing.

The key question about tuition is: How much should it be? That is, How much tuition revenue do we need to make ends meet? Ideally, an institution will charge as much tuition as necessary to cover its operating expenses. Add up the expected expenses, subtract the expected nontuition revenue, and charge sufficient tuition to cover the difference. For that to occur, the institution must have full control over its tuition rates. Realistically, however, the extent of this control is influenced by market, political, and social forces that can introduce uncertainty into the tuition-setting process. Indeed, setting tuition rates is a surprisingly complicated process, with little margin for error.[7]

For public universities, market forces may be secondary to political considerations. Public university administrators may propose sizable tuition rate increases to meet financial needs, but state legislatures generally strive to keep tuition low, thus making college affordable to a large number of students. In return for accepting state-mandated low tuition rates, the universities plead for more generous state appropriations, seeking to balance tuition rates and state appropriations. In times of tight budgets, state legislatures may couple reduced state support with increased institutional control over tuition rates.

Social forces also affect the process of setting tuition rates. In general, tuition rates affect accessibility to higher education, with correlative social implications. Thus, senior management may seek input from key stakeholders, such as the faculty, admissions and financial aid counselors, current students, alumni, and interested members of the general public. Ostensibly, the tuition-setting process takes into account multiple viewpoints to create tuition policies that are in line with the unique needs and mission of an institution. Stated idealistically, the goal is to set tuition rates at levels that benefit society. Stated less nobly, the goal is to generate "buy-in."

Regardless of political and social forces, tuition and enrollment obey the law of demand, one of the most fundamental laws of economics: as price goes up, demand goes down. Or, more appropriately for universities: as tuition goes up, enrollment goes down. Charge too much or offer too little financial aid, and the students will go elsewhere. At the community college level, too-high tuition rates may deter students from going to college altogether; at the elite university level, too-high tuition rates may convince students to apply to a less expensive competitor.

This inverse relationship between tuition and enrollment can be expressed in terms of elasticity. In this context, elasticity is the responsiveness of students to an increase in tuition. Arithmetically,

$$tuition\ elasticity = \frac{percent\ change\ in\ enrollment}{percent\ change\ in\ tuition\ rate}$$

An increase in tuition (the denominator) will usually cause a decrease in enrollment (the numerator), so tuition elasticity is usually negative. Sometimes, it is expressed as the absolute value, which is always positive. However, for pedagogical clarity, the negative sign will be retained in this discussion.

Most institutions predict their tuition elasticity by analyzing the impact of past tuition increases on enrollment. Values are usually in the −0.1 to −0.5 range. The average tuition and fee elasticity of total student headcount for all four-year institutions is −0.1072, which is relatively inelastic.[8] For research-intensive institutions, the average value is higher: −0.2357 for in-state students at the 120 public universities with the highest research expenditures. There is always an element of uncertainty when making predictions based on past data because elasticity can be affected by many factors that can change fairly quickly, including general economic conditions, supply and demand, and the school brand name. A public scandal can erode a university's market position quickly. These market forces can be a significant source of uncertainty in setting tuition rates.

Tuition elasticity is illustrated graphically in figure 3.2, which shows a classic demand curve with hypothetical enrollments for different values of tuition elasticity. The easiest way to interpret these curves is to begin at the top-left corner and "slide" downward: the faster the slide, the lower the elasticity. If enrollment does not change when tuition rates increase, the tuition elasticity is zero; tuition is perfectly inelastic. But, more realistically, if enrollment drops as tuition rises, tuition elasticity is negative, becoming more and more elastic as the value decreases (from 0 to −1.0 in this example). Less elasticity (in the 0 to −0.5 range) implies that raising tuition rates has limited impact on the number of students enrolled; more elasticity (in the −0.5 to −1.0 range) implies that raising tuition may have a substantial impact on the number of students enrolled. For example, if the tuition elasticity is −1.0, a 10 percent tuition increase, from $10,000 to $11,000, will result in a 10 percent drop in enrollment (from 11,111 to 10,000 students).

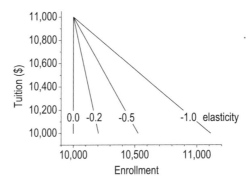

Figure 3.2. Demand curve. Tuition elasticity is given for each curve.

Table 3.1. Tuition increase model

Before tuition increase	
Tuition rate	10,000
Enrollment	10,000
Total tuition	100,000,000
Discount	30.00%
Net tuition	70,000,000
Proposed tuition increase	5.00%
Assumed tuition elasticity	−0.20
After tuition increase	
Tuition rate	10,500
Projected enrollment	9,900
Projected total tuition	103,950,000
Discount	31.50%
Projected net tuition	71,205,750
Projected total tuition increase	1,205,750
Cost savings from reduced enrollment	
Cost per student	2000
Total cost savings	200,000
Projected net increased revenue	1,405,750

Senior administrators often rely on models to analyze the revenue gained from raising tuition rates. The models range in complexity, from simply looking at data in a spreadsheet to sophisticated Monte Carlo simulations that account for factors such as demographic trends (that is, the number of high school students "in the pipeline"), overall economic conditions, and competition from other universities. A skeletal model is illustrated in table 3.1, which examines the impact of a proposed 5 percent tuition increase, assuming −0.20 tuition elasticity. After the tuition increase, enrollment dropped by 100 students ($500 increase in tuition times −0.2). To accommodate increased need for financial aid consequent to the tuition increase, the discount rate was increased by the same amount as the tuition, namely, 5 percent. The net increase in tuition revenue was $1,205,750. But there are further savings due to the reduced enrollment. Assuming that it costs $2,000 per student, the 100-student drop in enrollment saves the institution $200,000. When added to the net tuition increase, the total increased revenue generated by the tuition increase is $1,405,750.

There is a significant shortcoming to this simple model: it assumes that all students pay the same amount of tuition. In reality, this seldom occurs. Part-time students, for example, complicate enrollment projections. To account for variable enrollment in their tuition revenue projections, most universities develop a tuition schedule relating tuition charges and credit hours. From a management perspective, the university has control over this aspect of the tuition-setting process.

There are three standard schedules relating the tuition charged and the number of credits: credit-hour, unlimited, and tuition band.[9] These three schedules are illustrated in figure 3.3 (upper panel), which is based on the 2017–2018 undergraduate tuition rate schedules for Michigan State University, the University of California, Berkeley, and the University of Alabama in Huntsville, respectively.[10] The credit-hour schedule (open circles) is straightforward, charging for each credit. So, the total tuition cost increases for each additional credit; a student taking 18 credits pays twice the tuition charged for a student taking 9 credits. In contrast, the unlimited schedule (filled circles) charges a one-time fixed rate, so students taking 9 and 18 credits pay the same tuition; this schedule, known as the "all you can eat" schedule, is used commonly at private universities. The tuition band schedule (squares) is a hybrid of the credit-hour and unlimited schedules. In this example, the first 9 credits are charged by the credit-hour. The charge for the next 6 credits—up to 15—does not change; there is a plateau, with students taking between 9 and 15 credits all paying the same tuition. More than 15 credits are then charged on the credit-hour basis. The credit-hour and tuition band schedules are used primarily at universities that accommodate students who cannot take a full course load.

Apropos full load: the tuition band schedule implicitly defines a full load as the number of credits lying in the plateau (unlimited) range of the curve. In figure 3.3 (upper panel), the plateau extends from 9 to 15 credits per semester, implying that a full load is 9 to 15 credits per semester and that the university expects students to graduate within 4 to 7 years. If the plateau range, and therefore the

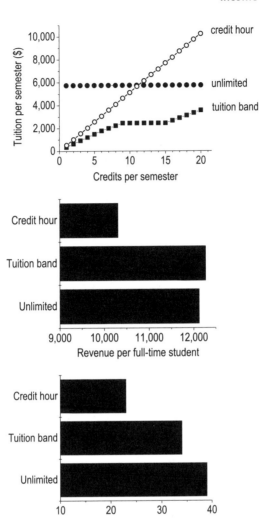

Figure 3.3. Three sample tuition schedules: (*upper panel*): credit hour (open circles), unlimited (filled circles), and tuition band (squares). The corresponding revenue per full-time student (*middle panel*) and four-year graduation rates (*lower panel*) are also shown. Full-time is defined as 15 credits per semester.

implicit full load, extended from 12 to 15 credits, the implication is that the university expects students to graduate within 4 to 5 years. Because of these implications, academic administrators often debate the exact plateau range when considering the tuition band schedule.

The choice of tuition schedule subtly impacts tuition revenue. In their study of 70 public institutions, David Holman et al. found that the revenue per full-time undergraduate student was significantly greater for universities using the tuition-band or unlimited schedules than for those using the credit-hour schedule (figure 3.3, *middle panel*).[11] They attribute this mainly to corresponding differences in the percentage of students taking the full-time load (15 credits) per semester and, therefore, graduating in four years (figure 3.3, *lower panel*). Furthermore, their six-year graduation rates remain comparably lower. So, by inference, the revenue per student does not "catch up" as students graduate over longer time frames.

The number of students enrolled hinges on numerous factors besides tuition rate, such as the number of graduating high school students, admissions selectivity, acceptance yield, retention, and graduation rate. Even the economy influences enrollment: when the economy is bad and jobs are few, enrollment generally increases, and vice versa. Many institutions recruit students actively, offer generous financial aid, and invest in attractive residence halls and student activity centers to boost enrollment and, therefore, increase tuition revenue. Of course, all of these incentives cost money, thus reducing the net tuition intake. Enrollment managers can estimate the "return" on these enrollment incentives, but the estimates always contain an element of uncertainty.

For public universities, the number of out-of-state students also makes a difference since they usually pay higher tuition rates. However, many states limit the number of out-of-state students that can be enrolled, thus putting a cap on this source of additional tuition revenue. In times of financial stress, public universities may ask the state legislature for permission to raise the number of out-of-state students to boost tuition revenue. Legislators may demur, however, if they perceive that out-of-state students will displace in-state students, thus denying them the opportunity to attend the state's tax-supported university.

Once enrolled, the number of credits taken per student depends in part on personal factors, such as the need for a job, family obligations, and so forth. The university has little control over some of these factors. However, the university has some control over academic requirements that can influence credit load. For example, it can require a student to enroll for at least nine credits to receive financial aid or adjust a curriculum that increases or decreases the number of credits needed for graduation. In some cases, accreditation standards may constrain an institution's flexibility to manipulate these requirements. The provost, deans, and faculty senate occasionally debate these issues in the context of tuition revenue.

Some universities allow individual colleges or schools to charge "differential tuition rates," most commonly in professional schools. That is, a university may not use the same model for all undergraduate, graduate, and professional programs. Even at the undergraduate level, some universities charge differential tuition depending on the college or major. The University of Texas at Austin, for example, charges a different tuition rate for each undergraduate college, ranging from $4,957 to $5,696 per semester for full-time students in the colleges of liberal arts and business, respectively.[12] The rationale may be a matter of cost of education or of market forces. On the one hand, for example, medical schools charge much higher tuition than most undergraduate colleges, ostensibly because of the higher costs of medical education. On the other hand, business schools, for example, charge higher tuition because students are willing to pay a premium on the presumption that they will obtain higher-paying jobs after graduation. Notwithstanding the University of Texas, differential tuition per se is less common in undergraduate and graduate programs in traditional liberal arts and sciences; philosophically, universities prefer not to influence most undergraduates' academic choices based on the cost of tuition.

Fees

Student fees constitute a small but significant source of revenue. For students, they can amount to hundreds of dollars per year. Until recently, most universities combined tuition and fees into a single number, "tuition and fees," thus masking the full impact of fees on affordability. However, nowadays, institutions provide information about their required fees separate from tuition via an online "net price calculator" that, according to federal law, each postsecondary institution in the United States participating in Title IV student aid programs (that is, almost all institutions) must post on its website.[13] Most institutions provide a table of other program-specific fees as well on their website.

By nature, fees pay for specific costs. Students pay a fee for a specific activity, and the university uses the fee income to support that specific activity. (This linkage is not a legal requirement; it is an ethical guideline.) Some fees are for extracurricular activities. For example, students are assessed a mandatory student-union fee; the money is then used solely to support student-union activities, which may include mortgage payments for a student-union building, thus benefiting the students. Others are curricular. Some universities charge fees to cover exceptional costs of instruction for specific programs of study. For example, Purdue University assesses a $1,025 fee per semester for students majoring in engineering.[14] The fee income goes directly to the College of Engineering to support activities benefiting the students. Other universities charge a fee for specific courses. For example, students may be assessed a fee when taking a motion-picture filmmaking course; the fees are used to pay for cameras and film-editing equipment, thus benefiting the students taking the course. To state the obvious, it would be unethical to use filmmaking course fees to pay for football uniforms or any other unrelated expense. An equally restrictive but more flexible usage of fees occurs, for example, when prospective students are assessed an application fee; in those cases, the fee income is used to offset the costs of processing the applications, including salaries, supplies, and other admissions office expenses. Overall, by charging fees, universities can cover the costs of specific activities without using tuition revenue.

Despite the philosophical argument for uniform undergraduate tuition rates, course fees make some fields of study more expensive than others. In that way, universities indirectly influence a student's academic choices on the basis of money. The question arises: Why doesn't the university simply include all fees in the overall tuition? The answer, according to the university, is that not all students should be expected to subsidize particularly expensive programs and courses. Why should a history student pay the additional costs of instruction incurred by an engineering student?

Usually, the governing board must approve fees, just as it must approve tuition rates. Because the fees affect affordability, they come under scrutiny by the administration and the board. But fees seldom attract as much public attention as tuition. Thus, "under the radar screen," universities can assess special fees to cover extracurricular or exceptionally high curricular costs. In that sense, this is a convenient revenue source to meet specific needs and to enrich university offerings.

State Financial Support
State Revenue Forecasts

How do states decide the amount of money to provide for higher education? To understand state support for higher education, this critical question should be answered first. The answer depends on the total revenue available for all state agencies, and that amount depends on revenue projections for the next one or more fiscal years. These projections are produced generally by the state budget office or a group composed of experienced economists representing the legislature (House and Senate), the governor, and, perhaps, the academic and private sectors. These groups sometimes are referred to as the "revenue estimating conference."[15]

The state of Hawaii provides a typical example of the forecasting process. In Hawaii, the revenue estimating group is known as the Council on Revenues.[16] It has seven members representing the legislature, the governor's office, academic institutions, and the private sector. Four times a year, the state's Department on Taxation asks each council member to provide a forecast for key economic variables that help determine General Fund tax revenues, such as construction, total personal income, inflation, and visitor arrivals. The department then enters these economic forecasts into econometric models to predict tax revenues over the budget period. The models also take account of things like tax law changes and collection lags. The Tax Department also enters further information on the recent trends in tax collections and any issues of tax administration that might affect General Fund tax revenues, such as unusual delinquent tax collections or lags in processing of returns and payments.

When the council meets, it evaluates the results of the econometric models and examines recent trends in tax collections. The council also considers other economic or political changes that might materially affect tax collections. The members then agree on their official forecasts for growth rates of overall General Fund tax revenues. The Tax Department takes the official growth forecasts and adjusts the variables in one of its econometric models to produce forecasts for the individual tax types that are consistent with the council's overall forecasts.

In addition, the council prepares estimates of the state's total personal income twice a year. These estimates, which predict tax revenue, are considered by the governor in preparing the state budget and controlling expenditures. And they are considered by the legislature when enacting revenue measures. The quarterly revenue reports provide feedback that can be used to adjust spending during the fiscal year if necessary.

Appropriations Process

As a matter of law, public money cannot be spent unless it has been appropriated by a legislature. This applies to all money, including tuition revenue and federal indirect cost reimbursements generated by universities as state agencies. Although public universities may collect this money, they cannot spend it without legislative appropriations. And they cannot spend any amounts generated in excess of the appropriation.

To understand the legislative appropriation process, it helps to review briefly a generic state appropriation process, based on the federal appropriation process.[17] It starts when the governor presents next year's (or two years' in states with biennial budgets) proposed executive state budget based on the revenue projections to the legislature at the beginning of its session. (The legislature's and the judiciary's budgets are not part of the executive budget and are submitted separately to the legislature.) The executive budget contains detailed funding proposals for each state agency, including public universities, and thus reflects their spending priorities. Importantly, the aggregate budgets of the executive, legislative, and judicial branches may not exceed an expenditure ceiling usually determined by adjusting the immediate prior fiscal year expenditure ceiling by the projected "state growth" in revenue for the next fiscal year. In Hawaii, for example, the state growth is established by averaging the annual percentage change in total state personal income for the three calendar years immediately preceding the fiscal year.

Both the state House of Representatives and the state Senate refer the governor's budget to two of their committees: the budget committee and the appropriations committee. Separately, the House and Senate budget committees analyze the governor's budget and, after consultative hearings with representatives of each state agency, arrive at a concurrent resolution that determines the amount of money needed to implement its proposed programs. This amount may not equal the revenue projections exactly, but it seldom differs by a significant amount. Based on their analyses, the budget committees provide each appropriations committee with a budget that covers mandatory entitlement allocations (for example, Medicaid) and discretionary allocations (for example, public universities). The discretionary programs include those requested in the governor's budget.

Meanwhile, the House and Senate appropriations committees refer the governor's budget to their subcommittees responsible for the various state activities, such as transportation, higher education, corrections, and others. Each subcommittee also is given its share of the overall appropriations committee's budget for the next fiscal year (or years). Within their budgetary constraints, the subcommittees draft the appropriations bills and report them to the full appropriations committees. Typically, senior university administrators testify before these committees, defending and answering questions about their request. The subcommittees are not obligated to honor any aspect of the governor's budget, although they usually pay close attention to it when drafting the final appropriations bill. At this critical stage, legislators' special interest items may be inserted into the bill, with or without additional funding for them—funded versus unfunded mandates, respectively. Most large universities have a full-time staff member and perhaps a professional lobbyist assigned to represent the universities' interest at this stage. In the final step, the executive branch—the governor's office—allocates the legislatively appropriated funds to the individual agencies, including public universities.

Individual states, of course, have variations on this process. Commonly, for example, the legislature has a single, nonpartisan legislative finance committee that prepares the revenue guidelines. Also commonly, the House of Representatives takes the lead, and after it has prepared a first-draft appropriations bill, it passes the bill over (the "cross-over") to the Senate for its consideration. The bill goes back and forth for up to three readings by each body before a consensus appropriations bill is reached. Regardless of these and other distinctions, the various state appropriations procedures follow more or less this basic protocol.

To control expenditure rates, some states require their agencies to prepare quarterly expenditure plans for their allocated funds. Accordingly, allocations by the governor's office are usually made in quarterly installments. To ensure solvency, the governor has the authority to withhold money from allocations if the expenditure rate is projected to exceed the state's revenues and unencumbered cash balances. This might occur, for example, if the economy takes an unanticipated downturn and tax revenues fail to meet projections. In those situations, universities must cope with mid-year adjustments to state support, through hiring freezes and other cost-cutting measures.

Most appropriations are available for obligation for a limited period of time. For general-purpose operational appropriations, this is usually the fiscal year. Capital appropriations and rare operational appropriations may extend for more than one year, but this longer period of availability must be stated explicitly in the appropriation. If appropriations are not obligated during the period of availability the funds expire. That is, they lapse, reverting to the state treasury. Notably, "private funds," such as endowment and interest income, do not lapse at the end of a fiscal year; they carry forward. Consequently, universities strive to spend all state-appropriated funds before the end of the fiscal year when they lapse. This usually involves transferring expenses charged to private funds to state funds as the fiscal year comes to a close. Caveat: some universities may have internal policies preventing the carry-forward of private funds, returning them to the university treasury if they're not obligated by the end of the fiscal year. Because this is an internal policy, the administration retains the authority to make exceptions, allowing some funds to carry forward.

Appropriations to Universities

States appropriate funding to universities through several mechanisms: general-purpose appropriations, research appropriations, and financial aid grants. This is illustrated in figure 3.4, which is based on 2013 data compiled by the Pew Charitable Trust.[18] The general-purpose appropriations, which constitute about 70 percent of all state support, supplement tuition and fees revenue to pay for university operations; in most contexts, the term "state appropriations" usually refers to the general-purpose appropriations. Research appropriations broadly encompass grants and contracts for a variety of projects, such as studies of weed control, highway traffic patterns, and other topics of specific interest to the state. Overall in the United States, the aggregate state spending on higher education was $72.7 billion in 2013.

Ideally, these appropriations come without restrictions on their use. For universities established in the state constitution (constitutional universities), there are necessarily few, if any, legislative provisions on how the money is spent. The University of Michigan is the enviable example of a constitutional university. However, for universities established by legislative statute (statutory universities), there may be legislative provisions on how the money is spent. Some state legislatures minimize provisions by appropriating funds as a "lump sum" for the university's governing board to administer; this limits legislative intrusion. But in less permissive states, legislatures appropriate by line-items, which can significantly dilute the governing board's authority over how to spend the money. The rationale for such tight legislative control over university appropriations re-

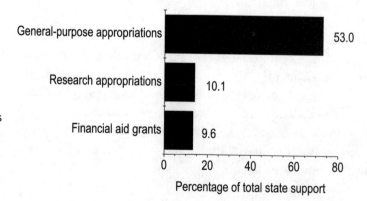

Figure 3.4. Mechanisms of state support to higher education, for FY 2013. The amounts, in $ billions, are shown to the right of each bar.

sides primarily in the legislature's commitment to public participation in the management of taxpayer money. "It's the people's money; why shouldn't their elected representatives have a say in how it's spent?"

As a quid pro quo for state financial support, public universities keep tuition rates low, certainly lower than the amount required to sustain operations. Historically, state appropriations have exceeded tuition and fees as a revenue source. This is illustrated in figure 3.5, which shows the percentages of total revenue derived from state appropriations and from tuition and fees for all two-year and four-year degree-granting institutions of higher education in the United States. Although the percentage of state support for all institutions has declined since 2008, it still exceeds tuition and fees as a revenue source for two-year institutions (figure 3.5, *upper panel*). However, since 2011, the percentage of total revenue from state appropriations has dropped below the percentage of revenue from tuition and fees for four-year institutions (figure 3.5, *middle panel*); in 2015, the corresponding values were 17.6 and 22.1 percent, respectively. And this is manifest in the percentages for all institutions (two- and four-year combined; figure 3.5, *lower panel*). For some large public research universities, the percentage of total revenue from state appropriations has dropped to 10 percent or less. At the University of Michigan, for example, the percentages of total revenue for operating activities (excluding revenues from the health system) from state appropriations and net tuition and fees in 2015 were 10 and 32 percent, respectively.[19]

Why has state support for universities declined? Nationally, state appropriations for higher education rank third behind elementary and secondary (K-12) education—that is, the public schools—and Medicaid, as shown in figure 3.6 (*left panel*).[20] Higher education consumes between 1 and 25 percent of a state's total expenditures; the average is 11 percent (figure 3.6, *right panel*).[21] At first thought, low appropriation percentages might reflect correspondingly low commitments to public higher education. Of course, that may be true. But they may also reflect particularly expensive state-specific mandatory commitments to elementary and secondary school education, Medicaid, or pension obligations. Because higher education is a discretionary budget item, it is secondary to these mandatory programs. Moreover, the actual amount provided by the state depends on the overall state economy. In good times, states usually provide more; in bad times, they provide less. Needless to say, this variability complicates long-range planning.

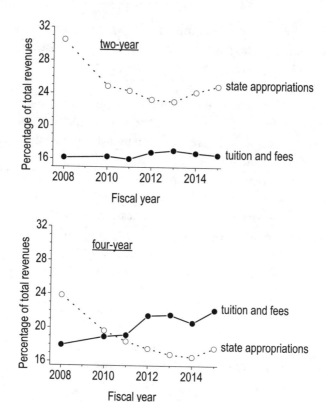

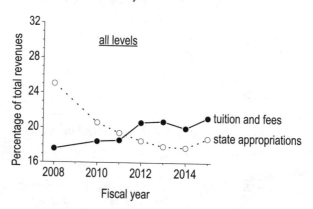

Figure 3.5. Percentages of total tuition and fees and of total state appropriations relative to total revenues for two-year (*upper panel*), four-year (*middle panel*), and all levels (*lower panel*) of public degree-granting institutions in the United States

Incidentally, most states appropriate money to in-state private universities as well as public universities. The rationale is to contribute to the private universities' costs of educating in-state students. On the one hand, the money may be given directly to the university, usually on a capitation basis, and the university records it as operating revenue. For example, the state of Pennsylvania appropriates about $600 million per year to four nominally private universities, the University of Pittsburgh, Pennsylvania State University, Temple University, and Lincoln University, which use the money to lower the

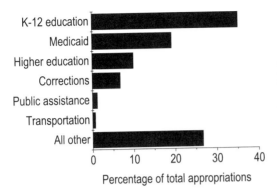
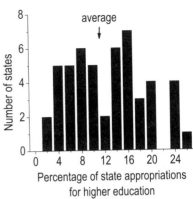

Figure 3.6. Major categories of total state general fund appropriations (*left panel*) and percentage of total state appropriations for higher education (*right panel*) for FY 2014

cost of tuition for in-state students. At the University of Pittsburgh, this state support enables in-state students to pay about $11,500 less tuition than out-of-state students.

On the other hand, the state money may be given as grants to in-state students attending a private in-state university. One example is the State of New York Scholarships for Academic Excellence program, which awards grants of up to $1,500 to students enrolled in New York universities, public or private.[22] Another example is the state of Wisconsin need-based tuition grants program that equalizes the net tuition paid by in-state students at the University of Wisconsin–Madison and the more expensive private universities in the state.[23] As shown by the example in table 3.2, the award amount equals the difference in tuition between Lawrence University (private) and the University of Wisconsin–Madison (public) minus the imputed family contribution.[24] Notably, the tuition difference ($34,056) is 62.49 percent of the total cost of education at Lawrence University. If the standard financial aid needs analysis determines that the family contribution to the total cost of education should be $10,000, then the family is expected to contribute 62.49 percent of that amount (that is, $6,249) toward the state tuition grant if the student were to attend Lawrence University. Therefore, the net state grant to the Lawrence student would be $27,807 ($34,056 − $6,249). In comparison, the total state appropriation per student to the University of Wisconsin–Madison is $14,768.

Federal Government
Student Financial Aid

Like state governments, the federal government provides revenue for higher education with the goal of increasing access for students and fostering research. In 2013, the total federal support for higher education was $75.7 billion, roughly the same as total state support

Table 3.2. Example of state appropriations to in-state private universities in Wisconsin

Tuition	
Lawrence University (private)	44,544
University of Wisconsin–Madison (public)	10,488
Tuition difference	34,056
Lawrence University total cost of education	54,498
Ratio of tuition difference to total cost of education	0.6249
Family contribution	
University of Wisconsin–Madison	10,000
Imputed, Lawrence University	6,249
State grant to Lawrence student	27,807
Comparison with appropriations to the University of Wisconsin–Madison	
State appropriation (general program plus specific purpose)	436,200,000
Undergraduate enrollment	29,536
State appropriation/undergraduate student	14,768

Note: All data are for the 2016–2017 academic year.

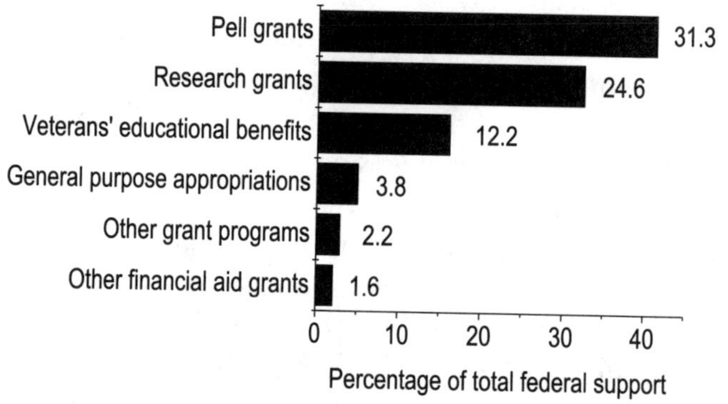

Figure 3.7. Mechanisms of federal support to higher education, for FY 2013. The amounts, in $ billions, are shown to the right of each bar.

($72.7 billion). However, the state and federal government support higher education in different ways: states typically fund the general operations of public institutions, with smaller amounts appropriated for research and financial aid (figure 3.4), while the federal government mostly provides financial assistance to individual students and funds specific research projects, as shown in figure 3.7.[25]

Technical notes: In this context, financial aid refers only to grants, not to loans, which will be considered separately. Also, these federal and state data are derived from the most recent (2015) report by the Pew Charitable Trust. Separate reports from various sources indicate that more recent data are not substantially different; the numbers vary from year to year, but the conclusions to be drawn from them are basically the same.[26]

Financial aid to students constitutes the largest source of revenue from the federal government (figure 3.7). Pell grants, which are need-based student financial aid, constitute the largest component of this source of revenue. These funds are awarded to individual students, but the money is disbursed by the federal government (US Department of Education) directly to the university, which then applies grant awards to the individual students' tuition and fees bills. The federal government also awards the university an allowance to cover the costs of administering the Pell grants. Other federal financial aid programs, such as the veterans' educational benefits under the GI Bill, operate in the same way: they pay students' tuition and fees awards directly to the institution.

Another financial aid program, the Federal Work Study Program, provides funds for part-time employment to help needy students.[27] Students may be employed by the institution itself; a federal, state, or local public agency; a private nonprofit organization; or a private for-profit organization. The institution applies each year to the US Department of Education for work-study funding. Using a statutory formula, the department allocates funds based on the institution's previous funding level and the aggregate need of eligible students in attendance in the prior year.

The government imposes some requirements. In most cases, the university or the employer must pay up to a 50 percent share of a student's wages under the work-study program. However, in some work-study jobs, such as reading or mathematics tutors, the federal share of the wages can be as high as 100 percent. Regardless, hourly wages must not be less than the federal minimum wage. Institutions must use at least 7 percent of their work-study allocation to support students working in community service jobs, including reading tutors for preschool age or elementary school children; mathematics tutors for students enrolled in elementary school through ninth grade; literacy tutors in a family literacy project performing family literacy activities; or emergency preparedness and response.

Universities use the same accounting methods for both state and federal financial aid grants. But the methods used by public and private universities differ because GASB and FASB guidelines differ in their underlying logic.[28] According to GASB accounting standards, public universities are required to treat Pell grants, for example, as scholarships because, logically, the institution is involved in the administration of the program (as evidenced by the administrative allowance paid to the institution). However, according to FASB accounting standards, private institutions have the option to treat Pell grants as scholarships (like the GASB) or as pass-through transactions because, logically, the federal government determines who is eligible for the grant, not the institution. Because of this difference in requirements, on the one hand, public institutions report Pell and similar state and federal financial aid grants as revenues and as allowances (like discounts) that reduce tuition revenues. On the other hand, private institutions may do this as well, but more commonly they treat these grants as pass-through (agency) transactions. As pass-through transactions, the university does not record them as revenue or expenses. Consequently, if the public and the private institutions receive the same amount of Pell grants, the public institution will appear to have less tuition and more federal revenue, whereas the private institution treating the Pell grants as pass-through (agency) funds will appear to have more tuition and less federal revenue.

Student Loans

The federal government is the nation's largest source of student loans. It lent $103 billion in student loans in 2013. This amount has declined a bit since then, to $95 billion in 2017.[29] Nonetheless, it is considerably more than the amount of loans issued by the states, which was only $840 million in 2013, less than 1 percent of the federal amount. Indirectly, student loans provide substantial revenue to the university because the students use the money primarily to pay tuition and fees.

There are five basic types of federal loans, as shown in table 3.3.

Table 3.3. Federal student loan programs

Loan type	Eligibility	Financial need	Interest rate (%)	Total lent in 2017 ($ millions)
Perkins	Undergraduate, graduate, and professional students	Yes	5.00	1,054
Subsidized direct	Undergraduates	Yes	4.45	21,715
Unsubsidized direct	Undergraduate	No	4.45	49,852
	Graduate and professional students	No	6.00	
ParentPLUS	Parents of dependent undergraduate students	No	7.00	12,610
GradPLUS	Graduate and professional students	No	7.00	9,630
Total				94,862

The first type, Perkins loans, is serviced by the university, which means that the students repay the loans to the university. Because the money is lent, repaid, and lent again, it is recorded in a revolving fund within the loan fund category and as notes receivable in the financial statements.

Private companies service the other four types under contract to the US Department of Education. The university disburses the loans, but they are repaid to these companies. Accordingly, they are recorded in clearing accounts within the agency fund group.

The most common types of these loans are the direct loans, also known as Stafford loans. They may be subsidized or unsubsidized by the federal government. Subsidized loans are based on financial need, as determined by the university. As a subsidy, the federal government pays all interest while the student is enrolled at least half-time and for the first six months after graduation. Unsubsidized loans are not based on financial need, although the university determines the maximum amount that can be borrowed based on the cost of attendance and other financial aid received by the student. Unlike the subsidized loans, the government does not pay any of the interest on these loans; the student must pay all interest, which begins to accrue when the loan is made. The PLUS awards are the only loan types that require a credit check.

Procedurally, the university administers federal loan funds. Initially, the university's financial aid office determines a student's eligibility for a federal loan based on financial need determined by the Free Application for Federal Student Aid (FAFSA).[30] The loan is part of an overall financial aid package. Upon accepting the financial aid package, the student then applies online to the federal government for the loan, signing an electronic promissory note. The university credits the loan directly to the student's tuition bill. If any money is left over, the university issues a check or credit to the student, who may use the money for any purpose. (They may even invest the loan, thus earning interest through arbitrage.) Because the money is lent to students and not spent on operations, loans are not posted as revenue or expenditures.

By the way, student financial-aid administration provides a good example of internal control by segregation of duties. The financial aid office is responsible for determining a student's need or eligibility for a loan. And it makes the award to the student. However, the treasurer's office disburses the aid through transfers to the student's tuition account or by check to the student.

The federal government reimburses the university for the cost of the loan disbursements through its G5 grants management system. Throughout the academic year, the university's financial aid office sends electronic files of the amounts disbursed for each individual student to the US Department of Education. Accordingly, the department authorizes draw-downs from its Federal Reserve account via letters of credit, and the university receives the money by wire transfer. For direct loans, the university does not receive any compensation to cover its administrative costs. Parenthetically, federal financial aid grant awards are processed in basically the same manner.

Research Grants

For many universities, grants and contracts from the federal government are a major source of revenue. Indeed, at research universities, they may be the largest source of revenue. For example, in FY 2013, federal grants and contracts comprised the largest portion (24 percent) of the University of Wisconsin–Madison's $2.9 billion in revenue, exceeding both tuition and fees (16 percent) and state appropriations (15 percent).[31] Even at much smaller research universities, they can constitute the largest revenue source. In 2013, at the University of Alabama in Huntsville federal grants and contracts were 48 percent of the $220 million total revenue; in comparison, state appropriations and tuition and fees comprised 20 and 24 percent, respectively, of the total revenue.[32] Grant and contract revenue may be less in other institutions—considerably less in many—but, nonetheless, it often comprises a meaningful fraction of the overall budget.

In most cases, revenue from federal grants and contracts is current and restricted. The money must be spent to achieve the specific aims and deliverables documented in the grant application and the contract, respectively. Use of the money for any other purpose constitutes fraud, which can have criminal consequences. There is little room for error in this regard. Thus, if federal funds awarded for one project are used, even inadvertently, to support some other project with different specific aims, this is considered fraud; it is comparable to theft of funds from an award. It doesn't matter that both awards came from the same federal agency. Likewise, if a researcher receives 20 percent of his salary from a grant award for a specific project but then dedicates only 15 percent of his effort to that project, he has committed fraud; in the eyes of the law, the researcher has stolen 5 percent of his salary from the government. This latter example illustrates the critical importance of accurate effort reporting.[33]

For individuals unfamiliar with these restrictions, grant and contract funds might appear to be a sizable pool of money available for general university purposes, especially in times of budget stress. Many university presidents can relate anecdotes about naive assertions that these funds can and should be used to alleviate planned increases in tuition and requests for more state support.

Because of the accounting complexity when administering federal grants, this subject will be considered in more detail in a separate chapter (chapter 8) in this book.

Land Grants

The Morrill Act of 1862 (also known as the Land-Grant Act) authorized the federal government to give each state a grant of federal land within its borders for the establishment of a public institution to provide a practical education in "such branches of learning as are related to agriculture and the mechanic arts, in such manner as the legislatures of the States may respectively prescribe, in order to promote the liberal and practical education of the industrial classes in the several pursuits and professions in life."[34] States could sell the land to finance the new institution or use the land as a site for the institution, which was designated as the state's land-grant institution. If the federal land within a state was insufficient to meet that state's land grant, the state was issued "scrip," which authorized the state to select additional federal lands in other states to fund its institution. For example, using scrip, New York carefully selected valuable timberland in Wisconsin to fund Cornell University.

Proceeds from the sale of the land must be invested in a permanent endowment to support the land-grant institution's operations. According to the act, "it must remain forever at the disposal of the institution entitled to the benefit of the fund. Nor may it ever be covered into the general State funds or used for general State purposes." Thus, land-grant institutions have this continuing source of revenue. The only restriction on the money is that it cannot be used for buildings: "no part of such income may be expended for the purchase, erection, preservation, or repair of any building or buildings, nor may this income be used for the purchase of land."

Notably, the state (not the university) received the land grant. Consequently, the state usually administers the grant and any related assets. Accordingly, the land-grant assets are reflected in the state's financial report, not the university's. Periodically, the state distributes investment income from the perpetual land-grant endowment to the university, which the university reports as revenue.

The money is generally unrestricted and can be used at the university's discretion. It is not targeted specifically for the College of Agriculture or experiment station, unless the state imposes this condition. Montana State University, for example, has pledged this income for the retirement of revenue bond indebtedness. Any money remaining after this obligation is met can be used for any "lawful purpose."[35]

A second Morrill Act (1890) appropriated additional endowments for all land-grant institutions but prohibited distribution of money to states that made distinctions based on race in admissions.[36] However, states that provided a separate land-grant institution for African Americans were eligible to receive the funds. Thus, institutions founded or designated as land-grant institutions for African Americans in each of the then-segregated southern states came to be known as "the 1890 land-grant institutions." In 1908, land-grant benefits were extended to Puerto Rico.

Additional institutions have been incorporated into the land-grant system. In 1967, the University of the District of Columbia was designated a land-grant institution, funded with a $7.24 million federal endowment. Then, in 1972, the US territorial and commonwealth islands of Guam, Micronesia, American Samoa, Northern Marianas, and the Virgin Islands became eligible to designate a land-grant institution, with each receiving a $3 million federal endowment. And in 1994, Native American tribal colleges were given similar land-grant status, financed by a $23 million federal endowment.[37] They are called the 1994 land-grant institutions. Significantly, despite their land-grant status, neither the 1890 nor the later land-grant institutions received a grant of land that they could sell to establish an endowment. Instead, they receive comparable federal support via annual appropriations.

All land-grant institutions receive so-called formula funds from the federal government, appropriated by the Hatch, Smith-Lever, and McIntire Stennis Acts, and the Animal Health and Disease Research (AHDR) program. These funds, known as capacity grants, provide operating revenue for agricultural research and extension programs.[38] They are restricted for these specific activities and cannot be used to support other university nonagricultural research or extension operations. Unlike most federal research grants, the formula funds are not awarded to the universities on a competitive basis. Instead, they are awarded only to land-grant institutions by a noncompetitive formula that takes into account the states' rural and farm population numbers and nonfederal forest operations. (However, the university must distribute its formula funds on a competitive basis.) These formula-funded capacity grants will be discussed in more detail in the context of federal grants in chapter 8.

Auxiliary Enterprises

The term "auxiliary" refers to the myriad enterprises outside the core academic mission common to most universities. Typically, auxiliary enterprises include food services, housing, the bookstore, the student center, intercollegiate athletics, and student health services. They also include non-degree-granting educational activities, where students receive instruction but not course credit toward a degree or certificate. Generally, the instruction takes the form of individual course offerings, executive education, or instructional conferences and workshops. Furthermore, this includes the sales and services of educational activities that provide goods and services that may be sold to students, faculty, staff, and the general public. Sources of revenues from these kinds of educational activities include teaching hospitals or hotels; executive education; sales of scientific and literary publications; testing, consulting, or other technical services; and sales of products and services of dairy operations, food technology divisions, or farms. Some institutions include their affiliated hospitals in this category.

Auxiliary operations are expected to cover all of their costs and, if there is any money left over, contribute net revenue to the institution. These self-supporting operations are funded by user fees and income that they generate through sales and services: food bills, rent, book sales, ticket sales, and so forth. In that sense, the auxiliary enterprises operate as businesses, each with their own budget and accounting system—their own set of books. In this context, they are expected to pay an overhead fee to cover the costs of support services provided by the institution, such as administrative support, facilities, and utilities. Accordingly, their revenue and expenses are recorded in enterprise funds. On average, a university's auxiliary enterprises generate approximately 20 percent of a university's total income (figure 3.1); if university hospital operations are excluded, this percentage decreases to about 8 percent.

Universities may hire outside contractors and vendors to run some auxiliary enterprises. Common examples are food concessions, bookstores, and other retail operations. The goal is to improve service levels or reduce costs, while freeing the institution to focus on its core activities. Vendors and the university frequently negotiate long-term exclusive contracts; that is, the university grants vendors exclusive rights to provide the services. In return, vendors may agree to pay a portion of the profits to the university and, perhaps, to improve the service facilities. For example, at the University of Hawaii, a private food vendor agreed to build a food-court dining facility on campus in return for an exclusive 10-year contract to provide all food services; this included all catering for university events, such as presidential receptions, department "coffee hours," and so forth. There are risks for the vendor, for once a contract is negotiated, the vendor, not the university, will incur any losses. Of course, these vendors expect to produce a profit, but they must also share some of the profit with the university.

This example raises an important point sometimes misunderstood on a campus: because an activity is accounted for as an auxiliary enterprise, it cannot necessarily operate as an independent entity, apart from the rest of the institution. The dining facilities are an auxiliary enterprise, but a portion of their profit can be transferred into the university's general operating fund (unless this is prohibited by a vendor contract). Likewise, intercollegiate athletics are—and should be—accounted for as auxiliary enterprises. But the intercollegiate athletics department is not free to operate as an independent business, spending whatever revenues it earns as it sees fit. Revenues earned by intercollegiate athletics can just as properly be transferred to the university's general operating fund as left in the auxiliary enterprise fund. In his accounting textbook, Michael Granof notes: "for purposes of budgeting, the need for a new training room can be weighed against that for a new chemistry lab."[39]

Gifts

By definition, a gift is a donor's contribution to a university of something with economic value, such as money or other asset. An asset donated to the university will be recorded at its fair market value at the time of the donation. The donor may be an individual, a corporation, or a nonprofit entity. Importantly, there is no reciprocal economic benefit provided by the university in return. Furthermore, the award is typically irrevocable, with no specified time limit for its expenditure. And there is no formal fiscal accountability beyond periodic progress and expenditure reports to the donor. These progress reports are generally considered to be reports on stewardship and not performance. The essential point is that a gift may not have a "scope of work" or other deliverable. Thus, the bene-

factor receives nothing in return other than recognition and disposition of the gift in accordance with the donor's wishes. Recognition
usually includes a thank-you note and, more important, a receipt.

Gift funds may be unrestricted or restricted, depending on the
donor's wishes. A gift may be designated for general operations or
restricted to a particular purpose, such as research in a defined area
or support of a professorship or a program. The donor may stipulate
the gift for specific purposes but may not have control over expenditures or over the work performed. Because there are no "deliverables," gifts from a private donor are not considered sponsored
research, even if the donor calls the gift a grant or the gift is used in
support of the research mission. Furthermore, a gift may be designated by the donor as expendable—immediately usable for current
purposes—or as an endowment to be invested, with the investment
returns available to support university purposes.

When donors give something to the university, they usually in-
tend to claim an income-tax deduction for the value of the gift. Not
surprisingly, the IRS has specific guidelines about what constitutes
a gift that qualifies for this deduction: "Generally, you can deduct
your contributions of money or property that you make to, or for
the use of, a qualified organization. A gift or contribution is 'for the
use of' a qualified organization when it is held in a legally enforceable trust for the qualified organization or in a similar legal arrangement. The contributions must be made to a qualified organization
and not set aside for use by a specific person."[40]

The last phrase, "not set aside for use by a specific person," means
that if donors specify the intended recipient of gift funds (who may
be themselves), the donation is not tax deductible. To get it straight: a
donor may be the beneficiary of a gift (a particular professor, for example, donates money for her own research program), but, the donor
may not claim a tax deduction for the gift. Indeed, the IRS has ruled
that in these cases the ultimate recipient is realistically the specific
person and not the university—even though the gift was given to the
university: "The organization must have control and discretion over
the contribution, unfettered by a commitment or understanding that
the contribution would benefit a designated individual. . . . The
donor's intent must be to benefit the organization and not the individual recipient."[41] Thus, the donor is not entitled to deduct the charitable contribution. Ultimately, it is the responsibility of the donor to
ensure that a donation meets the definition to qualify as a charitable
deduction for income tax purposes, regardless of whether or not a
gift receipt has been issued by the university.

As pointed out in *Managing the Research University*, there is a way around this IRS ruling:[42]

> The usual solution is to make the donation to the university to support research in the specific area that your favored professor studies, such as stem-cell research. If your person is the only one at the university in that field, then he or she will get the money, fair and square. And you get the tax deduction. If there are several faculty members studying in that area, then the university will have to devise some way to distribute your money among them. But it isn't obligated to give your person any of it—the university may decide to give it all to one or more of the other researchers.

Couldn't the area be narrowed so much that only one professor would qualify for the money? "Yes, but be careful. The IRS has a low tolerance for that kind of manipulation. They may disallow your deduction if they suspect that you're violating the spirit of the law."

The university's development office generally administers gifts. For its services, it charges a fee since universities seldom subsidize these offices. The amounts and fee structure differ among institutions. However, a common charge is a one-time service fee—for example, 5 percent of the original gift amount. Alternatively, the charge may be an annual management fee, such as a percentage (for example, 2 percent) of the gift's current market value. In general, gifts that restrict the collection of a management fee will be assessed the charge out of some other source of funds.

To conform to IRS and standard accounting procedures, the university must distinguish between sponsored projects—that is, a grant or contract—and gifts. As they come into the university, sponsored projects and gifts are usually identifiable as one or the other and are routed to the appropriate office. The chief research officer administers sponsored projects, and the chief development officer administers gifts. However, when ambiguities arise, the two offices must decide jointly whether it is a sponsored project or a gift. A subtle tension may lurk under the surface. The chief research officer naturally wants the university to bring in as many sponsored projects as possible; likewise, the chief development officer wants to maximize the number of gifts received by the university. However, competent staff members recognize this tension and do not allow it to cloud their judgment.

To stimulate giving, universities occasionally undertake a so-called capital campaign. They decide upon a goal—how much money to raise from gifts within a specific time period. For example, the goal might be to raise $500 million in five years. Moreover, the university decides a priori on its fundraising priorities, and potential donors will be encouraged to direct their gifts to these priority programs, such as undergraduate scholarships or named professorships. As a rule of thumb, capital campaigns are not announced publicly until about half of the targeted amount has been raised. Then, with much fanfare, the campaign goes public, often under the symbolic leadership of a well-respected, famous community leader.

During a campaign, universities usually try hard to control fundraising requests to potential donors. Using well-prepared lists of the donors' presumed wealth, personal interests, and past donations, campaign managers carefully match planned requests and potential donors. A cardinal sin in this context occurs when somebody, such as a dean or athletic director, ignores the campaign's priority list and errantly requests a small gift from a very wealthy donor. In the eyes of the development office, this constitutes a wasted opportunity for a large gift. For that reason, campaign managers try to assert control over all institutional fund-raising efforts, including those benefiting major athletic teams. Usually these efforts have limited success.

Capital campaigns are not always well understood by faculty members. Predictably, the setting of fund-raising priorities rankles academic programs not high on the list. Realistically, the university will accept a gift for any program designated by the donor, whether or not it is on the priority list. Fallaciously, a fund-raising priority also may be viewed as a university commitment of funding; it is not—unless the necessary funds designated for the priority program are actually raised. And that can seldom be guaranteed. In any capital campaign, expectations must be managed.

Endowments
University Endowments

Gifts, especially larger ones, are often targeted to establish an endowment. By definition, an endowment is "income or form of property given or bequeathed to someone."[43] For a university, it is "an aggregation of assets invested to support its educational mission in perpetuity."[44] To clarify the term "aggregation," an institution's endowment actually comprises hundreds or thousands of individual endowments given to an institution by donors. Each individual endowment is treated as a fund, usually with stipulations about its

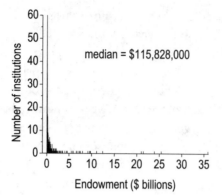

Figure 3.8. Endowments of 828 colleges and universities (2015). Bin size is $10 million.

management imposed by the donor. Thus, for example, Harvard University's endowment is made up of more than 13,000 individual funds invested as a single entity.[45] Characteristically, endowment funds are given to an institution by donors who have stipulated as a condition of the gift that its principal may not be spent, and they expect that its value will increase over time through a responsible balance between expenditure and reinvestment of its earnings.

Although some universities have legendary multibillion-dollar endowments, most colleges and universities have much smaller endowments. This is illustrated in figure 3.8, a histogram of 828 college and university endowments in FY 2015.[46] Only 9 institutions (for example, Harvard, Stanford, and Yale Universities) have endowments exceeding $10 billion. Tellingly, the median value is $115,828,000; half of the institutions have less than that. And, as seen by the highly skewed distribution, many have much less than that. Sixty institutions have endowments of less than $10 million. Indeed, most public colleges and universities have no substantial endowments. As of 2012, of the nation's 4,000 public and private nonprofit 2- and 4-year colleges and universities, only 657—about 16 percent—have endowments of more than $50 million.[47]

Incidentally, starting in 2018, colleges and universities with endowments exceeding $500,000 per student and more than 500 students are subject to a 1.4 percent tax on annual investment earnings. The roster of affected schools includes large universities such as Harvard, Stanford, and MIT as well as smaller colleges such as Pomona, Amherst, Swarthmore, Grinnell, and Williams. For Harvard, the tax obligation will exceed $40 million annually. Of course, this tax is not welcome by these institutions. Besides the immediate financial consequences, with the tax now in place, there is concern that future revenue-hungry legislators will increase the tax.

Endowment Types

There are three endowment types: permanent, quasi-, and term. Each can be either restricted or unrestricted, depending on the donor's wishes. Permanent (or true) endowments occur when the donor specifies that the principal is to be invested and maintained in perpetuity; only the income distributions may be expended. If the university rather than the donor determines that an account's funds are to be retained and managed like an endowment, the fund is called a quasi-endowment. The university may invest its own funds in a quasi-endowment, either as a sole donor or as a supplement to a private gift. Since quasi-endowments are established at the discretion of the institution rather than an external source, the principal also may be spent; these expenditures also must conform to the donor's wishes. If the donor specifies a time limit for an endowment's lifetime, it becomes a term endowment. At the end of the lifetime—for example, 10 years—the university may expend the principal in its entirety according to the donor's wishes.

Endowment Management

Endowments may be managed directly by the university or by an associated nonprofit corporation, usually called the university foundation. The latter arrangement—that is, the nonprofit foundation—is most common in public universities, for it can operate outside restrictive state regulations on investment strategies, property management, personnel, and other business activities. As separate corporations, these foundations have their own governing board. However, one or more members of the university administration (for example, a member of the governing board or the president) may sit on the foundation board to represent university interests. These may be nonvoting positions to reinforce the legal separation between the foundation and the university. These foundations are tax-exempt for one of two reasons: either they are part of a tax-exempt university or are a separate tax-exempt 501(c)(3) organization.

Ostensibly, donors may feel more secure making a major gift to a foundation governed by individuals with specialized legal, business, and financial management expertise.[48] Unlike college and university regents or trustees, who may be politically appointed or elected and have primary responsibility for institution policy, foundation board members are recruited for their ability to raise and manage private support for the benefit of the institution. Furthermore, they have a fiduciary responsibility to represent the donors' interests and to adhere to standards imposed by the IRS, various other regulatory agencies, and the donors themselves. This fiduciary responsibility can be critically important when political or budgetary pressures pervade the university.

Some private institutions utilize institutionally related foundations for many of the same reasons as public institutions. Although they are not subject to regulations governing state agencies, the foundation allows the university to separate support from private individuals and corporations from funding provided by churches or religious entities.

Although a foundation's primary purpose is to manage private support for its affiliated institution, many of them also raise money for the institution. According to the Council on Advancement and Support of Education (CASE), about one-third of institutionally related foundations solely manage and invest private support.[49] The remaining two-thirds also are responsible for soliciting private support to benefit their affiliated educational institution. In that capacity, they often work in conjunction with alumni organizations, athletic booster clubs, and other university-related fund-raising organizations.

Endowment Income

Endowment income originates from the return on the investment of principal. It comprises an important component of many universities' operating budgets, supporting expenditures on student financial aid, faculty research, maintenance of facilities, and other campus operations. Properly invested, an institution's endowment provides a source of income in perpetuity. An investment committee reporting to the university or foundation governing board generally oversees the investments. Although some institutions may have an internal investment office that manages their investment portfolio, more commonly they hire outside consultants to manage the investments.[50] In fact, they often hire several consultants in order to diversify investment strategies. Beyond that, they may even hire an additional consultant to evaluate the performance of the investment consultants.

The payout rate—the percentage of the endowment that contributes to the operating budget—is the maximum amount of the endowment that can be spent in a given year. The governing board (university or foundation, depending on management structure) usually sets the payout rates based on a three- to five-year average of the endowment's market value. Generally, rates vary between

Table 3.4. Average endowment payout rates (percentages) for 812 US colleges and universities and affiliated foundations

Institution type	Year					
	2015	2014	2013	2012	2011	2010
Public	4.0	4.1	4.1	4.0	4.5	4.1
Private	4.3	4.5	4.6	4.3	4.6	4.8
All institutions	4.2	4.3	4.4	4.2	4.6	4.5

Note: The rates represent the distribution for spending divided by the beginning market value (endowment value on or around the beginning of the fiscal year). They are calculated net of any investment fees and expenses for managing the endowment.

about 3 and 6 percent. Typically they are about 4 percent, as shown in table 3.4.[51] Payout rates seldom exceed 7 percent because the Uniform Prudent Management of Institutional Funds Act (UPMIFA) of 2006, which has been adopted by 49 states, includes a provision that the "appropriation for expenditure" of an amount greater than 7 percent of the fair market value of an endowment fund (calculated on the basis of market values averaged over a period of not less than three preceding years) creates a "rebuttable presumption of imprudence."[52] In FY 2015, Harvard's endowment paid out about $1.6 billion, roughly 35 percent of the university's total income. In contrast, the median endowment at private colleges and universities is roughly $7.9 million. At a typical spending rate of about 4 percent to 5 percent, this endowment would support an annual payout of between $316,000 and $395,000.

Ultimately, the goal is to maximize the payout while reinvesting a sufficient amount of the return as a safeguard against inflation. The actual payout rate depends heavily on the balance between investment performance and institutional need. An increased investment performance and a constant budgeted need (for example, $100 million per year) translate into a decreased payout rate, and vice versa. Thus, counterintuitively, a university may report a lower payout rate during a time of lucrative investment returns. Depending on the circumstances, the university may increase the payout rate, thus reducing the reinvestment amount, or leave it constant, thus increasing the rate of principal growth.

To ensure that an endowment's payout provides sufficient income for its intended purpose, many universities specify minimum threshold amounts for various endowment types. For example, the University of Texas at Austin's minimum threshold amounts to create various endowment types are shown in table 3.5.[53] At Duke University, the thresholds are about twice as large; moreover, "$5,000,000 will establish an endowment supporting the head coach of football, men's

Table 3.5. Minimum threshold amounts to create an endowment at the University of Texas at Austin, 2015

Endowment type	Threshold ($)
Book fund	10,000
Undergraduate research	20,000
Program support	25,000
Undergraduate scholarship	40,000
Graduate research	50,000
Endowed presidential scholarship	50,000
Endowed presidential fellowship	100,000
Faculty fellowship	150,000
Professorship	300,000
Chair	1,000,000

basketball, or women's basketball."[54] Thresholds for naming a department or college may be a bit more flexible, although the rule of thumb is that the endowment must be at least as large as its one-year operating budget.

Generally, gifts to the endowment begin to generate income the month after they are invested in the pooled endowment. Payout of gift income begins after the pledge is complete. For example, a $100,000 gift paid to the institution (or foundation) over five years would begin to pay out income the month after the last installment of $20,000 is received. An outright gift of $100,000 would begin to pay out the month after the $100,000 is received. Sometimes, payout is delayed until the endowment's value reaches the threshold for a particular endowment type through either reinvestment of its income or additional donor contributions.

Investment Costs

Endowments are subject to investment management fees and investment office operating costs. They also are subject to custody fees, which are charged by a bank or other financial institution for holding the endowment securities in safekeeping to minimize the risk of theft or loss. These investment fees are in addition to the one-time service fees (about 5 percent) charged when a gift is donated to the institution. Consequently, the university considers all these investment costs carefully to ensure that they are justified and appropriate. In fact, UPMIFA directs the institution to incur only "appropriate and reasonable costs" in managing its investment portfolio. Determination of what satisfies this standard is left to the endowment managers, who are expected to act "in good faith and with the care an ordinarily prudent person in a like position would exercise under similar circumstances."[55]

A portion of the gift or investment income is used to cover these costs. The amount varies widely among institutions. The practice of directing a portion of gifts or endowment returns to pay for costs not directly proscribed by the donor is common, and most colleges and universities explain and spell out that component of the gift. There are no summary statistics of these costs, but the amounts are often available from a university's website. For example, the University of Texas and Arizona State University charge 0.23 and 1.5 percent of the endowment's market value, respectively; the California Institute of Technology directs 15 percent of the endowment payouts to overhead costs.[56]

Sometimes this money goes to supporting fund-raising efforts in addition to administrative or overhead costs. The cost of fund-raising is quantified by the ratio:

$$fund\text{-}raising\ to\ contribution\ ratio = \frac{fund\text{-}raising\ expense}{contribution\ revenue}$$

The ratio depends on how the institution accounts for fund-raising expenses and contribution revenue. To standardize accounting, the FASB has issued GAAP covering the more salient situations.[57] For example, if presidents spend 20 percent of their time fund-raising for their institutions, then 20 percent of their salary would be included in fund-raising expenses. Other areas that tend to be allocated to fund-raising expenses include building occupancy, which should be calculated using estimates of square footage of space used; postage; and, of course, the development officers' salaries.

In addition, the CASE has developed standardized guidelines used by most universities when reporting fund-raising costs.[58] And it has prepared a compendium of data comparing fund-raising costs to money raised for 120 institutions.[59] In table 3.6, an example shows the amount raised per dollar of fund-raising operational expenses (the return on investment) and the reciprocal fund-raising to contribution ratio. On average, for every dollar spent on fund-raising, the institutions generated $7.98, corresponding to a fund-raising to contribution ratio of 0.13. Stated differently, the university spends 13 cents of every dollar donated to generate more donations. Similar data for nonprofit charities are available online.[60]

The ratios for all nonprofit organizations, including private universities and foundations affiliated with public universities, can be

Table 3.6. Total contributions raised per dollar of annual operating expenses for fund-raising (return on investment) and the reciprocal fund-raising-to-contribution ratio for 120 institutions

Institution category	Contributions raised per dollar of fund-raising expenses ($)	Fund-raising to-contribution ratio	Number of institutions
Public	7.97	0.13	57
Private	7.99	0.13	63
BA	10.44	0.10	38
MA	5.47	0.18	45
PhD	8.81	0.11	28
Start-up	9.44	0.11	18
Emerging	6.44	0.16	42
Mature	8.63	0.12	60
In a campaign	8.55	0.12	71
Not in a campaign	7.17	0.14	49
All	7.98	0.13	120

Note: Nine institutions did not award BA or higher degrees.

derived from their tax returns. Public universities per se do not file tax returns. But all other nonprofit organizations must report fund-raising expenses and revenue to the IRS using Form 990. These reports are readily available online.[61]

Using data from their income tax returns, the fund-raising to contribution ratios for 12 sample institutions are shown in table 3.7. The ratios ranged from 0.04 to 0.27, with an average value of 0.13, the same value reported by the CASE (table 3.6). However, unlike the CASE results, in this small sample, private institutions had a significantly higher expenses and more revenue (even without Harvard, the outlier). And they had a larger average ratio than the public institutions, 0.17 and 0.09, respectively. Collectively, these results from the IRS tax returns conform to the old adage that "it takes money to make money."

The costs of fund-raising vary by activity. In 1999, James Greenfield provided rules of thumb based on composite data from several groups of nonprofit organizations (charities, universities, foundations, etc.), shown in table 3.8.[62] Capital campaigns are among the least expensive; the ratio of 0.05 to 0.10 means that it costs about 5 to 10 cents to raise a dollar. In contrast, acquiring new donors via direct ("snail") mail requests is the most expensive, requiring more than a dollar to raise a dollar; the benefit of this "loss leader" is that it costs only 20 cents to raise additional dollars from existing donors.

Table 3.7. Fund-raising to contribution ratio for 12 sample institutions, using data from 2014 or 2015 IRS Form 990 tax returns

Institution	Fund-raising expenses ($)	Contribution revenue ($)	Fund-raising-to-contribution ratio
Private			
Brown University	22,260,355	184,187,457	0.12
Colorado College	5,278,531	29,730,967	0.18
Harvard University	167,510,150	1,593,868,204	0.11
Occidental College	6,914,686	25,489,189	0.27
University of Pittsburgh	15,927,960	66,083,820	0.24
Stanford University	82,049,632	785,631,869	0.10
Average ratio for private institutions			0.17
Public			
Auburn University Foundation	2,918,200	65,347,401	0.04
Georgia Tech Foundation	4,137,439	106,402,601	0.04
University of Hawaii Foundation	8,105,343	81,598,684	0.10
Montana State University Foundation	2,638,346	21,298,867	0.12
University of New Mexico Foundation	6,939,282	35,384,747	0.20
University of Wisconsin Foundation	18,818,436	388,508,377	0.05
Average ratio for public institutions			0.09
Average ratio for all institutions			0.13

Table 3.8. Fund-raising-to-contribution ratio for various fund-raising activities

Activity	Ratio
Capital campaign	0.05 to 0.10
Major gifts	0.05 to 0.10
Corporations and foundations	0.20
Direct mail renewal	0.20
Planned giving	0.25
Benefit/special events	0.50
Direct mail acquisition	1.00 to 1.25
National average	0.20

The cost of processing online donations is even less expensive, ranging from 3 to 7.5 percent of the amount of each gift.[63] The national average for these composite organizations is 20 cents per dollar raised, which is somewhat more than the average for public and private universities. In general, nonprofit organizations should spend no more than 35 percent of related contributions on fund-raising.[64]

Unrelated Business Income

According to the IRS, unrelated business income is income from an activity, trade, or business that is not substantially related to educational tax-exempt purposes. The IRS regulations state this clearly: "Unrelated business income is the income from a trade or business regularly conducted by an exempt organization and not substantially related to the performance by the organization of its exempt purpose or function, except that the organization uses the profits derived from this activity."[65] Sources of unrelated business income might include museum shop sales, golf course fees for nonuniversity players, advertising billboards in a parking garage, and so forth. Critically significant, the IRS does not consider income from externally sponsored research grants to be unrelated business income: "For a college, university, or hospital, all income from research, whether fundamental or applied, is excluded in computing unrelated business taxable income."[66]

Unlike a university's regular income, its unrelated business income is taxable. The tax is known as the unrelated business income tax (UBIT). It is not unusual for a university to generate—and pay tax on—unrelated business income, although the amount is usually a small percentage (less than 1 percent) of its total income. Importantly, having to pay unrelated business income tax does not jeopardize an institution's tax-exempt status.

Incidentally, the tax code states further that the unrelated business income tax "is imposed on the unrelated business income not only of the universities and colleges themselves, but also upon their wholly owned subsidiary organizations. Consequently, it is immaterial whether the business activity is conducted by the university or by a separately incorporated, wholly owned subsidiary. If the business activity is unrelated, the income in both instances will be subject to the tax."[67] Therefore, the university cannot escape the tax code provisions by relegating private use of its facilities to those housed in a building owned by a separately incorporated nonprofit entity that is demonstrably affiliated with the university. For this strategy to succeed there must be "blue water" between the university and the separate nonprofit entity. That is, the two cannot be linked organizationally in any perceptible way.

Unrelated business income is reported on IRS Form 990T, which looks like most other tax forms with income, expenses, deductions, and tax calculations based on corporate rates to fill out. Unlike an institution's Form 990 that reports nonprofit activities, its Form 990T reports private business activities and is not available for public scrutiny.

Summary

Income derives from two sources: revenue and gain. Revenue refers to income earned through regular business activities such as

teaching and research. Gain refers to investment returns and donations. Tuition and fees are a major revenue source. Tuition waivers
are recorded as a scholarship allowance if the institution provides a
student with institutional resources to pay part or all of the student's
tuition and fees but not if the institution simply discounts the tuition and fees according to a published rate structure. Tuition rates
obey the law of demand: as tuition increases, enrollment decreases.
The total revenue from tuition depends on the rates charged per
credit, which varies between and within institutions. For public universities, state funding primarily supports operations. The federal
government provides revenue for higher education in a different way.
States typically fund the general operations of public institutions,
with smaller amounts appropriated for research and financial aid,
while the federal government mostly provides financial assistance
to individual students via grants and loans and funds for specific
research projects. Auxiliary operations such as dormitories and dining halls are expected to cover their costs and contribute net revenue to the institution. These self-supporting operations are funded
by user fees and income generated through sales and services. Gifts
of money or assets are often targeted to establish endowments,
usually with stipulations about their management imposed by the
donors. Endowment income originates from the return on the
investment of principal. Endowments are subject to investment
management fees and one-time service fees charged when a gift is
donated to the institution. A portion of these fees may be used to support fund-raising efforts in addition to administrative or overhead
costs. Unrelated business income is taxable income from an activity,
trade, or business that is not substantially related to a university's
educational tax-exempt purposes.

Notes

1. Oxford University Press, "Oxford Dictionaries," http://www.oxforddictionaries
.com/?gclid=CMa5maK2p8kCFU1cfgodiXoNoA (accessed November 23, 2015).

2. National Center for Education Statistics, "Postsecondary Institution Revenues," http://nces.ed.gov/programs/coe/current_tables.asp (accessed October 11,
2016). Tables 333.1, 333.4, and 333.55.

3. State Higher Education Executive Officers Association, "SHEF—State Higher
Education Finance FY15," http://www.sheeo.org/projects/shef-fy15 (accessed
October 18, 2016).

4. National Association of College and University Business Officers, "Accounting and Reporting Scholarship Allowances to Tuition and Other Fee Revenues by Higher Education" (1997), http://www.nacubo.org/Business_and_Policy
_Areas/Accounting/Advisory_Reports/Advisory_Report_1997-1_Accounting_and

_Reporting_Scholarship_Allowances_to_Tuition_and_Other_Fee_Revenues_by _Higher_Education.html (accessed March 28, 2017).

5. Moody's Investor Service, "Public University FY 2014 Medians Highlight Sector Differentiation," https://www.moodys.com/research/US-Higher-Education -Public-University-FY-2014-Medians-Highlight-Sector—PBC_1006130 (accessed November 6, 2017); "Signs of Moderating Stress in Private University FY 2014 Medians," https://www.moodys.com/research/US-Higher-Education-Signs-of -Moderating-Stress-in-Private-University—PBC_1005678 (accessed November 6, 2017).

6. National Association of College and University Business Officers, "Private College Tuition Discounts Hit Historic Highs Again," http://www.nacubo.org/About _NACUBO/Press_Room/Private_College_Tuition_Discounts_Hit_Historic _Highs_Again.html (accessed November 6, 2017).

7. Paul Tullis, "How Do Colleges Set Tuition?" http://www.takepart.com /article/2014/06/12/how-colleges-set-tuition (accessed October 18, 2016).

8. Steven W. Hemelt and Dave E. Marcotte, "Rising Tuition and Enrollment in Pubic Higher Education," *Discussion Paper 3827, Institute for the Study of Labor* (2008), https://papers.ssrn.com/sol3/papers.cfm?abstract_id=1305811 (accessed February 28, 2018).

9. David Holman, Samuel Kissinger, and Robert Hammer, "An Investigation into University Tuition Models across the United States" (2017), https://assets .documentcloud.org/documents/3860781/An-Investigation-Into-University -Tuition-Models.pdf (accessed November 17, 2017).

10. Michigan State University, "Student Accounts," http://www.ctlr.msu .edu/COStudentAccounts/Tuition_FeesResident_Undergraduate.aspx (accessed November 17, 2017); University of Alabama in Huntsville, "Tuition and Fees," http:// catalog.uah.edu/grad/financial-information/tuition-fees/ (accessed November 17, 2017); University of California, Berkeley, "2017–2018 Fee Schedule," http://registrar .berkeley.edu/tuition-fees-residency/tuition-fees/fee-schedule (accessed November 17, 2017).

11. Holman, Kissinger, and Hammer, "An Investigation into University Tuition Models across the United States."

12. University of Texas at Austin, "Undergraduate Traditional Flat Rate Tuition," https://utexas.app.box.com/v/ug-tuition-17-18-long (accessed November 15, 2017).

13. Higher Education Opportunity Act, 110–315 § 132.

14. Purdue University, "Tuition and Fees," http://www.admissions.purdue.edu /costsandfinaid/tuitionfees.php (accessed Ocotber 19, 2016).

15. Iowa Department of Management, "What Is the Revenue Estimating Conference?" https://dom.iowa.gov/faq/what-revenue-estimating-conference (accessed October 29, 2016); Louisiana State Legisalture, "§ 10. Expenditure of State Funds," http://www.legis.la.gov/legis/law.aspx?d=206526 (accessed October 28, 2016).

16. State of Hawaii Department of Taxation, "Council on Revenues," http:// tax.hawaii.gov/useful/a9_1cor/ (accessed October 29, 2016).

17. Dean O. Smith, *Managing the Research University* (New York: Oxford University Press, 2011), 74–75.

18. Pew Charitable Trusts, "Federal and State Funding of Higher Education," http://www.pewtrusts.org/en/research-and-analysis/issue-briefs/2015/06/federal -and-state-funding-of-higher-education (accessed October 19, 2016). Figure 2.

19. University of Michigan, "2015 Annual Report," http://www.finance.umich.edu/reports/2015/ (accessed November 16, 2017).

20. National Association of State Budget Officers, "State Expenditure Report," https://www.nasbo.org/mainsite/reports-data/state-expenditure-report (accessed October 21, 2016). Table 3.

21. State Higher Education Executive Officers Association, "SHEF—State Higher Education Finance FY15." Table 11.

22. New York State Education Department, "The Scholarships for Academic Excellence," http://www.highered.nysed.gov/kiap/scholarships/sae.htm (accessed November 30, 2017).

23. Wisconsin State Legislature, "Statute 39.30: Wisconsin Grants; Private, Nonprofit College Students," http://docs.legis.wisconsin.gov/statutes/statutes/39/III/30 (accessed November 28, 2017).

24. Lawrence University, "Tuition & Fees," http://www.lawrence.edu/admissions/afford/financial#lu-tabs-2 (accessed November 29, 2017); University of Wisconsin–Madison, "Data Digest," https://apir.wisc.edu/data-digest/ (accessed November 29, 2017).

25. Pew Charitable Trusts, "Federal and State Funding of Higher Education." Figure 2.

26. College Board, "Trends in Student Aid 2017," https://trends.collegeboard.org/student-aid/figures-tables/grants#Pell%20Grants (accessed February 1, 2018).

27. US Department of Education, "Federal Work-Study (FWS) Program," http://www2.ed.gov/programs/fws/index.html (accessed December 29, 2016).

28. National Center for Education Statistics, "IPEDS Finance Survey Tips Scholarships, Grants, Discounts, and Allowances," https://nces.ed.gov/ipeds/Section/fct_ipeds_finance_03072007_3 (accessed November 30, 2017).

29. College Board, "Trends in Student Aid 2017."

30. US Department of Education, "Federal Student Aid, Free Application for Federal Student Aid (FAFSA)," https://fafsa.ed.gov/ (accessed February 1, 2018).

31. National Center for Education Statistics, "Integrated Postsecondary Education Data System," http://nces.ed.gov/ipeds/datacenter/InstitutionByName.aspx (accessed February 27, 2015).

32. National Center for Education Statistics, "Integrated Postsecondary Education Data System."

33. Smith, *Managing the Research University,* 139–143.

34. Association of American Universities and the Association of Public and Land-grant Universities, "The Land-Grant Tradition," http://www.aplu.org/library/the-land-grant-tradition/file (accessed November 8, 2016), 10.

35. Montana State University, "Montana State University 2016 Financial Statements, Note 2," www.montana.edu/ . . . /2016%20MSU%20Consolidated%20Financials%20- %20Final.pdf (accessed January 25, 2018).

36. Association of American Universities and the Association of Public and Land-grant Universities, "The Land-Grant Tradition," 13.

37. United States, "7 U.S.C. § 7601 Equity in Educational Land-Grant Status Act of 1994," https://www.law.cornell.edu/uscode/text/7/7601 (accessed November 27, 2016).

38. National Institute of Food and Agriculture, "Capacity Grants," https://nifa.usda.gov/program/capacity-grants (accessed November 29, 2016).

39. Michael H. Granof et al., *Government and Not-for-Profit Accounting: Concepts and Practices*, 7th ed. (Hoboken, NJ: John Wiley & Sons, Inc., 2015), 592.

40. Internal Revenue Service, "Publication 526 Charitable Contributions" (Washington, DC: Internal Revenue Service, 2009), 3.

41. "Letter Ruling Request Regarding a Charitable Contribution," *Number 200250029, Index number 170.12-06* (2002), 4.

42. Smith, *Managing the Research University*, 60–61.

43. Oxford University Press, "Oxford Dictionaries."

44. American Council on Education, "Understanding College and University Endowments," https://www.acenet.edu/news-room/Documents/Understanding -Endowments-White-Paper.pdf (accessed November 30, 2016).

45. Harvard University, "Endowment," http://www.harvard.edu/about-harvard /harvard-glance/endowment (accessed December 1, 2016).

46. National Association of College and University Business Officers, "U.S. and Canadian Institutions Listed by Fiscal Year (FY) 2015 Endowment Market Value and Change in Endowment Market Value from FY2014 to FY2015," http:// www.nacubo.org/Research/NACUBO-Commonfund_Study_of_Endowments /Public_NCSE_Tables.html (accessed November 30, 2016).

47. American Council on Education, "Understanding College and University Endowments."

48. Council for Advancement and Support of Education, "Foundation FAQs," http://www.case.org/Browse_by_Professional_Interest/Institutionally_Related _Foundations/Foundation_FAQs.html (accessed December 1, 2016).

49. Council for Advancement and Support of Education, "Foundation FAQs."

50. Commonfund Institute, "Understanding the Cost of Investment Management," https://www.inphilanthropy.org/sites/default/files/resources/2015%20 Understanding%20the%20Cost%20of%20Investment%20Management%20 -%20A%20Guide%20for%20Fiduciaries.pdf (accessed December 12, 2016).

51. National Association of College and University Business Officers, "2015 NACUBO-Commonfund Study of Endowment (NCSE) Results: Average Annual Effective Spending Rates for U.S. College and University Endowments and Affiliated Foundations, FY 2015 to FY 2006," http://www.nacubo.org/Research/NACUBO -Commonfund_Study_of_Endowments/Public_NCSE_Tables.html (accessed December 1, 2016).

52. National Conference of Commissioners on Uniform State Laws, "Uniform Prudent Management of Institutional Funds Act (UPMIFA)" (2006), http:// www.uniformlaws.org/Act.aspx?title=Prudent%20Management%20of%20 Institutional%20Funds%20Act (accessed January 23, 2018). § 4(d).

53. University of Texas at Austin, "What Is the Minimum Amount to Create an Endowment?", https://austin-utexas.custhelp.com/app/answers/detail/a_id/1168 /~/what-is-the-minimum-threshold-to-create-an-endowment%3F (accessed December 13, 2016).

54. Duke University, "Endowment Giving," https://dukeforward.duke.edu/ways -to-give/endowment/endowment-giving/ (accessed December 13, 2016).

55. National Conference of Commissioners on Uniform State Laws, "Uniform Prudent Management of Institutional Funds Act (UPMIFA)." § 3(c)(1).

56. Arizona State University Foundation, "Endowment FAQs," http://www .asufoundation.org/how-to-give/endowments/endowment-FAQs (accessed December 13, 2016); California Institute of Technology, "Budget Planning Variables,"

finance.caltech.edu/ . . . /393-budget_planning_variables_11_24_14.pdf (accessed December 13, 2016); University of Texas System, "Rule 60102: Fees for Endowment Admnistration and Management," https://www.utsystem.edu/board-of -regents/rules/60102-fees-endowment-administration-and-management (accessed December 13, 2016).

57. Financial Accounting Standards Board, "Statement of Financial Accounting Standards No. 117: Financial Statements of Not-for Profit Organizations" (1993), http://www.fasb.org/summary/stsum117.shtml (accessed February 19, 2016).

58. Council for Advancement and Support of Education, *CASE Reporting Standards and Management Guidelines for Educational Fundraising*, 4th ed. (Washington, DC: Council for Advancement and Support of Education, 2009).

59. Judith A. Kroll, "Benchmarking Investments in Advancement Results of the Inaugural CASE Advancement Investment Metrics Study (AIMS)" (Washington, DC: Council for Advancement and Support of Education, 2012).

60. Charity Watch, "Charity Ratings," https://www.charitywatch.org/home (accessed December 14, 2016).

61. Foundation Center, "990 Finder," http://foundationcenter.org/find-funding /990-finder (accessed December 14, 2016).

62. James M. Greenfield, *Fund Raising: Evaluating and Managing the Fund Development Process*, 2nd ed. (New York: John Wiley & Sons, Inc., 1999), 87.

63. Affinity Resources, "How Much Does Fundraising Cost?", http://www.affinity resources.com/pgs/articles/fundraising_costs.html (accessed December 14, 2016).

64. McGladrey LLP, "Key Benchmarks," http://www.nacubo.org/Documents /EventsandPrograms/2013PBF/NACUBO%20Key%20Benchmarks%20Presen-tation%20091713.pdf (accessed December 14, 2016).

65. Internal Revenue Service, "Taxation of Unrelated Business Income State and Municipal Colleges," in *Internal Revenue Manual 7.27.4* (Washington, DC, 2010).

66. "Publication 598 Tax on Unrelated Business Income of Exempt Organizations" (2017), https://www.irs.gov/pub/irs-pdf/p598.pdf (accessed March 24, 2017).

67. "Taxation of Unrelated Business Income State and Municipal Colleges." § 7.27.4.2.2.2.

Chapter 4
Expenses

Costs, Expenses, and Expenditures

Before embarking on a discussion of expenses, the exact meanings of three words—"costs," "expenses," and "expenditures"—require clarification. In common usage, these terms may be used interchangeably; they mean about the same thing: money spent. In the language of accountants, however, there are subtle but significant differences between these three words.

Costs. By definition, a cost is "an amount that has to be paid or spent to buy or obtain something."[1] Stated differently in accounting terms, a cost is the cash amount given up for an asset. In that context, costs relate to specific objectives, namely, cost objectives (or cost objects). For example, in a university, instruction is a cost objective; the associated costs of providing instruction, such as faculty salaries, instructional supplies, classroom depreciation, and so forth, may be assigned to this cost objective. Likewise, research and public service are cost objectives with associated costs.

Expenses. By definition, expenses are "the costs incurred in the performance of one's job or a specific task."[2] Although this definition implies equivalence between costs and expenses, they differ technically in accounting terms. This difference is predicated on time. Costs convert to expenses as soon as related revenue is generated or the costs are consumed. This occurs when a service is performed, a product is sold, or an acquisition is depreciated. Stated differently, an expense is a cost that occurs as part of an institution's operating activities during a specified accounting period. Thus, when a university hires faculty members, it incurs a cost, namely, their annual salary. This cost (that is, the salary payments) becomes an expense when students pay tuition to receive instruction from the faculty members—revenue is generated. Moreover, expenses also refer simply to using up (consuming) an item over time. For example, the university incurs a one-time cost when it constructs a new classroom building, which is recorded as an asset. Depreciation of the classroom building constitutes an expense that may extend for 50 years.

In general, under the accrual method of accounting, an expense is reported for the period when the cost best matches the related revenues or the cost is used up or expires. As in depreciation, an expense can occur in an accounting period that is different from the period when the institution pays for the item. So, the word "expense" has a meaning that is different from that of "payment."

Expenses are often divided into two major classifications: operating and nonoperating. Operating expenses involve an institution's main activities. For example, a university's operating expenses include faculty salaries, the cost of teaching supplies, and associated indirect costs (classroom and office utilities, building maintenance, and so forth). Nonoperating expenses pertain to incidental activities, such as interest expenses incurred by long-term debt.

Expenditures. By definition, an expenditure represents an outflow of money for the purpose of making a payment. It is a disbursement; money is spent. For example, on the one hand, payment of cash to purchase a piece of equipment constitutes an expenditure. On the other hand, depreciation of the equipment constitutes an expense but not an expenditure because depreciation does not involve a disbursement of cash. In that sense, expenditures relate closely to costs. Indeed, for most purposes, they mean the same thing. Both terms refer to a disbursement to acquire something or perform a service. The "costs of doing business," for example, refers to money that has to be spent (as expenditures) to conduct business, hire employees, buy parts to manufacture a product, and so forth.

The technical distinctions between these three terms may seem like needless nit-picking. And, for everyday usage, perhaps it is. Nonetheless, they are not always interchangeable in the accounting context, as will be seen.

Direct and Indirect Costs

Costs are classified as either direct or indirect costs. In the accounting realm, there are conventional definitions of direct and indirect costs. The Office of Management and Budget (OMB) gives details on the conventional definitions in a document known as the *Uniform Administrative Requirements, Cost Principles, and Audit*

Requirements for Federal Awards, commonly called the *Uniform Guidance.*[3] The definitions in the *Uniform Guidance* guide most university accounting of direct and indirect costs.

Direct costs. Direct costs are associated directly with an institution's specific activities or products. That is, they are incurred to achieve a specific objective. The direct costs of instruction include salaries of the teaching faculty and classroom supplies. The direct costs of a specific research project include the salaries of individuals working on the project, expendable supplies, equipment, travel, consulting services, and other project-related expenses.

Indirect costs. Indirect costs are related to an institution's activities or products but cannot be traced to specific activities or products. They are incurred by the institution on behalf of more than one specific project. That is, they are not associated with any single project; they are common or joint costs that benefit multiple objectives. They include the costs of accounting and financing, utilities, human resources, administrative personnel, building and equipment use, et cetera.

In the jargon of corporate contracts, indirect costs are subdivided into two separate categories: "overhead" and "general and administrative" (G&A) costs. Overhead is ordinarily used for costs incurred that are not direct costs but that can be attributed to a specific project or job. Stated differently, overhead costs support the direct cost or revenue-generating projects of the company. Examples of overhead costs are machine shop support, material handling, subcontract management, and so forth. All apply to a specific project, function, or cost within the organization. Notably, if the company had no jobs or projects, it would have no overhead costs. In contrast, G&A costs apply to the institution's overall operation; they include utilities, human resources, accounting, contract administration, and so forth. Thus, if the company had no jobs or projects, it would still have G&A costs. In summary, if employees work on direct labor projects such as a grant or contract, any indirect labor or costs they incur would be charged to an overhead account. However, if employees typically don't work on direct projects, their time would be considered G&A and should be charged accordingly, along with any other costs that they might incur. And, in some cases, an employee's costs might be apportioned to both account types.

In the jargon of federal grants and contracts, indirect costs likewise are separated into two separate categories: those incurred for facilities ("F"), such as buildings, equipment, et cetera, and those incurred for administration ("A"), such as departmental administration, sponsored projects administration, et cetera. Therefore, collectively the indirect costs of government-sponsored research are known as "F&A" costs. Accordingly, academic institutions commonly refer to their indirect costs as F&A costs, or more simply as F&A. Details of indirect cost allocation and calculation methods are presented in chapter 9.

Expense Classifications

Both the GASB and the FASB recognize two different ways of classifying expenses: natural or functional. In the *natural* classification scheme, expenses are sorted by type; that is, by the nature of the expense. In the FASB's words, natural classification sorts expenses "according to the kinds of economic benefits received in incurring those expenses. Examples of natural expense classifications include salaries and wages, employee benefits, supplies, rent, and utilities."[4] In the *functional* classification scheme, expenses are sorted by function. According to the FASB, functional classification is "a method of grouping expenses according to the purpose for which costs are incurred. The primary functional classifications are program services and supporting activities."[5] As the NACUBO puts it, natural classifications tell *what* was purchased and functional classifications tell *why* an expense was incurred.[6]

Within these two classification schemes, the NACUBO recommends the natural and functional expense classifications listed in table 4.1.[7] The NACUBO adds that "many institutions may further refine these classifications into subclasses based on their particular needs and requirements and the requirements of regulatory bodies." The natural classifications tend to vary depending on institutional need. Consequently, the NACUBO provides only general guidelines for sub-classifications. However, functional classifications tend to be

Table 4.1. NACUBO-recommended expense classifications

Natural	Functional
Salaries and wages	Instruction
Employee benefits	Research
Scholarships and fellowships	Public service
Travel	Academic support
Supplies	Student services
Utilities	Institutional support
Other outside services	Operations and maintenance (O&M)
Depreciation	Auxiliary and self-supporting enterprises
Interest	Hospitals
Other	Independent operations

Table 4.2. Main functional expense subcategories

Function	Subcategory	Function	Subcategory
Instruction	General academic instruction Vocational/technical instruction Community education Preparatory/remedial instruction Instructional IT[a]	Institutional support	Executive management Fiscal operations General administration Public relations Administrative IT
Research	Institutes and research centers Individual and project research Research IT	O&M	Physical plant Repairs Security
Public service	Community services Cooperative extension services Public broadcasting services Public service IT		Environmental safety Space leasing Facility planning Central receiving Utilities
Academic support	Libraries Museums and galleries Educational media services Ancillary support Academic administration Academic personnel development Course, curriculum development Academic support IT	Scholarships/ fellowships	Landscape and grounds Grants-in-aid Trainee stipends Tuition and fee waivers Prizes to undergraduates
		Auxiliary enterprises	Dining, residence halls Student health
Student services	Student services administration Social and cultural development Counseling and career guidance Financial aid administration Student admissions Student records Student health services Student services IT		Faculty, staff services Intercollegiate athletics Auxiliary enterprises IT
		Depreciation (public universities only)	Buildings Capital improvements Equipment

[a]IT refers to information technology.

more uniform, mainly because the federal government has standard guidelines in this regard. Accordingly, the NACUBO recommends specific functional sub-classifications that conform to the federal guidelines; they are listed in table 4.2.

Guidelines for classifying depreciation differ for private and public universities.[8] According to FASB guidelines, private universities may report depreciation expenses as a natural but not a separate functional classification. Consequently, they allocate depreciation to the other functional classifications; for example, library depreciation will be included in the academic support classification. According to GASB guidelines, depreciation may be considered as either a natural or a functional classification. Therefore, depreciation may be allocated to the other functional classifications or reported separately (as shown in table 4.2). The majority of public institutions report depreciation as a separate functional classification.

For brevity in their financial reports, many institutions condense natural expenses into only four or five basic categories. Most commonly, they are:

- salaries and wages
- fringe benefits
- supplies and services (including utilities)
- depreciation (sometimes called capital expenses)
- scholarships and fellowships

In this abbreviated format, all of the nonsalary expenditures are bundled into a single natural "supplies and services" category.

Following a NACUBO recommendation, institutions may also link expenses in the natural and the functional categories in matrix form, providing additional information about the actual dedication of resources to the various university functions. An example is shown in table 4.3. The expense data in this example, derived from a composite of several public universities (listed in the preface), will be carried forward into financial calculations throughout all subsequent chapters. Totals for the natural and the functional classifications are in the bottom row and the right-hand column, respectively. Clearly, the matrix format provides the most information and is the most useful.

Although the matrix table contains all expense data, graphic presentation of the expense data in the two different classification schemes provides easier insight into university finances from two different points of view, as shown in figure 4.1. Natural expense classifications (*upper panel*) allow an analysis of the operational expenses for personnel relative to other operational expenses. Clearly, personnel (salaries and fringe benefits) constitutes the largest operational expense: 72 percent (55 percent and 17 percent, respectively) of all expenses. Functional expense classifications (*lower panel*) allow analysis of the full cost of program activities. In this example, research is the most expensive cost objective: 36 percent of total expenses are for research activities. Instruction is the second most expensive: 25 percent of total expenses.

The predominance of personnel costs (salaries, wages, and fringe benefits) is shown in more detail by retabulating the matrix data (table 4.3) in table 4.4. Overall, 72 percent of all expenses are for employee compensation, salaries, wages, and fringe benefits ($151,092,560/ $208,922,729). Notably, 92 percent of total instructional expenses are for employee compensation ($47,933,553). At most institutions, this includes many tenured faculty members. This observation raises

Table 4.3. Operating expenses in FY 2015 by functional and natural classifications

Functional	Salaries and wages	Fringe benefits	Supplies and services	Natural Depreciation	Scholarships and fellowships	Total
Instruction	36,079,255	11,854,298	4,119,168			52,052,721
Research	48,970,008	14,337,790	11,449,511			74,757,309
Public service	2,128,126	603,394	2,906,586			5,638,106
Academic support	6,091,175	1,814,676	2,924,953			10,830,804
Student services	6,427,408	1,976,915	6,185,770			14,590,093
Institutional support	10,531,518	3,423,856	5,263,182			19,218,556
Operations and maintenance	3,971,769	1,471,928	7,824,130			13,267,827
Scholarships and fellowships					1,101,624	1,101,624
Auxiliary enterprises	1,124,313	286,131	2,996,930			4,407,374
Depreciation				13,058,315		13,058,315
Totals	115,323,572	35,768,988	43,670,230	13,058,315	1,101,624	208,922,729

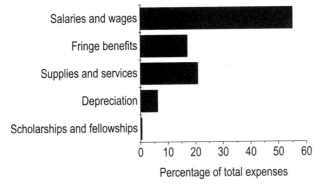

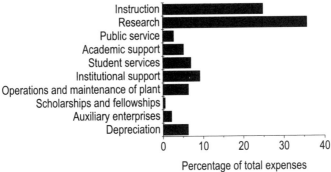

Figure 4.1. Percentages of total expenses for expenses classified in natural (*upper panel*) and functional (*lower panel*) categories

Table 4.4. Percentage of total expenses by function spent on salaries, wages, and fringe benefits for FY 2015

Function	Total expenses	Salaries, wages, and fringe benefits	% of total
Instruction	52,052,721	47,933,553	92.09
Research	74,757,309	63,307,798	84.68
Public service	5,638,106	2,731,520	48.44
Academic support	10,830,804	7,905,851	72.99
Student services	14,590,093	8,404,323	57.60
Institutional support	19,218,556	13,955,374	72.61
Operations and maintenance	13,267,827	5,443,697	41.03
Scholarships and fellowships	1,101,624		
Auxiliary enterprises	4,407,374	1,410,444	32.00
Depreciation	13,058,315		
Totals	208,922,729	151,092,560	

a warning flag: such a high percentage in faculty salaries leaves little "slack" for adjustments of the instructional budget if revenues were to decline appreciably, as can happen due to reduced state appropriations, decreased endowment income, or sharply declining enrollment.

The high proportion of salaries, wages, and fringe benefits warrants further attention. What drives these costs? The answer to this good question puts the spotlight on university personnel: how they're paid and what benefits they receive as university employees.

Salaries and Wages

A priori, it helps to understand the difference between salaries and wages. Although the two terms are sometimes used synonymously, there are significant differences with legal implications.

The fundamental difference between salary and wages is that a salaried employee is paid a fixed amount per pay period and a wage earner is paid by the hour. With a salary, there is no linkage between the amount paid and the number of hours worked; the salaried employee is not paid a smaller amount for working fewer hours or a larger amount for working more hours. In contrast, an employee who is paid wages receives a pay rate per hour, multiplied by the number of hours worked. For example, employees who are paid a wage of $25 per hour will receive a gross pay of $1,000 per week if they work a standard 40-hour week (that is, $25/hour × 40 hours) but only $500 if they work 20 hours in a week (that is, $25/hour × 20 hours). For comparison, assuming a standard work year of 2,080 hours (based on 260 8-hour days), wages of $25/hour equal an annual salary of $52,000.

Further differences between employees earning salaries and wages are regulated by the Fair Labor Standards Act (FLSA) of 1938.[9] This federal law includes provisions that:

- set a minimum wage
- require overtime pay
- require equal pay regardless of gender
- prohibit child labor
- require record keeping

However, the FLSA does not regulate:

- vacation, holiday, severance, or sick pay
- meal or rest periods during the workday, holidays, or vacations
- premium pay for weekend or holiday work
- pay raises or fringe benefits

Note: The FLSA does not regulate the number of hours an employee works per week, as long as overtime is paid appropriately.

Financially, the two major FLSA regulations cover minimum wage and overtime pay. In 2017, the FLSA mandated a minimum wage of $7.25/ hour and $8.25/hour for employees with and without health insurance coverage from the employer, respectively. Individual states may have higher minimum wage rates. Furthermore, employees who receive wages also are entitled to overtime pay of 1.5 times their normal rate of pay if they work more than 40 hours per week. In a university context, the overtime rule can have a significant financial impact.

Some employees are exempt from these FLSA requirements if they earn annual salaries exceeding $23,660 per year. (This threshold amount is expected to increase in 2018.) Stated in human resources parlance, employees are *nonexempt* unless they're *exempt* from FLSA requirements. In a university setting, the exemptions apply to executive, administrative, and professional employees (including faculty members and academic administrative personnel) and "learned professionals," such as researchers (including postdoctoral research fellows). However, if their salary is less than the threshold ($23,660), these employees are not exempt and must be paid overtime. Incidentally, employers may use nondiscretionary bonuses and incentive payments (including commissions) to satisfy up to 10 percent of the new standard salary level. Importantly for universities, most undergraduate and graduate students are exempt. Details and "fine print" concerning FLSA regulations for various university employees are available from the US Department of Labor.[10]

In financial reports, the expression "salaries and wages" refers to total cash expenditures paid to employees, the sum of all salaries and wages. This includes any money subsequently withheld by the employer on behalf of the employee for employee income taxes, contributions to retirement or other savings accounts, pre-tax health plans, Social Security payments, union dues, and so forth. But it does not include employer contributions to retirement plans, workers' compensation plans, health-care plans, and so forth. For many individuals, total salaries and wages income usually corresponds to taxable Medicare wages reported on an IRS W-2 wage and tax statement.

Within the university, salaries and wages are recorded on what is usually called a personnel action form (PAF). This form identifies the salaries and wages to be paid and the budgets (accounts) to be charged for the employees. It establishes the appointment and rate of pay. In addition, the form reflects the distribution of payroll charges to each budget (account) for a specified time period and, once entered into the system, controls the distribution of payroll charges.

Acknowledging these differences between salaries and wages, to simplify wording, the two terms will be used synonymously in

the ensuing discussion unless there are technical reasons to distinguish them.

Fringe Benefits

Fringe benefits are benefits provided by an employer to an employee or independent contractor. They have a price tag; they are expenses incurred by the employer. Some fringe benefits are paid
with general funds, and others are paid with nongeneral funds. Particularly, sponsored projects (grants and contracts) include the
costs of fringe benefits in their budgets, either as a direct cost or as
a component of reimbursable indirect costs. They are billed to the
sponsored project at the time the salary costs are incurred. Some
universities may provide fringe benefits supplementing those allowable on federal awards. Those universities must cover the unallowable costs of these additional benefits.

The major fringe benefits are:

- payroll taxes
    Social Security
    Medicare
- health-care benefits
- life insurance
- post-retirement benefits
    health-care and life insurance benefits
    pension plans
- paid time off
    vacations
    holidays
    sick leave

Generally, fringe benefits are available for employees with at least
a half-time appointment. That usually means that the employee
works at least 20 hours per 40-hour work week. The threshold varies between institutions, however. For example, Harvard University
provides full fringe benefits for employees who work at least 17.5
hours per week (corresponding to a 43.75 percent appointment),
but Woods Hole Oceanographic Institution provides full fringe
benefits only for employees who work at least 30 hours per week
(corresponding to a 75 percent appointment).[11] Moreover, some fringe
benefits, such as post-retirement benefits and paid time off, may
become available to employees only after a certain period of time.
This is known as *vesting*; when employees vest, they have ownership
of the benefit. The extent of fringe benefits may vary for different

employee groups. For example, employees exempt and nonexempt from FLSA provisions may earn paid vacation days or sick leave time at different rates.

Payroll Taxes

Federal Insurance Contributions Act (FICA) taxes pay for Social Security and Medicare. These flat-rate taxes are imposed on both the employee and the employer. The law requires the employer to withhold two separate taxes from the employee's wages: the Social Security tax and the Medicare tax. (In this context, wages refers to either salary or wages.) It also requires the employer to match the employee's contribution. Thus, the employer's matching payroll-tax contribution is considered a fringe benefit.

The *Social Security tax* is 6.2 percent of the employee's wages. But the Social Security tax is subject to a cap that is adjusted every year for inflation. In 2017, the maximum amount of taxable earnings was $127,200, which translates to a maximum social security tax withholding from the employee's paycheck of $7,886.40. This means that if an employee earned more than $127,200 in 2017, the Social Security tax did not exceed $7,886.40. If an employee has more than one job, each employer is required to withhold and contribute to the Social Security tax. Consequently, more than the maximum amount may be withheld. In that case, the excess withheld is refunded in the employee's tax return.

The *Medicare tax* is 1.45 percent of the gross wages. Plus, if an employee earns more than $200,000, an additional 0.9 percent Medicare surtax is withheld. There is not a wage cap on the Medicare tax paid, unlike the Social Security tax. To the contrary, as mentioned, the tax rate increases by 0.9 percent if the employee's wages exceed $200,000.

As a fringe benefit, the employer must match the employee's 6.2 percent Social Security tax and the 1.45 percent Medicare tax (plus the 0.9 percent supplement if that is levied). Therefore, each quarter, the employer must deposit the total amount (12.4 percent Social Security tax and 2.9 percent Medicare tax plus any supplement) into the employee's Social Security account via either a Federal Reserve Bank or an authorized commercial bank. Any excess amounts paid by employers are refunded in their tax returns.

Parenthetically, for-profit organizations also must pay taxes collected under the Federal Unemployment Tax Act (FUTA). Federal unemployment taxes provide benefits for a limited time to employees who lose their jobs through no fault of their own; the employees must be ready, willing, and able to work but cannot find work. Moreover, all states have complementary unemployment compensation programs, mandated by state unemployment tax acts (SUTA). Unlike the FICA taxes, these FUTA and SUTA taxes are paid entirely by the employer. Nonprofit organizations and government agencies, including most universities, are not subject to FUTA taxes. But they may be subject to SUTA taxes. For example, all employees are covered under the New York State Unemployment Insurance Law.[12] The costs (currently 5.4 percent of an employee's wages per year) are paid to the state entirely by the employer as a fringe benefit.

Health-Care Benefits

Like most employers, universities provide health-care benefits for their employees—at least for those with more than a half-time appointment. In general, coverage is offered to the employee plus eligible family members, such as a spouse or domestic partner, children, and other qualified dependents.

The *traditional plans* are administered by private health-care providers, such as Blue Cross-Blue Shield participants and health maintenance organizations (HMOs), such as Kaiser Permanente. They have a deductible amount that the employee must pay before insurance coverage "kicks in," as well as required co-insurance or co-payment costs. But they limit these out-of-pocket expenses, thus providing coverage against catastrophic expenses.

Because traditional health-care plans are so expensive, universities seldom pay the full cost; employees must pay part of the premiums. The university withholds the employees' share of the premium from their paychecks and then pays the entire premium bill directly to the provider. The employer's share of the premium varies widely between universities, although it hovers around 40 percent of the total cost.

Alternatively, universities may offer reimbursement-based *cafeteria plans*.[13] These plans allow employees to contribute a certain amount of their gross income before taxes are calculated to an account specifically for health-care expenses. Universities have the option to contribute into these accounts as well. As they are incurred, medical expenses not covered by insurance, as well as insurance premiums, can be reimbursed from these accounts throughout the plan year. These reimbursements also are tax-free. Because contributions are paid using pre-tax dollars, cafeteria plans reduce the employee's taxable gross income. And both employee and voluntary employer contributions are exempt from payroll taxes such as the Social Security and Medicare taxes (7.65 percent of wages).

Flexible spending arrangements (FSAs), which establish a flexible spending account, are the most common cafeteria plan. According to IRS regulations, the maximum employee contribution in 2017 was $2,600 per year, regardless of marital status. Any university contributions are independent of this limit. The contributions are generally spread over an entire year; so, for an employee receiving 26 paychecks, the maximum amount withheld for the FSA from each paycheck would be 1/26th of the $2,600, translated to $100 per paycheck. Of course, the maximum reimbursement is the amount contributed to the account during the year. Significantly, however, an employee may receive the maximum amount of reimbursement at any time during the coverage period (usually the calendar year), regardless of the amount actually contributed at the time of reimbursement. For the university, this provision poses a financial risk. For example, if an employee elects to contribute $2,600, makes only one payment ($100) before claiming the full $2,600 for a major medical procedure (such as Lasik surgery), and soon terminates employment before making any more contributions, then the university may be liable for the remaining $2,500—that is, will lose $2,500—unless the former employee surprisingly agrees to pick up the cost.

Although the FSA provides tax benefits, there is a catch: any unused balance at the end of the year is forfeited to the university. In other words, "use it or lose it." According to IRS regulations, if an employee forfeits an unused balance, the employer may not legally refund the balance directly to that employee. However, the employer may pool the balances of all employees and distribute the pooled amount evenly among all employees. Otherwise, the employer may use the balance only to offset the costs of administering the plan, which is a more common practice.

To mitigate the impact of this "use it or lose it" ruling, the IRS permits some flexibility with the deadline. With the university's approval, employees are allowed a two-and-one-half-month grace period (until March 15 for calendar years) to spend FSA money or to carry over $500 in unused funds to the next year and still contribute up to the maximum in the next plan year. But employees cannot do both. Actually, because of the tax advantage of contributing to an FSA, forfeiting a small balance may not be too damaging financially. Consider the math: for an employee in the 25 percent federal income tax bracket, a $2,600 FSA contribution in tax-free income results in a $650 tax savings ($2,600 × 0.25). Consequently, this employee could forfeit as much as $650 and still break even.

Consumer-directed health plans (CDHPs) are another way to minimize the health-care costs. These plans reduce premiums by raising the deductible amount and the out-of-pocket limits. Thus, by selecting a CDHP, the employee takes on more financial risk—a much higher deductible and out-of-pocket limit. To reduce the financial risk, CDHPs offer the opportunity for an employee to open a *health savings account (HSA)*. An HSA works like a typical bank account, earning interest and so forth, but the money can only be used for medical expenses. The employee and the university may add to the account up to a limit set by the IRS. In 2017, the limit for the combined university and employee contributions to an HSA was $3,400 for a single employee and $6,750 for the employee and family members.[14] Unlike an FSA, HSA accounts do not have to be spent within a specific time period; year-end balances are not forfeited. The HSA belongs to the employee, even after changing health plans or employers, and the employee's contribution uses pre-tax dollars, thus reducing federal tax obligations. Of course, the university stops contributing when an individual is no longer an employee.

Federal laws expand the protections available to health benefit plan participants and beneficiaries. One important law, the Consolidated Omnibus Budget Reconciliation Act (COBRA), provides some workers and their families with the right to continue their health coverage for a limited time after certain events, such as the loss of a job. Another law is the Health Insurance Portability and Accountability Act (HIPAA), which provides important protections for employees and their families who have preexisting medical conditions or might otherwise suffer discrimination in health coverage based on factors that relate to their health. Neither of these expanded protections has a significant impact on universities' finances, but they may have major impacts on individuals in need of them.

Self-insured health insurance programs have become more common during the past 20 years or so as a way to reduce costs. Indeed, according to the College and University Professional Association for Human Resources (CUPA-HR) *2016 Employee Health Benefits Survey of Higher Education*, 61 percent of the responding institutions have switched from fully insured (by a commercial insurance vendor) to self-insured plans for health-care coverage offered to their employees.[15] Although larger universities have an advantage over smaller institutions because they have more participants to share the risk, small colleges also have turned to self-insurance programs.

Moreover, to increase the number of participants, some small colleges have formed consortia to self-fund their health insurance programs.[16]

Unlike full insurance, with an insurance company assuming the risk, self-insurance means that the university takes on the risk and pays the actual health-care costs. The employees still pay fixed premiums, but the institution keeps the extra money that insurance companies charge for profit and taxes.[17] Plus, it saves on administrative costs. Under full-insurance plans, administrative costs constitute about 18 to 25 percent of the premium; under self-insurance plans, they drop to about 14 percent of the premium.[18] Notably, although self-insured health programs eliminate the need to pay as many third-party administrators, they do not eliminate third-party providers. Self-insured universities don't form their own network of doctors and hospitals; they still pay insurance companies like Blue Cross-Blue Shield to process claims. Just as with full insurance, medical-care providers (that is, physicians, hospitals, and so forth) send invoices to the insurance company. Then, these insurance companies submit employee insurance claims for payment by the university on a regular (for example, weekly) basis. In most self-insured programs, the university pays claims up to a maximum amount, such as $150,000 per individual per year. To protect against large, potentially catastrophic losses, universities usually purchase reinsurance policies, known as stop-loss insurance, which cover claims above their maximum amount.

Like full insurance, self-insurance charges premiums to cover the costs, which are determined by an actuary based on past claims. However, instead of paying a fixed premium to an insurance carrier, the university typically withholds the employees' contributions from their paychecks and deposits them and their contribution in a fund used only to pay claims and administrative costs. If these costs are lower than expected, the excess money flows into a reserve fund designed to protect the financial stability of the program and provide rate stabilization within the plan. Universities often document the magnitude of this reserve balance in their annual financial reports.

Understandably, the rationale for self-insured health plans is to save money. How much can they save? Of course, that depends on the number and costs of claims. In 2013, the University of New Hampshire reported cost savings of $10 million because of the switch to self-insured health care, which it invested in science, technology, engineering, and math education.[19] And, in 2016, Cornell University reported savings of about $14.5 million over the preceding 10-year period. So, the savings can be substantial. Notably, however, the savings are only in comparison to full insurance rates from commercial insurance companies. If overall health-care costs continue to go up, self-insured institutions only have limited ability to reduce employees' health-insurance costs.

Life Insurance

Like many employers, universities may provide basic term life and accidental death and dismemberment insurance policies at no cost to most full-time employees and perhaps their spouses. The policies are administered by independent insurance companies. Enrollment may be automatic when an employee is hired, implicitly waiving any requirement for a new employee to prove insurability. The insurance amount seldom exceeds about $50,000. However, many insurers offer employees the opportunity to buy supplemental insurance without the need to prove insurability—at least, if the supplemental coverage is purchased at the time of initial employment. Subsequent changes in the insurance amounts may require proof of insurability.

Employee-provided insurance coverage in excess of $50,000 is considered "imputed income" by the IRS and, therefore, is subject to federal income tax. According to the IRS, "there shall be included in the gross income of an employee for the taxable year an amount equal to the cost of group-term life insurance on his life provided for part or all of such year under a policy (or policies) carried directly or indirectly by his employer (or employers); but only to the extent that such cost exceeds the sum of (1) the cost of $50,000 of such insurance, and (2) the amount (if any) paid by the employee toward the purchase of such insurance."[20] Thus, the imputed income is reduced by the amount the employee paid toward the insurance; is taxable as a benefit; and is, therefore, added to the employee's applicable wage base for federal income tax, Social Security tax, and Medicare tax purposes. In practice, the amount of life insurance coverage above $50,000 is multiplied by a premium rate based on an employee's age at the end of the calendar year, which results in a monthly amount of imputed income. Fortunately, for most employees, this usually equates to a very small sum of money.

Post-Retirement Benefits

These benefits are provided by the employer to retired employees primarily for health care, life insurance, and pensions. Importantly, institutions account for all three of these benefits on the accrual basis. They estimate and record as expenses these post-retirement costs during the employees' working years because the institution benefits from the employees' service during this period.

Universities strive to provide generous coverage because these fringe benefits are magnets for attracting and keeping valued employees. However, these benefits have become a worrisome financial burden for most institutions. Soaring medical costs, early retirements, and prolonged longevity have added significantly to the expense. Many public university post-retirement benefits are administered by the state as part of a more general program for all retired public workers. That arrangement does not free the university from an obligation to pay its proportional share of the overall post-retirement costs, however. Private universities are more likely to contract outside vendors to administer parts or all of their post-retirement plans.

The federal Employee Retirement Income Security Act (ERISA) of 1974 sets minimum standards for most voluntarily established post-retirement health and pension plans in private organizations, including private universities, to provide protection for individuals in these plans.[21] ERISA requires plans to provide participants with plan information, including its features and funding; establish fiduciary responsibilities for administrators who manage and control plan assets; require plans to establish a grievance and appeals process for participants to get benefits from their plans; and give participants the right to sue for benefits and breaches of fiduciary duty. Although public universities are not subject to ERISA, many operate their post-retirement plans as if they were subject to ERISA, with many ERISA-like best practices in place.

Health-care benefits provided to active employees may continue into retirement. To be eligible for post-retirement health-care benefits, an individual must be employed by the institution long enough to become vested. The vesting period may vary for different types of appointments, but 10 years is quite common. If employment terminates before vesting occurs, the employee does not receive any post-retirement health-care benefits. Note that the vesting requirement not only reduces the long-term cost to the institution but also encourages employees to continue working for the institution.

While the insurance vendors and coverage may appear more or less unchanged after retirement, the underlying financial arrangements may differ significantly. A major change occurs when retirees become eligible for Medicare. Most universities require retirees to enroll in Medicare parts A, B, and D, covering in-patient hospital, out-patient medical (doctor's visits, etc.), and prescription drug costs, respectively. These are administered by the federal government. The government pays the cost of part A, but the retiree pays the costs of parts B and D, which are withheld from the retiree's monthly Social Security payments. As an alternative, universities may allow enrollment in Medicare part C, which lets private health insurance companies provide Medicare benefits. These Medicare private health plans are known as Medicare Advantage Plans; they offer at least the same benefits as standard Medicare but with different rules, costs, and coverage restrictions. Depending on the insurer, Medicare Advantage Plans may add a monthly premium in addition to the standard premium. Regardless of the plan option, Medicare becomes the primary insurer. The university-contracted vendor then becomes the secondary insurer, picking up some costs denied by Medicare. As a generous benefit, some universities refund the Medicare premiums to retirees.

University-paid *life insurance* policies generally expire when the employee retires. However, some insurers offer the opportunity for the retiree to continue coverage without proof of insurability. The retiree must pay the full premium, however. And the premium will undoubtedly be much higher due to the retiree's age.

Pensions obligate the university to provide benefits to employees after they retire. As such, the university and, in some plans, the employee contribute to a pool of funds set aside for the employee's future benefit. The pool of funds is invested by a plan administrator on the employee's behalf, and the earnings on the investments generate income for the employees when they retire. An employer's contribution to a pension plan is part of an employee's compensation as a fringe benefit, and the costs are recorded as operating expenses.

Generically, there are two types of pension plans: defined-contribution and defined-benefit.

In a *defined-contribution* plan, an employee and usually the employer (the university) contribute a certain percentage of the employee's pre-taxable pay to the employee's retirement account. Generally, the university sets up and makes deposits to the account, deducting the employee's contribution from the employee's paycheck through a salary reduction agreement. (The salary isn't actually reduced; a salary reduction agreement is the name of the agreement between employee and employer that allows for a portion of the employee's compensation to be invested directly into a retirement account.)

Table 4.5. Types of defined contribution retirement plans according to IRS code section 401(a)

Plan type	Common name	Eligible universities	Plan role
401(a)	Government plan	Public	Primary
403(b)	Tax-sheltered annuity	Private and public	Primary or supplemental
457(b)	Deferred compensation plan	Private and public	Supplemental

The IRS defines three different defined contribution plans, listed in table 4.5, which differ primarily in their target audience (public or private universities) and role in the overall institutional retirement benefits.[22] Thus, public universities offer 401(a) plans as their primary offering; both private and public universities may offer 403(b) plans as either the primary plan or supplementary to a 401(a) plan, respectively, and 457(b) plans supplementary to either 403(b) or 401(a) plans, respectively. Universities have some leeway in constructing their plans as long as they abide by the basic parameters established by the IRS.

Primary retirement accounts are usually mandatory; the employee has no choice in the matter. Typically, the university withholds the employee contribution (about 3 to 9 percent of the gross pay) from each pay period for deposit into the account. Supplementary accounts are voluntary; the employee may elect to have additional money withheld by the university for deposit in the supplemental account, which differs from the primary account.

In each plan, the contributions, which are not taxable at the time, are then invested by the plan administrator (for example, Fidelity, TIAA-CREF, or Vanguard). These funds cannot be withdrawn without a 10 percent penalty until the employee is age 59 1/2 years; this age limitation is waived if an employee becomes unemployed or disabled. When funds are withdrawn, they become taxable. The actual amount available for withdrawal depends not only on the amount contributed but also on investment performance. Thus, there is some uncertainty inherent in the employee's retirement benefit. One common solution is to establish an annuity through the plan administrator as a buffer against investment uncertainties. Regardless, these plans offer a major financial advantage because tax has been deferred until withdrawal; the money that would have been taxed—both the employee and the university contributions—has generated compound interest. Consequently, they are a good deal for the employee.

Money can be moved from one tax-deferred account to another without becoming taxable. This includes moving an account from one administrator to another. These changes are called transfers of interest. Money can also be moved into individual retirement arrangements (IRAs); these changes are called rollovers.

Importantly, the IRS limits the amount that can be contributed to these tax-deferred retirement plans. The maximum annual contribution, including both the university and employee contributions, for each plan in 2017 was $18,000. Furthermore, the maximum total amount that can be invested in all types of tax-deferred accounts, including traditional and Roth IRAs, was $54,000. Notably, however, universities have the option to allow employees older than age 50 to contribute an additional $6,000 per year in so-called catch-up contributions to each plan type. And, in 457b plans, for three years prior to the normal retirement age (as specified in the plan), an employee may contribute a special catch-up that is the lesser of:

- twice the annual limit (2 × $18,000 = $36,000 in 2017), or
- the basic annual limit plus the amount of the basic limit not used in prior years (only allowed if not using age 50 or over catch-up contributions)

Universities may select which, if any, of these catch-up options to include in their 457 plans. Significantly, these catch-up contributions are not included in the $54,000 regular contribution limit; they are "on top" of the limit. So, if an employee makes a $6,000 catch-up contribution, the actual limit increases to $60,000.[23]

Contribution calculations are illustrated in table 4.6 (*left panel*). In this example, an employee participates in a mandatory 401(a) retirement plan, with the employee and the university contributing 5 and 6 percent of the employee's total salary, respectively. The university has chosen not to provide for catch-up contributions to this 401(a). Thus, the total annual contribution to the 401(a) plan is $17,600. To supplement retirement savings, the employee contributes the maximum amount permissible, including catch-up, to a separate 403(b) retirement account; this amounts to an additional $24,000 in retirement savings per year. The annual contribution to these two plans equals $41,600 ($17,600 + $24,000). The IRS allows total tax-deferred contributions up to $54,000 plus any catch-up contributions. Taking advantage of this high limit, the employee contributed an additional $24,000 per year to a 457(b) account, including catch-up. The total tax-deferred contributions to the three plan types add up to $65,600, which is $400 below the $66,000 contribution limit.

Table 4.6. University and employee 2017 contribution calculations for tax-deferred retirement and tax deferral earning

Contribution calculations		Tax-deferral earnings	
Parameters		Parameters	
Employee age on December 31, 2016	55	Total tax-deferred income	65,600
Salary and wages		Investment rate (paid quarterly)	7.00%
Base salary (academic year)	120,000	Investment period (years)	10
Summer salary	40,000	Federal income tax bracket	25.00%
Total annual earnings	160,000	Tax-deferral savings	
		Federal tax savings	16,400
401(a) retirement account		Interest earned	16,426
Employee mandatory percentage	5.00%	Tax savings plus interest	32,826
Employee annual contribution	8,000	Federal tax on deferred savings	8,207
University match	6.00%	After-tax total	24,620
University annual contribution	9,600	Net earnings from tax deferral	8,220
Total annual contribution	17,600		
		Tax-deferred income	
403(b) supplemental account		Total tax-deferred income	65,600
Employee contribution		Interest earned	65,705
Regular	18,000	Deferred income plus interest	131,305
Catch-up	6,000	Federal tax on deferred income	32,826
Total annual contribution	24,000	After-tax total	98,479
		Net retirement amount	123,099
457(b) supplemental account			
Employee contribution		Earnings if not tax deferred	
Regular	18,000	After-tax principle	49,200
Catch-up	6,000	Interest earned	49,279
Total annual contribution	24,000	After-tax total	98,479
		Net savings from tax deferral	24,620
Total tax-deferred compensation			
401(a)	17,600		
403(b)	24,000		
457(b)	24,000		
Total annual contribution	65,600		
Contribution limit for all plans			
Regular contributions	54,000		
Catch-up contributions			
403(b)	6,000		
457(b)	6,000		
Total contribution limit	66,000		

Note: University and employee contribution calculations are shown in the left panel. The employee is contributing to three different plans. In this example, the 401(a) does not provide for catch-up, and the 403(b) and 457(b) supplemental plans do not provide for university contributions. The financial advantages of tax deferral are shown in the right panel.

These are sound investments, as shown in table 4.6 (*right panel*). Assuming that the employee is in the 25 percent federal income tax bracket, deferring tax on $65,600 saves $16,400 in tax payment (25 percent of $65,600). If this tax saving is invested at an annual rate of 7 percent, the principal plus investment interest (that is, the FV) will equal $32,826 in 10 years. Of course, when the money is withdrawn, it will be subject to federal income tax. After 10 years, if the tax rate remains at 25 percent, the tax will be $8,207, and the after-tax saving will be $24,620, which represents net earnings of $8,220 ($24,620 – $16,400). Plus, if the principal of the three retirement accounts (totaling $65,600) earned 7 percent interest, they also will approximately double in 10 years, adding an additional $65,705 to bring the total principal plus interest to $131,305. Upon withdrawal, taxes must be paid, lowering the net principal to $98,479. The combined tax saving and net principal yield a total retirement amount of $123,098. Even so, this is not a bad investment at all.

For comparison, if the original investment ($65,600) were not tax deferred, the net retirement amount after 10 years would be $98,479, which is $24,620 less than if tax were deferred. The advantage of deferring taxes continues to grow every year until retirement. For that reason, employees should try to maximize their contributions starting as young as possible.

The accounting for a defined contribution plan is straightforward. Each year (usually quarterly), the university makes a known contribution to the plan based on the plan's formula. As a result, the university knows the exact amount of the obligation, which it reports as a pension expense. The university reports a liability only if its contributions are not paid in full.

In contrast, a *defined benefit* plan specifies a specific amount paid to the employee after retirement. The actual amount paid usually depends on the employee's salary and years of service at the time of retirement. However, it cannot exceed an IRS limit, which was $215,000 in 2017. In these calculations, many defined-benefit plans calculate the annual benefit using the value of the employee's highest-paid annual salary (not including fringe benefits), the number of years in service, and a plan multiplier (usually between 1 and 3 percent). Stated algebraically:

$$annual\ defined\ benefit = highest\ annual\ salary \times years\ of\ service \times retirement\ multiplier$$

Instead of using only a single year's salary, some universities use the average of the employee's three highest annual salaries—the "high three." As an example, a university might define the benefit as 1.5 percent of the high three multiplied by the number of years in service. So, for an employee who has worked for 10 years and has an average high three salary of $100,000 per year, the annual defined benefit amount would be $15,000, equal to $1,250 per month. These plans are based on uncertain financial and actuarial variables such as how the fund investments will perform, employee turnover, length of service, compensation levels, and how long the retirees will live. Because of these uncertainties, many universities are phasing out defined-benefit plans in favor of defined contribution plans.

Experienced actuaries determine the cost of defined benefit plans to the university. Annually, they estimate a funding target that equals 100 percent of the present value of all benefit liabilities accrued to date and during the plan year (usually the fiscal year), including increases in past service benefits attributable to current year increases in compensation. Then, in accordance with IRS rules, they compare the funding target with the plan's assets (money already invested in the pension fund) to determine how much the university must contribute to the defined-benefit fund account that plan year.[24] If the value of the plan assets equals or exceeds the funding target for the plan year, then the university's minimum contribution requirement for that plan year is "equal to the target normal cost of the plan for the plan year reduced (but not below zero) by any such excess." If the value of the assets is less than the plan's funding target for the plan year, the funding shortfall must be made up. According to the IRS, in the case of a funding shortfall, the minimum required contribution for that year is "equal to the sum of the plan's target normal cost for the plan year plus any applicable shortfall amortization installments and waiver amortization installments." The shortfall is amortized over a seven-year period; that is, the shortfall is paid into the fund in regularly scheduled equal payments over a seven-year period.

Paid Time Off

For employees, paid time off refers to a pool of hours to be used as the desire or need arises. There are three predominant categories of paid time off:

- vacations
- holidays
- sick leave

Important exception: Faculty members normally do not receive vacation leave or sick leave. For them, short absences with full salary for personal business, illness, jury duty, and so forth are not considered paid time off from an accounting point of view.

Technically, salaries and wages are paid only for the time worked, so paid time off must be accounted for in some other way. For the accountants, paid time off refers to money, expressed in terms of expenses, payables, and cash. The equivalence of time and money in this context may not be obvious. After all, the university isn't paying employees anything extra during their time off. It may be paid from a separate account in a university's general funds or a sponsored project's award. Regardless of the source, paid time off is an expense that the university must cover.

As fringe benefits provided by the employer, paid time off, also called paid absences, is subject to GAAP established by both the FASB and the GASB.[25] According to GAAP, employers recognize paid time off as a liability when four conditions are met:

- The payment obligation for future absences is based on employee services already rendered.
- The amount of the obligation can be reasonably estimated.
- Payment is probable.
- The obligation is for employee rights that accumulate (that is, accrue).

The rationale for recording it as a liability stems from the institution's obligation to compensate employees for services already rendered through paid time off or some other means, such as cash payments at termination or retirement.

Vacations are a primary benefit granted to an employee. For employees, time is the currency of vacations; for example, "How many days of vacation do I have left this year?" For accountants, money is the currency of vacations, as vacation time translates into vacation pay. And this pay usually accrues over time, with a certain proportion of vacation pay earned for every hour worked. For example, an employee may earn one day (eight hours) of time—that is, vacation pay—per month. Characteristically, employees don't use vacation time as it is earned; they accumulate unused time, which means that the employer (the university) also accumulates a corresponding liability (vacation payable), payable as time off at some later date during the normal course of employment or as cash when an employee leaves the institution.

Parenthetically, financial institutions such as banks require employees to take all of their vacation time each year. The rationale is to deter fraud. When employees are on vacation, some other employees must take over their responsibilities. Presumably, this second set of eyes may detect any fraudulent activities.

Technically, *holidays* differ from vacation pay in several significant ways. Holidays are paid time off at full salary on government-declared holidays, such as Memorial Day, Labor Day, Thanksgiving, and

Christmas. Unlike vacation pay that accrues after services have been performed (usually at the end of the month), employees may receive holiday pay as soon as they become employees; they are vested immediately. Also unlike vacation pay, holiday pay does not accrue since employees are paid in the normal course of the month for holidays that arise during the month. Thus, there is no unpaid expense related to a holiday that rolls over into the following reporting period. In some cases, employees may work on holidays and be paid in cash for the missed day off. This situation usually arises where someone must be present at all times or when the work load is so high that it cannot be completed without working through the holiday. This provision does not apply to salaried employees, who are paid the same amount in every pay period, irrespective of the presence of any holidays. Despite the technical differences, vacation and holiday pay may be combined into a single vacation entity for bookkeeping purposes.

Sample bookkeeping calculations for vacation and holiday pay are shown in table 4.7. In this example, the employee earns 10 holidays and 12 vacation days per year. Thus, the employee works 238 days and earns 22 total vacation and holidays, which constitute 9.24 percent of the days worked. This percentage, known as the vacation accrual rate, is multiplied by the weekly pay to calculate the vacation expense for that week, which is recorded as a liability via a debit to the "vacation expense" account and a credit to the "vacation payable" account. (Because the university uses the accrual basis of accounting, the rate charges vacation as it is earned, rather than as it is taken.)

When an employee uses some of the accrued vacation time, the vacation payable liability is reduced accordingly. Three bookkeeping scenarios illustrate this: no vacation (40 hours worked per week), 1 day of vacation (32 hours worked per week), and 5 days (1 week) of vacation (0 hours worked per week). Note that no salary or fringe benefits are charged to the funding source for the duration of the vacation period. So, "wages payable" is debited and cash is credited by 800, 640, and 0 dollars, respectively. When 1 or 5 days of vacation are taken, the "vacation payable" liability is reduced accordingly by a debit equal to the wages for 1 ($160) and 5 ($800) days, respectively, with corresponding credits to cash.

In this example, the employee does not accrue vacation while on vacation. So, using the accrual rate (9.24 percent in the example), the university continues to debit and credit the "vacation expense" and "vacation payable" accounts only for each day worked during the

Table 4.7. Vacation and holiday pay bookkeeping calculations

Standard work load			
Weeks per year		52	
Working hours per week		40	
Working hours per year		2080	
Working days per year		260	
Vacation time			
Paid holidays		10	
Paid vacation days		12	
Total vacation days		22	
Net days worked		238	
Vacation accrual rate		9.24%	
Vacation expense			
Employee pay/hour		20	
Hours worked	40	32	0
Weekly pay	800	640	0
Vacation expense (pay × accrual)	74	59	0

Bookkeeping entries	Debit	Credit
No vacation (40-hour work week)		
Wages payable	800	
Cash		800
Vacation expense	74	
Vacation payable		74
One day of vacation (32-hour work week)		
Wages payable	640	
Cash		640
Vacation payable	160	
Cash		160
Vacation expense	59	
Vacation payable		59
One week of vacation (0-hour work week)		
Wages payable	0	
Cash		0
Vacation payable	800	
Cash		800
Vacation expense	0	
Vacation payable		0

Note: Three scenarios are shown: no vacation taken (40-hour work week); one day of vacation taken (32-hour work week); and one week of vacation taken (0-hour work week).

week. Notably, unlike this example, many universities allow vacation accrual while an employee is on vacation.

Similarly, further bookkeeping charges the appropriate funding source for the vacation expenses. Typically, these payments, whether from the general fund, a sponsored grant award, an endowment account, et cetera, are deposited into a central university fund to pay for vacation salary when employees either take vacation or leave the university.

As a corollary, if vacation pay is included as a fringe benefit, a sponsored project budget should include salary for only the time worked; vacation pay will be obtained as a fringe benefit. Harvard University, for example, advises its principal investigators: "When preparing proposal budgets to be submitted to a sponsor, it is not necessary to request salary dollars for exempt and nonexempt employees for the full 52 weeks. Any vacation an employee takes during the sponsored award period will not be charged to the award but will be charged against the central vacation pool."[26] So, for example, if 3 weeks of vacation pay are included in the fringe benefit budget, only 49 weeks of salary plus fringe benefits should be in the salary budget.

Standard accounting practice is to pay vacations at the current salary rate. Therefore, any pay raises between the accrual and payout dates will add to the liability, which must then be adjusted. As vacation pay accrues (accumulates) over time, it becomes a long-term liability that continues to increase. To reduce this long-term expense, some universities limit the amount of vacation pay that can be accrued. For example, they may not allow accrual of more than 30 days of vacation pay.

Sick leave accrues in much the same way as vacation pay. In general, sick leave accrues at about 8 to 12 hours per month (that is, 1 to 1 1/2 days per month) for a full-time employee and proportionally less for part-time appointments. Like vacation pay, paid sick leave carries over from year to year, usually with no cap on the number of days that can be accrued. And usually employees may use paid sick leave only after it has been accrued. Most universities do not compensate employees for unused sick leave when they terminate employment; unlike vacation pay, the sick leave is forfeited. According to GAAP, if there is no termination pay, then accrued paid sick leave is not considered a liability. In contrast, the few institutions offering termination pay for unused sick leave must report this accrued liability as it is earned.

For internal bookkeeping purposes, sick leave accrual rates and expenses may be calculated in the same way as vacation pay. For example, 8 and 12 hours per month correspond to accrual rates of 4.84 and 7.44 percent, respectively. Plugging these accrual rates into table 4.7 yields sick leave expenses of $39 and $60 per week. Like vacation pay, sick leave expenses are credited to the appropriate "sick leave payable" accounts as liabilities until sick leave is used, when the expenses are debited to the "sick leave payable" accounts.

Workers' compensation is a form of insurance providing wage replacement and medical benefits to employees sustaining occupational injuries or illness in the course of employment. It allows employees with a work-related injury or illness to receive benefits regardless of who was at fault—the employee, the university, a co-worker, a customer, or some other third party. Thus, the workers' compensation system is designed to provide benefits to injured workers, even if an injury is caused by the university's or employee's carelessness. In exchange for these guaranteed benefits, employees waive the right to sue the university in court for negligence or damages related to the injuries or illness, thus protecting the university from potentially costly lawsuits. In other words, the employee is prohibited from filing suit while the university is obligated to pay the mandated benefits. This compromise—known as "exclusive remedy"—is the foundational basis for the workers' compensation system.

In most states, workers' compensation is mandatory. Commonly, employers may develop a self-insurance program or purchase coverage from a private insurance company that competes on price and coverage in an open market. Some states also provide insurance plans in the open market. In a few states, known as monopoly states, all coverage is provided by a state agency, with no private insurers and no competition. States may limit the length of time that an employee can receive temporary benefits for an injury. These limitations are in the range of three to seven years. However, they generally do not limit the length of permanent disability benefits, with the exception that some states terminate weekly benefits when the employee reaches age 65.

Employers must pay the full cost of the insurance, which is included as a fringe benefit. Employees do not share in covering the cost of the premium. In addition, when an accident occurs to an employee, the insurance organization pays all the costs of that claim. Unlike other business activities, where the prices of goods and services are established after most costs of production and delivery are known, workers' compensation premiums are established long before the number, severity, duration, or cost of claims can be known. The insurance providers establish financial reserves based on actuarial and case data as claims occur, but the ultimate cost of those claims may remain unknown for many years, sometimes taking as long as 40 to 50 years. Catastrophic, unanticipated events also may occur, which can greatly exceed a policyholder's annual premium. Thus, the insurers must build a substantial reserve to cover potential claims, and this adds to the cost for the employer.

Premiums vary by the employees' type of work. To quantify the risk of injury and, therefore, a claim, the National Council on Compensation Insurance, an independent entity, has developed a system of classification codes to categorize the kinds of work people do and the associated risk.[27] Understandably, riskier professions cost more to insure. Thus, workers' compensation insurance for office workers will be less than for construction workers—0.9 and 3.1 percent of compensation costs, respectively. So, an institution's workers' compensation costs depend on the nature of its workforce.

Sabbaticals are a special case of paid time off and are subject to the same GAAP. Accrual rates depend on the university's calendar. In a semester calendar, the rate is usually about 2.5 days per month of service. Therefore, in 6 years (72 months), 180 days will accrue, corresponding to roughly half of a year at full salary. In a quarter academic calendar, the rate is usually about 1 credit per quarter of service, with a maximum of 3 credits per year; the number of credits required for 2 quarters of sabbatical at full salary varies between about 18 and 24, meaning 6 to 8 years of service.

The appropriate accounting for sabbatical leave depends on the purpose of the leave. On the one hand, if the leave is to perform services or activities determined by the university, the sabbatical pay is for services performed and must be recorded as an accrued liability, just like vacation pay. The accrual amount should be based on the periods during which the rights to sabbatical leaves are earned and the probable amounts that will be paid through time off to the employee. On the other hand, if the leave is granted only to perform research or to enhance the reputation of the institution, the leave is not attributable to services already performed by the employee and is not reportable as a liability. In this case, there is no accrual, and the costs associated with the leave should be reported as current expenses in the period that the employee is on sabbatical.

Fringe Benefit Rates

All employees do not necessarily receive the same fringe benefits. For example, faculty members do not receive paid vacations or sick leave. Moreover, some fringe benefits, such as health care and retirement plans, provide choices that incur varying costs to the institution. Therefore, the costs of fringe benefits vary between employees. In principle, the fringe benefit costs for each employee could be calculated, but this would be cumbersome and time-consuming. Therefore, to simplify accounting and budget administration, employees are grouped (classified) according to the fringe benefits available to them. For each group, the costs of each fringe benefit are combined into a single pool. A fringe benefit rate is then determined for each pool by dividing the fringe benefits costs paid by the university by the total salaries and wages of that group:

$$pooled\ fringe\ benefit\ rate = \frac{total\ cost\ of\ fringe\ benefits\ in\ a\ pool}{total\ salaries\ and\ wages\ in\ that\ pool}$$

Consequently, each employee group has a different rate because different benefits are offered. The pooled rates spread fringe benefit costs over the institution's total salary base and funding streams, which greatly simplifies accounting and budget administration. Plus, the impact of an employee's fringe-benefit choices is kept within the pool rather than the employing departments. Procedurally, the use of pooled rates also minimizes incentives to hire based on an employee's potential benefits needs. Note that the pooled rates have no impact on the cost of the benefits to employees.

By using the pooled fringe benefit rate, a department easily can calculate the fringe benefit cost of a new employee at the time of hire rather than after the new employee makes benefit choices. The fringe benefit cost can be calculated by multiplying the employee's salary by the appropriate pooled fringe benefit rate. This is done routinely in the budgets of grant and contract applications. In fact, because of the financial implications, the federal government must approve an applicant institution's fringe benefit rates prior to issuing the institution any awards.

The pooled fringe benefit rates are prepared annually by the budget or controller's office. At the end of a fiscal year, the fringe benefit costs estimated for that year are compared with the actual costs incurred. Unpredictable factors, such as employee turnover, usually introduce variances between estimated and actual costs. Following the *Uniform Guidance*, these variances are carried forward.[28] If actual costs were more or less than the estimated costs, the under or over recovery is added or subtracted, respectively, to the next year's fringe benefit rate. With the inclusion of carry-forward, the benefit pools are designed to break even in the long run.

The calculation process for FY 2016 pooled fringe benefit rates is illustrated in table 4.8. Because the rates for next year (FY 2016) are based on costs from the current year (FY 2015), the cost data for each employee group are derived from the revised 2015 budget (salaries and wages are shown in table 6.1). Notice that the FICA tax rates

Table 4.8. Calculation of fringe benefit rates for separate employee classifications

Employee classification	Salaries and wages	FICA taxes	Health insurance	Life insurance	Retirement	Paid time off	Workers' comp.	Fringe benefits pool	(Under)/ over recovery	Net fringe benefits pool
					Fringe benefit costs					
Faculty	28,714,716	1,559,640	4,077,490	43,072	2,572,839	86,144	51,686	8,390,871	(75,518)	8,466,389
Exempt staff	2,000,615	114,785	284,087	3,001	179,255	14,004	3,601	598,734	(1,796)	600,530
Nonexempt staff	73,198,989	5,599,723	10,394,251	109,798	6,558,629	512,393	131,758	23,306,553	(23,307)	23,329,860
Postdocs	6,825,629	522,161	969,239		611,576	27,303	12,286	2,142,565	(2,143)	2,144,708
Teaching assistants	6,825,629		631,883				12,286	644,169	(4,509)	648,678
Student hourly	117,683						212	212		212
Totals	117,683,261	7,796,308	16,356,950	155,871	9,922,299	639,844	211,830	35,083,103	(107,272)	35,190,376

	FICA taxes	Health insurance	Life insurance	Retirement	Paid time off	Workers' comp.	Fringe benefits pool	Pooled rates (%)
				Fringe benefit rates (%)				
Faculty	5.43	14.20	0.15	8.96	0.30	0.18	29.22	29.48
Exempt staff	5.74	14.20	0.15	8.96	0.70	0.18	29.93	30.02
Nonexempt staff	7.65	14.20	0.15	8.96	0.70	0.18	31.84	31.87
Postdocs	7.65	14.20		8.96	0.40	0.18	31.39	31.42
Teaching assistants		9.26				0.18	9.44	9.50
Student hourly						0.18	0.18	

for faculty and exempt professionals are reduced because some salaries in these groups exceed the maximum for social security taxes. Also, the paid time off rate for faculty members is reduced because they do not receive vacation pay or sick leave benefits. Following the calculations, the faculty group, for example, accumulated $8,390,871 in pooled fringe benefits. To this, under-recovered fringe benefits from the previous year ($75,518) were added, yielding a net fringe benefit pool of $8,466,389. This value was divided into the total faculty salaries and wages ($28,714,716) to obtain the pooled fringe benefit rate, 29.48 percent. Therefore, a new faculty member's salary (for example, $100,000 per year) would be multiplied by 29.48 percent to determine the fringe benefit cost ($29,480). And so forth for employees in each group.

Supplies and Services

The costs of supplies and services associated with an organization's main operating activities (instruction, research, and public service) constitute operating expenses. These operating costs include the costs of administration, supplies, libraries, utilities, plant maintenance, rent, advertising, and other items necessary for operating the university according to its mission. Some of these costs are variable; they vary depending on the number of students, research activities, and related activities. Other costs are fixed; they tend to remain the same regardless of the number of students, et cetera. Examples include utilities and classroom and physical plant maintenance. Of course, salaries and wages and fringe benefits are significant operating costs, but they are recorded separately.

Operating costs are paid promptly using revenue generated during the current fiscal year, thus converting them immediately to expenses in accounting terms. In that sense, they constitute so-called revenue expenditures; they are matched with revenue earned during the current fiscal year. For example, routine repairs are revenue expenditures because they are charged directly to a repairs and maintenance expense account.

Scholarships and Fellowships

From an accounting perspective, financial aid comes in two different forms: scholarship allowances and direct student aid. (In this context, fellowships are considered the same as scholarships.) As described in chapter 3, scholarship allowances are subtracted directly from a student's tuition bill, thus reducing the amount paid by the student and earned by the institution. They are an offset to tuition and fees and are subtracted from the tuition and fees revenue; the resulting net tuition and fees are reported as revenue. These scholarship allowances constitute "forgone revenue," money earned but not collected. Consequently, they are not reported as expenses. In contrast, direct student aid is paid in cash to the student and is recorded as a "scholarship and fellowship" expense. That is, the student pays full tuition and fees but receives financial aid via cash from the university. This type of financial aid does not constitute forgone revenue since the full tuition and fees are collected from the student.

Summary

By definition, costs and expenditures are amounts to be paid or were spent to buy something. Costs convert to expenses as soon as related revenue is generated or the costs are consumed. Direct costs are associated directly with an institution's specific activities, such as salaries of the teaching faculty. Indirect costs are incurred on behalf of more than one specific project and cannot be traced to specific activities. Fringe benefits are provided by the university (the employer) to an employee. From an accounting perspective, they are expenses incurred by the employer. However, employees usually contribute part of the total costs of the fringe benefits. For example, Social Security and Medicare are funded by flat-rate taxes imposed equally on both employer and employee. Both employers and employees contribute to health-care plans. Post-retirement benefits, such as pensions, are recorded as expenses during the employees' working years because the university benefits from the employees' service during this period. Vacations and sick leave are paid as a fringe benefit and are recorded as a liability; notably, faculty members normally do not receive vacation or sick leave time. To simplify accounting, all employees are grouped according to the fringe benefits available to them. A fringe benefit rate is then determined for each group by dividing the fringe benefits costs paid by the university by the total salaries and wages of that group. The costs of supplies and services are paid using revenue generated during the current fiscal year, thus converting them immediately to expenses in accounting terms. In that sense, they constitute revenue expenditures; they are matched with revenue earned during the current fiscal year. Scholarship allowances subtracted directly from a student's tuition bill constitute "forgone revenue," not expenses. In contrast, direct student aid paid in cash to the student is recorded as a "scholarship and fellowship" expense.

Notes

1. Oxford University Press, "Oxford Dictionaries," http://www.oxforddictionaries.com/?gclid=CMa5maK2p8kCFU1cfgodiXoNoA (accessed November 23, 2015).

2. Oxford University Press, "Oxford Dictionaries."

3. Office of Management and Budget, "Uniform Administrative Requirements, Cost Principles, and Audit Requirements for Federal Awards, 2 C.F.R. §200," http://www.ecfr.gov/cgi-bin/text-idx?tpl=/ecfrbrowse/Title02/2cfr200_main_02.tpl (accessed June 19, 2017).

4. Financial Accounting Standards Board, "Not-for Profit Entities Presentation of Financial Statements Glossary," https://asc.fasb.org/glossarysection&trid=2209788&id=SL49203516-112866 (accessed April 21, 2016).

5. Financial Accountin Standards Board, "Not-for Profit Entities Presentation of Financial Statements Glossary."

6. National Association of College and University Business Officers, "Financial Accounting and Reporting Manual for Higher Education" (2016), http://efarm.nacubo.org/farm (accessed February 29, 2016). ¶704.1.

7. "Recommended Disclosure of Alternative Expense Classification Information for Public Higher Education Institutions," http://www.nacubo.org/Business_and_Policy_Areas/Accounting/Advisory_Reports/Advisory_Report_2000-8_Recommended_Disclosure_of_Alternative_Expense_Classification_Information_for_Public_Higher_Education_Institutions.html (accessed February 6, 2015).

8. "Financial Accounting and Reporting Manual for Higher Education." ¶703.13.

9. 29 U.S.C. Chapter 8.

10. US Department of Labor, "Guidance for Higher Education Institutions on Paying Overtime under the Fair Labor Standards Act," https://www.dol.gov/whd/overtime/final2016/highered-guidance.pdf (accessed January 19, 2017).

11. Harvard University, "Types of Employment," https://hr.harvard.edu/staff-personnel-manual/requirements-conditions-employment/types-employment (accessed June 20, 2017); Woods Hole Oceanographic Institution, "Definitions/Types of Employment," https://www.whoi.edu/HR/page.do?pid=16309&ct=901&cid=224 (accessed June 20, 2017).

12. State of New York, "Unemployment Insurance Law, Articles 18 & 25-B," https://labor.ny.gov/ui/dande/article18.shtm (accessed January 20, 2017).

13. Internal Revenue Service, "Publication 969 Health Savings Accounts and Other Tax-Favored Health Plans," https://www.irs.gov/pub/irs-pdf/p969.pdf (accessed January 20, 2017).

14. "Revenue Procedure 2016-28" (2016), https://www.irs.gov/pub/irs-drop/rp-16-28.pdf (accessed January 18, 2017).

15. College and University Professional Association for Human Resources (CUPA-HR), "2016 CUPA-HR Healthcare and Other Benefits Survey" (2017), http://www.cupahr.org/surveys/benefits.aspx (accessed May 9, 2017).

16. Priyanka Daya McCluskey, "Colleges across Region Team up to Cut Health Care Costs," August 25 (2015), https://www.bostonglobe.com/business/2015/08/24/local-colleges-form-consortium-lower-health-care-costs/fxm2hfOBtXoUAx1AleamkM/story.html (accessed May 9, 2017).

17. Justin Zackal, "Why Institutions Self-Insure Their Health Care Coverage" (2014), https://www.higheredjobs.com/Articles/articleDisplay.cfm?ID=498 (accessed May 8, 2017).

18. Audrey Williams June, "More Colleges Turn to 'Self Insurance' to Deal with Rising Health-Care Costs," *Chronicle of Higher Education* 49, no. 34 (2003) (accessed May 9, 2017).

19. University of New Hampshire System, "USNH Saves $10 Million by Moving to Self-Insured Health Care; Savings," https://www.usnh.edu/about/usnh -saves-10-million-moving-self-insured-health-care-savings (accessed May 9, 2017).

20. 26 U.S.C. § 79—Group-term life insurance purchased for employees.

21. 29 U.S.C. Chapter 18—Employee retirement income security program.

22. 26 U.S.C. § 401—Qualified pension, profit-sharing, and stock bonus plans.

23. Claire Boyte-White, "Are Catch-up Contributions Included in the 415 Limit?", http://www.investopedia.com/ask/answers/112415/are-catchup-contributions -included-415-limit.asp (accessed January 26, 2017).

24. Internal Revenue Service, "Determination of Minimum Required Pension Contributions: T.D. 9732, RIN 1545-BH71," http://federalregister.gov/a/2015-20914 (accessed January 24, 2017).

25. Financial Accounting Standards Board, "Statement of Financial Accounting Standards No. 43, Accounting for Compensated Absences," http://www.fasb.org/jsp /FASB/Document_C/DocumentPage?cid=1218220130511&acceptedDisclaimer =true (accessed January 31, 2017); Governmental Accounting Standards Board, "Statement No. 16 of the Governmental Accounting Standards Board, Accounting for Compensated Absences," http://www.gasb.org/jsp/GASB/Document_C/Docum entPage?cid=1176160030155&acceptedDisclaimer=true (accessed January 31, 2017).

26. Harvard University, "Absence Management Guidance," http://osp.finance .harvard.edu/absence-management-guidance (accessed February 6, 2017).

27. National Council on Compensation Insurance, "About Us," https://www .ncci.com/Pages/AboutUs.aspx (accessed February 15, 2017).

28. 2 C.F.R. § 200.431 Compensation—fringe benefits.

Chapter 5
Capital Assets

Definition of Capital Assets

In generic accounting terms, capital assets are "property that is expected to generate value over a long period of time."[1] They are also known as long-term assets, fixed assets, or property plant and equipment. In this context, long-term means longer than one year. Thus, capital assets differ from supplies, maintenance costs, and other items that are acquired, paid for, and used within a single year. (Of course, items purchased near the end of a fiscal year may carry over to the next fiscal year; but, if they are intended for use within the next year, they are not capital assets.)

Characteristically, capital assets:

- have a useful life of more than one year
- cost more than a minimum amount, known as the capitalization limit
- are not expected to be sold as a normal part of operations
- tend not to be convertible into cash easily

Capital assets may be tangible or intangible. Examples are land, buildings, computer and laboratory equipment, machinery, vehicles, and intellectual property "acquired by purchase, construction, manufacture, lease-purchase, exchange, or through capital leases."[2] Incidentally, as intellectual property, the institution's financial accounting software system (which may have cost millions of dollars) is a capital asset. Further examples are "additions, improvements, modifications, replacements, rearrangements, reinstallations, renovations or alterations to capital assets that materially increase their value or useful life (not ordinary repairs and maintenance)." Capital assets are considered investments needed to fulfill the institution's objectives. Stated differently, they are assets that add to the institution's value. Thus, the purchase of a capital asset adds to the institution's value.

Capitalizing

Capitalizing (that is, to capitalize) is an accounting method used to delay the recognition of the cost of acquiring a capital asset by recording it as a long-term, capital expense. In other words, when an institution purchases a capital asset, it incurs a capital expense that is written off incrementally over a number of years; the expense is capitalized. Cash is paid "up front" to acquire the asset, but the total cost is not recorded as an expense in the current year; it is spread out over the expected lifetime of the asset. Improvements to capital assets such as land, buildings, and infrastructure (for example, utilities) that significantly increase the value or extend their useful life are also capitalized. However, routine repairs and maintenance are reported as an operating expense in the year when the expense was incurred.

Conceptually, capitalizing derives from one of the most important principles in accounting: the matching principle. The matching principle requires the matching of revenues and expenses to the fiscal year when they occurred. Matching is a simple task with the cost of office supplies; they are typically used within one year, so the associated revenues and expenses are easily matched to that year. But capital assets such as a building or a computer bring value to the institution for many years. Therefore, instead of converting the entire cost of the building or computer to an expense when they are purchased, institutions convert the original cost of capital assets to expenses over their many years of useful life, thus matching revenue and expenses. In accounting terms, the expense is capitalized to match revenue. In colloquial terms, the asset is written off as it is used to generate revenue over its useful life.

Capitalizing also derives from the related principle of inter-period equity. (In this context, the term "period" usually refers to a year.) According to the GASB, inter-period equity is "the state at which current-year taxpayers have provided adequate resources to pay for the cost of current-year services. Another way to look at it is as a state of equilibrium in which a government is neither deferring costs to the future nor using accumulated resources to provide current-period services."[3] Because capital assets provide benefits over more than one year, it is usually assumed that the costs should be spread over more than one year. That way, future beneficiaries of the assets share in the costs.

Most institutions have a threshold value for asset capitalization. Accordingly, assets valued over a certain amount are treated routinely as a capitalized asset. For example, a university may capitalize any asset with an acquisition value greater than $5,000. Automatically, that would include all buildings and major renovations. Moreover, that would include many common laboratory pieces of equipment, such as microscopes, centrifuges, et cetera. In contrast, regular operating expenses valued at less than the threshold would not be capitalized. Indeed, that would be fraudulent if the intent were to make the current year's expenses appear smaller than they really are.

Depreciation

Depreciation is the process of converting the cost of a capital asset into an operational expense (called a depreciation expense) over the asset's estimated useful life. That is, depreciation spreads a large expenditure (the purchase price of the asset) proportionately over a fixed period of multiple fiscal years to match revenue received from it. Thus, depreciation deducts a certain value from the asset every year until the full value of the asset has been "written off." The annual depreciation expense comes out of that year's net income. Technically, only tangible or physical assets such as buildings and equipment (except for the cost of land) are depreciated. Intangible assets, such as patents and software, are amortized. The two terms, "depreciation" and "amortization," refer to the same process: proration of the cost of a specific type of capital asset over the asset's lifetime. Indeed, in some parlance the terms are used interchangeably.

For how many years is a capital asset depreciated? Or, asked differently, how long is the useful life (or lifetime) of a capital asset? In financial terms, the useful life of an asset "is an estimate of the number of years an asset is likely to remain in service for the purpose of cost-effective revenue generation."[4] Buildings and equipment usually have lifetimes ranging from 35 to 50 years and 3 to 8 years, respectively. Specialized research facilities may have components with useful lifetimes ranging from 10 to 45 years. Approximate useful lifetimes of common capital assets are shown in table 5.1. Most universities have a master list of useful lifetimes for all capital assets, including laboratory equipment, computers, and furniture, where specific items can be looked up.[5]

As a capital asset depreciates over its useful life, losing some of its value each year, the depreciation is subtracted from an asset's

Table 5.1. Approximate useful lifetimes of capital assets

Capital asset	Useful lifetime (years)
Buildings	35–50
Building improvements	5–40
Specialized research facilities	10–45
Land	Infinite (cannot be depreciated)
Land improvements	10
Infrastructure	10
Library books	10
Computer software	10
Office and laboratory equipment	5–15

original acquisition cost to yield its depreciated value. If the asset has any salvage (or residual) value at the end of its useful life, that salvage value may be deducted from the acquisition cost to obtain the depreciation base:

$$depreciation\ base = acquisition\ cost - salvage\ value$$

In this context, the salvage value may be the market value of a fully depreciated building or the scrap-metal value of a fully depreciated truck. The salvage value may be zero if the asset has no monetary value at the end of its useful life.

There are several ways to calculate depreciation, but the most common in university settings is the "straight-line" method. In this method, the depreciation base is divided by the number of years of useful life. That is:

$$annual\ depreciation = \frac{depreciation\ base}{useful\ life}$$

The annual depreciation is deducted from the depreciation base of the item each year, and these deductions accumulate over the useful lifetime of the item. Thus, at the end of its useful life, the item has no value as a capital asset other than any salvage value; the accumulated depreciation equals the depreciation base. The item is fully depreciated. (An asset cannot be depreciated to less than its salvage value.) At that point, the item is "taken off the books"—it is no longer considered a capital asset.

Major renovations also can be capitalized. Basically, depreciation of the renovation cost is added to the depreciation of the asset's cost. For this addition, there are two procedures that depend on whether the renovation extends the asset's useful life. If the renovation extends the asset's useful lifetime, the cost of the renovation is subtracted from the accumulated depreciation at the time of the renovation, thus increasing the depreciated value by the same amount. The depreciation amount per year doesn't change, but the number of years of depreciation increases. If the renovation does not extend the useful life, the cost of the renovation is added to the depreciated value of the asset at the time of the renovation, with a corresponding increase in the annual depreciation amount. Either way results in the same accumulated depreciation amount—the original cost plus the renovation cost minus the salvage value.

These two procedures are illustrated in figure 5.1, which presents depreciation calculations for an asset such as a building, without (*upper panel*) and with (*middle and lower panels*) renovations. In this example, the original cost of the building was $32 million. After a useful lifetime of 40 years, the residual salvage value will be $2 million. As shown in the upper panel, the $32 million building depreciates to its salvage value in 40 years.

Therefore, using straight-line depreciation:

$$annual\ depreciation = \frac{\$32,000,000 - \$2,000,000}{40\ years}$$
$$= \$750,000\ per\ year$$

Now add the renovations. On the one hand, assume that a $12 million renovation was completed in year 20, extending the building's useful life for at least another 20 years, illustrated in the middle panel. The renovation cost is subtracted from the accumulated depreciation at year 20, with a corresponding increase in the building's depreciated value. The renovated building can then be depreciated by $750,000 for an additional 16 years:

$$additional\ depreciation\ time = \frac{\$12,000,000}{\$750,000/year} = 16\ years$$

The total useful life is extended from 40 to 56 years. Consequently,

$$total\ accumulated\ depreciation = \frac{\$750,000}{year} \times (40+16)\ years$$
$$= \$42,000,000,$$

which is the original cost less salvage value ($30,000,000) plus the renovation cost ($12,000,000).

On the other hand, assume that the renovation did not extend the building's useful life. In that case, shown in the lower panel, the renovation cost, $12 million, is added to the building's depreciated value at the time of the renovation (year 20), raising it from $17

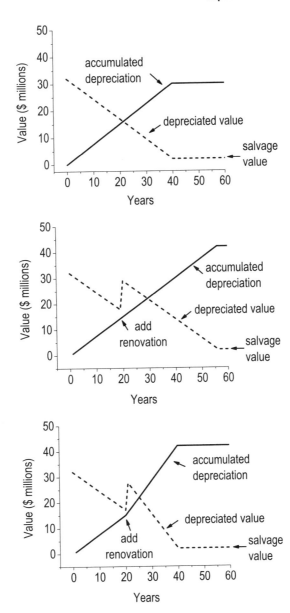

Figure 5.1. Straight-line depreciation without (*upper panel*) and with (*middle and lower panels*) renovations

million to $29 million. Because of this increase in asset value, the annual depreciation amount from year 21 to year 40 also increases accordingly:

$$annual\ depreciation\ after\ renovation = \frac{\$29,000,000 - \$2,000,000}{20\ years}$$
$$= \$1,350,000\ per\ year$$

Thus, at year 21, the annual depreciation increases from $750,000 per year to $1,350,000 per year. After 40 years, the total accumulated depreciation equals $42,000,000. As these figures show, the total accumulated depreciation cannot exceed the cost of the building less salvage value plus renovations.

As a reminder: the cost of a capital asset is not recorded as an expense at the time of acquisition. Instead, the depreciation is recorded as an expense for each year of the asset's useful life. In that sense, depreciation represents "real money"—the money used to pay for the capital asset when it was acquired—just like any other expense, such as salaries and wages and other operating expenses.

Allocation of Depreciation

In some situations, an institution may want to allocate a capital asset's depreciation to specific cost pools. For example, if a building is occupied by departments in two different colleges, the institution may want to determine the amount of the building's depreciation assignable to each college. Likewise, the institution may want to determine the amount of the building's depreciation assignable to instruction or research. These situations arise in the context of indirect cost assignments to specific cost objectives in some institutional budget models, such as responsibility center management (chapter 6), and federal grants and contracts (chapter 9).

For buildings, depreciation is usually allocated to various cost objectives (sometimes called cost pools in this context) on the basis of usable square feet of space. Depending on the specific purpose of the allocation, this may or may not include common areas such as hallways, stairwells, and restrooms. The number of square feet occupied by each cost pool (usually referred to as assignable net square feet, or ANSF) is tabulated, and the depreciation is allocated according to the percentage of space occupied by each cost pool relative to the building's total ANSF:

$$\frac{allocated\ pool\ depreciation}{total\ building\ depreciation} = \frac{ANSF\ benefiting\ the\ pool}{total\ building\ ANSF}$$

Rewritten more simply:

$$allocated\ depreciation = percentage\ of\ ANSF \times total\ building\ depreciation$$

If individual rooms are used jointly by more than one function, depreciation is allocated further based on some appropriate metric, such as the number of FTE occupants or their salaries and wages.

Allocation of depreciation is illustrated for a single building, namely, the life sciences building, in table 5.2. The building's total

Table 5.2. Allocation of a building's depreciation to the colleges using the building

Location	Users	College	ANSF	% of total ANSF	Annual depreciation
First floor	Classrooms	All-campus	20,000	16.67	40,000
Second floor	Biology department	Arts and sciences	20,000	16.67	40,000
Third floor	Biology department	Arts and sciences	20,000	16.67	40,000
Fourth floor	Biotechnology institute				
		Arts and sciences	10,000	8.33	20,000
		Agriculture	10,000	8.33	20,000
Fifth floor	Bacteriology department	Agriculture	20,000	16.67	40,000
Sixth floor	Plant Pathology department	Agriculture	20,000	16.67	40,000
Totals			120,000	100.00	240,000

	First-floor classrooms		
College	FTE usage	% FTE usage	Annual depreciation
Agriculture	1,063	20.74	8,297
Arts and sciences	2,438	47.59	19,036
Education	284	5.55	2,220
Engineering	1,338	26.12	10,447
Totals	5,123	100.00	40,000

	Colleges				
Location	Agriculture	Arts and science	Education	Engineering	Annual depreciation
First floor	8,297	19,036	2,220	10,447	40,000
Second floor		40,000			40,000
Third floor		40,000			40,000
Fourth floor	20,000	20,000			40,000
Fifth floor	40,000				40,000
Sixth floor	40,000				40,000
Totals	108,297	119,036	2,220	10,447	240,000

Note: Life science building's total annual depreciation = $240,000.

depreciation for this fiscal year is $240,000, based on the cost of the building and capitalized equipment within it, such as heating and air conditioning units, cabinetry, plumbing fixtures, and so forth. Depreciation of department-specific equipment, such as microscopes, centrifuges, and other laboratory capital assets, is not included. Initially, the building's depreciation is allocated by floor on the basis of square footage occupied by the colleges (*upper panel*). All common space, such as hallways, et cetera, is included. The allocation calculations are straightforward for the second through sixth floors. However, for the first-floor classrooms, the allocation must be further calculated based on classroom usage by the various colleges. In this example (*middle panel*), the number of FTE students enrolled in courses taught in these rooms during the fall semester constituted the base. So, 1,063 students attended courses taught by the College of Agriculture in these first-floor classrooms; this represents 20.74 percent of all students taking courses in these rooms (5,123). Consequently, 20.74 percent of the first floor's total depreciation ($40,000) is allocated to the College of Agriculture: $20.74\% \times \$40,000 = \$8,297$. The colleges' total allocations for all floors are then added up (*lower panel*). For example, the College of Agriculture's allocation of the life science building's depreciation is $108,297 for this fiscal year.

The algorithms for allocating depreciation of other kinds of capital assets use bases that most accurately (and fairly) represent the benefits to the particular cost objectives.

Debt Financing: Bonds

Capital assets, such as buildings, major renovations, and the like, are very expensive. They cost much more than a typical university can pay from its operating fund. So, some other way must be found to pay for them. Some universities may save money in a reserve account to pay cash for future capital assets. Or, a donor may give cash to pay for the asset. But, more commonly, universities borrow money to pay for them. Even when a donor pledges money for a new building, universities often borrow money to pay for the building "up front" and use the donation proceeds to make the periodic interest plus principal payments over the duration of the long-term debt. This compares to a prospective homeowner taking out a mortgage from a bank to finance a house purchase or remodeling. Like a homeowner, a university can borrow money from a bank. Accordingly, most universities have a line of credit with a local bank to cover short-term needs. But, unlike homeowners, they seldom borrow from a bank to finance long-term capital projects. Indeed, for long-term financing, banks are considered the "lender of last resort."

Instead, universities rely on bonds, a form of long-term debt, to finance new capital assets. A bond issue is generally less expensive than borrowing money from a bank and is subject to fewer restrictive covenants—rules placed on debt to reduce the lender's risk. Nonetheless, some aspects of bond financing can become fairly complex, especially when bonds are bought and sold during unstable financial conditions. Because of the large amounts of money at stake, bond financing represents a topic of considerable interest to CFOs and governing boards. They are constantly on the lookout for ways to reduce this debt, usually through refinancing when interest rates decline. Any savings in this regard become available for other academic priorities. To show what university financial officers look for, we will examine bonds in some depth.

Bonds are formal certificates of indebtedness. Individual bonds represent a fixed amount of debt or, stated differently, a fixed amount of money to be borrowed. Individuals or institutional investors known as bondholders purchase them. Commonly, the value of one bond, known as its face (or par) value, is $1,000. So, to raise $10 million, the institution would issue (sell) 10,000 bonds (10,000 × $1,000 = $10,000,000). The institution (the issuer) is obligated to repay to the bondholders the face value when the bond matures; when they are paid off, the bond is "redeemed." The maturity date must extend more than a year into the future and usually extends between 5 and 30 years into the future. During this time, the institution also pays interest, known as coupon, to the bondholders at a rate (the coupon rate) that may be fixed or variable. (The word "coupon" originated before the days of computerized banking transactions, when coupons attached to the bonds were presented to a bank to redeem the periodic interest payments.) In general, the coupon rate increases as the maturity date extends farther into the future.

Incidentally, after purchasing the bonds, the bondholders may sell them on the secondary market at a price that depends on market forces. For the university, the sale doesn't change any of the terms of the bond; it continues to pay the new owners of the bond interest at the coupon rate until the maturity date stated on the bond itself.

The bond certificate states contractually the interest rate that will be paid and the time when the loaned funds (the bond principal) must be repaid to the bondholders. A document called an indenture accompanies the bond, spelling out the agreement between the issuer and the bondholders.[6] Within the indenture are covenants designed to protect the university and the bondholders, specifying what the issuing institution may or may not do during the life of the bond. For example, the university may be required to maintain adequate insurance on the capital asset. Or, it may be required to establish a special fund specifically for the maintenance and repair of the capital asset.

Most bond indentures have a provision, known as the call provision, allowing the institution to buy the bonds back from the bondholders before the maturity date. This is known as calling the bonds. The call provision gives the university (the borrower) the right to retire (pay off) all or a portion of the outstanding bonds at a stipulated price (the call price), usually at a premium over face value, but never less than face value. The premium is designed to compensate the bondholders for the institution's right to pay off the debt earlier than the holders expected. Many bond issues have a deferred call, which means the institution cannot call in the bond until the expiration of the deferment period, usually between 5 and 10 years.

To ensure that a bond issue is properly framed, the issuing institution retains legal counsel, known as bond counsel. After all, a lot of money is changing hands. Bond counsels are lawyers engaged to provide an objective legal opinion with respect to the validity of bonds and other aspects such as the tax treatment of interest on the bonds. Accordingly, the bond counsel confirms that the university is allowed legally to issue the bonds and obligated to repay them. Furthermore, the bond counsel ensures that the issue has been announced properly and that the bond certificates have been printed legally. These confirmations and assurances are documented in a formal legal opinion that must be attached to every bond certificate.

The institution's credit risk affects the price and, therefore, the interest rate of the bonds. Credit risk (also called default risk) is the possibility that the issuing institution will be unable to pay off the principal or even make the interest payment: the higher its credit risk, the lower the price and the higher the yield (the interest rate) on its bonds. Companies such as Moody's, Standard & Poor's, and Fitch evaluate the likelihood that a debt issuer will be able to meet scheduled interest and principal payments.[7] Their ratings are compared in table 5.3. The highest ratings, such as AAA, AA, and A, are awarded to issuers with a solid, proven record of paying interest and principal in a satisfactory manner; lower ratings, such as BB, B, CCC, and so on down the line, indicate less trustworthy issuers. (In the jargon, one rating step is called a notch; so, moving from AAA to AA+ is downgrading one notch.) Bonds issued by institutions rated Baa and BBB and higher are considered "investment grade" and sell at prices close to face value—that is, they pay interest at rates close to face value. However, bonds issued by institutions with lower ratings are considered "speculative," and cost less (that is, pay higher interest rates) to offset the higher perceived risks. Stated in different terms, bond yields increase as credit ratings decrease. And increased yields mean that the issuer pays higher interest rates on the bonds. *Note:* Although credit risk refers formally to the institutions issuing the bonds, as a shortcut the term refers informally to the bonds themselves. Thus, bonds issued by an institution with a AA credit risk are rated AA bonds.

Table 5.3. Credit ratings and default risk

Bond rating			Grade	Risk
Moody's	Standard and Poor's	Fitch		
			Investment grade	
Aaa	AAA	AAA	Investment, highest quality	Lowest
Aa1	AA+	AA+	Investment, very high quality	Low
Aa2	AA	AA		
Aa3	AA–	AA–		
A1	A+	A+	Investment, high quality	Low
A2	A	A		
A3	A–	A–		
Baa1	BBB+	BBB+	Minimum investment grade	Medium
Baa2	BBB	BBB		
Baa3	BBB–	BBB–		
			Speculative	
Ba1	BB+	BB+	Junk, speculative	High
Ba2	BB	BB		
Ba3	BB–	BB–		
B1	B+	B+	Junk, very speculative	Higher
B2	B	B		
B3	B–	B–		
Caa1	CCC+	CCC+	Junk, default possible	Even higher
Caa2	CCC	CCC		
Caa3	CCC–	CCC–		
Ca	CC	CC+	Junk, default probable	Extreme
	C	CC	Junk, in imminent default	Highest
		CC–		
D	D	DDD		

In general, all bond ratings are compared to the benchmark US Treasury bonds because the US government is considered the least likely to default. That is, they carry the lowest credit risk and, accordingly, pay the lowest interest (yield). The difference in yield between a US Treasury bond and a non-US Treasury bond of comparable maturity is called the spread. The spread is measured in basis points (bp), with one bp equaling 0.01 percent (100 bp equals 1 percent), or in percentage yield.

The importance of a university's credit rating on the cost of borrowing is shown by the relationship between rating, bond yields, and interest payment in table 5.4, which is based on rating data published by New York University.[8] In this example, the US Treasuries yield 3.00 percent, and the highest rated bonds (AAA) yield 3.65 percent. With a face value of $1,000, each AAA bond pays $36.50 of interest per year; for 10,000 bonds, this totals $365,000 in interest payments per year and $7,300,000 at maturity. Stepping down one notch to AA+, the yield increases to 3.80 percent. This

Table 5.4. Relationship between bond rating and interest paid

Rating	Spread (%)	Yield (%)	Yearly interest per bond	Yearly total interest	Total interest at maturity	Interest increment per rating notch	Interest increment relative to US Treasury
US Treasuries	0.00	3.00	30.00	300,000	6,000,000		
Aaa/AAA	0.65	3.65	36.50	365,000	7,300,000	1,300,000	1,300,000
Aa1/AA+	0.80	3.80	38.00	380,000	7,600,000	300,000	1,600,000
Aa2/AA	0.95	3.95	39.50	395,000	7,900,000	300,000	1,900,000
Aa3/AA−	1.05	4.05	40.50	405,000	8,100,000	200,000	2,100,000
A1/A+	1.15	4.15	41.50	415,000	8,300,000	200,000	2,300,000
A2/A	1.20	4.20	42.00	420,000	8,400,000	100,000	2,400,000
A3/A−	1.45	4.45	44.50	445,000	8,900,000	500,000	2,900,000
Baa1/BBB+	2.00	5.00	50.00	500,000	10,000,000	1,100,000	4,000,000
Baa2/BBB	2.30	5.30	53.00	530,000	10,600,000	600,000	4,600,000
Baa3/BBB−	3.10	6.10	61.00	610,000	12,200,000	1,600,000	6,200,000
Ba1/BB+	3.75	6.75	67.50	675,000	13,500,000	1,300,000	7,500,000
Ba2/BB	4.50	7.50	75.00	750,000	15,000,000	1,500,000	9,000,000
Ba3/BB−	4.75	7.75	77.50	775,000	15,500,000	500,000	9,500,000
B1/B+	5.50	8.50	85.00	850,000	17,000,000	1,500,000	11,000,000
B2/B	6.50	9.50	95.00	950,000	19,000,000	2,000,000	13,000,000
B3/B−	6.75	9.75	97.50	975,000	19,500,000	500,000	13,500,000
Caa/CCC	8.75	11.75	117.50	1,175,000	23,500,000	4,000,000	17,500,000
CC	9.50	12.50	125.00	1,250,000	25,000,000	1,500,000	19,000,000
C	10.50	13.50	135.00	1,350,000	27,000,000	2,000,000	21,000,000
D	12.00	15.00	150.00	1,500,000	30,000,000	3,000,000	24,000,000

Note: Yield and interest are computed using the following bond issue parameters: face value, 1,000; maturity, 20; number of bonds issued, 10,000; total issue, 10,000,000.

increases the total interest paid at maturity by $300,000 (from $7,300,000 to $7,600,000). As the rating declines, the incremental yield increases, as does the total interest paid at maturity. And this increases the cost of borrowing money.

Most university bonds are investment grade, reflecting the university's low credit risk. Indeed, historically, universities default on less than 0.3 percent of investment-grade bonds. Nonetheless, ratings do change occasionally, and even a one-notch downgrade costs money that must be taken from other academic priorities. Consequently, university financial officers always pay attention to the bond credit ratings to minimize the cost of borrowing money.

In reality, when issuing the bonds, the university may not get the bonds' exact face value. When the bonds are printed (in hard-copy or digital format), the face value represents the prevailing interest rates for comparable bond issues in the overall bond market. However, during the time intervening between printing the bonds, finding buyers, and selling them, the market interest rates may change, thus changing the value of the bonds. The university always must pay the interest stated on the bond (the coupon rate), so it accommodates changes in the market interest rate by adjusting the actual price of the bond: if market interest rates go down, the price goes up, the bonds are more valuable, and the institution receives more than the face value, and vice versa. In financial terms, if market interest rates are lower than face value, the bonds are sold at a premium, and if market interest rates are higher than face value, the bonds are sold at a discount. Factoring in the market price of the bond, the actual rate of interest received by the purchaser, known as the yield, may differ from the coupon rate. Indeed, the yield will equal the coupon rate only if the bond is purchased at face value.

The concept of variable bond prices is illustrated in table 5.5. The institution issued 10,000 bonds with a face value of $1,000—nominally, a $10 million bond issue. And it agreed to pay 5 percent interest on the $10 million semiannually until the bonds mature in 20 years; that commitment equals $250,000 per payment. But the actual market value of the bonds when sold may be more or less than $10 million due to interest rate fluctuations. In this illustration, the bonds' market value was computed for three different interest rates, known as discount rates in this context.

The bonds' market value equals the sum of the present values of the interest payments and the principal amount. Stated as a question: For a given discount rate, what must the bonds' value be today for them to be worth $10,000,000 at maturity? To answer this

Table 5.5. Costs of borrowing for bond issues at face value, a discount, and a premium

Parameters			
Number of bonds issued	10,000		
Face value (par)	1,000		
Total amount issued	10,000,000		
Date issued	3/7/2017		
Maturity date	3/7/2037		
Number of years	20		
Number of payments/year	2		
First interest payment date	9/7/2017		
Coupon rate	5.00%		
Interest per payment	250,000		
Total interest	10,000,000		

Calculations			
	Bond values		
	Face value	Premium	Discount
Discount (market) rate	5.00%	4.00%	6.00%
Present value of interest	6,275,694	6,838,870	5,778,693
Present value of principal at maturity	3,724,306	4,528,904	3,065,568
Market value of bonds (amount received from bondholders)	10,000,000	11,367,774	8,844,261
Premium		1,367,774	
Discount			1,155,739
Market price per bond	1,000	1,137	884
Yield to investor	5.00%	3.08%	7.09%
Cost of borrowing			
Interest	10,000,000	10,000,000	10,000,000
Subtract premium		(1,367,774)	
Add discount			1,155,739
Total cost of borrowing	10,000,000	8,632,226	11,155,739
Payments per period			
Interest	250,000	250,000	250,000
Amortization (straight-line)		(34,194)	28,893
Interest expense	250,000	215,806	278,893

question, the present value of the interest and the principal at maturity were computed and added together to obtain the present value of the bonds, which is the market value, for each of three different discount rates. When the discount rate equals the coupon rate (5 percent), the market value of the bonds equals the face value, $10,000,000. However, when the discount rate is 4 percent, the market value is more, $11,367,774; consequently, the bond issue generated an extra $1,367,774 (a premium) for the institution ($11,367,774 – $10,000,000). Conversely, when the discount rate is 6 percent, the market value of the bonds is less, $8,844,261; the bond issue generated $1,155,739 less (a discount) than the face-value amount. *Note:* The market price per bond (market value divided by the number of bonds issued) adjusts accordingly. Thus, an investor pays (and the institution generates) $137 more per bond when they sell at a premium and $116 less per bond when they sell at a discount, with corresponding changes in the yield to the investors. Usually, the premium or discount is not paid in one lump sum; it is amortized over the lifetime of the bond. Therefore, the interest payments per period adjust to the bonds' market values by subtracting or adding the amortized premium and discount amounts, respectively. So, in the example, the interest payment per period decreases by $34,194 ($1,367,774 divided by 40, the total number of payments) when the discount rate drops to 4 percent.

Municipal Bonds
Tax-Exempt Bonds

To minimize the cost of borrowing money, universities often take advantage of an IRS provision that allows state and local governments to issue tax-exempt bonds.[9] More exactly, the interest paid to the bond purchasers is tax-exempt; the bondholder does not have to pay federal taxes on the interest income. Moreover, most states do not tax the interest income from tax-exempt bonds issued within that state; however, virtually all states tax the interest from tax-exempt bonds issued in another state.

Definitionally, bonds issued by state and local governments are known commonly as municipal bonds (or "munis"). Since tax-exempt bonds are always issued by a government agency, university tax-exempt bonds are always municipal bonds. Notably, the interest on some municipal bonds is taxable because the federal government will not subsidize the financing of activities that do not provide significant benefit to the public. For example, bonds issued to finance things like stadiums or replenishment of an underfunded pension plan would not qualify for federal tax exemption.

How much lower are the yields to the bondholder for tax-exempt bonds? Of course, that depends on the market—how much of a premium a potential buyer will offer in return for the tax exemption. But, as a rule of thumb, the equivalent tax-exempt bond yield depends on the bondholder's marginal tax rate:

$$equivalent\ tax\ exempt\ bond\ yield = taxable\ bond\ yield$$
$$\times (1 - bondholder's\ marginal$$
$$tax\ rate)$$

Assuming the bondholder's marginal tax rate is 28 percent (0.28) and the yield on comparable taxable bonds is 5 percent (0.05),

$$equivalent\ tax\ exempt\ bond\ yield = 0.05 \times (1 - 0.28) = 0.036 = 3.6\%$$

In the long run, investors may not reap significant financial advantage from tax-exempt bonds because they are bought at a premium. But, in the short run, they benefit financially (and perhaps emotionally) because of reduced tax payments.

Parenthetically, bond brokers quote after-tax yields on municipal bonds using the highest individual federal income tax rates in effect at the time of each distribution. So, their quotes are the maximum available.

For public universities, issuing tax-exempt bonds is a fairly straightforward process: once the debt has been authorized by the legislature, the state treasurer issues the bonds and allocates the proceeds to the university. These are known as governmental bonds. For private universities, the process is a bit more complicated since only governments can issue tax-exempt bonds. To help private universities get around this provision, state and local governments issue tax-exempt bonds, known as "qualified 501(c)(3)" bonds, on behalf of the nonprofit private institutions in the state.[10] The bonds may be issued directly by a city, county, or state treasurer or through a government agency established for this purpose, such as the California Educational Facilities Authority (CEFA).[11] Regardless, the government acts merely as a conduit, assuming no financial responsibility on behalf of the institution. For convenience, the government usually assigns management of the bond issue to a private trust company. Then, it lends the proceeds to the institution or undertakes the capital project itself. It builds the dormitory, for example, and subsequently leases it to the institution. In the latter case, when the bonds are mature (the debt is paid) ownership of the building transfers to the institution.

Incidentally, the Municipal Securities Rulemaking Board (MSRB) provides detailed information about all municipal bond issues at its Electronic Municipal Market Access (EMMA) website, where a university's bond issues can be looked up easily.[12]

There are two different categories of municipal bonds: general obligation bonds and revenue bonds.

General Obligation Bonds

General obligation bonds are issued mainly by a state to benefit its public universities. They are backed by the "full faith and credit of the state," and their issuance usually must be authorized by legislative action. Future state general-fund appropriations guarantee the bonds. Ultimately, the state may use any taxation power in its authority to repay them: income taxes, corporate taxes, property taxes, sales taxes, and any other tax that can be levied. This is why they are called general obligation bonds: the issuer is generally obligated to tap any resource to repay the bonds. Most states have upper limits on the amount of general obligation bonds that can be issued.

Revenue Bonds

Revenue bonds are the most common debt issued by both private and public universities. A revenue bond is an obligation issued to finance a revenue-producing enterprise. Both the principal and interest are paid exclusively from the earnings of the enterprise. That is, a university's revenue bonds are backed by a general or specific revenue pledge by the university. For example, bonds are issued to raise $10 million for building a new student dormitory; income from the dormitory will be used (pledged) to pay the principal and interest on the bonds. Thus, the revenue bonds are secured by a specific revenue source.

There are two main reasons for the issuance of revenue bonds, rather than general obligation bonds. First, revenue bonds are based on the concept that only the users of a facility financed by the sale of bonds should pay for that facility. They are distinguished by their guarantee of repayment from revenues generated by a specified self-supporting entity associated with the purpose of the bonds. As a general rule, revenue bonds do not have any claim on the general credit or taxing power of the state. Typically, since holders of revenue bonds can rely only on the specific project's income, revenue bonds carry a higher risk than general obligation bonds and, therefore, pay a higher rate of interest. Second, they are not subject ordinarily to statutory or constitutional debt limitations. However, some states limit the total amount of debt that a public university may issue. And, most states, such as Hawaii, must appropriate all debt issues; the University of Hawaii may not issue revenue bonds without the legislature's prior approval.

Revenue bonds are usually issued as "serial bonds." The bonds within an issue mature periodically rather than all at once at the maturity date, in contrast to term bonds that mature all at the same time. In the simplest example of a serial bond issue, a university issues $10,000,000 in bonds with $500,000 maturing every year for 20 years (that is, in 20 groups of 500 bonds), plus interest. In effect, along with the regular interest payments, this resembles straight-line amortization of the debt over a 20-year period. But, in most cases, the number of bonds maturing each year varies with time, depending on factors such as the institution's overall debt-payment schedule and anticipated revenue flow, usually with more coming due in the last several years of the issue. Importantly, the continuing revenue stream is used to make continuing interest and principal payments on the serial bonds, paying off bonds within the issue as they mature, until the entire bond issue is paid off.

Note on nomenclature: Serial bonds are usually identified by the year they were issued. Since more than one series may be issued in a year, the year is followed by the suffix A, B, C, and so forth, indicating the order of issuance. So, two series issued in 2011 are known as Series 2011A and Series 2011B.

An example of a serial bond issued on November 15, 2011 (Series 2011A), is illustrated in table 5.6.[13] The total issue, $14,100,000, is broken into 15 different groups maturing at 1-year intervals, starting in the second year, over a 16-year period. The first 5 issues have been redeemed (paid in full), leaving an outstanding principal balance of $13,640,000 (on June 30, 2017). *Note:* These amounts do not include interest payments.

In their financial reports, some universities document the sources of revenue pledged to repay revenue bond debt. An example is shown in table 5.7.[14] In this example, 25 percent of student fees are pledged to repay bonds, presumably those used to construct or improve a student center. All housing and residence-hall dining revenues are pledged to repay bonds, presumably those used to finance construction of a dining hall. And 9 percent of sponsored research F&A costs reimbursed by the federal government are used to pledge bonds issued presumably to improve research infrastructure (to modernize research buildings, for example). The universities might also affirm that "all of the above revenues are cross-pledged to repay any and all of the secured debt."[15] In other words, if one source provides insufficient revenue for some reason, the other sources will be used to cover the debt. In this example, the overall pledged revenue ($37,074,748) exceeds the annual debt payments ($16,031,764) by a margin of $21,042,984, which is good.

Table 5.6. Serial bond issue, with payments through 2017

Payment due date	Series 2011A			
	Interest rate (%)	Original issue	Redeemed	Outstanding
November 15, 2012				
November 15, 2013	2.00	75,000	75,000	
November 15, 2014	2.00	55,000	55,000	
November 15, 2015	2.00	90,000	90,000	
November 15, 2016	2.00	65,000	65,000	
November 15, 2017	2.25	175,000	175,000	
November 15, 2018	2.50	185,000		185,000
November 15, 2019	3.00	195,000		195,000
November 15, 2020	3.00	190,000		190,000
November 15, 2021	3.00	190,000		190,000
November 15, 2022	5.00	1,895,000		1,895,000
November 15, 2023	5.00	1,995,000		1,995,000
November 15, 2024	5.00	2,095,000		2,095,000
November 15, 2025	5.00	2,205,000		2,205,000
November 15, 2026	3.75	2,300,000		2,300,000
November 15, 2027	4.00	2,390,000		2,390,000
Totals		14,100,000	460,000	13,640,000

Note: The bonds were issued on November 15, 2011. Payments began in the second year, on November 15, 2013.

Table 5.7. Pledged revenues to repay secured bond debt (FY 2015)

Revenue source	Total revenue	Pledged revenue	% pledged
Student fees (no tuition pledged)	37,856,446	9,410,196	24.86
Housing and residence hall dining revenues (net)	12,739,569	12,739,569	100.00
Foundation gift revenue related to Series B debt service	3,039,053	3,039,053	100.00
Grant and contract F&A cost recoveries	16,027,616	1,380,027	8.61
Athletic events revenue	3,305,133	3,205,020	96.97
Campus parking revenues	2,250,641	2,250,641	100.00
Bookstore and museum lease income	700,121	700,121	100.00
Land grant income	3,572,401	3,572,401	100.00
Investment income	1,188,545	777,720	65.43
Total	80,679,525	37,074,748	45.95
Less debt service requirements		(16,031,764)	
Excess of pledged revenue over debt service requirements		21,042,984	

The revenue guaranteeing the bond issue is distributed according to a protocol known as the "flow of funds." Initially, all receipts and income derived from the operation of the entity (such as a dormitory) are deposited into a bond reserve fund. The first claim on the reserve fund usually is a prorated amount to meet the cost of operation and maintenance, as set forth in the annual budget. The rationale is that without proper operations and maintenance, the facility may not generate sufficient income to cover the debt. Therefore, revenue bonds most commonly are payable from net revenues: gross receipts less operating and maintenance costs. The second claim is a bond service account, which constitutes an amount that will be sufficient to pay the next semiannual interest payment, as well as the next maturing principal payment. The third claim is payment into a debt service reserve fund, which contains an amount equal to one or two years' maximum interest and principal payments. The fourth claim is payment into a renewal and replacement fund, sometimes called a replacement reserve, established to replace equipment or provide necessary repairs beyond normal maintenance. This fund also may be used to meet unusual or extraordinary maintenance charges that have not been budgeted. As a rule of thumb, this fund should equal about one-tenth of a year's gross revenues to cover unforeseen contingencies. Any money left over after these distributions goes into a surplus fund that can be used for general purposes, such as improving the facility or retiring bonds in advance of their maturity.

Importantly, according to IRS regulations, revenue bonds must be spent in a timely manner on the specific project described in the bond issue. In this context, timely means "not later than 18 months after the later of the date each expenditure is paid or the date the project, if any, that is financed by the issue is placed in service. This allocation must be made in any event by the date 60 days after the fifth anniversary of the issue date or the date 60 days after the retirement of the issue, if earlier." Implicitly, this time limitation means that the bond proceeds cannot be used to make money through arbitrage—using the proceeds of an issue to acquire investments that earn a yield that is materially higher than the yield on the bonds that were issued. Indeed, the IRS explicitly requires the borrower to refund to the government any gains earned through arbitrage. Thus, the university cannot use bond proceeds to make money.

Taxable Bonds

Despite the lower interest rates paid on tax-exempt bonds, universities sometimes issue taxable bonds. In these cases, the interest earned by the bondholders is taxable. Therefore, as compensation for the taxed income, the bond purchasers expect and the university pays an interest rate higher than for tax-exempt bonds. The bondholders receive roughly the same amount of net interest regardless of bond type; the amount of additional interest earned at the higher rate with taxable bonds approximates the amount of interest paid in tax. However, the university (the issuer) pays more interest. Why, then, would a university ever issue taxable bonds?

Despite their greater cost to the university, taxable bonds have several advantages over tax-exempt bonds. Most importantly, taxable bonds are not subject to many of the restrictions imposed on tax-exempt bonds. For example, the money need not be spent within five years, and it may earn interest exceeding the debt on the bonds (that is, arbitrage). With current (2017) low interest rates, the difference in coupon rates between tax-exempt and taxable bonds is quite small, generally less than 0.5 percent. Therefore, the flexibility and the opportunity for arbitrage provide attractive enticements to issue taxable-bond proceeds. In a real example, a university issued 30-year taxable bonds. The bond proceeds were invested in fixed income securities to cover future capital expenses and in the endowment with the payout available to support the debt service payments. The flexibility of taxable bonds outweighed the small financial advantages of tax-exempt bonds. Other universities have been making similar decisions in this era of low interest rates.

Bond Redemption

Redemption of a bond refers to the return of the bond's principal to the bondholders, the investors. Bonds can be redeemed at maturity and before maturity. When the final interest payments and principal have been paid to the investors, the bonds are said to be retired. They are off the books, reducing the institution's long-term debt.

At Maturity

When bonds reach maturity, the institution must pay the bondholders the face value, regardless of the issue price (face value, a premium, or a discount). After that payment, the bonds are retired. Looking at this another way, at maturity, the institution redeems the bonds by buying them back at face value and then retires them. The debt is off the books.

To ensure that money is available to pay the bondholders when term bonds (as opposed to serial bonds) mature, the covenants may require the institution to establish a fund, called a *sinking fund*, for the sole purpose of paying the bond principal when it comes due at maturity. In fact, some states require public universities to establish these sinking funds. Accordingly, the university transfers money periodically into the sinking fund, which may be administered by an independent trustee. If there are no set rules on the timing of these payments into the sinking fund, they may be delayed until the final several years before the maturity date. The trustee may invest the money, but all investment income must be used for redeeming or buying back the bonds. *Note:* Because serial bonds are paid off at regular intervals, usually yearly, they generally don't require a sinking fund.

In addition, universities generally have a more inclusive *debt service reserve* fund as a requirement of bond covenants for their outstanding bond issues. Debt service reserve funds are retained in case the university defaults on a bond payment. The specific bond covenants determine the type of reserve funds held by the university and any limitations on the income earned on those funds.

The university's financial records may report large sinking fund and debt service reserves, prompting questions like "Why can't we use that money to raise faculty salaries?" These reserves are restricted by bond covenants and cannot be used for any other purpose: not faculty salaries, not graduate assistants, not lab supplies. Furthermore, all investment income earned on bond sinking funds and debt service reserve funds must be used for debt payments.

Before Maturity

A bond is said to be retired early when it is retired at any time before its maturity date. Some of the reasons for redeeming bonds before the maturity date are to take advantage of lower interest rates, to shorten or lengthen the debt payout period, or to get rid of restrictive bond covenants. The primary reason is to refinance the debt to save money. Existing debt is retired before maturity and replaced with new debt. This is known as bond *refunding*, which is somewhat comparable to refinancing a home mortgage. Usually, bonds are refunded when interest rates decline. Because institutions can then borrow money at lower interest rates, they pay the outstanding debt on their bonds using money generated from a new bond issue at the lower rates. In this way, the debt has been refinanced. Restated differently, new bonds are issued, and the proceeds are used to retire bonds that have been issued already. To be effective, refunding occurs primarily when the new bond issue is at a lower rate of interest than the refunded issue, ensuring significant reduction in interest expense for the institution.

One way to redeem bonds is for the institution to repurchase its own bonds on the secondary market. The institution will recognize a gain on the repurchase if the outstanding bond is selling at a market price lower than the face value (at a discount). Conversely, the institution will recognize a loss on the repurchase if the market value is above the book value (at a premium). Of course, the institution would not repurchase the bonds if it would lose money in the deal. Importantly, the institution will not recognize any gain or loss if it issues new bonds to pay for the repurchase of outstanding bonds, regardless of how low interest rates are. That is because the premium paid to purchase the existing bonds to be retired would exactly offset the present value of future interest savings consequent to the lower interest rates.

The only sure way to save money when refunding is to call the bonds when the call price per bond is lower than the economic value of the bonds at current market prices. Then, the present value of the interest savings will exceed the premium paid to call the bonds. As a result, to refinance a bond issue, institutions almost always need to exercise the call option. That is why virtually every new bond issue contains a call provision.

If the bonds cannot be called, or at least not until after a certain period of time, the institution can lock in savings due to lower interest rates, effectively refunding in advance, by a process known as *defeasance*. In this method, the institution sets aside sufficient cash designated specifically for retirement of the bond when it matures. The cash may be raised by issuing new bonds at a lower interest rate, pledging them to pay outstanding bond issues when they mature. Technically, defeasance is "the action or process of rendering something null and void."[16] In that context, a defeased bond is treated as if it has been redeemed already. In accounting terms, the defeased bond becomes null and void, both legally and financially, thus removing the debt from the university's books. One advantage of defeasance is that an institution may free itself from having to pledge revenue, such as tuition or dormitory income, to guarantee a revenue bond issue. Defeasance of the bonds makes the pledged revenue available for other purposes. Of course, if the funds deposited in defeasance prove insufficient to make future payment of the outstanding debt, the institution remains obligated to make payment on the debt from the pledged revenues.

Examples of these three methods of refunding bonds, repurchasing, calling, and defeasing, are shown in table 5.8. In the original issue on July 1, 2012, $10 million was raised by issuing 10,000 bonds at a face value of $1,000. The coupon rate was 5 percent, paid semiannually for 20 years until maturity. According to the indentures, the bonds could not be called until year 10, on July 1, 2022, at a call price of $1,050. On July 1, 2017, the interest rates dropped to 4 percent,

Table 5.8. Economic gain from three different methods of refunding bonds

| | Original issue | Refunding | | |
		Repurchase	Call	Defease[a]
Bond issue				
Number of bonds issued	10,000	10,000	10,000	10,000
Face value	1,000	1,000	1,000	1,050
Total amount issued	10,000,000	10,000,000	10,000,000	10,000,000
Coupon rate	5.00%	4.00%	5.00%	4.00%
Issue date	7/1/2012	7/1/2017	7/1/2022	7/1/2017
Maturity date	7/1/2032	7/1/2032	7/1/2032	7/1/2022
Number of years	20	15	10	5
Number of payments per year	2	2	2	2
Earliest call date	7/1/2022			
Call price	1,050			
Current bond market (July 1, 2017)				
Interest rate	4.00%	4.00%	4.00%	4.00%
Interest payments per period	250,000	227,355	210,000	250,000
Present value				
Principal	4,528,904	6,275,817	7,066,199	8,613,657
Interest	6,838,870	5,091,957	3,433,801	2,245,646
Market value of bonds	11,367,774	11,367,774	10,500,000	10,859,303
Market price per bond	1,136.78	1,136.78	1,050.00	1,050.00
Economic gain			867,774	508,471

Note: In each method, new bonds were issued to finance the refunding. Bonds issued for the defeasance were invested for the time between issue and the call.
[a]Invest new defeasance bond issue:

Amount available at time of call	
Rate	4.00%
Principal	10,859,303
Interest accrued	2,171,861
Total at time of call	13,031,164

Amount payable at time of call	
Interest accrued	2,500,000
Principal	10,500,000
Total at time of call	13,000,000

which raised the market value of the bonds (the cost of purchasing outstanding bonds) to $11,367,774; therefore, the market price for each bond rose to $1,136.78.

The first approach to refunding the original bond issue, by repurchasing them, requires a new bond issue to raise money for the repurchase. Although it was not necessary, the institution maintained the same schedule for retiring the original debt by setting the maturity date for the new bonds at July 1, 2032; they are 15-year bonds. Because of the lower interest rates, the interest on the new bond issue decreased from $250,000 to $227,355 per payment. But the corresponding decrease in the present value of the interest is matched by a corresponding (and equal) increase in the present value of the principal, bringing the cost of the new bonds, $11,367,774, equal to the market value of the original issue. So, there is no economic gain to the institution by refunding the bonds via repurchase. (In fact, there would be a cost due to the underwriter's fees of issuing new bonds.)

The second approach, calling the bonds at the earliest call date, after 10 years, at the stated call price, $1,050, requires a new bond issue costing $10,500,000, paying 4 percent interest. Like the re-purchase, the maturity date was set to July 1, 2032, to maintain the same debt repayment schedule. In this case, the interest on the new bond issue decreased, from $250,000 to $210,000 per period, with the present value of the interest decreasing accordingly. How-ever, unlike the repurchase, the corresponding increase in the present value of the principal did not offset the interest savings because the call price was less than the market price of the bonds. And this resulted in an $867,774 economic gain for the institution ($11,367,774 − $10,500,000).

Defeasance is the third approach to refunding. The earliest call date is July 1, 2022. So, when interest rates dropped to 4 percent on July 1, 2017, the institution defeased the bonds using proceeds from a new 5-year bond issue. The amount of the issue ($10,859,303) was based on the present value ($8,613,657) of the $10,500,000 needed to redeem the bonds after the 5-year period plus the present value ($2,245,646) of the $250,000 interest paid per period on the out-standing bonds during that period before the call (July 1, 2017, to July 1, 2022). Importantly, until they were needed for the call, the new bond proceeds were invested at 4 percent interest (table 5.8, *bot-tom panel*). At the time of the call, principal plus interest on this investment yielded $13,031,164, which was just enough to offset the interest paid on the original bonds before the call ($2,500,000) plus the redemption price ($10,500,000), $13,000,000. With these costs offset, the institution realized a $508,741 economic gain from the defeasance ($11,367,774 − $10,859,903).

As shown in table 5.8, the actual economic gain from refinanc-ing debt depends on numerous factors: market interest rate versus coupon rate, the call provisions, time to maturity of new bond is-sues, and so forth. Moreover, administrative and underwriters' fees (known collectively as the flotation costs) also must be taken into consideration. Of course, all of these factors determine the ultimate benefits of refinancing long-term debt. But the financial benefits from refunding a bond issue are usually newsworthy.

Certificates of Participation

Sometimes, an institution needs financing for a capital asset but cannot issue long-term debt because of state-mandated debt ceilings, for example. Or it wants to circumvent certain bond limitations. Therefore, the institution structures financing in a way that is not considered debt under state law, such as lease-backed financing. In this method, called lease financing for short, instead of buying a capital asset with bond debt, the institution leases the capital asset, with lease payments coming from its operating budget. In a lease-purchase agreement, the lease payments apply toward the purchase price of the asset; at the end of the lease, the institution owns the asset. Leases are not considered debt because the institution can theoretically stop making lease payments at any time—just walk away, relinquishing the asset. Of course, this seldom happens.

This alternative method of acquiring a capital asset often involves issuance of so-called *certificates of participation* (COPs). In COP financing, the institution enters into a lease or lease-purchase agreement for a proposed facility owned by another party. For example, the facility may be an existing building or a new building constructed according to the institution's specifications. Typically, the agreement is between the institution and a trustee, such as a commercial bank. The trustee agrees to buy the facility from the owner and then lease it to the institution, which makes regular lease payments to the trustee. To generate money to pay for this purchase of the facility, the trustee issues COPs that entitle the investors who bought them to receive a participation, or share, of the lease payments made by the institution to the trustee. The term of the COPs equals the term of the lease. Restating this procedure for clarity, the principal received by the trustee from the purchasers of the COPs is used to buy the facility from the owner, thus transferring ownership to the trustee for the term of the lease. The trustee collects lease payments from the institution and makes payments to the investors. Note that it is not necessary for the trustee to be a nonprofit organization.

Although COPs and bonds are fundamentally different, they share some common attributes. The documentation in a COP transaction is similar to that in a regular revenue bond transaction; instead of a loan agreement, there is a lease agreement. And COPs are accompanied by an indenture that directs the trustee's execution of the COPs. Like bonds, COPs have a face value (principal) and a stated interest rate, with the actual sales price of the COP depending on the market at the time. Furthermore, like municipal bonds, COPs issued by a government agency can be tax-exempt. However, because they are inherently riskier than bonds, COPs have a lower credit rating than municipal bonds and, therefore, pay higher interest rates.

Public universities are more likely to use COPs than private universities. They are likely to use COPs for infrastructure projects including utility infrastructure projects or utility chilled water or steam loops.[17] Private universities are not subject to state debt limitations, so they have less of an incentive to use COPs. Also, asking a government conduit to issue COPs adds to the extra cost relative to more traditional financing methods.

Private Business Use of Facilities

Interest on state and local government bonds and on qualified 501(c)(3) bonds is exempt from federal taxes as long as the proceeds from the bonds are used for activities benefiting the public. If the proceeds from these bonds are used for private business activities, the bonds become known as private activity bonds. And the interest on private activity bonds is not tax-exempt. If the bonds' tax-exempt status were lost, the university must redeem the bonds (through defeasance if necessary) and reissue them as taxable bonds paying higher interest. Of course, the university considers that undesirable.

Within a university context, examples of private business activities include:

- use by for-profit entities of property, such as laboratory space or equipment, which is built, improved, or purchased with tax-exempt bond proceeds
- lease agreements for the use of space, such as parking space or cellular towers, even if the lessee is a nonprofit organization
- improvements to plant facilities, such as utilities, benefiting campus buildings that have private use activity

There are exceptions to these activities. For example, lease agreements do not constitute private business activities if the term of use does not exceed 100 days and the property is made generally available to third parties. Likewise, rental of the property is excluded if rent is negotiated at fair market value and the term of use does not exceed 50 days. Management or service contracts are exempt if the services provided are "incidental to the exempt uses of the facilities"; examples are janitorial services or office equipment repair services. And "non-possessory" facilities such as vending machines, mobile-device charging stations, and small kiosks are exempt if they comprise less than 2.5 percent of the bond proceeds.

The IRS has specific financial criteria that determine whether bonds are private activity bonds. Collectively, they are known as the private business use test. Most importantly for public and private universities, if more than 10 or 5 percent, respectively, of the bond proceeds are used for private business activities, the bonds pass the private business use test and lose their tax-exempt status. Stated conversely, for public universities, up to 10 percent of the proceeds from a tax-exempt bond issue may be used for private business activities without jeopardizing the bonds' tax-exempt status. And for private nonprofit universities, up to 5 percent of the proceeds from a qualified tax-exempt bond issue may be used for private business activities.[18] Realistically, the private university limit is only about 3 percent because the cost of the bond issuance (about 2 percent of the total) is also considered a private business activity. (The cost of bond issuance is neutral for public universities.) As Cornell University states in its guidelines for private business use of its facilities, "five percent or less of tax-exempt bond issue proceeds may be used for private business purposes, including the costs incurred to issue the debt, and such use may occur only if it is in accordance with tax certificate provisions and in compliance with applicable federal law."[19] These 10 and 5 percent allowances for private business activities constitute "wiggle room" within so-called safe harbors.[20]

Before proceeding, it may help to clarify what "10% [or 5%] of the amount of the bond issuance" really means. The IRS has several methods for translating the amount of bond issuance measured in money to capital asset parameters, based on how the bond funding was used, the nature of the private use, and the square footage. Ideally, the university has kept track of how the bond proceeds were allocated within the building, so the amount used to finance the site of private business activity is known exactly. Then, the percentage calculations are straightforward and simple. However, the exact dollar allocations to specific sites within a building may not be known; in fact, they probably aren't. In that more realistic situation, alternative methods must be used to estimate the allocations. In its simplest form, assuming that all space within the building costs the same amount, bond issuance (denoted in money) translates 1:1 into square-footage (ANSF) of a building financed by tax-exempt bonds. So, 10 percent of the bond issuance translates into 10 percent of the ANSF in the building.

This translation is illustrated in table 5.9. In this example, a university constructed a $100 million building housing classrooms (40,000 sq. ft.), research laboratories (40,000 sq. ft.), vendor space (1,500 sq. ft. for snack and soft-drink vending machines, etc.), and common space (18,500 sq. ft. for hallways, restrooms, and building utilities). To finance the cost of the new building, it issued $80 million in tax-exempt bonds and raised $20 million from private donors, giving it 20 percent equity in the building. The common space was allocated to the classrooms, research, and vending spaces according to relative square footages and added to their respective ANSF, resulting in adjusted ANSF values. The classroom's adjusted ANSF (49,080 sq. ft.) comprised 49.08 percent of the total adjusted ANSF (100,000 sq. ft.). Bond proceeds and equity then were allocated to the three functions based on their proportion of the adjusted ANSF. Thus, bond proceeds allocated to the classrooms ($38,478,528) equal 49.08 percent of the net bond proceeds ($78,400,000).

The institution set aside a percentage of classroom and research space for private business use (table 5.9, *middle panel*). For each function, the dollar amount allocated to private business use equals the percentage set aside for private business use (PBU) times the total financing (bond proceeds plus equity) allocated to that function. For classrooms:

$$
\begin{aligned}
\textit{amount allocated to PBU} &= \textit{\% of ANSF allocated to PBU} \\
&\times (\textit{bond proceeds} + \textit{equity}) \\
&= 10\% \times (\$38,478,528 + \$9,815,951) \\
&= \$4,829,448
\end{aligned}
$$

Adding the corresponding amount for research ($19,317,791) yields the total amount allocated to PBU, $24,147,239. (The same result is obtained by calculating the cost per square foot times the square footage set aside for private business use.) To minimize the impact of PBU on the tax-exempt bond issue, the amount allocated to PBU is first applied to equity. Any remainder is applied to the bonds. So, in this example, the first $20,000,000 of the amount allocated to PBU is applied to equity. The remainder, $4,147,239, which is 5.29 percent of the net bond proceeds ($78,400,000), is applied to bonds.

So far, the calculations have been the same for both public and private universities. At this point, however, they diverge when the cost of bond issuance is factored into the calculations, as shown in table 5.9 (*lower panel*).

On the one hand, for a public university's bonds, the cost of issuance is prorated like the bonds for private business use. So,

Table 5.9. Private business use (PBU) allocation to bonds

Financial parameters

	Amount	% of total		Amount	% of total
Building cost	100,000,000	100.00	Bond issue	80,000,000	80.00
Equity	20,000,000	20.00	Cost of issue	1,600,000	2.00
			Net bond proceeds	78,400,000	78.00

PBU parameters

Function	ANSF	Prorated common space	Adjusted ANSF	% ANSF	Bond proceeds	Equity	% for PBU	Amount allocated to PBU	PBU allocated to bonds
Classroom	40,000	9,080	49,080	49.08	38,478,528	9,815,951	10.00	4,829,448	
Research	40,000	9,080	49,080	49.08	38,478,528	9,815,951	40.00	19,317,791	
Vendor	1,500	340	1,840	1.84	1,442,945	368,098			
Sub-total	81,500	18,500	100,000	100.00	78,400,000	20,000,000		24,147,239	4,147,239
Common space	18,500								
Total	100,000								

Allocations to PBU

	Public	Private
% of cost of issuance allocated to PBU	5.29	100.00
Cost of issuance allocated to PBU	84,638	1,600,000
PBU allocated to bonds	4,147,239	4,147,239
Total bond costs allocated to PBU	4,231,877	5,747,239
% of total bond cost allocated to PBU	5.29	7.18
Safe harbor	10.00%	5.00%

Note: Common space and equity were prorated based on square footage.

the percentage of the total cost of issuance ($1,600,000) allocated to PBU is the same as for the net bond proceeds, corresponding to $84,638 allocated to PBU (5.29 percent of $1,600,000). Thus, the total bond costs allocated to PBU are $4,231,877, which is 5.29 percent of the total bond issue ($80,000,000). This equals the percentage of the net bond proceeds allocated to the cost of issuance. In other words, the cost of issuance does not factor into the PBU calculations. The bottom line: at 5.29 percent, the public university's private business activity is well within the 10 percent safe harbor.

On the other hand, for a private university's qualified 501(c)(3) bonds, the full cost of issuance ($1,600,000) is added to the proceeds used for private business activity, and the total ($5,747,239) is divided into the total bond issue to get the percentage used for private business use, 7.18 percent (table 5.9, *lower panel*). This exceeds the safe harbor limit of 5 percent, so the tax-exempt status of the private university's bond issue is in jeopardy.

Potential complications for public and private research universities arose from an IRS code ruling that "an agreement by a nongovernmental person to sponsor research performed by a governmental person may result in private business use of the property used for the research based on all the facts and circumstances."[21] In other words, the IRS ruled that a university research project sponsored by an external party (a company or even the federal government) may be considered private business activity. As a consequence, sponsored research could invalidate the tax-exempt status of bonds used to finance a research facility. This could have significant financial implications for the university.

Fortunately, to the immense benefit of academic institutions, the IRS modified this ruling by adding an additional safe harbor where a federally sponsored research agreement does not result in private business use and therefore invalidate the tax exemption.[22] But there's a catch: the safe harbor applies only to "basic research," which is defined as "original investigation for the advancement of scientific knowledge not having a specific commercial objective." This describes most federally sponsored research performed in academic institutions. Exceptions that fall outside the safe harbor include "product testing supporting the trade or business of a specific non-governmental party" and clinical trials, which are not basic research.

This safe harbor also applies to basic research funded by corporate sponsors. However, as a condition of this safe harbor protecting basic research, corporate sponsors of research using tax-exempt facilities must pay a fair market price for any intellectual property license arising from its sponsorship, and that price should be determined at the time the technology is available for use, not beforehand. This may be an exclusive license, but only as long as the sponsor pays the same license fee as would be charged to a nonsponsor. Conceivably, a sponsor might object: "I paid for the research that developed this product, so why can't I get the license to use it at a discounted price?" To stay within the safe harbor, the university's answer to that question is: "We can sell you an exclusive license, but we cannot sell the license at a below-market price."

In addition, this safe harbor applies to cooperative research arrangements between "industry, government, and university researchers." (In this context, the word "industry" refers to corporate sponsors.) For the research to be within the safe harbor, the university must determine the research to be performed and the manner in which it is to be performed (for example, selection of the personnel to perform the research), and title to any patent or other product incidentally resulting from the basic research lies exclusively with the university. Furthermore, the sponsor or sponsors are entitled to no more than a nonexclusive, royalty-free license to use the product of any of that research. Thus, the university has title to any intellectual property generated by the research. Incidentally, the IRS has ruled that this safe harbor also applies to any inventions made with federal support, which are subject to the provisions of the Bayh-Dole Act (1980).[23]

From the university's financial perspective, it is critical to maintain the tax-exempt status of its bonds. Consequently, in cooperative research arrangements most institutions steadfastly negotiate provisions for the use of inventions and facilities by private partners that are consistent with the safe harbor provisions. Specifically, they require that the nature of the work should fit the IRS definition of "basic research" and that the sponsor should receive no more intellectual property rights than an option for a nonexclusive, royalty-free license or an exclusive royalty-bearing license. In that context, funding support for a research project may not be considered as payment toward a license of future intellectual property.

Two concluding questions about private business activity arise in *Managing the Research University*.[24] First: Why don't universities avoid these problems by using buildings that were constructed without tax-exempt bond funding for privately sponsored research? The answer is that, in fact, they would if they could. But on many campuses nearly all university buildings suitable for modern research have been constructed, remodeled, or refinanced using tax-exempt bonds. Second: How about buildings endowed by a private donor? The answer to that question depends on the donor's commitment. If the donor has agreed to fund all initial costs, then bonding isn't required. However, in many cases, the up-front construction costs are financed by a tax-exempt bond issue. The endowment then pays the bond debt over a 20- or 30-year period.

These tax issues epitomize the aphorism "the devil is in the details." Because the stakes are so high, most experienced administrators consult with the university's lawyers and bond counsel whenever they contemplate allowing a private party to use university facilities or departing from the safe harbors in a cooperative agreement.

Summary

Capital assets are property that is expected to generate value over a long period of time—that is, longer than one year. When an institution purchases a capital asset, it incurs a capital expense that is written off incrementally over a number of years; the expense is capitalized. Depreciation converts the cost of a capital asset into an operational expense, called a depreciation expense, over the asset's estimated useful life. Universities usually pay for capital assets by incurring long-term debt. To minimize the cost of borrowing money, universities often issue tax-exempt bonds, known as municipal bonds; because the interest paid to municipal bond purchasers is tax-exempt, the bonds pay commensurately lower interest. Commonly, universities issue revenue bonds to finance an enterprise (for example, a dining hall), with both the principal and interest paid exclusively from the earnings of the enterprise. By law, revenue bonds must be spent within 18 months on the specific project described in the bond issue, and the bond proceeds cannot be reinvested to earn money. Because of these limitations, universities sometimes issue taxable bonds, despite their higher interest rates. If interest rates decline, bonds may be paid off before the maturity date, and new bonds are issued to take advantage of the lower rates. If an institution needs financing for a capital asset but cannot or prefers not to issue bonds, it may enter into a lease or lease-purchase agreement for an asset owned by another party, which issues certificates of participation that guarantee a fraction of the lease payments to pay for the asset's cost. Private business use of a facility financed with tax-exempt bonds could invalidate the tax-exempt status of the bond issue, thus subjecting the interest income to taxation and raising the cost to the university. Fortunately, the IRS provides safe harbors for limited private business use.

Notes

1. Accounting Tools, "Capital Asset," http://www.accountingtools.com/dictionary-capital-asset (accessed February 23, 2017).

2. 2 C.F.R. § 200.12.

3. Governmental Accounting Standards Board, "Interperiod Equity and What It Means to You," http://gasb.org/cs/ContentServer?c=GASBContent_C&pagename=GASB%2FGASBContent_C%2FUsersArticlePage&cid=1176156731381 (accessed June 28, 2017).

4. Investopedia, "Useful Life," http://www.investopedia.com/terms/u/usefullife.asp (accessed August 24, 2016).

5. University of California, "Useful Life Indices for Equipment Depreciation," http://eulid.ucop.edu/ (accessed June 8, 2015).

6. Sunita Lough and Debra Kawecki, "Understanding Bond Documents" (1996), https://www.irs.gov/pub/irs-tege/eotopic96.pdf (accessed March 22, 2017).

7. Fitch Ratings Inc., "Fitch Ratings," https://www.fitchratings.com/site/home (accessed June 28, 2017); Moody's, "Moody's Corporation," https://www.moodys.com/Pages/atc.aspx (accessed June 28, 2017); Standard & Poor's Financial Services LLC, "S&P Global Ratings," http://www.standardandpoors.com/en_US/web/guest/home (accessed June 28, 2017).

8. Aswath Damodaran, "Defining and Estimating the Cost of Debt" (2014), www.stern.nyu.edu/~adamodar/podcasts/BVR/BVR7ppt.ppt (accessed March 5, 2018); New York University, "Ratings, Interest Coverage Ratios and Default Spread," http://pages.stern.nyu.edu/~adamodar/New_Home_Page/datafile/ratings.htm (accessed March 5, 2018).

9. Internal Revenue Service, "Publication 4079 Tax-Exempt Governmental Bonds" (Washington, DC, 2016).

10. "Publication 4077 Tax-Exempt Bonds for 501(c)(3) Charitable Organizations" (Washington, DC, 2016).

11. State of California, "California Education Facilities Authority," http://www.treasurer.ca.gov/cefa/ (accessed December 23, 2016).

12. Municipal Securities Rulemaking Board (MSRB), "Electronic Municipal Market Access," http://emma.msrb.org/ (accessed March 22, 2017).

13. Montana State University, "Consolidated Revenue Bond Report and Supplemental Schedules" (2015), https://mus.edu/board/meetings/2016/Mar2016/AdminBudget/AuditReports/MSU%20Consolidated%20Revenue%20Bond%2015.pdf (accessed March 22, 2017).

14. "Montana State University 2015 Financial Statements," www.montana.edu/opa/budget-finance/FY15financialsaudited.pdf (accessed August 11, 2016). Note 17.

15. "Montanta State University 2015 Financial Statements."

16. Oxford University Press, "Oxford Dictionaries," http://www.oxforddictionaries.com/?gclid=CMa5maK2p8kCFU1cfgodiXoNoA (accessed November 23, 2015).

17. State of Illinois, "State University Certificates of Participation Act" (2017), http://www.ilga.gov/legislation/ilcs/ilcs3.asp?ActID=3090&ChapterID=18 (accessed March 23, 2017).

18. 26 U.S.C. § 141 (b)(3).

19. Cornell University, "Private Use Policy and Guidelines," https://www.dfa.cornell.edu/treasurer/debt/private-use-compliance/guidelines (accessed March 23, 2017).

20. Internal Revenue Service, "Revenue Procedure 2016-44" (2016), https://www.irs.gov/pub/irs-drop/rp-16-44.pdf (accessed March 22, 2017).

21. 26 U.S.C. § 141-3 (b)(6).

22. Internal Revenue Service, "Revenue Procedure 2007-47" (2007), https://www.irs.gov/irb/2007-29_IRB/ar12.html (accessed March 26, 2017).

23. 35 U.S.C. § 200-212.

24. Dean O. Smith, *Managing the Research University* (New York: Oxford University Press, 2011), 292.

Chapter 6
Budgets

University Budgets

To understand university financing, another important question requiring an answer is: How does the university divide up its money? More aptly: How does the governing board distribute the money under its control? Or, from a dean's or faculty member's perspective: Who gets how much?

The straightforward answer to these questions is that the university's budget delineates who gets how much money. But that leaves a more important—but difficult—question to answer: Who constructs the budget? That is, who decides what is in the budget and how much money is allocated to each item? The answer to this question gets to the core of university finance and governance. As Michael Granof states in his classic textbook on nonprofit accounting, "Budgets are to governments and not-for-profits what the sun is to the solar system. Trying to understand government and not-for-profit accounting without recognizing the centricity of the budget would be like trying to comprehend the earth's seasons while ignoring the sun."[1] Stated less grandiloquently, to understand university finances, it is necessary to understand the budget.

For starters, to understand the budget, it helps to know exactly what a budget is. The Oxford Online Dictionary provides two simple definitions of a budget: "an estimate of income and expenditure for a set period of time" and "the amount of money needed or available for a purpose."[2] Thus, in its simplest form, a budget is an itemized summary of estimated or intended expenditures for a given period along with estimated resources for financing them. Accordingly, a budget is a relatively straightforward document. For a given time period (such as a fiscal year), it tabulates items or services to be purchased and the proposed amount of money available for these purchases—that is, the budgeted amount for each purpose. It can be as simple as that.

The Business Dictionary provides a more nuanced definition: "An estimate of costs, revenues, and resources over a specified period, reflecting a reading of future financial conditions and goals. One of the most important administrative tools, a budget serves also as a (1) plan of action for achieving quantified objectives, (2) standard for measuring performance, and (3) device for coping with foreseeable adverse situations."[3] The simple definition conforms to the standard notion of a budget in most contexts, including households. However, the nuanced definition captures the more far-reaching significance of a budget in an academic setting. Budgets are, indeed, essential elements of the financial planning process at many different levels of the university's hierarchy.

The significance of a budget to the university cannot be overstated. Through the budgeting process, an institution aligns its resources with its priorities, bringing together income and expenses. Connecting the university's strategic plan to the budget and then to university operations is primarily the responsibility of the president and the provost. But how this strategically developed budget is ultimately financed is left to the CFO. As the NACUBO notes, "He or she must bring together the streams of revenue—unrestricted tuition dollars and other revenues, restricted funds available for spending, and endowment spending—with the plans of the institution, matching donor intent with actual spending in support of good stewardship and with fidelity to the gifts' requirements."[4]

On an institutional scale, universities usually have three budget types: operating, capital, and auxiliary. Each is a separate budget. However, the budgets are not necessarily independent. A cost in one budget may affect the costs in another budget. For example, a new building in the capital budget may result in higher maintenance and utility costs in the operating budget. Each of these budget types will be examined. But first, the basic accounting methods used for budgets, budgetary accounting, will be introduced.

Budgetary Accounting

The term "budgetary accounting" is defined as accounting "in accordance with an estimate of income and expenditure."[5] A more comprehensive definition states this a bit differently: "a method of accounting in which the amounts that a company planned to spend and the amounts it really spent are included in the accounts, so that you can see how much of the budget is left."[6] Both definitions refer to the forward-looking aspect of a budget. In that sense, budgetary accounting differs from financial accounting that looks backward at income and expenditures already received and incurred, respectively.

Neither the FASB nor the GASB has established GAAP for budgetary accounting, in contrast to financial accounting. Indeed, they lack the authority to establish budgetary accounting GAAP. Nonetheless, they can (and do) make recommendations about several aspects of budget accounting. Some states have established principles for state agencies, including public universities. But, for the most part, budgetary accounting principles are determined primarily by the institution to suit its particular planning needs.

For their budgetary accounting, most universities use a cash basis or a slightly modified cash basis that accounts for encumbrances as if they were equivalent to the actual cash purchases. The reason is that the cash basis has practical advantages. It ensures that cash is available to pay for any expenditure; this favors the maintenance of a balanced budget, which is mandatory for many public institutions. Conversely, the university is not required to have cash available to pay for an expenditure that is deferred, such as unused vacation "payout" when an employee resigns or retires; this frees up revenue for other, current needs. It also allows a university to balance its budget by delaying payments into the next fiscal year; for example, a cash-strapped university may delay issuing the final paycheck by one day, from the last day of one fiscal year to the first day of the next fiscal year. And money can be transferred from a fund with a positive balance to offset a negative balance in another fund. These transfers, which resemble a loan, usually occur near the end of a fiscal year to balance the budget. After the beginning of the new fiscal year, the reverse transfers may occur to "repay the loans."

Although university budgets adhere to a fairly standard format that lists at minimum the revenues and expenditures, there are no specific principles that specify which of the two expenditure-classification schemes to use in university budgets: natural or functional. However, the NACUBO recommends reporting expenditures using both classification schemes. Thus, some universities report their budgets using both classifications for clarity.

Operating Budget

The institutional operating budget supports the primary mission of the university. It lists the revenues and expenditures necessary to fund the general operations of the university. Thus, it is of utmost interest to administrators and faculty members, for it relates to basic academic operations. How many faculty members can be hired this year? How many students can be given scholarships? How much money is available for new lab supplies?

The primary revenue sources for the operating budget are tuition and fees, state appropriations, and endowment income. The funds are usually unrestricted, so they can support most aspects of the institutional operations. In many institutions, these unrestricted operating funds are called *general funds*. Consequently, the operating budget is sometimes known as the *general fund budget*. General funds in the operating budget can be used for any university purpose, but they are designated primarily for academic purposes, including administration and campus maintenance. In addition, some institutions must allocate a small fraction of the general funds to support auxiliary programs such as intercollegiate athletic teams.

Importantly, the institutional operating budget actually derives from a large variety of budget documents. Most organizational units in the hierarchy have their own operating budget. In this context, an organizational unit with an operating budget is known as a "budget unit." Thus, every department, school, college, center, administrative and service unit with its own operating budget is a budget unit. They are controlled by the chairs, deans, directors, and so forth down into the hierarchy. And, within each of these budget units, specific funds may have their own operating budget; each sponsored research grant, for example, has its own budget. All of these budgets are combined into the operating budget of the next higher unit in the organizational hierarchy. So, the departments' budgets are incorporated into the colleges' budgets, the colleges' budget are incorporated into the provost's budget, and the provost's budget is consolidated into the institution's master operating budget. This hierarchy is illustrated in figure 6.1. The university's chief budget officer, who reports to the CFO, oversees coordination and maintenance of the master budget.

Potential source of confusion: Operating budgets within the hierarchy do not represent a transfer of university money. They represent transfers of authority to commit university money. Accordingly, when a provost gives a college dean the college's budget, the provost is giving the dean the authority to commit university money according to the budget. The provost has not made an expenditure; no money has changed hands. The dean may hire an employee, thus committing university money. But a fiscal officer spends the money (makes the expenditure) when issuing the employee's paycheck.

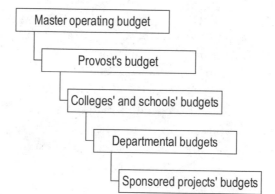

Figure 6.1. University master (consolidated) operating budget, illustrating the hierarchical structure

The hierarchical structure of the operating budget focuses attention on individual university programs, such as academic departments and colleges. The alternative would be an operating budget for the entire institution, without regard to the individual programs. This kind of top-down budgeting generally would focus on cost-containment rather than program effectiveness and efficiency. From an academic perspective, this top-down approach is much less desirable than the hierarchical, bottom-up approach.

When publishing their annual operating budget report for external audiences, most institutions generally include only a summary of the master budget for the institution as a whole, sometimes broken down by major fund groups. But, for internal audiences, they usually publish a summary of each of the individual units' budgets. Some institutions also may publish the detailed budgets for individual units, including the names and salaries of specific personnel. But access to these details is usually limited to current university employees. The individual sponsored grant and contract budget details are generally a separate document that is available through the office of sponsored projects, although total grant and contract revenues and expenditures are summarized in the master budget. For a large university, the entire operating budget document—even without all of the details—can be very big. Indeed, the comprehensive annual budget report for the University of Texas at Austin exceeds 700 printed pages, not counting the 500-page index.[7] And it doesn't include the sponsored grant and contract budgets.

A simplified master operating budget for FY 2015 with natural expenditure classification is illustrated in table 6.1. As shown in this example, most operating budgets throughout the hierarchy tabulate not only the current-year budget that is based on projected revenue

Table 6.1. Master operating budget for FY 2015

	2014 actual	2015 original	2015 revised	Change Amount	%
Revenues					
Tuition and fees	68,185,645	76,062,318	76,579,542	517,224	0.68
State appropriations	42,710,964	43,102,390	43,102,390		
Grants and contracts	82,440,473	84,991,396	89,375,698	4,384,302	5.16
Auxiliary	10,687,450	10,972,200	10,972,200		
Other sources	3,809,020	5,439,020	5,439,020		
Totals	207,833,552	220,567,324	225,468,850	4,901,525	2.22
Expenditures					
Salaries and wages	110,825,886	115,932,678	117,683,261	1,750,583	1.51
Fringe benefits	31,029,260	34,777,065	35,083,103	306,038	0.88
Operating	62,291,241	67,787,919	71,156,979	3,369,060	4.97
Capital	1,482,164	1,494,664	1,499,895	5,231	0.35
Totals	205,628,551	219,992,326	225,423,239	5,430,913	2.47
Fund balance	2,205,001	574,998	45,611	(529,387)	−92.07

Note: The revised budget was reported at the end of the fiscal year, noting changes from the original budget (2015 original) to the revision (2015 revised).

and expenditures but also the actual amount of revenues and expenditures from the previous year (2014), consistent with the more comprehensive definition of budgetary accounting. These two basic elements of the budget are shown in the two left columns.

Furthermore, the GASB recommends that public universities report their original budget and a revised, final budget that accounts for any changes during the budget year, along with their actual expenditures for the year.[8] Therefore, in that spirit, both public and private university budgets usually are revised at least once during the fiscal year to account for changes in state appropriations or allocations, updated tuition and fee income, and any other sources of revenue or anticipated major expenditures. The example in table 6.1 includes the revised budget, which was reported at the end of the fiscal year, along with the amounts and percentage of changes between the original and the revised budgets. Analysis and explanation of changes from the previous to the current fiscal year may be provided in footnotes to the budget. In this example, the major revision in revenue can be attributed to an unexpected 5.16 percent increase in grants and contracts during the year. The increased expenditures can be attributed mainly to sizable increases in personnel and operating costs, which are probably associated with the increased grants and contracts.

Variances

The GASB also encourages public universities to report any differences—called variances—between the budgeted amount and the actual spending during a fiscal year, along with an analysis of the variances. Private universities generally adhere to these guidelines as well. In fact, most public and private universities issue budget-variance reports for the schools and colleges not only at the end of a fiscal year but also at least two, and often four, times each year. As Stanford University notes: "Periodically through the year, as determined by University management, budget officers provide analysis and explanation of the variance between actual income and expense (or projected income and expense) and the Consolidated Budget in accordance with the guidelines provided by the University Budget Office."[9] These budget variance reports play an important role in maintaining financial stability. They alert administrators about any deviations between the budgeted and actual expenditures, highlighting any needed financial or managerial adjustments.

Technical note: The convention for reporting variances differs between universities. In the ensuing discussion, by convention,

$$variance = actual - budgeted.$$

Often the variances are reported as percentages. By convention,

$$variance \% = \frac{variance}{budgeted}.$$

Also by convention, a variance is considered favorable when the actual revenue is more than the budgeted revenue or the actual expenditures are less than the budgeted expenditures. Vice versa, a variance is considered unfavorable when the actual revenue is less than the budgeted revenue or the actual expenditures are more than the budgeted expenditures. By this convention, favorable revenue variances are positive and favorable expenditure variances are negative. In budget shorthand, the descriptors "favorable" and "unfavorable" are denoted simply by F or U, respectively.

Fiscal year-end variance reports identify budget items that may require attention in the next year's budget. Indeed, year-end variances are always looked at when preparing next year's budget. Of course, large variances attract the most attention. They may indicate faulty forecasting or fiscal mismanagement by the budget unit, requiring additional staff training. Also, they may occur due to unexpected fluctuations in revenue or expenditures, such as those following the loss of a large grant, a major hurricane, et cetera. Although positive variances in the expense category represent saved money, they are not necessarily desirable. They may indicate the budget unit's under-investment in its academic programs, which represents academic mismanagement. And, of course, they raise questions about how much money the budget unit actually needs, which portends a reduction in next year's budget allocation. Alternatively, negative variances may indicate poor fiscal management. Indeed, deans or department chairs who report sizable negative variances several years in a row risk losing their jobs.

Ideally, variances are zero, manifesting competent budget forecasts and management. Realistically, small deviations from zero are expected. As an expedient, universities may impose a threshold for detailed explanations of a variance from the budget unit director. For example, according to Stanford University's policy, "An explanation is required if a variance exceeds the greater of ±$500,000 or ±10%."[10]

These thresholds do not necessarily imply that a unit may keep the money reported by the variance (the year-end fund balance). In fact, it is not uncommon for the provost to "sweep" (take away) the money unless the unit can argue persuasively that it has a greater need for it. Nor is it uncommon for the provost to reduce next year's budget by the amount reported as a negative variance unless the unit can argue persuasively that the university benefited from over spending its budgeted amount.

A sample year-end variance report for a graduate school budget is illustrated in table 6.2. Although they do not represent money per se, the imputed dollar amounts of allowable tuition waivers (tuition discounts) are included in this budget. The variances are expressed as a percentage of the original budget issued at the beginning of the fiscal year. Notably, the faculty salaries are fixed; they seldom vary. Most other items vary to some extent. Two salary items (the classified employee and other compensation items) incurred large unfavorable variances that certainly warrant explanation by the unit director. Unfavorable variances incurred by office supplies and travel were relatively small in terms of dollar amounts but large in percentages. They, too, may require an explanation. Fortunately, these unfavorable variances are counter-balanced by large favorable variances in the graduate research assistant and tuition waiver items. Ironically, however, the tuition waiver's favorable variance may also warrant an explanation, for it indicates under-investment in graduate student

Table 6.2. Graduate school FY 2016 budget with year-end variances

Description	Original budget	Actual	Variance Amount	%
Revenues				
Revenue allocation	1,048,695	1,048,695		
Allowable tuition waivers	2,245,614	2,245,614		
Total revenues	3,294,308	3,294,308		
Expenditures				
Salaries				
Faculty	91,806	91,806		
Professional	213,211	216,664	3,453	1.62
Administrative	162,887	148,493	(14,394)	−8.84
Classified employee	134,545	165,488	30,943	23.00
Graduate research assistant	178,144	130,162	(47,982)	−26.93
Student and temporary wages	9,137	7,575	(1,562)	−17.10
Other compensation	26,593	40,268	13,675	51.42
Subtotal salaries	816,323	800,456	(15,867)	−1.94
Operations				
Contracted services	26,825	23,994	(2,831)	−10.55
Office supplies	3,772	10,434	6,662	176.62
Communications	8,525	5,588	(2,937)	−34.45
Travel	16,785	22,853	6,068	36.15
Subscriptions		719	719	
Repairs and maintenance	1,464	965	(499)	−34.08
Recruiting	55,000	52,426	(2,574)	−4.68
Subtotal operations	112,371	116,980	4,609	4.10
Financial aid				
Scholarships/fellowships	120,000	119,243	(757)	−0.63
Tuition waivers (discounts)	2,245,614	2,106,543	(139,071)	−6.19
Subtotal financial aid	2,365,614	2,225,786	(139,828)	−5.91
Total expenditures	3,294,308	3,143,222	(151,086)	−4.59

support. Nonetheless, the overall variance of −4.59 percent is reasonably close to zero. In fact, if the tuition waivers are excluded from the arithmetic, the variance is 1.15 percent, which is quite close to zero, indicating good budget management.

More frequent variance reports issued during the fiscal year serve a controlling function by alerting the budget unit about any significant deviations from the budget. Some deviations may be cyclical and, therefore, predictable. Tuition revenue, for example, may spike at the beginning of each semester. Other deviations may be less predictable, and they are the ones requiring attention. This may involve either adjustments to the budget (for example, shifting money from one item to another) or, alternatively, corrections in the spending pattern (for example, curtailing travel, freezing hiring, etc.). In the budget vernacular, these two alternative approaches represent flexible and static budgeting, respectively.

A sample mid-year variance report for the graduate-school budget (table 6.2) is shown in table 6.3. In this example, encumbrances are included in the actual expenditure amounts. The variance report was issued at the beginning of the fourth quarter of the fiscal year, April 1, 2016. Assuming a "straight-line" budget, the year-to-date (YTD) budgeted amounts were assumed to be three-fourths of the original budgeted amount. Since the encumbered cash has not yet been spent, some universities "break out" the encumbrances and list them in a separate column. The variances are reported relative to the year-to-date budget and the original budget. In the former case (YTD actual-YTD budget), there are noteworthy favorable and unfavorable variances for the graduate research assistant and office supplies items, respectively. It may be too late in the year to invest in more graduate research assistants, but, clearly, the dean must reduce the spending rate for office supplies. The variance between the YTD actual and the original budget equals the amount of money available for variable items during the remainder of the fiscal year. Faculty salaries are fixed, so all of the money in that line has been committed. But, for the variable student and temporary wages, there is $3,532 available for the fourth quarter.

Modern accounting software can generate variance reports in "real time." (Historically, prior to enterprise accounting software, budget units would keep up-to-date "shadow" accounting systems that were independent of the main institutional accounting system.) This real-time control feature is useful for deans, department chairs, and principal investigators as they manage their finances. They list the budgeted amount, the actual amount spent up to the time of the report, any outstanding encumbrances, and the remaining unencumbered balance of the budgeted amount (the variance). From a practical vantage point, the unencumbered balance of an expenditure account is the uncommitted amount of budgeted money that remains for use.

Operating Budget Preparation

Now, back to the important, opening question: Who constructs the operating budget? Or, stated differently, who decides how the university's money for academic purposes is distributed? The answer to this question will depend on the institution: its type (public or private), leadership style, governance culture, financial situation, and various other attributes. Furthermore, the budget-construction

Table 6.3. Graduate school FY 2016 budget with third-quarter variances

Description	Original budget	YTD (April 1, 2016)		Variances			
				YTD actual-YTD budget		YTD actual-original budget	
		Budget	Actual	Amount	%	Amount	%
Revenues							
Revenue allocation	1,048,695	786,521	786,521			(262,174)	−25.00
Allowable tuition waivers	2,245,614	2,245,614	2,245,614				
Total revenues	3,294,308	3,032,135	3,032,135			(262,174)	−7.96
Expenditures							
Salaries							
Faculty	91,806	68,855	69,169	315	0.46	(22,637)	−24.66
Professional	213,211	159,908	160,331	423	0.26	(52,880)	−24.80
Administrative	162,887	122,165	112,855	(9,310)	−7.62	(50,032)	−30.72
Classified employee	134,545	100,909	122,461	21,553	21.36	(12,084)	−8.98
Graduate research assistant	178,144	133,608	98,923	(34,685)	−25.96	(79,221)	−44.47
Student and temporary wages	9,137	6,853	5,606	(1,247)	−18.20	(3,532)	−38.65
Other compensation	26,593	19,945	30,603	10,659	53.44	4,010	15.08
Subtotal salaries	816,323	612,242	599,949	(12,294)	−2.01	(216,374)	−26.51
Operations							
Contracted services	26,825	20,119	17,756	(2,363)	−11.75	(9,069)	−33.81
Office supplies	3,772	2,829	7,930	5,101	180.31	4,158	110.23
Communications	8,525	6,394	4,135	(2,258)	−35.32	(4,390)	−51.49
Travel	16,785	12,589	17,368	4,780	37.97	583	3.48
Subscriptions			719	719		719	
Repairs and maintenance	1,464	1,098	733	(365)	−33.21	(731)	−49.90
Recruiting	55,000	41,250	38,795	(2,455)	−5.95	(16,205)	−29.46
Subtotal operations	112,371	84,278	87,437	3,159	3.75	(24,934)	−22.19
Financial aid							
Scholarships/fellowships	120,000	90,000	90,625	625	0.69	(29,375)	−24.48
Tuition waivers (discounts)	2,245,614	1,684,211	1,579,907	(104,303)	−6.19	(665,707)	−29.64
Subtotal financial aid	2,365,614	1,774,211	1,670,532	(103,679)	−5.84	(695,082)	−29.38
Total expenditures	3,294,308	2,470,731	2,357,917	(112,814)	−4.57	(936,391)	−28.42

Note: The original budget was issued at the beginning of FY 2016 (July 1, 2015).

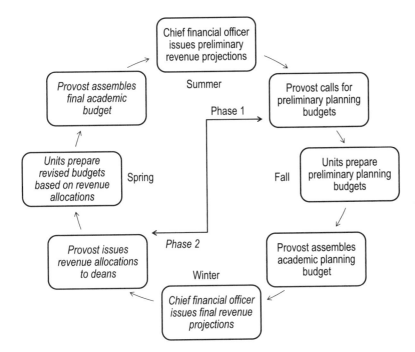

Figure 6.2. Sample academic budget planning process. Phase 1 begins when the chief financial officer issues preliminary revenue projections, and phase 2 (in italics) begins when the chief financial officer issues final revenue projections.

process usually involves the participation of numerous individuals and groups, which can obfuscate the exact source of specific decisions about how money is budgeted to be spent. Nonetheless, there is one clear element in all of this: ultimately, the governing board has the final decision because it must approve the university's master operating budget.

Despite the variability in details from one institution to another, budget preparations usually follow a common skeletal paradigm, illustrated in figure 6.2. It is a cyclical two-phase, annual process where decisions must be made: What programs or services will be offered? How much will they cost? Where will the money to support them come from?

The first phase (figure 6.2, *right*) starts with the development of preliminary revenue and expenditure projections for the upcoming budget year. In what will be called *incremental projections*, the chief financial officer usually requests revenue projections (and any unusual expenditure projections) from the deans, directors, and the chief research and chief investment officers (or whoever oversees the university's endowment and investments). Usually, these projections consist of incremental changes to the previous year's budget.

Examples are shown in Table 6.4, which, for comparison, presents the projected revenue for next year (2017) as well as the actual revenues for the past four years. The 2017 projections reflect the

Table 6.4. Budget revenue and expenditure projections

Sources	Actual budget revenues				Incremental projections	
	2013	2014	2015	2016	2017	Rationale
Tuition and fees	62,555,223	68,185,645	76,579,542	77,285,797	79,604,371	2016 amount plus 2%[a]
State appropriations	43,240,587	42,710,964	43,102,390	43,997,235	44,959,223	State estimate[b]
Contracts and grants	83,243,514	82,440,473	89,375,698	106,619,417	109,926,150	Deans' estimates
Endowment and other	2,179,020	3,809,020	5,439,020	5,366,699	4,866,699	Foundation estimates
Auxiliary services	10,704,330	10,687,450	10,972,200	11,480,500	12,869,708	Directors' estimates
Total	201,922,674	207,833,552	225,468,850	244,749,648	252,226,151	
	Actual budget expenditures					
Salaries and wages	103,700,958	110,825,886	117,683,261	118,868,276	121,245,642	2016 plus 2% raise[a]
Fringe benefits	29,041,284	31,029,260	35,083,103	35,657,748	36,370,903	
Operating	67,179,221	62,291,241	71,156,979	88,153,960	92,061,658	Deans' estimates
Capital	1,426,211	1,482,164	1,499,895	1,494,664	1,516,664	Director's estimate
Total	201,347,674	205,628,551	225,423,238	244,174,648	251,194,866	
Fund balance	575,000	2,205,001	45,612	575,000	1,031,285	

Note: Incremental projections for 2017 were derived by methods shown in the notes. Linear regression projections for 2017 are as follows:

Number of years in regression	2	3	4	
Revenue	268,931,972	261,299,604	254,071,973	
Expenditures	268,356,970	261,811,272	253,496,974	
Fund balance	575,002	(511,668)	574,999	

[a]Pending board approval
[b]Pending final appropriation

deans' and directors' estimates based on predicted adjustments to the current year's budget (2016). The rationale for these adjustments is noted in the right-hand column. Senior, experienced financial officers usually have a fairly good "feel" about the accuracy of these projections and may tweak the numbers up or down. As shown in the footnotes to the rationale, a projected 2 percent tuition increase and salary raise must await governing board approval, and the projected state appropriation must await the governor's signing of the appropriations bill (which may not occur until several weeks into the budget year). Notably, in these preliminary projections for 2017, revenue exceeds expenditures by $1,031,285. For a prudent financial officer, this projected surplus provides a welcome buffer for unexpected expenditures.

In an alternative, more quantitative (but not necessarily more accurate) method, *linear regression projections* are used to forecast revenue and expenditures. A straight line is fit to total revenue or expenditure amounts from the past several years, and the line is extrapolated to the upcoming budget year. The extrapolation yields the projected values. Mathematically, using standard least-squares regression methods, the linear fit with y intercept a and slope b is described by the equation:

$y = a + (b \times x)$,

where x and y refer to the year and the projected value, respectively. So, the equation for extrapolation to the projected value is:

projected value = *intercept* + (*slope* × *year*)

This method is shown graphically in figure 6.3, which compares three different linear regressions of the revenue and expenditures shown in table 6.4 based on the past two, three, or four years (2013 to 2016). *Note:* Because revenues and expenditures are nearly in balance most years, the revenue and expenditure projection curves predictably are quite similar. The shorter time period (two years) reflects recent trends, and the longer time period (four years) reflects historical trends. Incidentally, the same procedure could be used to obtain projections for any other time-dependent variable, such as tuition and state appropriations.

The linear regression projections for revenue and expenditures also are tabulated in table 6.4 (*lower panel*). Each of the linear regression projections of both revenue and expenditures exceed the incremental projections. However, their predicted fund balances were considerably smaller, leaving less of a buffer. Indeed, the three-year

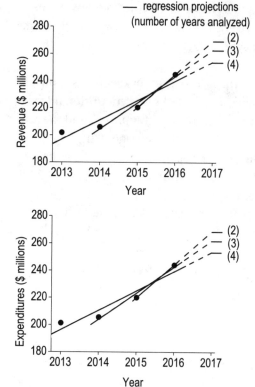

Figure 6.3. Revenue (*upper panel*) and expenditure (*lower panel*) projections for 2017 derived from linear regression of budget revenues in the past two (2015-2016), three (2014-2016), and four (2013-2016) years

regression projected a negative fund balance, which adds a note of caution to the planning of next year's budget. Confronted with such disparate projections, what should a prudent financial officer do? Most probably, issue the lowest revenue projection ($252,226,151) as the target in the preliminary budget.

The advantage of the linear regression method is that it reflects statistical trends, short-term or longer-term. The example shows trends over two, three, and four years. It "looks beyond" one-time anomalies in revenue or expenditures. But that is also its main disadvantage; the regression does not account for one-time circumstances that might affect the next year's revenue or expenditure projections. It is blind, so to speak, to a stock market crash or natural disaster that impacts university revenues. In that sense, linear regressions are more suitable for long-term projections. Accordingly, they (and more sophisticated statistical techniques) are used primarily for long-term forecasting by large organizations and government agencies (such as the OMB). Although the statistical method removes human bias from the projections, pragmatically, it should be used in conjunction with—not in lieu of—the more conventional, incremental projection method.

With preliminary revenue and expenditure projections in hand, the provost moves to the next step, issuing calls to each budget unit for preliminary planning budgets. In times of financial uncertainty, the CFO may issue several different revenue projections, requiring different budgets for each revenue scenario. The provost asks each unit to prepare a budget that aligns with its strategic plans based on these preliminary projections. So, at each level in the hierarchy, the budget units construct a budget that reflects their programmatic priorities. Conservative practice is to constrain the budget units' proposed expenditures to match the preliminary revenue projections. This tends to maintain status quo. More liberal practice is to allow the budget units' proposed expenditures to exceed the revenue that they can reasonably expect to get. Although this "pie in the sky" approach might seem unrealistic, it promotes thoughtful planning for future program growth and quality enhancement. Thus, it is not necessarily discouraged. These preliminary budgets then flow up to the top; the deans assemble departmental budgets and their own priorities into an overall school or college budget that they transmit to the provost, who merges them into a campus academic planning budget. Finally, the university's chief budget officer consolidates the institutional master planning budget that goes to the governing board for information and, sometimes, approval.

The second phase (denoted by italics on the left-hand side in figure 6.2) begins when the CFO issues final institutional financial parameters, including updates of projected revenues from tuition and fees, endowment pay-out, state appropriations, grants and contracts, and any other sources. Based on these projections, the provost must decide how the available revenue will be allocated, generally with advice and support of an institutional budget committee composed of faculty members, staff, and students. The deans and directors usually present their projected goals and needs to this committee in so-called budget hearings, basically lobbying the provost for support. Ultimately, the provost distributes revenue allocations down the hierarchy, via the deans and directors. At each level, the units revise their preliminary planning budget based on their allocated revenue and programmatic priorities. These revised budgets then flow back to the top; the deans assemble department budgets into an overall school or college budget that they transmit to the provost. At this stage, the provost prepares the final budget, and the university's chief budget officer consolidates the final institutional operating budget that goes to the governing board for approval. This overall institutional budget is sometimes called the consolidated budget because it consolidates the budgets developed by units lower in the hierarchy.

Despite its tedious nature, the budget process is quite important to the viability of an organization. This importance is recognized by the regional accrediting associations, which have a common standard requiring the alignment of resources—that is, the budget—with educational purposes and objectives. For example, the Southern Association of Colleges and Schools Commission on Colleges requires an institution to have "an annual budget that is preceded by sound planning, is subject to sound fiscal procedures, and is approved by the governing board."[11] Accordingly, there have been numerous books and articles written about the budget planning process and its role in the university.[12]

Revenue Allocation

Revenue allocation by the provost (or the chief budget officer), in the second step of phase 2 in figure 6.2, is the keystone to the operating budget process. This is the point when department aspirations meet financial reality. Also, it is the point when the provost has the opportunity to reallocate funds, rewarding well-performing or particularly high-priority units. In that context, this is the point where institutions can implement changes in a programmatic direction. And it is the point when the provost decides how much revenue to keep in reserve for unexpected situations, a common practice known as "under-allocation."

Sometimes, especially in times of unstable state appropriations, tuition income, or endowment income, the CFO or the provost apportions revenue allocations at various times in the fiscal year: quarterly or semi-annually. Not all revenue is given out at once. This is good practice, for an apportionment can be adjusted if the available revenue decreases unexpectedly during the fiscal year, due to a state tax shortfall or a drop in enrollment in the second semester, for example. Moreover, apportioned allocations also ensure that the entire year's allocation is not used up early in the budget year. On the downside, the apportionment process limits flexible use of the money.

Seldom does a provost decide on revenue allocations willy-nilly. More often than not, the institution has adopted formal guidelines for making these decisions. These guidelines are usually based on some model for budget allocations. Within academia, there are four standard budget allocation models:

- zero-based
- incremental
- formula-based
- revenue-based

The principles of each model will be discussed. In practice, however, the allocation procedures may not follow any model precisely; there may be some overlap between two or three of these models.

Zero-Based Budgeting

In this, the harshest, most centralized budget model, each unit must justify from the ground up all of its proposed expenditures. This is tantamount to justifying its very existence every fiscal year. On the one hand, this allocation model is responsive to current performance and needs. On the other hand, it seriously hampers any long-range planning. In this model, tenure guarantees a job but not a salary. Plus, the budget hearings expand into full-scale performance reviews, which consume a lot of time and faculty effort. Consequently, academic institutions seldom adhere to a zero-based budget model. At most, they may reduce the base relative to last year by a more manageable amount, such as 10 or 15 percent, and require expenditure justifications from that reduced base.

Incremental Budgeting

In this extensively used model, funding increments are added to (or subtracted from) the previous year's budget. The underlying assumption is that the institution's fundamental goals and objectives will not change markedly from this year to the next. Like zero-based budgeting, this model depends on budget hearings and committee reviews, where the budget unit directors (for example, department chairs and deans) essentially negotiate the changes to their annual budgets. However, unlike zero-based budgeting, the prior year's budget is the base. Because the provost ultimately decides on increments to the base, this model is known cynically as the "history and mystery" budget model.

An across-the-board incremental budgeting model is the easiest to implement. The provost simply adds or subtracts a percentage increment from each unit's previous year's budget. The incremental amount depends on the overall amount of revenue available to the institution. Thus, if the university's state appropriations increase by 2 percent, each unit's allocation increases by 2 percent less any amount withheld by the CFO or the provost for special purposes; commonly, both the CFO and the provost under-allocate their available revenue. A common example of incremental budgeting occurs if the state or the governing board includes a 2 percent increase in the budget specifically to fund 2 percent salary increases. The incremental allocation (2 percent) is simply added to each unit's budget. Department chairs may have the discretion to base an individual's salary raise on performance metrics, budget hearings, committee recommendations, and other criteria. In that case, the overall incremental amount available for pay raises is constant (2 percent), but not all individuals necessarily get equal incremental raises.

Incremental budgeting has advantages and disadvantages. On the one hand, its simplicity reduces the administrative burden of extensive budget hearings and consultations. A unit's continued existence is not at stake. Also, its stability eases long-range planning; although the exact magnitude of future increments may be unknown, at least the units know that they won't be "singled out" with hugely disproportional budget cuts because of decreased performance or enrollment. On the other hand, incremental budgeting lacks incentives. This is the serious downside to its stability; units aren't rewarded for exceptional performance. For this reason, a unit's enthusiasm for incremental budgeting depends on its expected performance. Furthermore, incremental budgeting maintains a school's or college's relative share of the total revenue available, with little regard for changes in teaching load or sponsored research activity. In a sense, prior-year base budgets become "entitlements"; past expenditures, not strategic plans, drive budget preparation.

Formula-Based Budgeting

Formula-based budget models allocate revenue according to selected productivity metrics. The formulas vary in complexity, but most base allocations on several standard metrics. Semester credit hours, full-time equivalent students, or total number of students are the most prevalent bases in the instruction, academic support, and institutional support areas; square footage is used most often in the operation and maintenance of the physical plant; and total student enrollment ("headcount") is the base unit most often in student services and financial aid. Thus, in the simplest formula, instructional allocations depend on a college's enrollment, such as $100 per student. Or, they might depend on the number of semester credit hours taught: for example, a college teaching 10 percent of the credit hours would receive 10 percent of the overall instructional budget. Formulas also may be based on specific performance measures, such as in-creased retention and graduation rates, reductions in time to degree, number of grant applications submitted, and number of papers published.

The metrics, semester credit hours, square footage, et cetera, measured at a specific time, such as the end of the fall semester, commonly are averaged over a three-year period to damp out any unusual fluctuations. Then, they are multiplied by a base rate to attain the allocation. So, if the base rate is $50 per semester credit hour, a college that taught 800, 1,000, and 1,200 semester credit hours in the fall semester of fiscal years 2013, 2014, and 2015 would receive an allocation of $50,000 ($1,000, the 3-year average, × $50) in the FY 2016 budget. The base rate depends on the projected revenue—if the projected revenue available for budgeting increases, then the base rate increases, and vice versa.

Formulas become more complicated if they account for differences between student level (freshman, sophomore, graduate, and so forth) and academic disciplines (liberal arts, engineering, business, and so forth) by adding a weighting scheme. Usually, the relative weights account for differential costs for delivering instruction. For example, the least expensive cost of instruction might be for lower-level undergraduates in the liberal arts; thus, it is assigned a baseline weight of 1.0. However, if the cost of instruction in the College of Engineering is 1.8 times more expensive, the College of Engineering might be assigned a weight of 1.8 in the allocation formula. Therefore, for each semester credit hour taught, the College of Engineering would be allocated 1.8 times as much as the college of liberal arts. In practice, weighting schemes generally introduce bookkeeping complications. Nonetheless, institutions that use a formula-based model for revenue allocations tend to adopt a more-or-less complicated weighting scheme.

A majority of states use a formula-based process for allocating appropriations to the public institutions of higher education. At the state level, the weighting schemes can become quite detailed, for the weights reflect the myriad educational, political, economic, and public policy factors that influence the financing of higher education. Texas provides an example of a complicated algorithm, with more than 100 different weights in the instructional allocation formula.[13] To illustrate this complexity, their relative weights for FY 2017 are shown in table 6.5. The base rate is $55.39; thus, with a weight of 1.00, an institution receives $55.39 for every semester credit hour that is taught to a lower-level (freshman and sophomore) undergraduate

Table 6.5. Texas Higher Education Coordinating Board formula funding weights for 2016–2017

Discipline	Undergraduate lower-level	Undergraduate upper-level	Master's	Doctoral	Professional practice
		Relative weights			
Liberal arts	1.00	1.76	4.00	10.77	
Science	1.78	3.02	7.53	20.61	
Fine arts	1.47	2.52	6.03	7.95	
Teacher ed.	1.63	2.08	2.56	7.42	
Agriculture	2.07	2.75	7.80	11.77	
Engineering	2.38	3.52	7.10	17.98	
Home economics	1.10	1.75	3.01	8.67	
Law					5.13
Social services	1.68	2.05	2.93	18.18	
Library science	1.49	1.57	3.60	12.06	
Veterinary medicine					22.03
Vocational training	1.45	2.64			
Physical training	1.51	1.26			
Health services	1.07	1.65	2.79	9.86	2.64
Pharmacy	1.86	5.02	28.29	35.14	4.32
Business admin.	1.19	1.88	3.39	23.92	
Optometry			37.52	55.92	7.58
Teacher ed. practice	2.28	2.13			
Technology	2.26	2.41	3.89	5.20	
Nursing	1.72	2.11	3.34	8.99	
Developmental ed.	1.00				

Note: Base rates are:

$55.39   Funding rate per weighted semester credit hour

10%   Teaching experience supplement for tenure and tenure track faculty members

student in the liberal arts. However, with a weight of 1.78, it receives $98.59 for every semester credit hour taught to a lower-level undergraduate in science. And, with a weight of 20.61, it receives $1,141.60 for every doctoral student in the sciences. In addition, Texas adds an additional weight of 10 percent to lower-division and upper-division semester credit hours taught by tenured and tenure-track faculty members. Of course, astute campus administrators cannot ignore the financial implications of these various weights when planning long-term enrollment and academic strategies.

Practical usage of the weighting algorithm for five different colleges within a university is illustrated hypothetically in table 6.6, reading from top to bottom. Initially, a matrix of weights is prepared (*upper panel*), and the semester credit hours are tabulated (*middle panel*). As in most cases, the semester credit hours represent the average of the fall semester data for the preceding three years to smooth out large fluctuations. The semester credit hour values are multiplied by the corresponding relative weights to attain the weighted semester credit hours (*lower panel*). Finally, the weighted semester credit hours

Table 6.6. Formula funding based on weighted semester credit hours

| | Weights | | | |
College	Undergraduate lower-level	Undergraduate upper-level	Master's	Doctoral
Liberal arts	1.0	1.5	4.0	8.0
Science	2.0	3.0	7.5	15.0
Engineering	2.5	3.5	8.0	20.0
Education	1.6	2.2	2.5	7.5
Business	1.2	1.8	3.4	18.0

| | Semester credit hours | | | |
College	Undergraduate lower-level	Undergraduate upper-level	Master's	Doctoral
Liberal arts	45,979	40,544	1,918	5,755
Science	23,077	4,710	423	2,065
Engineering	1,677	4,543	2,558	5,115
Education	459	9,201	4,166	2,777
Business	2,544	9,750	2,796	311

| | Weighted semester credit hours | | | |
College	Undergraduate lower-level	Undergraduate upper-level	Master's	Doctoral
Liberal arts	45,979	60,816	7,672	46,040
Science	46,154	14,130	3,173	30,975
Engineering	4,193	15,901	20,464	102,300
Education	734	20,242	10,415	20,828
Business	3,053	17,550	9,506	5,598

| | Allocations ($) | | | | |
College	Undergraduate lower-level	Undergraduate upper-level	Master's	Doctoral	Total
Liberal arts	2,758,740	3,648,960	460,320	2,762,400	9,630,420
Science	2,769,240	847,800	190,350	1,858,500	5,665,890
Engineering	251,550	954,030	1,227,840	6,138,000	8,571,420
Education	44,064	1,214,532	624,900	1,249,650	3,133,146
Business	183,168	1,053,000	570,384	335,880	2,142,432
Totals	6,006,762	7,718,322	3,073,794	12,344,430	29,143,308

Note: Allocations equal the base rate times the weighted semester credit hours. Base rate ($ per weighted semester credit hour) = $60.00

are multiplied by the base rate to calculate the allocated revenue for each college. So, for example, the 40,544 semester credit hours taught to upper-level undergraduates in the liberal arts generate 1.5 times as many weighted semester credit hours (60,816). Therefore, at $60.00 per weighted semester credit hours, the liberal arts college receives $3,648,960 for its upper-level undergraduate education.

Using comparable methodology, utilities and operations and maintenance budget allocations can be calculated. Weights may be applied, depending on the building's use; energy-hungry laboratories and computing facilities may be assigned higher weights. And the square footage for each building is multiplied by the appropriate weight en route to the final allocation.

Some units are not suitable for formula-based allocations. Central administration activities, for example, don't have quantifiable activities. Consequently, they may not be included in the formula-based allocation process. Instead, they may be funded incrementally, which decreases funds available for distribution according to the formula. This is not desirable, because reducing the fraction of resources allocated via the formula in this way weakens incentives and impedes reallocations needed to meet demand.

On the one hand, formula-based funding has two major advantages. Importantly, formula funding introduces objectivity into the allocation process. Politics may be involved, but political influence will be expressed in the relative weights, not the application of the formula. Thus, by relying on quantitative algorithms for distributing revenue, the allocation process is not politicized at the campus level. Equally important, formula-based budget models respond to changes in teaching loads, research productivity, or other formula parameters. Input formulas can promote internal funding equity and redistribute resources from shrinking to growing programs if they are applied symmetrically. As John R. Curry, Andrew L. Laws, and Jon C. Strauss note, formula-funded budgets "ebb and flow with demand."[14]

On the other hand, formula-based funding has two major disadvantages. First, unless performance measures are included in the formula, this model does not necessarily incorporate quality in the resource allocation process. Second, the formula-based allocations do not necessarily align with an institution's strategic plan. They may favor anomalous, nonstrategic programs, which can raise discontent among "slighted" high-priority programs. Indeed, a differential weighting scheme, as in table 6.6, has the potential to pervert strategic planning. This can place the provost in the awkward position of having to over-ride the strict formula-based allocations in order to favor strategic goals.

Revenue-Based Budgeting

This model allocates the revenue generated by a unit back to the unit. Thus, it is called the revenue-based return or, alternatively, the activity-based return model. In a typical scenario, a school, college, or department generates revenue for the university from five main sources (sometimes called lines):

- tuition (based on semester credit hours taught by the unit)
- student fees
- grants and contracts
- indirect cost reimbursement
- outreach revenue (for example, summer school, extension courses, workshops, etc.)

The revenue-based model returns to the school, college, or department the revenue that it generates from each of these sources. In other words, revenues generated from instructional, research, and outreach activities are allocated directly to the unit responsible for the activity. In that sense, the unit gets to keep what it earns. This model is described colloquially as "eat what you kill."

There is a significant catch, however: the provost usually imposes a "tax" on the returned revenue. The tax is sometimes called "participation."[15] (The term "participation" refers to the units' membership in the university, enabling them to use the university's name and goodwill.) The provost uses the tax to supplement whatever other revenue might be available (such as state appropriations, endowment income, etc.) to pay for centrally provided institutional infrastructure, such as the library, central administration, and special programmatic priorities. Thus, the units actually receive a fraction of the total revenue that they have generated. The tax rate depends on the availability to the provost of income from other sources and the extent of the centralized infrastructural costs. Of course, from the units' perspective, the lower the tax rate, the better. Some institutions base the tax on a three- to five-year running average of past years' infrastructure expenses to damp out unusual fluctuations in any single year.

In this model, the provost or dean may supplement a unit's revenue return using funds derived from a variety of sources: the revenue (participation) tax, state appropriations, endowment income, indirect cost reimbursement, licensing income, interest income, and so forth. These supplements, called subvention, are an important element of the model because they are leverage points where the provost and deans can exert control over the allocation process. Stated in pragmatic terms, "it keeps them in the game." For example, the campus subvention provides the opportunity to subsidize strategically important programs that cannot generate sufficient operating revenue through tuition or indirect cost reimbursement because they cannot accommodate large enrollments or compete for large federal research grants. Examples might include a school of architecture or an honor's college. In addition, subvention provides the opportunity to reward or punish some program without selectively changing its percentage of revenue return, which is generally a very bad idea; the same goal can be reached simply by adjusting the subvention amount.

Depending on an institution's culture, the provost may or may not have sole discretion over the allocation of subvention funds. There are no general rules. However, it is safe to assume that most provosts do not make the decisions in a vacuum; they consult with various constituencies, such as other senior administrators and a campus budget committee, and adhere closely to institutional strategic plans when allocating subvention funds.

A sample revenue-based return budget for a college is illustrated in table 6.7. In this example, as shown in the footnotes, tuition revenue generated by the college is based on the number of semester credit hours taught by the college relative to those taught by the entire university. In this case, that was 18 percent. Thus, the college receives 18 percent of the total tuition collected by the university. Implicitly, the college receives all of the tuition from courses taught by its faculty members. Alternatively, a model could allocate a portion of the tuition to the colleges where the students major (for example, 20 percent), recognizing that they attracted the students' interest and incur advising costs. Tuition, indirect cost reimbursement (primarily from federal grants and contracts), and outreach (summer school, extension, etc.) revenue is taxed at rates varying from 33 percent to 67 percent, as documented in the footnotes. Notably, in this example, scholarships and fellowships are considered expenditures; thus, they do not affect the tuition tax. Alternatively, financial aid may be subtracted (discounted) from the tuition revenue, thus reducing the tuition tax. On first thought, this might seem to benefit the college. However, on further thought, ultimately, it might not benefit the college because it triggered a higher tax rate to generate the revenue needed for the provost's subvention pool.

In general, revenue-return models provide strong incentives for the department to generate more revenue through teaching, research, and outreach activities. Presumably, the higher the percentage returned to the unit, the greater the incentive to generate more revenue. As the University of Washington summarizes the advantages of revenue- (activity-) return models, "activity-based budgeting 'empowers' greater local planning and accountability and creates incentives for units to manage resources and expenditures more efficiently. Further, direct control of resources generated from activities

Table 6.7. College revenue-based budget for FY 2016 (actual) and FY 2017, with the change from 2016 to 2017

Revenue	2016 (actual)	2017	Change Amount	%
Tuition[a]	12,219,449	12,397,876	178,427	1.46
Central administration tuition tax[b]	(4,887,780)	(4,959,150)	(71,371)	1.46
Student fees	432,710	443,528	10,818	2.50
Subtotal tuition and fees	7,764,379	7,882,253	117,874	1.52
Sponsored programs				
Grants and contracts	4,607,380	4,964,531	357,151	7.75
Indirect cost reimbursement	1,290,066	1,390,069	100,002	7.75
Central administration reimbursement tax[c]	(864,344)	(931,346)	(67,002)	7.75
Subtotal sponsored programs	5,033,102	5,423,254	390,152	7.75
Outreach revenue	990,076	1,014,828	24,752	2.50
Central administration outreach tax[d]	(326,725)	(334,893)	(8,168)	2.50
Subtotal outreach	663,351	679,935	16,584	2.50
Subtotal revenue	13,460,832	13,985,442	524,609	3.90
Campus subvention	1,000,000	1,000,000		
Total	14,460,832	14,985,442	524,609	3.63
Expenditures				
Salaries and wages	9,046,374	9,514,627	468,253	5.18
Fringe benefits	2,985,303	3,139,827	154,523	5.18
Operating	232,876	238,713	5,837	2.51
Scholarships and fellowships	2,092,275	2,092,275		
Total	14,356,829	14,985,442	628,613	4.38
Fund Balance	104,004			

Note: SCH refers to semester credit hours.
[a]Tuition calculation:

Total university SCH (fall semester)	170,368	174,627	4,259	2.50
College SCH (fall semester)	30,275	31,032	757	2.50
% college SCH/university SCH	17.77%	17.77%		
Total university tuition revenue	68,763,108	69,767,177	1,004,069	1.46
College tuition (based on SCH percentage))	12,219,449	12,397,876	178,427	1.46

[b]Tuition tax = 40% × total tuition revenue
[c]Indirect cost tax = 67% × indirect cost reimbursement
[d]Outreach tax = 33% × outreach revenue

creates incentives to set priorities and develop new activities consistent with the overall mission and strategic goals of the institution."[16]

Responsibility Center Management

The decentralization inherent in the revenue-based budget model is expanded in responsibility center management (RCM). In this management-accounting model, each budget unit in the organizational hierarchy is considered a "responsibility center." By definition, "a responsibility center is a functional entity within a business that has its own goals and objectives, dedicated staff, policies and procedures, and financial reports. Such a center is used to tie specific responsibility for revenues generated, expenses incurred, and/or funds invested to individuals."[17] Thus, in an academic setting, this definition of RCM implies that each responsibility center—college, school, department, service center, and so forth—is responsible for its generated revenues and incurred expenses. Indeed, that is the core foundation of this budgeting model.

Within the university, there are two basic categories of responsibility centers: academic and administrative. On the one hand, the academic responsibility centers comprise the colleges, schools, departments, centers and institutes, and other revenue-generating units. Some universities include athletics and auxiliary units, such as housing and food services, in this category. The main attributes of the academic responsibility centers are the abilities to:

- generate revenue
- cover direct costs with generated revenue
- cover fully allocated indirect costs
- retain both surpluses and losses

On the other hand, the administrative responsibility centers comprise financial services, the registrar, facilities and real estate services, information technology, human resources, and other support operations. In general, these units:

- cannot generate revenue
- provide services and support to the academic responsibility centers
- are accountable for optimal service levels and fiscal performance

Some institutions include resource centers such as museums, libraries, theaters, and so forth in this category. Collectively, the administrative centers provide services that benefit the academic centers. They are known as indirect services. And the costs of providing these services are considered indirect costs. Even the imputed cost of occupying a university-owned building—the equivalent of rent—is included as an indirect cost.

Characteristically, the manager of the responsibility center, such as a provost, dean, or director, is responsible for the activities and performance of the center—in short, for managing the center. Although this may seem tautological, it bears emphasis in slightly different terms: the responsibility center manager has the authority and the responsibility for managing the unit's revenues and expenses. In the other budget models, the manager is responsible for the direct activities (such as teaching, research, and public service) and perhaps the revenue generated by these activities, but the central administration is responsible for providing (and paying for) the indirect services (such as utilities, building maintenance, human resources, and so forth). In RCM, the manager is responsible for the direct activities and the expenses of the indirect services incurred by the unit.

In RCM, therefore, the academic responsibility centers must pay out of their revenue their share of the indirect costs incurred by the administrative centers. Unlike the other budget models, the central administration doesn't pay for the indirect services. Accordingly, like the revenue-based model, the RCM model allocates all revenues generated by the academic responsibility center to the center. But it also "charges" the unit for its use and consumption of indirect services.

Also, like the revenue-based model, the central administration imposes a tax on the revenue to fund a subvention pool. Indeed, RCM depends on campus subvention to achieve a balance between responsibility center priorities and the best interest of the university as a whole. As in the revenue-based model, funds in the subvention pool are used to supplement units needing assistance and to support university priorities. However, the central administration does not require much if any tax to pay for the indirect services; those costs have been decentralized to the responsibility centers. Therefore, the RCM-based tax rate, sometimes called the participation fee, rarely exceeds 20 percent.

If a responsibility center's revenues exceed expenditures, it retains the positive fund balance. These positive fund balances can be carried over into subsequent years. In contrast, if expenditures exceed revenue, the negative fund balance must be repaid either through reduced expenditures during the next year, dipping into positive fund balances from previous years, or borrowing from the provost with a promise to repay the loan from future years' budgets.

Ideally, all indirect services provided by the administrative responsibility centers could be charged directly to the user. And, in some cases, that is possible. For example, if each academic center's building has separate utility meters (for electricity, gas, water, internet access, and so forth), then the indirect costs of these utilities can be billed directly to the center. However, this is not always possible or practical. Thus, in most cases, the indirect costs incurred by each responsibility center are based proportionately on some quantitative measure of their benefit to the center, such as ANSF,

Table 6.8. Responsibility center management FY 2017 budget, with changes from FY 2016 (actual) to FY 2017

Revenue	FY 2016 actual	FY 2017	Change Amount	%
Tuition	12,219,449	12,397,876	178,427	1.46
Central administration tuition tax[a]	(1,832,917)	(1,859,681)	(26,764)	1.46
Student fees	432,710	443,528	10,818	2.50
Subtotal tuition and fees	10,819,242	10,981,722	162,480	1.50
Sponsored programs				
Grants and contracts	4,607,380	4,964,531	357,151	7.75
Indirect cost reimbursement	1,290,066	1,390,069	100,002	7.75
Central administration reimbursement tax[b]	(193,510)	(208,510)	(15,000)	7.75
Subtotal sponsored programs	5,703,936	6,146,089	442,153	7.75
Outreach revenue	990,076	1,014,828	24,752	2.50
Central administration outreach tax[c]	(99,008)	(101,483)	(2,475)	2.50
Subtotal outreach	891,068	913,345	22,277	2.50
Subtotal generated revenue	17,414,247	18,041,157	626,910	3.60
Campus subvention	1,000,000	1,000,000		
Total	18,414,247	19,041,157	626,910	3.40
Expenditures				
Direct				
Salaries and wages	9,046,374	9,514,627	468,253	5.18
Fringe benefits	2,985,303	3,139,827	154,523	5.18
Operating	232,876	238,713	5,837	2.51
Scholarships and fellowships	2,092,275	2,092,275		
Subtotal direct expenditures	14,356,829	14,985,442	628,613	4.38
Indirect[d]				
Facilities	564,478	560,052	(4,426)	−0.78
Administration	3,044,096	3,058,701	14,605	0.48
Library	397,889	383,135	(14,754)	−3.71
Subtotal indirect expenditures	4,006,464	4,001,889	(4,575)	−0.11
Total	18,363,292	18,987,330	624,038	3.40
Fund balance	50,954	53,826	2,872	5.64

[a]Tuition tax = 15% × total tuition revenue.
[b]Indirect cost tax = 15% × indirect cost reimbursement.
[c]Outreach tax = 10% × outreach revenue.

student headcount, salaries and wages, et cetera. For example, if the College of Engineering uses 20 percent of the institution's total energy consumption, it pays for 20 percent of the total energy bill using revenue that it generated through its activities. Thus, the institution calculates each responsibility center's share of the total indirect costs and expects the centers to pay for their share out of the revenues that they have generated. Detailed examples of these indirect cost allocations are provided in chapter 9.

Table 6.8. *continued*

[d]Indirect expenditure calculations:

Indirect service	FY 2016 actual	FY 2017	Change Amount	%
Facilities				
University				
Total sq. ft.	1,667,819	1,667,819		
Expenditures	14,995,177	14,381,529	(113,648)	−0.78
College				
Assigned sq. ft.	64,949	64,949		
% of university total sq. ft.	3.89	3.89		
Assessed cost	564,478	560,052	(4,426)	−0.78
Administration				
University				
Total FTEs (faculty and staff)	706	785	79	11.19
Expenditures	22,386,792	23,087,312	800,521	3.13
College				
FTEs	96	104	8	8.33
% of university total FTEs	13.60	13.25	−0.35	−2.57
Assessed cost	3,044,096	3,058,701	14,605	0.48
Library				
University				
Total number of faculty	260	319	59	22.69
Total number of students	7,348	7,866	518	7.05
Total number faculty and students	7,608	8,185	577	7.58
Expenditures	2,011,390	1,923,902	(87,488)	−4.30
College				
Number of faculty	80	97	17	21.25
Number of students	1,425	1,533	108	7.58
Number of faculty and students	1,505	1,630	125	8.31
% of university faculty and students	19.78	19.91		0.67
Assessed cost	397,889	383,135	(14,754)	−3.71

A prototypical college RCM-based budget is illustrated in table 6.8. This simple RCM example expands the revenue-based model in table 6.7. Revenues and expenditures are averaged over a three-year period to damp unusual fluctuations (revenues for FY 2013–FY 2015 are not shown). The actual revenues are the same for both models (tables 6.7 and 6.8), but in the RCM model (table 6.8), the central administration taxes are considerably less, resulting in more net revenue. Likewise, the direct expenditures are the same for both models. However, in the RCM model, the indirect costs of facilities (space, utilities, maintenance, and so forth), administrative support (central payroll, purchasing, and so forth), and the library are added to the expenditures, resulting in considerably greater expenditures. Incidentally, the derivation of these indirect costs is shown in the footnotes to table 6.8. The facilities, administration, and library expenditures (that is, indirect costs) were allocated on the basis of square footage, total personnel (faculty and staff FTEs), and total faculty members plus student enrollment in the fall semester, respectively.

In "real life," of course, the RCM budget easily can become more complicated than this simple example, as other revenue sources are incorporated. They include endowments, state appropriations, licensing revenue, auxiliary enterprises, and so forth. Also, the tax basis for the subvention pool and the algorithms for calculating indirect expenditures generally vary between institutions, usually in attempts to account more accurately for differences in usage patterns among the different responsibility centers.[18] Indeed, in an unusual algorithm, the Medical University of South Carolina bases the campus facilities costs on the fair market value for leasing either "dry" or "wet" space in the local economy.[19]

RCM's underlying premise is that the decentralized nature of the model entrusts academic units with more control of financial resources, leading to more informed decision-making and better results or outcomes for the university as a whole. In principle, RCM couples authority and responsibility wherever it is applied down into responsibility centers within the hierarchy. This coupling is one of its main attributes, for it creates a number of potentially powerful incentives. As Curry, Laws, and Strauss put it:[20]

- Centers are responsible for meeting revenue projections and living within their planned operating margins.
- Incentives for growth include retention of new revenues.
- Incentives for prudent management include retention of operating surpluses and repayment of operating deficits.
- Incentives to optimize space usage and to limit central overhead costs reside in the abilities of the centers to spend dollars saved in reduced space usage and administrative costs allocated to them.

Thus, by allowing responsibility centers to control the revenues they generate, colleges are better able to evaluate the academic and financial impacts of their decisions. For these reasons, numerous universities, including the University of Pennsylvania, Indiana University, and the University of Michigan, have adopted RCM, and the momentum indicates that more will in the near future.[21]

Despite its attractions, RCM has its detractors. They assert that the inherent competition between responsibility centers for revenue undermines institutional integrity.[22] For example, they foresee departments offering duplicate courses to attract students such as "English for engineers," "calculus for economics majors," and so forth; duplication of services to generate revenue; a decline in selectivity as colleges lower admissions and enrollment standards to boost tuition revenue; and departments discouraging students from changing majors because of lost revenue. And they foresee other potentially injurious side effects. Leroy Dubeck summarizes his objections: "In short, RCM would pit the profit motive against academic considerations of which courses a student should take and where these courses could best be taught."[23] In fact, several universities have adopted RCM but then pulled back for one reason or another. Examples include the University of Miami and the University of South Carolina.[24]

These same apprehensions also apply to any budget model that places incentives on student enrollments and course credit hours. That includes both the revenue- and the formula-based allocation models. These concerns warrant attention, to be sure, although there are few anecdotal reports of abuse by predatory responsibility centers. Nonetheless, prudence dictates the need for central monitoring of these potential problems by the provost or the faculty senate.

Every Tub on Its Own Bottom

In the context of budget models, the extreme of decentralization is known as "every tub on its own bottom" (ETOB). Every school or college owns 100 percent of its revenue, runs its own central administration, and adheres to its own strategic plan. At most, they contract with the university for utilities, investment management, and perhaps financial accounting. Unlike RCM and other revenue-based models, ETOB does not rely on subvention to force investment in shared strategic objectives. For all intents and purposes, therefore, in ETOB the schools and colleges are independent members of an overall university-based federation.

Harvard University is the most prominent example. (In fact, former Harvard president Nathan Pusey coined the expression ETOB to describe the university's budget model.) At Harvard, each school and college is fully dependent on its own revenues and in turn responsible for its own expenses. Operationally this results in a weak central administration. From a Darwinian perspective, individual units at Harvard must achieve financial self-sufficiency if they are to survive.

Few universities have adopted an ETOB model. This model is simply impractical for public universities that depend on state appropriations. And the extreme decentralization has proved to be an obstacle to efficient use of university resources in times of financial stress. Consequently, both the University of Pennsylvania and Vanderbilt University pulled back from the extreme decentralization of ETOB to the less extreme RCM.[25]

Financial Reserves

Functionally, positive fund balances in the operating budget constitute discretionary reserve money. Conservatively, the CFO may under-allocate revenues in the original budget to create a positive fund balance as a buffer in case revenues come in lower than projected or expenditures come in higher than projected. This original fund balance is sometimes called the margin. Absent any restrictions, these reserves can be used for any purpose. Therefore, fund managers at all levels of the hierarchy (ranging from a department chair to the CFO) also try to build up unrestricted reserves derived from fund balances, as well as excess investment returns and other sources, to provide a "cushion" against unforeseen financial needs—so-called rainy-day funds. In the worst case when revenue drops unexpectedly, these reserves can be used to pay bills. Or, in less dire cases, they can be used to expand high-priority programs, take advantage of unexpected opportunities, or pay for deferred maintenance.

On the down side, these financial reserves take money out of the institution's everyday operations, thus imposing constraints. For example, a vacant faculty position may go unfilled or routine building maintenance may be curtailed in order to build up the reserves. Thus, the amount of money set aside in reserve can be a contentious issue on campus. Questions arise: "Why does the vice president for finance need all that money in reserve when our department is so broke?"

Consequently, some governing boards impose restrictions on the amount and the source of money held in reserve. In most nonprofit organizations, the rule of thumb is to maintain a reserve sufficient to pay operating expenses for at least two months. Recognizing the need for an operating reserve, the University of Hawaii Board of Regents policy, for example, calls for the university to maintain operating reserves "sufficient to provide for continued operations of the university for a minimum of two months."[26] Significantly, however, the operational reserves must be derived from non-general fund revenues. Other universities impose similar guidelines. These operational reserves usually are administered by the CFO.

It is not unusual for a provost, dean, department chair, or faculty member to build up sizable fund balances through under allocation of revenues, as well. Sizable is a loose word, but more than about $100,000 is sizable in this context. For a provost, dean, or department chair, a common rationale is for future start-up packages, which can be very costly. Principal investigators also may hold grant money in reserve to cover a reduced grant budget, unexpected opportunities, and other emergencies. In general, the existence of these reserves explains why a provost, dean, or department chair can appear to have a stash of discretionary money. In fact, they do.

These are among the many good reasons for deans, department chairs, and principal investigators to set aside a reserve pool of money. But in times of budgetary stress, these reserves look very attractive to cash-hungry CFOs, legislative budget personnel, and governing board members. Unspent funds can be swept to cover other university needs. These administrators (the "sweepers") may acknowledge that a sweep punishes what might seem to be solid conservative management by the account holders. However, in tight times, there may be few other alternative sources of cash to meet budgetary shortfalls. Indeed, in 2013, the issue of how much funding the University of Wisconsin System should keep in reserve became a contentious topic in the state legislature. In the 2013–2015 budget, legislators required the university to spend tuition dollars held in reserve to cover state funding cuts.[27] As pointed out in *Managing the Research University*, "experienced chief research officers routinely keep an eye on these unspent research-related balances and issue warnings about potential sweeps. One common ploy against 'the sweep' is to distribute unspent money into many smaller reserve accounts to reduce their visibility on the CFO's radar screen."[28]

Budget Cuts

Universities must occasionally confront periods of budgetary stress. And these periods must be managed in ways that do not seriously derail normal operations. Many books on university administration document various strategies for managing these situations. The unavoidable fact, however, is that when expenditures exceed revenues, universities must either raise additional revenue or decrease expenditures. Raising additional revenue may require the institution to increase tuition, endowment pay out, state appropriations, or debt. Each of these can be difficult to manage in the short term, especially in public universities where other state agencies compete for state appropriations. Often the public response to the university's plea for increased appropriations is "reduce expenditures by increasing efficiencies." And the belt-tightening begins.

In contrast, decreasing operating expenditures can be accomplished quickly by hiring freezes, deferring building and grounds maintenance, reducing library acquisitions, et cetera. But these measures are not sustainable in the long run. Longer-term solutions must be found.

A routine solution is to cut operating budgets, either selectively or across-the-board. And neither is easy to accomplish without rancor. On the one hand, selective cuts are generally more difficult to make because they require programmatic decisions to be made, usually with extensive faculty involvement. And that is always difficult in a university environment. On the other hand, across-the-board cuts are generally very unpopular, especially among the academic units (colleges and departments) that consider themselves among those favored in the strategic plan or ranked highly in national rankings.

Ironically, when budgets must be cut, restricted funds may become more valuable than unrestricted funds because they are immune to cuts. As the NACUBO puts it: "Although most money is 'green,' restricted funds may have the effect of allowing budget owners in those areas to escape the competitive fray for resources that other programs without restricted funds must enter. This does not necessarily enable an institution to maximize its resources."[29]

The relative impact of a budget cut on restricted and unrestricted funds is illustrated in table 6.9. In this example, restricted funds constitute 25 and 50 percent of the arts and sciences and business colleges' budgets ($5,000,000), respectively. A 10 percent cut in their

Table 6.9. Impact of a 10 percent budget cut on unrestricted and restricted funds

	Arts and sciences	Business
Original budget		
Restricted	1,250,000	2,500,000
Unrestricted	3,750,000	2,500,000
Totals	5,000,000	5,000,000
10% budget cut		
Restricted		
Unrestricted	(375,000)	(250,000)
Totals	(375,000)	(250,000)
Budget after cut		
Restricted	1,250,000	2,500,000
Unrestricted	3,375,000	2,250,000
Totals	4,625,000	4,750,000

Note: Difference between A&S and Business after cut = 125,000

general funds budget must come out of their unrestricted budget component. Consequently, the arts and sciences cut ($375,000) is $125,000 more than the business cut ($250,000). Thus, because of its greater percentage of restricted funds, business has a distinct advantage when budget cuts occur.

Significantly, in this example, the budget cuts were across-the-board. To equalize the impact of budget cuts, the business budget would have to be cut more than the arts and sciences budget, resulting in a selective budget cut. As the NACUBO notes further: "financial officers have a mandate to responsibly link mission, strategy, budgets, and assessment, without allowing their thinking to become confused by the changing exigencies of funding source."

In the most severe budget crises, the governing board often calls for "downsizing," which is code for laying off personnel and terminating academic units. Therefore, in crisis situations, universities consider consolidating or eliminating programs to reduce overall expenditures. The usual process involves analyses of various cost objects within the university (departments, degree programs, athletic teams, and so forth) in the context of the strategic plan by committees composed mainly of faculty members but also including staff and student representatives. Particular attention focuses on programs with declining enrollment, accreditation problems, or low academic productivity (publications, grants, doctoral degrees awarded, etc.). These are not easy analyses because they set faculty members against each other. Nonetheless, decisions must be made, and specific programs are designated for consolidation or closure.

As most administrators and governing board members in this situation have discovered, consolidating or closing programs can be devilishly difficult if not impossible. Every cost object seems to have its protective constituents, and, one way or another, they can exert strong pressure to maintain the status quo, regardless of budgetary implications. In that context, "university faculty members are far more comfortable with allocations since they are additive; they are constructive, not destructive. Anything beyond that additive comfort zone lies outside the acceptable limits of their shared authority."[30] Ultimately, however, the process must go forward if operational costs are to be reduced.

Pragmatically, department or program closure is phased over several years. Students "in the pipeline" must be accommodated, which usually means that they remain enrolled in the department until they finish their program of study. As a result, the department must continue to teach relevant courses until the students finish. Similarly, sponsored projects must be brought to an orderly conclusion: experiments completed, manuscripts written, reports filed, et cetera. Furthermore, personnel contracts must be honored. Nontenure-track employees must be allowed to complete the terms of their contract, which may extend up to three years. Tenured faculty members must be transferred to another department, unless the university decides to declare a fiscal emergency, which is tantamount to setting aside tenure. Regardless, these arrangements also take time. Therefore, the actual cost savings from the phased closure may not be recognized for several years.

An anecdotal phase-out is illustrated in table 6.10. In the base year, 2016, expenses exceeded revenues by $2,854,079. Obviously, the department spent a lot more than it brought in. This over-spending has been a recurrent problem, so the governing board directed the president to close the department. The closure will be phased-out

Table 6.10. Phased close-out of a department

| | 2016 | Phase-out | | | | |
		2017	2018	2019	2020	2021
Revenues						
Tuition	944,450	708,337	472,225	236,112	4,382,734	
State appropriation	1,446,951	1,446,951	1,446,951	1,446,951	1,446,951	1,446,951
Sponsored projects	5,976,456	5,578,026	5,179,595	4,781,165	4,382,734	4,382,734
F&A recovery	1,393,746	1,300,830	1,207,913	1,114,997	1,022,081	1,022,081
Transfer						(6,851,766)
Totals	9,761,603	9,034,144	8,306,685	7,579,225	6,851,766	
Expenses						
Salaries and wages[a]	5,834,858	4,554,428	3,461,756	2,306,497	1,151,239	1,151,239
Fringe benefits	1,750,460	1,366,330	1,038,528	691,950	345,372	345,372
Operating	5,025,364	3,769,023	2,512,682	1,256,341		
Capital	5,000					
Transfer						(1,496,611)
Totals	12,615,682	9,689,781	7,012,966	4,254,788	1,496,611	
Fund balance	(2,854,079)	(655,637)	1,293,719	3,324,437	5,355,155	

Note: In 2021, tenured faculty members (associate and full professors) and their associated revenues and expenses will be transferred to another department, thus concluding closure of the department.
[a]Salary and wage calculations:

Personnel	Number of FTEs	Average salary	Total salary
Research appointments	72	60,100	4,327,217
Lecturer	1	62,586	62,586
Assistant professors	4	73,454	293,816
Associate professors	5	98,681	493,405
Professors	6	109,639	657,834
Total	88		5,834,858

over a five-year period, starting in 2017. In the first year, no more students are admitted to the department, thus reducing tuition revenue by 25 percent. And as students complete their programs over the next three years, tuition revenue continues to decline. As their three-year contracts expire, nontenured faculty members are laid off at a rate of 25 percent per year, thus reducing personnel expenditures. (The lecturer position was eliminated in the first year, 2017.) The number of sponsored projects also declines as nontenured faculty members are laid off. Likewise, the operating budget declined by 25 percent per year. By 2020, only the 11 tenured faculty members remain in the department, with their sponsored project revenue ($4,382,734) and salary and fringe benefit expenses ($1,496,611). In 2021, these tenured faculty members are transferred to another department, along with their sponsored project revenue, salary and fringe benefit costs, and the state appropriation revenue, thus concluding the phase out. The department is now closed. Notably, the university doesn't recognize positive fund balances until the second year of the phase out (2018). Moreover, the ultimate savings ($5,355,155) is only 42.4 percent of the total expenditures in 2016, due to revenue lost because of the closure. Incidentally, in a private institution, "endowment income" could replace "state appropriations" in this setting.

These calculations assume that all personnel ultimately will be taken off the department's payroll. For soft-money research appointments supported by sponsored grants and contracts, this is doable. But faculty members, especially those with tenure, will resist dismissal, and, as in the example (table 6.10), the university may end up reassigning some or all of them to unfilled faculty positions in other departments. Any litigation will consume time and legal fees. This and other imaginable scenarios can erode seriously the actual net savings from departmental closure to the point where the question arises: Is it worth all of this?

Capital Budget

The capital budget is a plan, separate from the operating budget, for spending large sums of money for investment in plant and machinery: projects that will have ongoing effects on the institution's operations, such as buildings, renovations, roads, and major equipment items. Stated more simply, the capital budget is a spending plan for capital assets. Most institutions limit inclusion in the capital budget to proposed capital-asset expenses greater than a threshold value, for example, $100,000. Any project costing less than that threshold is included in the operating budget. Unlike an auxiliary or operating budget, which pertains to a single fiscal year, the capital budget extends for several years, the time span for planning, design, and construction of a new building or for scheduled major maintenance or infrastructure projects. Revenue sources include cash, state appropriations, endowment income, and debt. And, usually, these funds are restricted to capital projects; they cannot be used for academic operations.

Capital budgets usually are developed and controlled by CFOs. Various constituencies recommend items for inclusion in the budget. For example, the provost might recommend specific new buildings and renovations to meet academic demands for space; the physical plant director might recommend specific upgrades to heating, ventilation, and air-conditioning (HVAC) systems to meet modern efficiency standards. The capital budget is nearly always subject to approval by the governing board, mainly because of the large amounts of money involved. Realistically, in public institutions, state legislatures often exert de facto control of the capital budget through the appropriations process; they determine whether state funding will be available for specific projects. Although political considerations may influence the actual appropriations, most legislatures honor capital-project priorities submitted by the university administration.

The skeletal elements of a capital budget are illustrated in table 6.11. In this example, which was submitted in FY 2015, various capital asset projects ranging from equipment upgrades to new construction are listed in priority order along with their planned funding sources and estimated costs. It's not unusual for capital budgets to include more detail about the funding sources along a timeline similar to that for estimated expenditures shown in this example.

Because of the long time-frame of most capital asset projects, costs will change from year to year. Thus, as shown in table 6.12, capital budgets often include updates on specific project expenditures. In this example, the first two stages of a new engineering laboratory addition (priority item 3 in table 6.11) have been approved by the governing board and completed at a cost of $3,357,500. The updated capital budget now lists the net budget available for completing the addition ($26,345,813), which equals the original estimated cost ($29,703,313) less the amount already spent ($3,357,500). For informational and planning purposes, the remaining costs are presented in further detail.

Table 6.11. Capital budget, submitted in FY 2015

Priority	Project	Funding source	Estimated total cost	Expenditures prior to 2015	Estimated expenditures			
					2015	2016	2017	2018 and beyond
1	Library fire and safety upgrade	Reserves	6,400,000		2,133,333	2,133,333	2,133,333	
2	Dormitory fire and safety upgrade	Program revenue bonds	6,000,000		186,647	1,813,353	2,000,000	2,000,000
3	New engineering laboratory addition	General fund revenue bonds	29,703,313	3,357,500	10,837,706	8,100,405	7,407,702	
4	Chemistry building renovation	General fund revenue bonds	19,400,000	12,933,333	6,466,667			
5	Old Main utilities upgrade	General fund reserves	7,000,000			2,333,333	2,333,333	2,333,333
6	Football stadium expansion	Program revenue bonds and gift	21,000,000	2,574,931	15,000,000	3,425,069		
7	New parking structure	Program revenue bonds	8,000,000			745,000	3,627,500	3,627,500
8	New life sciences building	Gift and grant	45,000,000			589,164	19,000,000	25,410,836
9	Performing arts theater	Gift and grant	24,700,000				720,000	23,980,000
10	Stage 1 design of new dormitory	Program revenue bonds	350,000		350,000			
	Totals		167,553,313	18,865,764	34,974,353	19,139,657	37,221,869	57,351,669

Table 6.12. Update of item 3 in the capital budget (shown in table 6.11)

New engineering laboratory addition	
Total project budget	29,703,313
Previously approved	
Stage 1 Planning and design	452,500
Stage 2 demolition and abatement	2,905,000
Sub-total previously approved	3,357,500
Net budget	26,345,813
Remaining costs	
Construction	20,251,012
Professional services	854,168
Fixed fixtures and equipment	3,157,222
Administrative cost	362,453
Public art, landscape enhancement	1,214,683
Contingency	506,275
Total remaining costs	26,345,813

In addition to the costs of new buildings or land improvements, the costs of repairing major deficiencies, such as replacing a boiler, removing asbestos, installing a new roof, and so forth, normally are included in the capital budget. As part of the capital budget, the timeline for correcting these deficiencies may extend over several years. For items financed by revenue bonds, the necessary funding may be in a capital assets "repairs and maintenance" reserve account mandated by the bond covenants. Or, to finance particularly costly repairs, the funding may be raised by issuing new debt, usually bonds. Although the repair work may be performed by "in-house" personnel, larger projects are frequently contracted to outside vendors. In those cases, university (and state) policies usually require obtaining at least three competitive bids.

When preparing the capital budget, the facilities department must estimate the anticipated costs of major maintenance projects. This is not particularly daunting. For most routine projects, cost estimates for materials and local union labor are available readily from commercial data sources such as RSMean.[31] They are accessible via hardcopy or online.

In the capital budget, projects usually are listed in order of priority. The highest-priority project is the next to be undertaken and on down the list. Every year or so, the list is revised, with some projects coming off or moving onto, up, or down in priority. These revisions depend on the seriousness of maintenance or repair issues, funding availability, programmatic changes, and political considerations. Only a few top-ranked items are actually approved for funding in each year's capital budget. Some items lower on this list may never reach the top. However, a major donation for the construction of a specific new building usually can move that building quickly up in priority.

As part of the prioritization process, the facilities office staff must determine the nature and seriousness of any capital asset deficiencies—that is, repairs that must be made. To keep track of each capital asset's condition, they maintain a capital asset condition inventory by routinely inspecting each capital asset on a regular basis—once every three years, for example.

Sample entries in a building condition inventory are shown in table 6.13. This example shows only a few deficiencies in two buildings. In the full inventory, similar data are tabulated for every building. The "percent deficient" refers to the percentage of the component needing repair. So, 40 percent of the footings around the administration building need repair, at an estimated cost of $3,387.

The priority of specific repairs on the list depends on the nature of the deficiencies. Their usual order of priority is:

- health and safety issues
- building code violations
- damage or wear out
- environmental improvements
- energy conservation
- aesthetics
- building enhancements

Within each of these categories, the order follows the deficiency percentage. So, repairs affecting health and safety issues always take top priority. For example, the top priority is the plumbing in the business building's fire suppression system, which is a matter of safety. The second priority is the circuit distribution of the administration building's electrical system, which is in violation of code. Since none of the other items on this sample list is a health and safety item or code violation, the business building's HVAC system, which is 100 percent deficient, will be the third item repaired. Next will be the business building's roof, which is 90 percent deficient. And on down the list until the budgeted money runs out.

In times of budgetary stress, institutions may defer costly maintenance, putting off replacing an aging ventilation system, delaying replacing a roof, et cetera. This results in so-called deferred maintenance. Importantly, deferred maintenance refers to building system deficiencies that affect the long-term renewal costs of the building—"big-ticket" items. It does not refer to relatively minor

Table 6.13. Sample entries in a building condition inventory

Building	System	Component	Deficiency type	Percent deficient	Renewal cost	Description
Administration	Foundation	Footings	Damage	40	3,387	Repair settling and cracks
	Electrical system	Circuit distribution	Code	20	148,962	Replace system
	Envelope	Exterior walls	Damage	70	17,861	Patch, caulk, and paint
	Envelope	Exterior walls	Damage	5	1,276	Repaint chimney
	Finishes	Ceilings	Damage	5	424	Repair ceiling cracks
	Finishes	Floor finishes	Damage	80	9,843	Replace carpet
Business	Envelope	Exterior doors	Damage	33	17,581	Replace doors at entry
	Finishes	Flooring	Damage	10	30,508	Replace flooring
	HVAC	Ventilating	Damage	100	785,804	Replace entire HVAC
	Plumbing	Fire suppression	Safety	100	77,602	Replace sprinkler valves
	Roof system	Covering	Damage	90	152,046	Replace roof

Note: Percent deficient refers to the percentage of the component needing repair.

repairs covered by routine work orders. Left unchecked, deferred maintenance can erode campus facilities, with insidious consequences for teaching effectiveness and research capacity. Indeed, deferred maintenance costs are a lurking menace to a university's academic and financial wellbeing. Significantly, buildings financed with revenue bonds are much less likely to have deferred maintenance since bond covenants often require the institution to set aside money to pay for repairs needed to keep the building in good condition.

To reduce a backlog of deferred maintenance, universities resort to myriad funding plans.[32] These plans include issuing debt, directing donor gifts and endowment income, leasing or selling real estate. And universities may even tap into their operating funds to address particularly critical maintenance needs. Moreover, public universities often appeal to the state government for special funding to mitigate deferred maintenance.

Auxiliary Budget

An auxiliary budget is developed for an auxiliary enterprise—that is, an operation that directly or indirectly provides a service to students, faculty, staff, or the general public and charges a fee for these services. Most institutions have separate auxiliary budgets for auxiliary activities such as residence facilities (dormitories and dining halls), hospitals, clinical practice plans, intercollegiate athletic programs, and specialized research centers. Auxiliary budgets resemble the academic units' operating budgets. They are developed and controlled similarly by directors, such as the hospital director, the center directors, the athletic director, et cetera. Furthermore, auxiliary enterprises usually have their own advisory board, which must approve the fee structure and budget.

The most distinguishing characteristic of an auxiliary enterprise is that it must be managed as a self-supporting activity, which is manifest in its budget. As a self-supporting activity, auxiliary enterprise fees are set to match expenses—to "break even." That is, revenue generated by the service, such as dormitory room and board fees, hospital fees, athletic-event ticket income, and so forth, generally equals expenditures. Furthermore, as a self-supporting activity, auxiliary enterprises earn all interest income gained from the investment of its excess cash. Thus, in principle, an auxiliary's budget is straightforward, with user fees matching expenses.

Nonetheless, some services may require revenue subvention if the fees prove to be inadequate to meet expenses. For example, a university press may occasionally require subvention from the operating budget to offset a revenue shortfall. In those cases, the subvention is treated like a loan, to be repaid to the university's operating budget. Moreover, some auxiliary enterprises, such as specific athletic programs, may depend on donated revenue from groups like booster clubs to supplement fees to meet expenses. In contrast, revenue may flow in the opposite direction, from an auxiliary enterprise to the university's operating budget. The most notable example is a highly successful football program that generates income exceeding its budgetary needs, resulting in a fund balance that can be transferred into the operating budget. More commonly, a successful university bookstore may transfer a fund balance into the operating revenue.

Because they are self-supporting, auxiliary enterprises often establish reserve funds to pay for maintenance and repair expenses or cyclical expenses when the need arises. Money designated for the reserve funds may be built into the fee structure. Indeed, this is quite common. And it is recorded as an expense in the budget.

Budget Limitations

Despite their central role in university financial and strategic planning, budgets provide limited information about a university's overall financial condition. This limitation occurs mainly because budgets by definition are planning documents that project into the future. They depend on inherently imprecise projections regarding enrollment, pay raises, inflation, state tax revenue, and other financial variables. Changes in any of these parameters alter a budget, sometimes quite significantly. As Rudy Fichtenbaum notes, "evaluating a university's finances by looking at its budget would be the equivalent of evaluating the performance of a for-profit company by looking at its business plan."[33]

Moreover, universities are not obligated legally to spend money in accordance with their budget, which is just a planning document. For example, a budget may allocate a certain amount of salary for faculty positions. However, in any given year some faculty members leave the institution for one reason or another. Therefore, the budgeted amount for faculty salaries is not necessarily the actual amount spent on salaries. As a result, some percentage of the budgeted faculty salaries either gets re-budgeted to some other item or accumulates and becomes part of the university's net assets (reserves).

There are other limitations that can be quite misleading. In the realm of fund accounting, budgets normally are based only on the unrestricted current fund. But universities have the ability to transfer money from one fund to another. Therefore, looking only at the unrestricted current fund does not necessarily give a true picture of a university's finances. Furthermore, budgets usually are balanced, which creates the impression that universities spend every dollar of revenue that they take in. As Fichtenbaum notes, "this is far from true for most universities. In general, most universities and colleges will have balanced budgets and yet in most years they will have revenues that are substantially in excess of expenses."[34]

If the budget doesn't give a true picture of a university's finances, what does? The answer is: the financial statements, which represent the actual revenues and expenses of a university. And that is the topic of the following chapter.

Summary

Budgets itemize estimated expenditures for a given period along with estimated resources for financing them. In many institutions, the operating budget is known as the general fund budget. Each unit in the organizational hierarchy (for example, colleges and departments) has its own operating budget, and they are all combined into the operating budget of the next higher unit in the hierarchy, culminating in the university's master operating budget. For their budgetary accounting, most universities use a cash basis that accounts for encumbrances as if they were equivalent to the actual cash purchases. Budgets are revised at least once during the fiscal year to account for changes in anticipated revenue or expenditures. For control purposes, budgets also report variances, the differences between budgeted and actual amounts of revenue and expenditures. Protocols for budget preparation vary between institutions, but most of them involve a two-stage process based on initial and then updated estimates of available revenue. Zero-based budgeting requires each unit to justify from the ground up all of its proposed expenditures. In incremental budgeting, funding increments are added to (or subtracted from) the previous year's budget on the assumption that the institution's fundamental goals and objectives will not change markedly from one year to the next. Formula-based models allocate revenue according to selected productivity metrics. Revenue-based models allocate revenue generated by a unit back to the unit, less a fraction levied by the provost. Responsibility center management returns a large fraction of revenue but requires the units to cover their own indirect costs. Positive fund balances in the operating budget constitute discretionary reserve money. When expenditures routinely exceed revenues, budget must be cut, sometimes by the difficult process of closing programs. The capital budget and auxiliary budgets are spending plans for capital assets and auxiliary enterprises, respectively. They are separate from the operating budget.

Notes

1. Michael H. Granof et al., *Government and Not-for-Profit Accounting: Concepts and Practices*, 7th ed. (Hoboken, NJ: John Wiley & Sons, Inc., 2015), 90.

2. Oxford University Press, "Oxford Dictionaries," http://www.oxforddictionaries.com/?gclid=CMa5maK2p8kCFU1cfgodiXoNoA (accessed November 23, 2015).

3. BusinessDictionary.com, http://www.businessdictionary.com/ (accessed March 17, 2016).

4. National Association of College and University Business Officers, "Financial Aid: Does It Matter Whether It's Funded?" (2005), http://www.nacubo.org/Business_Officer_Magazine/Magazine_Archives/July_2005/Financial_Aid_Does_It_Matter_Whether_Its_Funded.html (accessed March 28, 2017).

5. Oxford University Press, "Oxford Dictionaries."

6. Cambridge University Press, "Cambridge Dictionary," http://dictionary.cambridge.org/us/dictionary/english/budgetary-accounting (accessed July 6, 2017).

7. University of Texas at Austin, "2015–2016 Operating Budget, Vol I and Vol II," http://www.utexas.edu/business/budget/ (accessed April 12, 2016).

8. Governmental Accounting Standards Board, "Statement No. 34: Basic Financial Statements—and Management's Discussion and Analysis—for State and Local Governments" (1999), https://www.google.com/search?q=gasb+statement+34&ie=utf-8&oe=utf-8 (accessed January 27, 2016).

9. Stanford University, "Budgeting," https://adminguide.stanford.edu/chapter-3/subchapter-1/policy-3-1-2 (accessed April 13, 2016).

10. "Year End Variance Reporting," https://web.stanford.edu/group/fms/fingate/docs/budget/howto/Tidemark_BBudget_YearEnd_VarRept.pdf (accessed March 7, 2018).

11. Southern Association of Colleges and Schools Commission on Colleges, "Principles of Accreditation: Foundation for Quality Enhancement" (2012), http://www.sacscoc.org/principles.asp (accessed May 4, 2016). § 2.11.1.

12. Margaret J. Barr and George S. McClellan, *Budgets and Financial Management in Higher Education*, 2nd ed. (San Francisco: Jossey-Bass, 2011); Larry Goldstein, *A Guide to College and University Budgeting: Foundations for Institutional Effectiveness*, 4th ed. (Washington, DC: National Association of College and Business Officers, 2012).

13. Texas Higher Education Coordinating Board, "Formula Funding: Basis for Legislative Appropriations, General Academic Institutions," http://www

.thecb.state.tx.us/index.cfm?objectid=4EA741D3-C76D-FBC5-04F664C233E8802B (accessed July 6, 2016).

14. John R. Curry, Andrew L. Laws, and Jon C. Strauss, *Responsibility Center Management: A Guide to Balancing Academic Entrepreneurship with Fiscal Responsibility*, 2nd ed. (Washington, DC: National Association of College and University Business Officers, 2013), 16.

15. Curry, Laws, and Strauss, *Responsibility Center Management*.

16. University of Washington, "Activity Based Budgeting," http://opb.washington .edu/activity-based-budgeting (accessed July 3, 2016).

17. Accounting Tools, "What Is a Responsibility Center?" http://www.account ingtools.com/questions-and-answers/what-is-a-responsibility-center.html (accessed May 9, 2016).

18. Curry, Laws, and Strauss, *Responsibility Center Management*.

19. Medical University of South Carolina, "Understanding the Space Allocation Driver," http://academicdepartments.musc.edu/vpfa/rcm/presentations .html (accessed May 12, 2016).

20. Curry, Laws, and Strauss, *Responsibility Center Management*, 8.

21. Indiana University Bloomington, "RCM at Indiana University," http:// www.indiana.edu/~obap/rcm-iub.php (accessed May 12, 2016); University of Michigan, "About the U-M Budget Model," http://obp.umich.edu/root/budget /budget-about/ (accessed July 18, 2016); University of Pennsylvania, "Responsibility Center Management," http://www.budget.upenn.edu/dlDocs/rcm.pdf (accessed May 12, 2016).

22. Mallory Barnes and Kyle Clark, "Responsibility Center Management: The Good, the Bad, and the Ugly," http://www.nacubo.org/Documents/Eventsand-Programs/2013PBF/Responsibility%20Center%20Management%20Presentation .pdf (accessed May 12, 2016); Leroy W. Dubeck, "Beware Higher Ed's Newest Budget Twist," http://www.nea.org/assets/img/PubThoughtAndAction/TAA_97Spr _07.pdf (accessed March 19, 2018).

23. "Beware Higher Ed's Newest Budget Twist."

24. Curry, Laws, and Strauss, *Responsibility Center Management*, 59.

25. Curry, Laws, and Strauss, *Responsibility Center Management*, 23, 79–80.

26. University of Hawaii, "Operating Reserves; Non-General Funds," http:// hawaii.edu/policy/?action=viewPolicy&policySection=rp&policyChapter =8&policyNumber=203&menuView=open (accessed December 28, 2016).

27. Karen Herzog and Patrick Marley, "Outrage Grows as University of Wisconsin System Admits It 'Did Not Draw Attention' to Cash," *Milwaukee Journal Sentinel* (2016), http://www.jsonline.com/news/education/outrage-grows-as-uw -admits-it-did-not-draw-attention-to-cash-r59lh2e-204159081.html (accessed December 28, 2016).

28. Dean O. Smith, *Managing the Research University* (New York: Oxford University Press, 2011), 58.

29. Ron Allan, Lucie Lapovsky, and Loren Loomis Hubbell, "Financial Aid: Does It Matter Whether It's Funded?" *Business Officer* (2005), http://www.nacubo .org/Business_Officer_Magazine/Magazine_Archives/July_2005/Financial_Aid _Does_It_Matter_Whether_Its_Funded.html (accessed May 10, 2017).

30. Dean O. Smith, *Understanding Authority in Higher Education* (Lanham, MD: Rowman and Littlefield, 2015), 45.

31. Gordian, "RSMeans Data," https://www.rsmeans.com/?gclid=CJmFmN6J2t MCFUtNfgodn0IH4g (accessed May 5, 2017).

32. Marcia Layton Turner, "Budgeting for Building Upkeep: Strategies for Tackling Deferred Maintenance across Campus," *University Business*, August (2015), https://www.universitybusiness.com/article/budgeting-building-upkeep (accessed May 5, 2017).

33. Rudy Fichtenbaum, "Understanding College and University Financial Statements," http://www.hawaii.edu/uhmfs/Understanding%20University%20%20College%20Financial%20Statements%20updated.pdf (accessed January 29, 2016).

34. Fichtenbaum, "Understanding College and University Financial Statements."

Chapter 7
Financial Reports

Financial Statements

At least annually, for-profit and nonprofit organizations issue reports about their financial health. Unlike budgets, which are based on revenue and expenditure *projection*s, financial reports are based on *actual* revenue and expenditure data. Looking backward, they summarize the organization's financial status in four separate documents:

- management discussion and analysis
- balance sheet
- income statement
- statement of cash flows

As the first component of the financial report, the management discussion and analysis introduces the financial report and adds context to its various components. Together, the last three—the balance sheet, the income statement, and the cash flow statement—comprise the so-called financial statements. They report the institution's net worth, net revenue earned, and cash inflow and outflow, respectively. In addition, details about these financial statements—calculation methods, itemization, unusual circumstances, and other pertinent explanations—are documented in accompanying footnotes. These notes are an important component of the financial statements.

All publicly traded, government, and nonprofit organizations' financial reports are required to provide financial statements. They are meant to present the financial information as clearly and concisely as possible for audiences both internal and external to the institution. In the for-profit sector, the primary audience is the shareholders, whereas in the nonprofit sector, the primary audiences are the governing board, legislators, investors, and donors.

To maintain consistency, both the GASB and the FASB have established GAAP for the preparation and presentation of financial reports.[1] Despite numerous technical differences between GASB and FASB GAAP, the financial statements of public and private universities convey basically the same information, and they both use the accrual basis of accounting. Nonetheless, the formats may not always look the same.[2]

In addition, to ensure accuracy and compliance with GAAP, financial statements usually are audited by certified public accountants (CPAs) and, in some cases, government agencies. Financial statements that have been reviewed by an outside accountant are referred to as *certified financial statements*. They are considered definitive; their accuracy can be trusted because CPAs have reviewed them to ensure that the information is correct, true, and reliable. Because it may contain subjective, nonquantitative information, the management discussion and analysis is not included in the audit.

Certification can take a considerable amount of time. Therefore, to meet some deadline, financial statements that have not been certified, known as *compiled financial statements*, may be released. Because they are not audited, the accuracy and quality of compiled financial statements, also called unaudited statements, are not guaranteed. Accountants that compile a company's financial statements are not required to verify or confirm the records, and they do not need to analyze the statements for accuracy. However, if accountants discover erroneous, misleading, or incomplete information in the compilation of these financial statements, they must notify management or discontinue their involvement in assessing the company's financial statements. "Overall, certified financial statements can provide you with additional and more accurate information than compiled financial statements."[3]

The balance sheet and the statements of income and cash flows, along with the accompanying management discussion and analysis and footnotes, are the foundation of financial accounting. And they are a trove of information for anybody who is curious about the university's finances. Therefore, as a guide to understanding them, each of these documents will be examined in detail. Although FASB and GASB GAAP convey basically the same information, their formatting differences sometimes can obfuscate the similarities. Therefore, examples of both formats will be presented for comparison.

Management Discussion and Analysis

Financial reports open with a summary of the financial statements, known by the GASB-mandated term "management discussion and analysis." The FASB does not require this section, but most private universities include it anyway, with or without the title. This plain-language introduction to the financial statements presents basic information contained in the financial statements in textual form, usually illustrated with fairly simple tables, charts, and graphs. For example, income sources and expenditure types may be summarized in pie charts. The management discussion and analysis seldom adds financial information not contained in the financial statements. More importantly, however, it highlights various noteworthy elements of the financial statements in the context of the institution's mission and strategic goals.

Unlike the certified financial statements (balance sheet, income statement, and cash flow statement), which are audited for accuracy, the management discussion and analysis is not audited. It is written by the institution and added directly to the financial report. Consequently, there is no guarantee that the discussion and analysis accurately portray the institutional context for evaluating the financial data. Of course, few institutions would deliberately misrepresent the context, but readers must exercise judgment when interpreting the management discussion and analysis.

Balance Sheet

The balance sheet, referred to as the *statement of financial position* and the *statement of net position* by the FASB and the GASB, respectively, provides information about the institution's worth at a specific point in time, generally the last day of the fiscal year. For private institutions, it reports the total assets, liabilities, and net assets according to the basic accounting equation (chapter 2):

$$assets = liabilities + net\ assets$$

Or, for public institutions, according to:

$$assets + deferred\ outflows = liabilities + deferred\ inflows \\ + net\ position$$

Regardless of institution type, the equation and, therefore, the balance sheet always must be in balance. This follows the same principle of double-entry accounting governing the general ledger. However, instead of showing individual accounting transactions, as in the general ledger, the balance sheet presents a snapshot summarizing the institution's accounts at the end of an accounting period.

Statements of financial position (FASB format) and of net position (GASB format) for private and public institutions are shown in tables 7.1 and 7.2, respectively. At first glance, the GASB format appears more detailed. Indeed, the GASB imposes several requirements related to the balance sheet that distinguish it from the FASB. In particular, for explicit clarity, the GASB requires that the statement be categorized with current assets presented separately from noncurrent assets and current liabilities presented separately from noncurrent liabilities. The FASB allows such a presentation but does not require it in the balance sheet. Thus, unlike the FASB format, the GASB format divides assets and liabilities into current and noncurrent categories.

Table 7.1. Private university balance sheet: statement of financial position (FASB format)

	FY 2015	FY 2014
Assets		
Cash and cash equivalents	13,036,353	14,017,939
Short-term investments	14,991,289	14,159,750
Accounts receivable, net	1,262,503	1,064,133
Inventories	1,387,028	1,328,748
Prepaid expenses and other assets	2,663,356	2,685,788
Pledges receivable, net	24,713,405	24,653,447
Student loans receivable, net	3,395,586	3,455,443
Long-term investments, at market	311,441,121	300,929,306
Land, buildings, and equipment, net	137,033,214	120,264,146
Total assets	509,923,854	482,558,699
Liabilities		
Accounts payable and accrued expenses	7,379,859	8,985,593
Deposits and deferred revenues	3,621,391	3,449,851
Post-retirement benefits	7,890,763	7,538,378
Federal student loan funds	3,539,324	3,478,509
Long-term debt	60,724,626	62,150,579
Total liabilities	83,155,963	85,602,909
Net Assets		
Unrestricted	196,516,091	184,177,891
Temporarily restricted	129,421,395	116,903,674
Permanently restricted	100,830,405	95,874,225
Total net assets	426,767,891	396,955,790
Total liabilities and net assets	509,923,854	482,558,699

Note: Statement of financial position is for last day of fiscal years 2015 and 2014.

Table 7.2. Public university balance sheet: statement of net position (GASB format)

	FY 2015	FY 2014
Assets		
Current assets		
Cash and cash equivalents	31,104,680	39,038,391
Operating investments	75,903,732	79,970,449
Accounts receivable, net	29,035,339	28,905,228
Other current assets	9,096,833	7,994,178
Total current assets	145,140,584	155,908,246
Noncurrent assets		
Restricted cash and cash equivalents	679,439	660,436
Endowment investments	30,699,638	27,595,094
Investments for capital activities	42,264,500	50,567,259
Capital assets, net	239,892,467	220,844,717
Legal settlement receivable	951,113	1,855,729
Other noncurrent assets	171,882	219,742
Total noncurrent assets	297,019,329	301,742,977
Total assets	442,159,913	457,651,223
Deferred outflows of resources		
Deferred outflows from pension	17,639,710	
Total deferred outflows of resources	17,639,710	
Total assets and deferred outflows of resources	459,799,623	457,651,223
Liabilities		
Current liabilities		
Accounts payable and accrued liabilities	23,214,476	18,565,766
Unearned revenues	28,689,929	28,444,114
Current portion of long-term debt	4,698,600	4,603,600
Deposits held for others	3,584,017	3,365,561
Total current liabilities	60,187,022	54,979,041
Noncurrent liabilities		
Long-term debt	103,084,078	107,792,600
Pension liability	135,283,004	
Total noncurrent liabilities	238,367,082	107,792,600
Total liabilities	298,554,104	162,771,641
Deferred inflows of resources		
Deferred inflows from pension	10,964,998	
Total deferred inflows of resources	10,964,998	
Net position		
Net investment in capital assets, net of related debt	128,446,531	124,034,324
Restricted:		
Nonexpendable	9,368,566	9,055,754
Expendable	9,951,078	9,051,983
Unrestricted	2,514,346	152,737,521
Total net position	150,280,521	294,879,582
Total liabilities, deferred inflows of resources, and net position	459,799,623	457,651,223

Note: Statement of net position is for last day of fiscal years 2015 and 2014.

However, a second glance reveals that both formats convey basically the same information. Assets are listed in the order of liquidity: cash, short-term investments, accounts receivable, notes receivable, inventory, and prepaid expenses. These are followed by less liquid assets: long-term assets such as investments, fixed assets, real property, other assets, and intangible assets such as goodwill. Liabilities are listed in the order of their due date. In both cases, debt is considered "long-term" if it will be liquidated some time beyond the current fiscal year.

Notably, in the FASB format (table 7.1), net assets are listed in three categories: unrestricted, temporarily restricted, and permanently restricted. By identifying whether assets are restricted or unrestricted, the actual amount of money available for operational use is presented much more clearly. Beginning in 2018, FASB guidelines will change. Net assets should be reported in just two categories: "with" or "without" donor restrictions.[4] The total net assets will be the same either way. In addition, the FASB will require institutions to disclose the nature and amounts of donor restrictions. This includes any designations by the governing board on how net assets without donor restrictions are to be used. For example, although an external donor has not imposed any restrictions on a gift, the institution may have placed its own restrictions on the intended use of the money. The unrestricted funds are "designated" or, in a slight variation of the term, "committed." In other words, the term "net assets without restrictions" does not mean "uncommitted net assets."

Pension liabilities, which can be quite sizable, are reported in several different ways. For defined contribution plans, the university's contribution is usually included as an expense in the "salaries and benefits" account, which *does not* appear in the balance sheet. Any difference between the pension expense and actual employer contributions is reported as a pension liability, which *does* appear in the balance sheet. For defined benefit plans, the difference between a pension plan's assets and obligations based on actuarial data constitutes a pension liability; it represents the additional amount the university will have to contribute to the current pension fund to meet future obligations. If a public university participates in a plan administered by the state, the university reports its proportionate share of the liability, which is usually based on the present value of its projected benefit payments. The FASB has traditionally required universities to report pension liabilities in the "post-retirement benefits" account (table 7.1).[5] The GASB began requiring universities to report pension liabilities directly beginning in fiscal years starting after June 15, 2014.[6] Therefore, they began showing up as noncurrent liabilities in most FY 2015 balance sheets, accompanied by a comparable decrease in unrestricted net assets (table 7.2). Notably, with this new GASB reporting requirement, annual pension expenses are no longer recorded as cash contributions made to the plans; those contributions are simply subtracted from the pension liability.

The pension plan's liability, based on actuarial data, is determined for a specific date, known as the measurement date. The FASB requires that date to coincide with the date of the university's financial statement. However, the GASB permits the measurement date to be up to one year prior to the date of the university's financial statement, which allows the plan administrators more time to prepare their financial reports. Therefore, if the measurement date precedes the financial statement date, any assets accrued or liabilities incurred during the intervening period are recorded as deferred outflows or deferred inflows, respectively.[7] Deferred outflows (from the plan) occur, for example, if actual earnings on plan investments exceed projected earnings. Conversely, deferred inflows (into the plan) occur, for example, if the university contributes to the plan subsequent to the measurement date.

Understandably, pension plans can be a major liability if they are underfunded. This occurs if the plan's assets are less than the projected benefit payments, resulting in a net pension liability. Ultimately, the university must allocate the assets required to mitigate the pension liability. If the plan has assets that equal or exceed the projected benefit payments, it is considered "funded," so no net liability appears on the balance sheets. When evaluating a university's financial position, details about its pension funds, usually found in footnotes to the balance sheet, always should be examined carefully.

Because the balance sheet presents the university's net worth, it answers the question: Is the university solvent? Asked differently, it answers the question: Can the university pay its debts? Theoretically, the answer is yes if assets exceed liabilities. However, reality may differ from theory if the university cannot convert all of its assets into cash. Selling a university's physical assets such as classroom buildings and specialty equipment can become quite complicated; there may not be a ready buyer. Consequently, some liabilities may become due before sufficient cash can be raised by liquidating assets. Even worse, if liabilities exceed assets, the university cannot possibly pay its debts; it is bankrupt.

Income Statement

The income statement, called the *statement of activities* and the *statement of revenues, expenses, and changes in net position* by the FASB and the GASB, respectively, illustrates the financial viability of an organization. It provides information that explains how assets, liabilities, and net assets change with time. Unlike the balance sheet, which focuses on assets and liabilities, the income statement focuses on revenues and expenses and how they affect net assets. And, unlike the balance sheet's one-day time frame, the income statement covers a longer time frame such as a fiscal year. Overall, it presents financial information about an institution's operating activities, investments, and fund-raising during the reporting period.

Accordingly, a university's income statement reports the amount of revenue earned over a specific time frame, usually a fiscal year, as well as the expenses directly related to earning that revenue. Revenue minus expenses yields the change in net assets for the reporting period that is reflected on the balance sheet; in equation form,

$$revenue - expenses = change\ in\ net\ assets$$

Income statements in FASB and GASB formats are presented in tables 7.3 and 7.4, respectively. Superficially, they look about the same. The revenues and expense categories roughly are similar. Prima facie, the main difference in these two examples is the format for expense reporting. The FASB requires expenses to be reported by functional classification (table 7.3), whereas the GASB allows expenses to be reported by either functional or natural classifications. Most public universities report them by natural classification in the income statement and by functional classification in the footnotes. In table 7.4, they are reported by natural classification. Three additional features warrant attention.

First, the FASB requires institutions to list their data in three categories according to restrictions on the use of the funds: unrestricted, temporarily restricted, or permanently restricted. (As on the balance sheet, after 2018, the data will be listed in only two categories: with donor restrictions and without donor restrictions.) However, the FASB considers all expenses unrestricted; "you can't spend the money unless it's unrestricted." To account for expenses financed with temporarily restricted resources, the FASB requires institutions to report shifts of net assets from temporarily restricted to unrestricted categories ("net assets released from restrictions"). These shifted net assets enter into the overall computation of the

Table 7.3. Private university income statement: statement of activities (FASB format)

	Unrestricted	Temporarily restricted	Permanently restricted	2015 total	2014 total
Operating revenues					
Tuition and fees	67,872,561			67,872,561	61,345,243
Student financial aid	(18,917,630)			(18,917,630)	(16,672,781)
Net tuition and fees	48,954,931			48,954,931	44,672,461
Sales and services of auxiliaries	15,124,561			15,124,561	13,286,099
Government grants and contracts	2,489,380			2,489,380	2,105,811
Private gifts and grants	5,105,788	3,299,936		8,405,724	7,059,380
Long-term investment income	5,137,734	6,179,018		11,316,751	12,690,788
Investment gains used for operations	1,489,280	1,821,179		3,310,459	1,203,984
Other income	1,642,801			1,642,801	1,606,780
Net assets released from restrictions	7,833,663	(7,833,663)			
Total operating revenues	87,778,138	3,466,470		91,244,608	82,625,303
Operating expenses					
Instruction	31,617,495			31,617,495	29,322,805
Research	1,900,451			1,900,451	1,762,523
Public service	1,230,919			1,230,919	1,141,583
Academic support	7,959,105			7,959,105	7,902,358
Student services	7,607,388			7,607,388	7,054,259
Institutional support	13,085,408			13,085,408	13,090,030
Auxiliary enterprises	20,027,530			20,027,531	17,930,494
Total operating expenses	83,428,296			83,428,296	78,204,051
Increase in net assets from operating activities	4,349,841			7,816,311	4,421,251
Nonoperating activities					
Investment gain reinvested	6,280,325	10,215,564		16,495,889	2,241,978
Capital gifts	1,167,754	2,401,699	4,956,180	8,525,633	10,639,730
Other	(1,496,383)	(1,529,349)		(3,025,731)	10,837,506
Net assets released from restrictions	2,036,663	(2,036,663)			
Increase in net assets from nonoperating activities	7,988,359	9,051,251	4,956,180	21,995,790	23,719,214
Net change in net assets	12,338,200	12,517,721	4,956,180	29,812,101	28,140,465
Net assets at beginning of year	184,177,891	116,903,674	95,874,225	396,955,790	368,815,325
Net assets at end of year	196,516,091	129,421,395	100,830,405	426,767,891	396,955,790

Table 7.4. Public university income statement: statement of revenues, expenses, and changes in net position (GASB format)

	FY 2015	FY 2014
Operating revenues		
Tuition and fees	72,713,243	69,207,640
Student financial aid	(19,244,242)	(18,612,696)
Net tuition and fees	53,469,001	50,594,944
Grants and contracts		
Federal	79,902,565	90,653,370
State	9,150,735	5,223,746
Private	1,976,343	2,074,302
Sales and services of educational departments	3,678,370	3,530,514
Auxiliary	6,686,732	6,135,066
Total operating revenues	154,863,746	158,211,942
Operating expenses		
Salaries and benefits	151,092,560	143,546,057
Supplies and services	43,670,230	50,498,859
Depreciation	13,058,315	12,416,766
Scholarships and fellowships	1,101,624	1,090,063
Total operating expenses	208,922,729	207,551,745
Operating gain (loss)	(54,058,983)	(49,339,803)
Nonoperating revenues (expenses)		
State appropriations	43,102,390	42,710,964
Private gifts	6,175,489	4,043,840
Net investment income (loss)	6,926,302	6,334,687
Pell grant revenue	7,395,098	7,615,679
Loss on disposal of capital assets	(1,461,846)	(276,840)
Interest expense	(3,454,765)	(2,435,540)
Net nonoperating revenues before capital additions	58,682,668	57,992,790
Capital gifts	28,000	637,197
Net nonoperating revenues	58,710,668	58,629,987
Change in net position	4,651,685	9,290,184
Net position		
Beginning of year	294,879,582	285,589,398
Cumulative effect of adopting new accounting guidance	(149,250,746)	
Beginning of year as restated start of FY 2015	145,628,836	285,589,398
End of year	150,280,521	294,879,582

change in net assets. Consequently, for private institutions, the equation becomes:

$$revenue - expenses + net\ assets\ released\ from\ restrictions$$
$$= change\ in\ net\ assets$$

The GASB doesn't have a similar concept; expenses can be restricted or unrestricted.

Second, the GASB requires explicit identification of the net results from operations and prescribes categorizing some revenues used to finance operations as nonoperating revenues. Specifically, state operating appropriations, investment income (except interest income on student loans), and gifts all must be reported as nonoperating revenues because they were not generated by normal university operations (teaching, research, etc.). As a result, because the state appropriations (which help pay for operating expenses) are not included in the operating revenue, public institutions always report a loss from operations. The FASB allows but does not require private institutions to identify operating activities; if the institution does, it may determine which items are operating and which are nonoperating.

Third, the GASB-mandated reporting of pension liabilities in the balance sheet after June 15, 2014, necessitated a restatement of net position for FY 2015 in the income statement. The unrestricted portion of the net position—that is, the net assets—decreased to offset the increased pension liability. Because the current pension liability is accumulated over previous reporting periods, the adjustment to net position appears as a one-time "cumulative effect of adopting new accounting guidance" (table 7.4).

Universities typically hold various agency funds in a fiduciary capacity for campus organizations such as classes and clubs. These organizations raise funds on their own and spend the funds on their organization's behalf. Therefore, the revenues and expenses of these agency funds are not included in the statement of activities.

The change in net assets manifest in the income statement measures the institution's financial viability and answers the question: Is the university spending within its means? An increase in net position indicates that the university is spending within its means; it is taking in more than it is spending. Any surplus can be reinvested in the institution. In contrast, a decrease in net position indicates that the university is not living within its means; it is spending more than it is taking in. Consequently, the university must find a way to meet the operating deficit in the short term. Possible solutions include dipping into cash reserves, increasing endowment payout, and taking out loans. In the examples, the private and the public universities reported positive net assets for both 2014 and 2015; in both years, they brought in more money than they spent. Thus, they appear to be healthy financially.

Noticeably, income statements look somewhat like university master operating budgets. Indeed, the income statement is a measure of institutional operations, much like the budget. They both report revenue and expenses in about the same categories. Actually, the operating budget can be converted to the income statement. The conversion requires certain revenue and expense reclassifications, transfers, and adjustments to the budget, such as removing capital equipment purchases and recording the current year's depreciation. In its budget plan, Stanford University provides a good example of the conversion process.[8]

The similarities relating the income statement and the budget might imply that corresponding revenue and expenditure amounts are the same in both documents. This may, in fact, occur in some entries. But, more often than not, corresponding amounts differ, as can be seen when comparing tables 6.1 (budget) and 7.4 (income statement). These discrepancies manifest the fundamental difference between a budget, a planning document for internal use with no GAAP guiding its construction, and a certified financial statement for external audiences that must abide by GAAP. For example, the budget may use a cash basis of accounting, whereas the income statement must use the accrual basis of accounting. Thus, despite their similar appearances, the income statement and the budget are two distinct documents with separate purposes.

Statement of Cash Flows

Stated formally, the statement of cash flows provides information about an institution's cash receipts and payments during a specific period, usually the fiscal year. It highlights the net increase and decrease in total cash on hand for the accounting period, indicating actual cash received or spent. In this context, cash includes currency and bank deposits as well as cash equivalents such as highly liquid US Treasury bills, money market accounts, and commercial paper. Other less liquid investments such as stocks and bonds are not considered cash equivalents.

Stated informally, the statement of cash flows addresses the mandate "Show me the money." To understand this assertion, it helps to remember that the income statement uses the accrual basis of accounting. Accordingly, it reports revenues as they are earned and expenses as they are incurred, whether or not cash has been received or paid. In that sense, the income statement provides a full accounting of the university's revenues and expenses. But, because it doesn't account for the timing of cash exchanges, the accrual method masks the flow of actual cash into and out of the university, leaving unanswered questions about the amount of ready cash available to pay bills. For example, on the income statement, the institution might report substantial revenue. But, if the revenue is primarily in accounts receivable and not cash on hand, the university might not be able to pay its bills if the receivables cannot be collected in a timely way.

To unmask the true flow of cash, the statement of cash flows converts net income from the income statement from the accrual basis to the cash basis. It does this by making adjustments (usually subtractions in this case) for noncash items in various accounts. These accounts include accounts receivable, inventory, prepaid assets, payable liabilities, and unearned revenues. Therefore, the cash flows statement will not include the accounts receivable et alia because they are not cash. In addition, changes that neither provide nor consume cash are removed. So, the income statement may show depreciation as an expense, but depreciation doesn't require a cash outlay and doesn't appear on the cash flows statement. Likewise, items that increase net assets but are long term in nature are removed from operations and reclassified to financing or investing activities. These includes contributions for long-term investments, whether in the form of new funds for endowment or funds to be expended for the acquisition or construction of property, plant, or equipment. In general, cash flows from investing and financing activities are not considered part of ongoing regular operating activities. However, they still represent cash that can be used to pay bills. Therefore, cash from investing and financing is added to cash flow from operations to arrive at the net change in cash and cash equivalents for the year. After making these adjustments, the statement of cash flows bottom line measures short-term viability: Will the university have money available to pay daily operating expenses and short-term debt obligations?

FASB and GASB accounting principles for statements of cash flows differ fundamentally in one main aspect: the reporting of cash flows from operating activities either indirectly or directly. In the indirect method, net assets based on the accrual method are shown, followed by the adjustments needed to convert the total net income to the cash amount from operating activities. Thus, reconciled cash flows are arrived at indirectly. In the direct method, those adjustments have been made "behind the scenes," so the statement of cash flows reports directly the reconciled cash flows from operating activities, including tuition and fees, grants and contracts, et cetera. The FASB allows the use of either method, although most private universities use the indirect method. The GASB requires use of the direct method. There are no further differences in the cash flows reported in the investing and financing activities sections.

Sample statements of cash flows in FASB and GASB formats are presented in tables 7.5 and 7.6, respectively. In both formats, the starting point at the top is the total change in net assets, as reported in the income statement. In the FASB format (table 7.5), these changes are summarized in the top line, "change in net assets," which is taken straight from the bottom of the income statement ("Net increase in net assets" in table 7.3). Then, following the indirect method, the various adjustments needed for reconciliation to the cash method are tabulated. For example, accounts receivable ($199,408) and pledges receivable ($60,895) are subtracted because the cash hasn't yet been received. However, following the direct method in the GASB format (table 7.6), the revenues and expenses expressed in the income statement (table 7.4) have already been reconciled in this report. From a pedagogical perspective, the FASB indirect method provides better insight into the reconciliation methods underlying the statement of cash flows. *Technical note:* Because the statements of income and cash flows are prepared using different accounting bases (accrual and cash, respectively), corresponding numbers for most line items in the two statements will not match exactly. Indeed, differences like these are to be expected.

The operating cash flows indicate the institution's financial viability. High positive operating cash flows usually correlate with high revenues, low overhead, and efficient operations. Negative operating cash flows mean that the institution must meet this deficit through revenue from some other source or by borrowing money. In both 2014 and 2015, the private university had positive operating cash flow ($8,436,390 in 2015; table 7.5). In contrast, in both 2014 and 2015, the public university had negative operating cash flow (−$39,902,853 in 2015; table 7.6). But this is expected because state appropriations, an important source of revenue, are not counted as operating revenue. Fortunately, in both years, the state appropriations ($43,102,390 in 2015) exceeded the operating deficit (table 7.6), so the combination of operating revenue and state appropriations is positive. Thus, both universities appear to be healthy from this financial point of view.

Cash flows from investing and financing activities can have a significant impact on the institution's overall net cash flow. Indeed, cash flows from these activities can offset otherwise positive operational results. For example, the private university had a negative net cash flow from investing activities in both 2014 and 2015, mainly because of large investments in plant facilities and equipment ($22,521,236 in 2015). The public university had negative investment

Table 7.5. Private university statement of cash flows (FASB format)

	FY 2015	FY 2014
Cash flows from operating activities		
Change in net assets	29,812,101	28,140,465
Adjustments to reconcile change in net assets to net cash provided by operating activities:		
Depreciation and amortization	5,856,198	4,832,731
Gains on investments	(19,806,590)	(3,445,671)
Gain on equipment disposals	(124,573)	(78,879)
Capital gifts	(7,358,270)	(8,939,259)
Other operating activity	2,123,340	321,438
Changes in assets and liabilities that provide (use) cash:		
Accounts receivable	(199,408)	(89,616)
Pledges receivable	(60,895)	(19,106,885)
Student loans receivable	60,554	58,256
Short-term investments	(832,965)	(276,281)
Inventories	(59,199)	(70,478)
Prepaid expenses and other assets	82,331	(93,534)
Accounts payable and accrued expenses	(1,606,985)	1,993,448
Deposits and deferred revenues	172,890	206,653
Post-retirement benefits	354,385	7,536,674
Other changes	23,475	(1,847,658)
Net cash used in operating activities	8,436,390	9,141,404
Cash flows from investing activities		
Purchases of plant and equipment, net	(22,521,236)	(23,637,358)
Purchases of investments	(332,418,139)	(422,169,166)
Proceeds from sales and maturities of investments	341,712,668	421,212,105
Other nonoperating activity	(2,122,605)	(321,346)
Net cash provided by (used in) investing activities	(15,349,313)	(24,915,765)
Cash flows from financing activities		
Proceeds from contributions for:		
Investment in endowment	4,956,776	6,064,563
Investment in long-lived assets	2,401,849	2,875,575
Proceeds from issuance of long-term debt		
Payments on long-term debt	(1,427,289)	(1,335,800)
Net cash provided by financing activities	5,931,336	7,604,338
Net decrease in cash and cash equivalents	(981,586)	(8,170,024)
Cash and cash equivalents, beginning of year	14,017,939	22,187,963
Cash and cash equivalents, end of year	13,036,353	14,017,939
Supplemental data		
Noncash investing and financing activities—gifts in kind	515,263	725,876
Interest paid	3,690,561	2,643,513

cash flows in 2014 and 2015 due to a large contribution to the university system's investment pool ($2,540,591 in 2015) and negligible proceeds from sales and maturities of investments ($3,153 in 2015), respectively. Moreover, it had negative cash flows in capital

Table 7.6. Public university statement of cash flows (GASB format)

	FY 2015	FY 2014
Cash flows from operating activities		
Tuition and fees	52,919,538	51,365,503
Federal grants and contracts	78,477,050	87,437,398
State and local grants and contracts	8,902,979	4,965,143
Private grants and contracts	1,922,834	1,971,613
Sales and services of departmental activities	4,952,753	2,862,834
Auxiliary enterprises	7,075,559	8,168,042
Payments to suppliers	(43,611,364)	(47,200,483)
Payments to employees and related fringe benefits	(148,519,009)	(145,666,222)
Payments for scholarships and fellowships	(2,023,193)	(716,714)
Net cash used in operating activities	(39,902,853)	(36,812,886)
Cash flows from investing activities		
Income distribution from system investment pool	1,370,660	1,348,408
Proceeds from sales and maturities of other investments	3,153	15,002,758
Contributions to system investment pool	(2,540,591)	(22,738,307)
Net cash provided by (used in) investing activities	(1,166,778)	(6,387,141)
Cash flows from capital and related financing activities		
Proceeds from issuance of bonds		32,005,000
Proceeds from issuance of notes payable		1,843,000
Purchase of capital assets	(31,074,731)	(28,952,466)
Proceeds from sale of capital assets	(77,478)	263,236
Principal payments on capital debt	(4,603,600)	(3,450,000)
Interest payments on capital debt	(3,969,323)	(3,407,068)
Net cash used in capital and related financing activities	(39,725,132)	(1,698,298)
Cash flows from noncapital financing activities		
State educational appropriations	43,102,390	42,710,964
Private gifts	4,536,825	3,084,760
Student direct lending receipts	27,906,543	28,230,308
Student direct lending disbursements	(28,466,907)	(28,425,788)
Amounts received from affiliates	244,939	123,341
Amounts paid to affiliates	(26,483)	(29,496)
Legal settlement	860,391	818,329
Pell grant revenue	7,395,098	7,615,679
Net cash provided by noncapital financing activities	55,552,796	54,128,097
Net increase (decrease) in cash and cash equivalents	(25,241,967)	9,229,772
Cash and cash equivalents, beginning of year	57,026,086	47,796,314
Cash and cash equivalents, end of year	31,784,119	57,026,086
Reconciliation of cash and cash equivalents to the statement of net position		
Cash and cash equivalents in current assets	31,104,680	39,038,391
Cash and cash equivalents for capital activities		17,327,259
Restricted cash and cash equivalents	679,439	660,436
Total cash and cash equivalents	31,784,119	57,026,086

and related financing activities due to large purchases of capital assets. In 2014, however, the purchase of capital assets was funded to a large extent by the proceeds of a bond issuance (table 7.6), which reduced the impact of the purchases on the cash flow. Again, negative net cash flow in investment and financing activities is not necessarily a sign of financial trouble in the university's operational activities.

Notes to Financial Statements

The phrase "See accompanying notes to financial statements" is typically at the bottom of each financial statement. Footnotes are an important element of the financial report. Indeed, they are considered essential to understanding the financial statements. Generically, the footnotes amplify information presented in the financial statements. They report details and explanations that were omitted in the main documents because of their length or their complexity. This informative supplementary information purportedly makes it easier to understand specific aspects of the financial statements.

Both the FASB and the GASB have guidelines for preparing the footnotes, with particular emphasis on what should be included in them.[9] State governments also may impose specific guidelines.[10] The actual list of topics depends on a particular institution's financial reporting structure. Typically they include at least the following items in this order:

- organization and summary of significant accounting policies
- cash
- investments
- accounts receivable
- operating expenses by function
- capital assets
- capital lease obligations
- endowment
- long-term debt
- post-employment benefits
- retirement plan
- contingencies and commitments

Furthermore, starting in 2018, the FASB requires private universities to document the amounts and intended purposes of funds designated by the governing board for specific uses. This includes disclosure of any board-imposed limits on the use of resources independent of any donor-imposed restrictions.[11]

Most of the items in this list are discussed in context in the other chapters. So, all of them will not be recapitulated here. It is worth pointing out, however, that the initial note on accounting policies documents the auditor's accounting methodologies in "boiler-plate" detail. Subsequent notes work through various topics from the financial statements, sometimes with rigor that mainly experts in the field can appreciate. Pragmatically, an easy approach to the footnotes is to look up those of interest rather than to read them systematically from beginning to end.

Three examples will be presented to illustrate the general format and content of footnotes: investments, capital assets, and long-term debt.

Investments

The footnotes explain details of the investments listed in the balance sheet. This includes all long-term investments and certain short-term investments, such as some money-market funds. (For simplicity, however, only long-term investments will be considered in the example presented below.) These explanations concentrate on three issues:

- investment strategies (how is the money invested?)
- valuation (how much are the investments worth?)
- liquidity (how easily can the investments be turned into cash?)

The investment strategies range from investments in stocks (equity) and bonds (fixed-income) to sophisticated alternatives, including hedge strategies, private equity investments (for example, venture capital and angel investments), real estate, and derivatives. The amount invested in each of these kinds of instruments is usually listed in two tables according to valuation and liquidity.

To standardize valuation, both the FASB and the GASB require universities to document how they determined the value of their investments.[12] According to GAAP, these determinations are based on inputs to a "fair value hierarchy" that has three levels:

1. Level 1 is based on quoted prices for *identical* assets on an active market (for example, stocks listed on the New York Stock Exchange, registered mutual funds, or money market securities).
2. Level 2 is based on quoted prices for *similar* assets in active markets, quoted prices for identical or similar instruments in markets that are not active, or inputs other than quoted prices (for

example, corporate and municipal bonds and interest and yield curves).

3. Level 3 is based on unobservable inputs for the assets (for example, private equity such as venture or angel investments and nonstandard derivatives).

Thus, if the university holds an investment and an active market with quoted prices exists, the market price of an identical security is used to report the fair value (level 1).

In addition, the value of some pooled and alternative investments can be reported more expediently by using the net asset value (NAV). The NAV is the asset's value minus any liabilities. Pooled funds from multiple campuses in a university system and arbitrage funds are reported at NAV, for example.

In the footnotes, universities report their investments according to this fair value hierarchy. The point is to answer the question: How did you determine the worth of these investments? This is not a trivial question because of the potential uncertainty in some level 3 valuations. To reduce the uncertainty, acquisitions, dispositions, and net gain of investments valued in level 3 must be reported (reconciled) separately, allowing a "look under the hood."

A valuation report based on the private university's balance statement (table 7.1) is shown in table 7.7. In this example, a sizable percentage (83 percent) of the investments is valued according to NAV, mainly because of the extensive investment in hedge funds (*top panel*). The level 3 investments are reconciled according to GAAP (*bottom panel*). This reconciliation summarizes the activity of these investments during the past year.

Universities also report their investments according to liquidity. In this context, liquidity is measured by how long it usually takes to convert the investment instrument into cash, that is, to redeem the investment. The point in this case is to answer the question: How quickly can the university cash in its investments in an emergency? An example is shown in table 7.8. Some equities and fixed-income investments can be converted to cash very quickly if they are in an active market; these include stocks in major US corporations, for example. Other assets are not liquid. Angel investments in a start-up company (private equity) are a good example.

The investment footnotes may include more tables containing further investment details, such as asset class allocation (capitalization levels, international stocks and bonds, etc.), credit risks, and so forth that provide useful information for professional investment

Table 7.7. Investment valuation methods and level 3 reconciliation

| | Valuation methods | | | | |
| | | Fair level hierarchy | | | |
Investments	NAV	Level 1	Level 2	Level 3	Totals
Equities	56,886,339	25,355,424	642,483	13,790	82,898,035
Fixed income	12,473,963	522,129	10,191,643	4,342,787	27,530,523
Hedge funds	110,759,978				110,759,978
Private equity	65,896,860				65,896,860
Real estate	23,979,653	163,412	115,476	97,184	24,355,724
Subtotal long-term	269,996,794	26,040,964	10,949,602	4,453,761	311,441,121
Cash and cash equivalents		13,036,353			13,036,353
Total investments	269,996,794	39,077,317	10,949,602	4,453,761	324,477,474

Level 3 reconciliation	Equities	Fixed income	Real assets	Total
Fair value as of June 30, 2014	49,530	4,658,916	97,184	4,805,630
Acquisitions		2,902,477		2,902,477
Dispositions		(3,497,400)		(3,497,400)
Net realized and unrealized gains	(35,740)	278,794		243,054
Fair value at June 30, 2015	13,790	4,342,787	97,184	4,453,761

Note: Investment valuation methods are shown in the *top panel*. Level 3 investments are described in more detail (reconciled) according to GAAP in the *bottom panel*.

managers. For nonaccountants, the best strategy is to focus initially on the valuation and liquidity tables. They provide core information needed to evaluate the financial health of the university's investments, the source of a vital component of many universities' operating income.

Capital Assets

Capital assets footnotes generally indicate changes in net capital assets during the fiscal year. An example from the public university's footnotes is shown in table 7.9. In this example, additions, retirements, and adjustments to capital assets are listed. Additions represent new purchases or improvements, and retirements occur when a long-term asset is no longer useful but cannot be sold. (Sales are accounted for separately.) Remember: land does not have a definable lifetime and, therefore, does not depreciate. Adjustments represent accounting changes; for example, in FY 2015, construction of a new building was completed, so its value ($21,523,729) was transferred from "construction in progress" to "buildings." Accumulated depreciation, from the income statement, is then subtracted to yield the net capital assets, listed in the balance statement (table 7.2), at the end of the fiscal year.

Table 7.8. Investment liquidity, based on the frequency of redemption opportunities

	Redemption opportunities					
Investments	Daily	Monthly	Quarterly	Annually	Multi-year lock-ups	Not liquid	Totals
Equities	26,328,951		19,853,184	16,968,718	18,994,476	752,706	82,898,035
Fixed income	14,680,488	4,871,014			7,602,856	376,165	27,530,523
Hedge funds		18,581,163		12,659,982	76,637,837	2,880,995	110,759,978
Private equity						65,896,860	65,896,860
Real assets	278,888	6,767,694				17,309,143	24,355,724
Subtotal long-term	41,288,327	30,219,871	19,853,184	29,628,700	103,235,169	87,215,870	311,441,121
Cash and cash equivalents	13,036,353						13,036,353
Total investments	54,324,680	30,219,871	19,853,184	29,628,700	103,235,169	87,215,870	324,477,474

Table 7.9. Changes in capital assets during FY 2015 and FY 2014

Capital assets	Start of FY 2015	Additions	Retirements	Adjustments	End of FY 2015
Land	7,552,605	38,543			7,591,148
Land improvements	14,870,571	1,895,615			16,766,186
Buildings and improvements	290,629,408	2,447,308	(3,416,722)	21,523,729	311,183,723
Construction in progress	18,454,776	25,786,071		(21,523,729)	22,717,118
Equipment	65,428,773	3,193,435	(6,679,817)		61,942,391
Library books	25,945,675	129,461	(51,298)		26,023,838
Computer software	2,939,750				2,939,750
Collections	1,124,402				1,124,402
Total cost of capital assets	426,945,960	33,490,433	(10,147,837)		450,288,556
Less accumulated depreciation	206,101,243	13,058,315	(8,763,469)		210,396,089
Capital assets, net	220,844,717	20,432,118	(1,384,368)		239,892,467

Capital assets	Start of FY 2014	Additions	Retirements	Adjustments	End of FY 2014
Land	3,960,290	3,653,083	(60,768)		7,552,605
Land improvements	11,174,484	3,696,087			14,870,571
Buildings and improvements	287,330,900	3,597,740	(299,232)		290,629,408
Construction in progress	2,224,158	16,956,124		(725,506)	18,454,776
Equipment	63,744,811	2,773,646	(1,089,684)		65,428,773
Library books	25,878,434	145,788	(78,547)		25,945,675
Computer software	2,939,750				2,939,750
Collections	510,305	614,097			1,124,402
Total cost of capital assets	397,763,132	31,436,565	(1,528,231)	(725,506)	426,945,960
Less accumulated depreciation	194,672,632	12,416,766	(988,155)		206,101,243
Capital assets, net	203,090,500	19,019,799	(540,076)	(725,506)	220,844,717

Long-Term Debt

The footnotes also provide details about changes in a university's long-term debt. To indicate the level of detail, changes in the public university's long-term debt are illustrated in tables 7.10 to 7.12. The initial table (table 7.10) identifies new long-term debt incurred during the fiscal year and principal repayments on existing long-term debt according to the type of debt and the source of revenue for repaying the bonds, namely, student housing revenue and general fee revenue. In this example, the university did not incur any new long-term debt in FY 2015. Notice that the long-term (noncurrent) and current debt amounts in the footnotes correspond to the noncurrent and current long-term debt liabilities in the balance statement (table 7.2). Remember: the current portion refers to payments on long-term debt that are due this fiscal year.

Also, this sample footnote refers to a "(Discount) or premium." As explained in chapter 5, discounts or premiums were incurred when the bonds were issued, as the bonds' interest rates were aligned

Table 7.10. Long-term debt activity for FY 2015

| Type/supported by | Long-term debt activity | | | |
	End of FY 2014	New debt	Principal repayment	End of FY 2015
Bonds				
Student-housing revenue	41,911,000		2,055,000	39,856,000
General-fee revenue	68,360,000		2,180,000	66,180,000
Note payable	1,843,000		368,600	1,474,400
Sub-total long-term debt	112,114,000		4,603,600	107,510,400
Less current portion	(4,603,600)			(4,698,600)
(Discount) or premium	282,200			272,278
Total long-term debt	107,792,600			103,084,078

to the market value of interest paid by similar bonds. On the one hand, the debt (that is, the amount received by the university) is reduced by a discount if the interest paid by the university is less than the market value; on the other hand, the debt is increased by adding a premium if the interest paid by the university is more than the market value. Discounts and premiums are usually amortized for the duration of the debt, as either additions or reductions of the amount the university pays periodically to the bondholders. The amortized payments are included in the income statement. The remaining, unamortized balance of the discount or premium is subtracted or added to the total long-term debt, respectively. In this example, the unamortized premium at the end of FY 2014 increased the value of the debt by $282,200, to a total long-term debt of $107,792,600 (table 7.10), which is reported in the balance sheet (table 7.2).

Further details about the debt are provided in a subsequent table (table 7.11) typically found in the footnotes that itemizes the specific debts, their purpose, dates of issue and maturity, interest rate, and outstanding indebtedness at the end of the fiscal year. As shown in the table, revenue generated by issuing the Series 2012A and Series 2012B bonds was used to refinance and retire Series 2001A and 2002A bonds. The financial benefits of this refinancing might be explained further in the accompanying text; for example: "In December 2012, the university refinanced the Student Housing Revenue Bonds Series 2001A and Series 2002A, which resulted in a reduction of future principal and interest payments of $1.5 million. This savings will average $75,000 per year for the next 20 years. The amounts outstanding on the 2001A and 2002A bonds were paid in January 2013, and the bonds were removed from the financial statement."

Table 7.11. Detailed schedule of long-term debt

Description and purpose	Date issued	Final maturity	Interest rate (%)	Original indebtedness	Outstanding indebtedness, end of FY 2015	Outstanding indebtedness, end of FY 2014
Bonds payable						
Series 2000A						
Dormitory remodeling	5/1/1980	5/1/2020	3.00	2,180,000	525,000	605,000
Series 2000B						
Dormitory remodeling	7/23/1982	5/1/2021	3.00	2,602,000	686,000	776,000
Series 2004A						
Student housing construction	9/30/2004	9/1/2034	3.00–4.625	13,130,000	10,390,000	10,705,000
Series 2004B						
Student housing remodeling	9/30/2004	9/1/2016	3.00–3.625	7,515,000	1,505,000	2,215,000
Series 2005A						
Dining hall construction	10/1/2005	6/1/2025	3.00–4.375	8,580,000	5,425,000	5,810,000
Series 2009A						
Upgrade campus utilities	8/4/2009	7/1/2029	3.00–4.50	8,115,000	6,585,000	6,905,000
Series 2010A						
Student housing construction	7/14/2010	6/1/2042	2.85–6.125	27,990,000	27,220,000	27,610,000
Series 2012A						
Refinance Series 2001A	4/3/2012	10/1/2031	0.73–4.28	11,170,000	10,230,000	10,700,000
Series 2012B						
Refinance Series 2002A	9/5/2012	12/1/2026	0.74–3.84	13,700,000	12,175,000	12,940,000
Series 2013A						
Student union construction	4/4/2013	4/1/2023	1.57	7,550,000	6,840,000	7,550,000
Series 2013B						
Physical sciences building construction	4/4/2013	4/1/2043	4.00	24,455,000	24,455,000	24,455,000
				128,830,000	107,510,400	112,114,000
Note payable						
University foundation	7/10/2013	7/1/2018		1,843,000	1,474,400	1,843,000
Total note payable				1,843,000	1,474,400	1,843,000
Total debt				128,830,000	107,510,400	112,114,000

Table 7.12. Principal and interest on long-term debt for the next five years and subsequent five-year periods, covering the period 2016 to 2045

Fiscal year	Revenue bond payables		
	Principal	Interest	Total
2016	4,698,600	3,873,870	8,572,470
2017	4,818,600	3,767,720	8,586,320
2018	4,143,600	3,651,535	7,795,135
2019	4,253,600	3,555,142	7,808,742
2020	3,995,000	3,450,047	7,445,047
2021–2025	21,716,000	15,312,746	37,028,746
2026–2030	22,005,000	10,958,209	32,963,209
2031–2035	16,060,000	7,107,397	23,167,397
2036–2040	13,920,000	4,036,084	17,956,084
2041–2045	11,900,000	988,483	12,888,483
Total cash requirements	107,510,400	56,701,233	164,211,633

Looking forward, the cash required to make payments on the revenue bonds, which comprise about 99 percent of the long-term debt, for the next 30 years is summarized in table 7.12. For the first 5 years (2016–2020), principal plus interest ranges from about $7.4 to $8.6 million per year. But, in subsequent years, annual payables decline steadily to about $2.6 million in the 5-year period from 2041 to 2045 ($12,888,483 over 5 years). More likely than not, during the 2021 to 2045 period the university will issue new debt, thus increasing the annual payables.

Financial Statement Analysis

Formally, financial statement analysis refers to evaluation of financial statement data. In this context, evaluation means "the making of a judgement about the amount, number, or value of something."[13] Therefore, financial statement analysis involves more than just looking at the raw data presented in the financial statements; it involves comparisons and manipulations of the data to extract information useful for determining an institution's past, current, and projected performance.

These analyses are not part of the financial statements. That is, the institution is not required to prepare or provide them for members of the public. The analyses are primarily for managerial use. Consequently, the exact nature of any analysis of financial statement data depends on the specific inquiry: "What do you want to know?" Because of the effort involved in preparing an analysis (mainly, entering the data into a spreadsheet), it helps to determine beforehand exactly what questions the analysis is designed to answer.

Three standard analytical techniques are used in financial statement analysis: horizontal, vertical, and ratio. Common questions addressed by each of the three techniques will be illustrated below.

Horizontal Analysis

This method analyzes trends in financial statement data over time by comparing two or more years of financial data in dollar and percentage form. That is, it relates the institution with itself over time by comparing the current year with a base year. The variance refers to the difference in dollars between the two years. The percentage change between the current and the base years is calculated according to the formula:

$$\% \text{ increase (decrease)} = \frac{\text{current year amount} - \text{base year amount}}{\text{base year amount}}$$

A horizontal analysis of an income statement is illustrated in table 7.13. This example covers three fiscal years, with the corresponding variance and percentage changes relative to the prior year (the base year). Comparisons are between one fiscal year (corresponding to the current year in the calculation formula) and the prior fiscal year, such as 2014 versus 2013. But comparisons could as easily extend for two or more years earlier. For example, if the university announced in FY 2013 that tuition would increase by 10 percent per year for the next two years, it might want to compare tuition revenue in FY 2012 versus 2014—that is, two years after the tuition increase was announced.

The easiest way to spot meaningful information in analyses like this that involve lots of numbers is to focus initially on the "variance %" columns. When scanning these percent change columns in table 7.13, one large change stands out: a 428 percent loss on the disposal of capital assets in FY 2015. Certainly, an analyst would want to look into this change. For an anomalous variance this large, one question might be whether there was an error in the data entry. Also, the change in net position became progressively larger in FY 2014 and FY 2015, decreasing by 47.96 and 49.93 percent, respectively. An analyst would want to look into those changes as well. Monetarily, much of the decrease in the FY 2015 net position (minus $4,638,499) can be attributed to the $10.75 million drop in revenue from federal grants and contracts.

Quite significantly, in 2015, the net position at the end of the year, which corresponds to the total net position on the balance sheet (table 7.2), dropped dramatically, −49.04 percent, due to the huge cumulative effect of adopting new accounting guidance associated with the recently required inclusion of pension liabilities on the income statement. Fortunately, that is a one-time correction, not a persistent trend. Excluding that one-time liability, the net position in 2015 increased by 1.58 percent compared to the higher education inflation rate, which has been less than 3 percent since 2012.[14] Most of the other data varied from year to year, but there were few consistent trends that might sound alarms. Indeed, despite the sizable decrease in net assets, the university looks healthy in most categories.

Similarly, the balance sheet is often analyzed horizontally. Like the sample analysis of the income statement, a first glance at the variance percent columns will identify significant changes that might require more rigorous consideration. Trending decreases in net assets (net position), especially cash and cash equivalents, or increases in accounts receivable or various liabilities, for example, would probably trigger attention. Importantly, net assets should increase at a rate exceeding inflation for the institution to sustain growth.

Vertical Analysis

Vertical analysis, also known as common-size analysis, compares financial statement data with a reference base in the same fiscal year. As a proportional analysis, each item in a financial statement is expressed as a percentage of the same base. Although the choice of a reference base depends on the information sought, common choices are the total assets and the total revenue on the balance and the income statements, respectively. Thus, on the income statement, the revenue generated by tuition, federal grants, investment income, and other sources is expressed as a percentage of the total revenue for the year. And, on the balance sheet, each asset is expressed as a percentage of total assets in the same year. For public institutions, the revenue base should not include deferred outflows of resources, nor should the expenses base include deferred inflows of resources. According to the GASB: "If you are analyzing whether a government has sufficient resources to satisfy its liabilities, for instance, the ratios you calculate ought not to include deferred outflows of resources among the assets, because they are not resources that can be used to pay off a liability. Likewise, the ratios should not include

Table 7.13. Horizontal analysis of income statements over three years: Statement of revenues, expenses, and changes in net position (GASB format)

	2015	Variance Amount	%	2014	Variance Amount	%	2013
Operating revenues							
Tuition and fees	72,713,243	3,505,603	5.07	69,207,640	989,111	1.45	68,218,529
Student financial aid	(19,244,242)	(631,546)	3.39	(18,612,696)	(426,968)	2.35	(18,185,728)
Net tuition and fees	53,469,001	2,874,057	5.68	50,594,944	562,143	1.12	50,032,801
Grants and contracts							
Federal	79,902,565	(10,750,805)	−11.86	90,653,370	6,916,587	8.26	83,736,783
State	9,150,735	3,926,989	75.18	5,223,746	1,157,572	28.47	4,066,174
Private	1,976,343	(97,959)	−4.72	2,074,302	218,443	11.77	1,855,859
Sales and services	3,678,370	147,856	4.19	3,530,514	79,169	2.29	3,451,345
Auxiliary	6,686,732	551,666	8.99	6,135,066	(583,832)	−8.69	6,718,898
Total operating revenues	154,863,746	(3,348,196)	−2.12	158,211,942	8,350,082	5.57	149,861,860
Operating Expenses							
Salaries and benefits	151,092,560	7,546,503	5.26	143,546,057	6,754,407	4.94	136,791,650
Supplies and services	43,670,230	(6,828,629)	−13.52	50,498,859	4,321,750	9.36	46,177,109
Depreciation	13,058,315	641,549	5.17	12,416,766	245,325	2.02	12,171,441
Scholarships and fellowships	1,101,624	11,561	1.06	1,090,063	483,699	79.77	606,364
Total operating expenses	208,922,729	1,370,984	0.66	207,551,745	11,805,181	6.03	195,746,564
Operating gain (loss)	(54,058,983)	(4,719,180)	9.56	(49,339,803)	(3,455,099)	7.53	(45,884,704)

Nonoperating revenues (expenses)						
State appropriations	43,102,390	391,426	0.92	42,710,964	(529,623)	−1.22	43,240,587
Private gifts	6,175,489	2,131,649	52.71	4,043,840	(1,981,323)	−32.88	6,025,163
Net investment income (loss)	6,926,302	591,615	9.34	6,334,687	(2,748,706)	−30.26	9,083,393
Pell grant revenue	7,395,098	(220,581)	−2.90	7,615,679	(502,484)	−6.19	8,118,163
Loss on disposal of capital assets	(1,461,846)	(1,185,006)	428.05	(276,840)	283,097	−50.56	(559,937)
Interest expense	(3,454,765)	(1,019,225)	41.85	(2,435,540)	909,740	−27.19	(3,345,280)
Net before capital additions	58,682,668	689,878	1.19	57,992,790	(4,569,299)	−7.30	62,562,089
Capital gifts	28,000	(609,197)	−95.61	637,197	(538,136)	−45.79	1,175,333
Net nonoperating revenues	58,710,668	80,681	0.14	58,629,987	(5,107,435)	−8.01	63,737,422
Change in net position	4,651,685	(4,638,499)	−49.93	9,290,184	(8,562,534)	−47.96	17,852,718
Net position							
Beginning of year	294,879,582	9,290,184	3.25	285,589,398	285,589,398		267,736,680
Effect of new accounting guidance	(149,250,746)	(149,250,746)					
Beginning of year (as restated)	145,628,836	(139,960,562)	−49.01	285,589,398	17,852,718	6.67	267,736,680
End of year	150,280,521	(144,599,061)	−49.04	294,879,582	9,290,184	3.25	285,589,398

Note: Variances and percent changes are relative to the prior year.

deferred inflows of resources among the liabilities, because they are not amounts the government owes and will need resources to satisfy."[15]

Fundamentally, vertical analysis applies to the single time frame of the financial statement, namely, the fiscal year. However, also it is useful for timeline analysis to see relative changes in accounts over more than one time frame—that is, several fiscal years.

An example of vertical analysis of a public university's income statement is shown in table 7.14. The percentage of each item relative to the reference base of total revenue (operating plus nonoperating) is tabulated for three fiscal years. The percentages vary by only a small amount during this time frame, indicating stability. Year after year, the operating revenues and state appropriations constitute about 73 and 20 percent of total revenue, respectively. And the total operating expenses consume between 92 and 98 percent of the total revenue during this time frame. All in all, the analysis indicates a financially stable operating environment.

Vertical analysis of a balance sheet usually uses total assets as the reference base. Because total assets equals liabilities plus net position (or net assets for a private institution), this is comparable to using total liabilities plus net position as the base. And, indeed, this is a better way of thinking about vertical analysis of liability line items.

Vertical analysis of the balance sheet using total assets as the base is illustrated in table 7.15. Therefore, the percent changes for each line item are relative to liabilities plus net position; for example, in 2015, total net position ($150,280,521) is 33.99 percent of "total assets" ($442,159,913). Again, scanning the percent change columns, this analysis demonstrates financial stability with one glaring exception: a large decrease in "unrestricted" net position between 2014 and 2015. The unrestricted net position decreased from 33.37 and 34.96 percent of total assets in 2013 and 2014, respectively, to 0.57 percent of total assets in 2015 as money was transferred to cover pension liabilities. (*Accounting note:* Net position and liabilities are on the same side of the accounting equation, so this transfer does not unbalance the equation.) Clearly, in 2015, the pension liability has a major impact on the institution's total net position. Otherwise, however, the composition of the balance sheet indicates financial stability.

Ratio Analysis

Ratio analysis compares the amounts for one or more line items to the amounts for other line items in the same year. Stated differently, ratio analysis examines proportional relationships between various items in the financial statements. Unlike horizontal and vertical analyses, which examine proportional relationships between single line items relative to a standard reference bases, ratio analysis can use sums or differences between various line items in the numerator, the denominator, or both. And the items may come from more than one financial statement. Consequently, there are myriad possible ratios that could be calculated.

To avert a distracting information overload, the purpose of any ratio analysis must be clearly defined beforehand: What is the question needing an answer? From a business perspective, these questions are in three basic categories: *profitability*, the organization's ability to generate income; *liquidity*, the organization's ability to use current assets to repay liabilities as they come due; and *solvency*, the organization's ability to repay lenders when debt matures and to make the required interest payments prior to the date of maturity. Accordingly, ratios in these three categories have been translated into a university context.[16]

Seven commonly used examples, listed in table 7.16 along with their desirable target values, will be presented. *Note on convention:* Ratios may be expressed as decimal numbers or percentages. In the examples, they are expressed as percentages. However, there is no rule of thumb, and the two formats can be used interchangeably.

Profitability. Of course, nonprofit institutions are not concerned with profit per se. But they are concerned with generating sufficient revenue to finance operations. In the nonprofit context, profitability ratios are called more accurately *operating ratios*. Generally, operating ratios use data in the income statement to evaluate revenue generation.

The *net operating revenues ratio* indicates whether the university is generating sufficient income to operate within its available resources. Basically, it compares net operating revenue to total unrestricted revenue. In this context, net operating revenue includes operating income (loss) plus net nonoperating revenue for public universities and increase in unrestricted net assets from operating activities for private universities. Accordingly, for public universities:

$$\text{net operating revenues ratio} = \frac{\text{operating gain (loss)} + \text{net nonoperating revenue}}{\text{total operating revenues} + \text{total nonoperating revenues}}$$

Table 7.14. Vertical analysis of the income statement for FY 2013 to FY 2015

	2015	%	2014	%	2013	%
Operating revenues						
Tuition and fees	72,713,243	34.05	69,207,640	32.01	68,218,529	32.11
Student financial aid	(19,244,242)	−9.01	(18,612,696)	−8.61	(18,185,728)	−8.56
Net tuition and fees	53,469,001	25.04	50,594,944	23.40	50,032,801	23.55
Grants and contracts						
Federal	79,902,565	37.42	90,653,370	41.93	83,736,783	39.42
State	9,150,735	4.29	5,223,746	2.42	4,066,174	1.91
Private	1,976,343	0.93	2,074,302	0.96	1,855,859	0.87
Sales and services	3,678,370	1.72	3,530,514	1.63	3,451,345	1.62
Auxiliary	6,686,732	3.13	6,135,066	2.84	6,718,898	3.16
Total operating revenues	154,863,746	72.52	158,211,942	73.18	149,861,860	70.55
Operating expenses						
Salary and benefits	151,092,560	70.75	143,546,057	66.39	136,791,650	64.40
Supplies and services	43,670,230	20.45	50,498,859	23.36	46,177,109	21.74
Depreciation	13,058,315	6.11	12,416,766	5.74	12,171,441	5.73
Scholarships and fellowships	1,101,624	0.52	1,090,063	0.50	606,364	0.29
Total operating expenses	208,922,729	97.83	207,551,745	96.00	195,746,564	92.15
Operating gain (loss)	(54,058,983)	−25.31	(49,339,803)	−22.82	(45,884,704)	−21.60

Nonoperating revenues (expenses)						
State appropriations	43,102,39	20.18	42,710,964	19.75	43,240,587	20.36
Private gifts	6,175,489	2.89	4,043,840	1.87	6,025,163	2.84
Net investment income (loss)	6,926,302	3.24	6,334,687	2.93	9,083,393	4.28
Pell grant revenue	7,395,098	3.46	7,615,679	3.52	8,118,163	3.82
Loss on disposal of capital assets	(1,461,846)	−0.68	(276,840)	−0.13	(559,937)	−0.26
Interest expense	(3,454,765)	−1.62	(2,435,540)	−1.13	(3,345,280)	−1.57
Net before capital additions	58,682,668	27.48	57,992,790	26.82	62,562,089	29.45
Capital gifts	28,000		637,197		1,175,333	
Net nonoperating revenues	58,710,668		58,629,987		63,737,422	
Change in net position	4,651,685		9,290,184		17,852,718	
Net position						
Beginning of year	294,879,582		285,589,398			
Effect of new accounting guidance	(149,250,746)					
Beginning of year (as restated)	145,628,836		285,589,398		267,736,680	
End of year	150,280,521		294,879,582		285,589,398	

Note: Each item is expressed as a percentage of the total revenue (operating plus nonoperating) for that year.

Table 7.15. Vertical analysis of the balance sheet for FY 2013 to FY 2015

	2015	%	2014	%	2013	%
Assets						
Current assets						
Cash and cash equivalents	31,104,680	7.03	39,038,391	8.53	47,178,224	11.41
Operating investments	75,903,732	17.17	79,970,449	17.47	69,164,239	16.73
Accounts receivable, net	29,035,339	6.57	28,905,228	6.32	22,643,397	5.48
Other current assets	9,096,833	2.06	7,994,178	1.75	8,841,125	2.14
Total current assets	145,140,584	32.83	155,908,246	34.07	147,826,985	35.76
Noncurrent assets						
Restricted cash and cash equivalents	679,439	0.15	660,436	0.14	618,090	0.15
Endowment investments	30,699,638	6.94	27,595,094	6.03	25,386,159	6.14
Investments for capital activities	42,264,500	9.56	50,567,259	11.05	33,536,897	8.11
Capital assets, net	222,252,757	50.27	220,844,717	48.26	203,090,500	49.12
Legal settlement receivable	951,113	0.22	1,855,729	0.41	2,716,120	0.66
Other noncurrent assets	171,882	0.04	219,742	0.05	268,124	0.06
Total noncurrent assets	297,019,329	67.17	301,742,977	65.93	265,615,890	64.24
Total assets	442,159,913	100.00	457,651,223	100.00	413,442,875	100.00
Deferred outflows of resources						
Deferred outflows from pension	17,639,710	3.99				
Total deferred outflows	17,639,710	3.99				
Total assets and deferred outflows	459,799,623	103.99	457,651,223	100.00	413,442,875	100.00

Liabilities						
Current liabilities						
Accounts payable and accrued	23,214,476	5.25	18,565,766	4.06	18,353,188	4.44
Unearned revenues	28,689,929	6.49	28,444,114	6.22	24,824,073	6.00
Current portion of long-term debt	4,698,600	1.06	4,603,600	1.01	3,450,000	0.83
Deposits held for others	3,584,017	0.81	3,365,561	0.74	3,271,716	0.79
Total current liabilities	60,187,022	13.61	54,979,041	12.01	49,898,977	12.07
Noncurrent liabilities						
Long-term debt	103,084,078	23.31	107,792,600	23.55	77,954,500	18.85
Pension liability	135,283,004	30.60				
Total noncurrent liabilities	238,367,082	53.91	107,792,600	23.55	77,954,500	18.85
Total liabilities	298,554,104	67.52	162,771,641	35.57	127,853,477	30.92
Deferred inflows of resources						
Deferred inflows from pension	10,964,998	2.48				
Total deferred inflows	10,964,998	2.48				
Net position						
Net investment in capital assets	128,446,531	29.05	124,034,324	27.10	125,072,139	30.25
Restricted:						
Nonexpendable	9,368,566	2.12	9,055,754	1.98	7,598,871	1.84
Expendable	9,951,078	2.25	9,051,983	1.98	8,362,708	2.02
Unrestricted	2,514,346	0.57	152,737,521	33.37	144,555,680	34.96
Total net position	150,280,521	33.99	294,879,582	64.43	285,589,398	69.08
Total liabilities, deferred inflows of resources, and net position	459,799,623	103.99	457,651,223	100.00	413,442,875	100.00

Note: The percent changes are relative to total assets for each year.

Table 7.16. Ratios that analyze financial stability, along with their desirable target values

Ratio	Target values (%)
Profitability	
Net operating revenue	2 to 5
Net tuition and fees contribution	≤60
Liquidity	
Current	200
Quick (acid test)	≥100
Primary reserve	≥40
Solvency	
Viability	≥100
Debt burden	≤7

For private universities:

$$\textit{net operating revenues ratio} = \frac{\textit{increase in net assets from operating activities}}{\textit{total unrestricted operating revenue}}$$

Sample calculations based on income statement data in tables 7.3 and 7.4 are shown in table 7.17. An exception: As shown in Table 7.3, the past year's (2014) income data are not normally categorized according to restricted, temporarily restricted, or unrestricted in the current year's (2015) income statement. Therefore, the 2014 unrestricted revenues were obtained from the 2014 income statement, which is not shown.

For both universities, the ratios are positive. A positive ratio indicates that the institution had an operating surplus for the fiscal year. As a rule of thumb, the target ratio falls preferably within the 2 percent to 5 percent range, so these two universities meet this positive target.[17] Note, however, that consistently higher values are not necessarily desirable because they could mean that the institution is underspending on programs critical to its mission. Conversely, a negative ratio indicates a loss for the year. A pattern of large deficits can quickly force an institution to restructure its programs.

Contribution ratios are another useful type of operating ratios. They measure revenues by sources, indicating their relative contribution to university operations. In general, for both public and private institutions, the numerator may be any source of revenue, such as tuition and fees (net financial aid), grants and contracts, state appropriations, and so forth. The denominator is total expenses. So, to assess the institution's reliance on tuition and fees to meet its operating expenses, the *net tuition and fees contribution ratio* is calculated:

Table 7.17. Net operating revenues ratios for public and private universities

	2015	2014
	Public	
Operating gain (loss)	(54,058,983)	(49,339,803)
Net nonoperating revenue	58,682,668	57,992,790
Total net revenues	4,623,685	8,652,987
Total operating revenues	154,863,746	158,211,942
Total nonoperating revenues	63,599,279	60,705,170
Total revenues	218,463,025	218,917,112
Net operating revenues ratio	2.12%	3.95%
	Private	
Increase in unrestricted net assets from operating activities	4,349,841	3,282,237
Total unrestricted operating revenue	87,778,138	81,486,288
Net operating revenues ratio	4.96%	4.03%

Note: Nonoperating revenue excludes capital gifts.

Table 7.18. Net tuition and fees contribution ratio for public and private universities

	Public		Private	
	2015	2014	2015	2014
Net tuition and fees	53,469,001	50,594,944	48,954,931	44,672,461
Total expenses	208,922,729	207,551,745	83,428,296	78,204,051
Net tuition and fees contribution ratio	25.59%	24.38%	58.68%	57.12%

$$\text{net tuition and fees contribution ratio} = \frac{\text{net tuition and fees revenues}}{\text{total expenses}}$$

Sample calculations for both public and private universities, using data from tables 7.3 and 7.4, respectively, are shown in table 7.18. The public university depends on tuition and fees to pay for about 25 percent of its operating expenses. The private university is considerably more dependent on tuition and fees to cover its operating expenses; the ratio is about 59 percent. The higher the ratio, the more the institution depends on tuition and fees to meet its costs, implying that there are fewer other alternative sources of revenue. Particularly high ratios (greater than 60 percent) raise the need to keep an eye on admissions policies, including selectivity, acceptance rate, yield on acceptance, and retention rate, to ensure adequate enrollment to meet expenses.

High ratios also draw attention to the amount of financial aid as a source of forgone revenue. The ratios of financial aid to total tuition and fees in the examples (calculated from tables 7.3 and 7.4) are 26 and 28 percent for the public and private universities, respectively. In both cases, this is less than the national averages of 31 and 36 percent, respectively. Thus, from a competitive viewpoint, neither university could reduce the tuition discount percentage by much.

An ancillary ratio, the *net tuition dependency ratio*, measures net tuition and fees as a percentage of total unrestricted operating income. It differs from the net tuition and fees contribution ratio only in the denominator: income instead of expenses. But, with that difference, the institution can assess the diversity of its revenue. Clearly, a downward trend in the ratio is beneficial—but only if it occurs because of an increasing denominator.

Liquidity. Liquidity ratios are used to measure the financial strength and viability of an institution by focusing on balance sheet items. They answer an important question: Does the institution have sufficient cash to meet current operating requirements and unrestricted reserves to meet future operating and capital requirements? Stated differently, does it have the resources needed to realize its strategic objectives?

Two ratios used commonly in the business sector, the *current ratio* and the *quick ratio* (also known as the acid-test ratio), measure the ability to meet current operating requirements with existing liquid assets.

The *current ratio* simply compares all current assets to current liabilities:

$$current\ ratio = \frac{current\ assets}{current\ liabilities}$$

A high current ratio indicates sufficient assets to cover current liabilities. Auditors prefer a value of about 200 percent. The *quick ratio* is a more conservative measure of the ability to pay current liabilities. Its comparison of current assets to current liabilities ignores current assets such as inventories and prepaid expenses because these items cannot be converted to cash quickly:

$$quick\ ratio = \frac{cash + current\ investments + accounts\ receivable}{current\ liabilities}$$

As a rule of thumb among auditors, the quick ratio should exceed 100 percent, indicating that the university has more readily avail-

Table 7.19. Current and quick (acid-test) ratios for public and private universities

	Public		Private	
	2015	2014	2015	2014
	Current ratio			
Current assets	145,140,584	155,908,246	61,449,519	61,365,247
Current liabilities	60,187,022	54,979,041	22,431,336	23,452,330
Current ratio	241.15%	283.58%	273.94%	261.66%
	Quick ratio			
Cash	31,104,680	39,038,391	13,036,353	14,017,939
Current investments	75,903,732	79,970,449	14,991,289	14,159,750
Accounts receivable	29,035,339	28,905,228	1,262,503	1,064,133
Total "quick assets"	136,043,751	147,914,068	29,290,144	29,241,822
Current liabilities	60,187,022	54,979,041	22,431,336	23,452,330
Quick ratio	226.04%	269.04%	130.58%	124.69%

able cash than liabilities. However, university administrators beware: a high ratio is not always good. It could indicate that cash is accumulating and sitting idly rather than being put to productive use. (This is a common source of tension between faculty members and the CFO.) Of course, this excess is better than the alternative (not enough cash), but it doesn't necessarily move the institution forward.

Examples of both ratios for the public and private universities are shown in table 7.19, which is based on balance sheet data in tables 7.1 and 7.2. Both universities exhibit ratios greater than the target values for these two tests. By inference, they are quite capable of meeting their immediate liabilities.

A third ratio, the *primary reserve ratio,* indicates how long the institution could function using its expendable reserves without relying on additional net assets generated by operations. Thus, it provides additional information about the institution's ability to meet its financial obligations. The primary reserve ratio compares expendable net assets to total expenses:

$$primary\ reserve\ ratio = \frac{expendable\ net\ assets}{total\ expenses}$$

The numerator includes all unrestricted and temporarily restricted or expendable restricted net assets for private and public institutions, respectively. In both cases, any net assets to be invested in the physical plant and any investment losses must be excluded from the numerator.

The general target for a primary reserve ratio is about 40 percent or higher. With a ratio of 40 percent, the institution can cover about 5 months (40 percent of 12 months) of expenses from reserves. As Lou Mezzina et al. point out, institutions operating at this ratio level have "the flexibility to transform the enterprise"; they rely on internal cash flow to meet short-term cash needs, can carry on a reasonable level of facilities maintenance, and appear capable of managing modest unforeseen adverse financial events.[18] Reserve funds are often needed for capital expansion, implementation of a major initiative, or, as in the public university example, a newly imposed pension liability, resulting in a temporary decline in the primary reserve ratio. Mezzina et al. note further that a ratio below 10 to 15 indicates that the institution's expendable net asset balances are in a position that generally requires short-term borrowing on a regular basis, since resources cover only one to two months of expenses, and that the institution tends to struggle to have sufficient resources for reinvestment. In addition, institutions with a low primary reserve ratio generally lack sufficient resources for strategic initiatives and may have less operating flexibility.

Primary reserve ratio calculations for the private and public universities are illustrated in table 7.20. Data came from their financial statements (tables 7.1, 7.2, 7.3, and 7.4). The bigger the ratio, the more financial flexibility an institution has. The private university's high ratios derive primarily from its low total expenses, its smaller denominator. The public university's negative primary reserve ratio in 2015 can be attributed to the inclusion of pension liability in its balance sheet, which depressed its unrestricted net assets and, therefore, its expendable net assets. Even so, the ratio was low (18 percent) in the preceding year. Thus, despite its favorable current and quick ratios, the primary reserve ratio paints a much less rosy picture of the public university's financial position.

Table 7.20. Primary reserve ratio for public and private universities

	Public		Private	
	2015	2014	2015	2014
Expendable net assets				
Expendable restricted net assets	9,951,078	9,051,983		
Unrestricted net assets	2,514,346	152,737,521	196,516,091	184,177,891
Net investment in plant	(128,446,531)	(124,034,324)	(137,033,214)	(120,264,146)
Total expendable net assets	(115,981,107)	37,755,180	59,482,878	63,913,745
Total expenses	208,922,729	207,551,745	83,428,296	78,204,051
Primary reserve ratio	−55.51%	18.19%	71.30%	81.73%

Importantly, however, the public university's low primary reserve ratios must be interpreted in its context as a government agency. Some states limit the amount of expendable net assets that public universities can accumulate, thus keeping the ratio low. Moreover, some states may exert tight control over the public universities' flexibility in financing large capital projects or major initiatives, thus reducing the rationale for a large primary reserve ratio. Private universities seldom have constraints such as these.

Solvency. Solvency refers to the ability to repay debt incurred to finance major projects, such as the construction of a new building or the purchase and installation of major equipment. Universities usually borrow money by issuing revenue bonds or, less often, taking out long-term loans. Naturally, this money must be repaid, with interest. Therefore, it becomes imperative to ensure adequate resources for repayment of debt when it comes due.

The *viability ratio* measures the availability of expendable net assets to cover debt on the balance sheet date. It compares expendable net assets to long-term debt:

$$viability\ ratio = \frac{expendable\ net\ assets}{long\text{-}term\ debt}$$

Long-term debt includes both the current and long-term portions but excludes short-term debt and bank-credit lines.

Sample calculations of the viability ratio are shown in table 7.21. Again, the 2015 pension liability depressed the public university's unrestricted net assets and, therefore, the viability ratio. Indeed, with a negative ratio, the university could not meet its debt obligation

Table 7.21. Viability ratio for public and private universities

	Public		Private	
	2015	2014	2015	2014
Expendable net assets:				
Expendable restricted net assets	9,951,078	9,051,983		
Unrestricted net assets	2,514,346	152,737,521	196,516,091	184,177,891
Net investment in plant	(128,446,531)	(124,034,324)	(137,033,214)	(120,264,146)
Total expendable net assets	(115,981,107)	37,755,180	59,482,878	63,913,745
Long-term debt:				
Current portion of long-term debt	4,698,600	4,603,600		
Long-term debt	103,084,078	107,792,600	60,724,626	62,150,579
Total long-term debt	107,782,678	112,396,200	60,724,626	62,150,579
Viability ratio	−107.61%	33.59%	97.96%	102.84%

with ready assets on the date of the balance statement. In contrast, with its larger positive ratios, the private university had more expendable assets to meet its obligation.

Ideally, the target viability ratio value is 100 percent, meaning that the expendable net assets equal long-term debt. Fortunately, all long-term debts seldom come due at the same time, which mitigates the real financial threat posed by a viability ratio less than 100 percent. The private university's ratios are close to this target value, so it has sufficient expendable assets to meet its obligations, albeit barely. Furthermore, many public institutions can operate effectively at a ratio considerably less than 100 percent because the financial benefit of state appropriations is not included in their expendable net assets. As Mezzina et al. note: "institutions often show a remarkable resiliency that permits them to continue long beyond what appears to be their point of financial collapse. In fact, institutions have been known to survive for a time with high debt levels and no expendable net assets, or even negative net asset balances. Frequently, this means living with no margin for error and meeting severe cash flow needs by obtaining short-term loans."[19] In the long run, a ratio less than 100 percent is not good, for it compromises an institution's ability to fulfill its mission.

A related ratio, the *debt burden ratio*, measures the institution's dependence on debt to finance its mission. It compares the current debt service with the total expenditures:

$$debt\ burden\ ratio = \frac{debt\ service}{adjusted\ expenses}$$

The debt service includes interest paid plus the current year's principal payments, which are presented in the statement of cash flows. The adjusted expenses are total expenses (operating and nonoperating) obtained from the income statement, minus depreciation expense, plus debt service principal payments.

The debt burden ratios for the public and private institutions are shown in table 7.22. The public university has a considerably lower debt burden ratio than the private university; its debt relative to adjusted expenses is less. This could be due in part to state support in financing capital acquisitions, such as buildings, or a governing board's lower tolerance for debt, or any of a number of other reasons. Also, it may reflect an institutional prioritization of financial aid or new academic programs over capital projects. Regardless of the root explanation, the lower debt burden ratio is advantageous because debt service payments come out of the op-

Table 7.22. Debt burden ratio for public and private universities

	Public		Private	
	2015	2014	2015	2014
Debt service				
Interest expense	3,969,323	3,407,068	3,690,561	2,643,513
Principal payments	4,603,600	3,450,000	1,427,289	1,335,800
Total debt service	8,572,923	6,857,068	5,117,850	3,979,313
Adjusted expenses				
Total operating expenses	208,922,729	207,551,745		
Total nonoperating expenses	4,916,611	2,712,380		
Total expenses	213,839,340	210,264,125	83,428,296	78,204,051
Depreciation expense	(13,058,315)	(12,416,766)	(5,856,198)	(4,832,731)
Principal payments	4,603,600	3,450,000	1,427,289	1,335,800
Adjusted expenses	205,384,625	201,297,359	78,999,388	74,707,120
Debt burden ratio	4.17%	3.41%	6.48%	5.33%

erating budget, thus reducing the institution's flexibility in achieving its goals. For both institutions, the ratio increased between 2014 and 2015. These increases can be acceptable for a short period of time—three or four years. However, a prolonged rising trend usually signifies an increasing demand on financial resources to repay debt.

As a rule of thumb, the upper threshold for this ratio is 7 percent.[20] That is, principal and interest payments should not exceed 7 percent of total expenditures. An institution may be tempted to undertake a higher debt burden if it finds that borrowing money through tax-exempt bond offerings is more beneficial than spending unrestricted net assets that might earn higher revenues through investments. However, with a high debt burden ratio, the institution may find it difficult to borrow additional money as agencies and lenders look at the overall financial condition with greater scrutiny. Also, an institution with great budget flexibility may be tempted to undertake a higher debt burden because it can allocate more money for debt payment than an institution with a tightly committed budget, such as an institution with a considerably restricted research budget.

Ultimately, debt is a limited resource that must be managed strategically in order to support the university's priorities in the best way possible. On the one hand, the use of debt plays a critical role in ensuring adequate and cost-effective funding for capital improvements. But, on the other hand, it reduces the amount of money available for other strategic priorities.

Summary

At least annually, universities issue financial reports. Unlike budgets, which are based on revenue and expenditure projections, financial reports are based on actual revenue and expenditure data. Looking backward, they summarize the organization's financial status in three key documents, the financial statements: the balance sheet, the income statement, and the statement of cash flows. Financial reports open with a summary of the financial statements, known as the "management discussion and analysis," which highlights noteworthy elements of the financial statements in the context of the institution's mission and strategic goals. The balance sheet, also referred to as the statement of financial position or the statement of net position, provides information about the institution's worth at a specific point in time, generally the last day of the fiscal year. The income statement, also called the statement of activities and the statement of revenues, expenses, and changes in net position, illustrates the financial viability of an organization by providing information that explains how assets, liabilities, and net assets change during a fiscal year. Unlike the balance sheet, which focuses on assets and liabilities, the income statement focuses on revenues and expenses and how they affect net assets. The statement of cash flows provides information about an institution's cash receipts and payments during a fiscal year. It highlights the net increase and decrease in total cash on hand for the accounting period, indicating actual cash received or spent. Information presented in the financial statements is amplified in footnotes that make it much easier to understand specific aspects of the financial statements. Data in the financial statements can be analyzed over time or relative to a reference base such as total assets or total revenue to evaluate an institution's past, current, and projected performance. Common ratio analyses measure the institution's profitability, liquidity, and solvency.

Notes

1. Financial Accounting Standards Board, "Project Update: Financial Statements of Not-for-Profit Entities," http://www.fasb.org/jsp/FASB/Document_C/DocumentPage?cid=1176168381847&acceptedDisclaimer=true (accessed June 15, 2016); Governmental Accounting Standards Board, "Statement No. 34: Basic Financial Statements—and Management's Discussion and Analysis—for State and Local Governments" (1999), https://www.google.com/search?q=gasb+statement+34&ie=utf-8&oe=utf-8 (accessed January 27, 2016).

2. Larry Goldstein and Sue Menditto, "GASB and FASB," *Business Officer*, January (2005), http://www.nacubo.org/Business_Officer_Magazine/Magazine_Archives/January_2005/GASB_and_FASB.html (accessed January 27, 2016).

3. Nicola Sargeant, "What Is the Difference between a Compiled and a Certified Financial Statement?" Investopedia, http://www.investopedia.com/ask/answers/06/compiledandcertifiedfinancialstatements.asp#ixzz4BZW73Dtl (accessed June 16, 2016).

4. Financial Accounting Standards Board, "Not-for Profit Entities (Topic 958): Presentation of Financial Statements of Not-for-Profit Entities," *FASB accounting standards update No. 2016-14* (2016), http://www.fasb.org/jsp/FASB/Document_C/DocumentPage?cid=1176168381847&acceptedDisclaimer=true (accessed November 27, 2017).

5. "Statement of Financial Accounting Standards No. 158: Employers' Accounting for Defined Benefit Pension and Other Postretirement Plans," http://www.fasb.org/jsp/FASB/Document_C/DocumentPage?cid=1218220125471&acceptedDisclaimer=true (accessed July 20, 2016).

6. Governmental Accounting Standards Board, "Statement No. 68: Accounting and Financial Reporting for Pensions—an Amendment of GASB Statement No. 27," http://www.gasb.org/jsp/GASB/Pronouncement_C/GASBSummaryPage&cid=1176160219492 (accessed July 20, 2016).

7. Governmental Accounting Standards Board, "Statement No. 68."

8. Stanford University, "Budget Plan 2015/2016," https://web.stanford.edu/dept/pres-provost/budget/plans/plan16.html (accessed September 28, 2016), 36–38.

9. Financial Accounting Standards Board, "Notes to Financial Statements," http://www.fasb.org/jsp/FASB/Document_C/DocumentPage?cid=1176163868268&acceptedDisclaimer=true (accessed August 11, 2016); Governmental Accounting Standards Board, "Touring the Financial Statements, Part IV: Note Disclosures," http://gasb.org/cs/ContentServer?c=GASBContent_C&pagename=GASB%2FGASBContent_C%2FUsersArticlePage&cid=1176156722430 (accessed August 11, 2016).

10. State of Texas, "Notes to the Financial Statements," https://fmx.cpa.texas.gov/fmx/pubs/afrrptreq/notes/index.php?menu=1 (accessed May 8, 2017).

11. Financial Accounting Standards Board, "Not-for Profit Entities (Topic 958): Presentation of Financial Statements of Not-for-Profit Entities."

12. "Statement of Financial Accounting Standards No. 157, Fair Value Measurements, Fair Value Hierarchy § 22." (2006), www.fasb.org/pdf/aop_FAS157.pdf (accessed January 23, 2018); Governmental Accounting Standards Board, "Statement No. 72, Fair Value Measurement and Application, Fair Value Hierarchy § 32." (2015), http://gasb.org/cs/ContentServer?c=Document_C&cid=1176165840291&d=&pagename=GASB%2FDocument_C%2FGASBDocumentPage (accessed January 23, 2018).

13. Oxford University Press, "Oxford Dictionaries," http://www.oxforddictionaries.com/?gclid=CMa5maK2p8kCFU1cfgodiXoNoA (accessed November 23, 2015).

14. Commonfund Institute, "Higher Education Price Index," https://www.commonfund.org/commonfund-institute/higher-education-price-index-hepi/ (accessed August 30, 2016).

15. Governmental Accounting Standards Board, "The User's Perpsective: A Plain-English Guide to Deferrals," http://gasb.org/cs/ContentServer?c=GASBContent_C&pagename=GASB%2FGASBContent_C%2FUsersArticlePage&cid=1176163674320 (accessed September 15, 2016).

    16. Lou Mezzina et al., *Strategic Financial Analysis for Higher Education: Identifying, Measuring and Reporting Financial Risks*, 7th ed. (San Francisco: Prager, Sealy and Co., LLC, 2010); University of California Los Angeles, "Thinking Strategically About University of California Finances," http://www.senate.ucla.edu/documents/2014Budget101ThinkingStrategically-Session3.pdf (accessed October 3, 2016).
    17. Mezzina et al., *Strategic Financial Analysis for Higher Education*.
    18. Mezzina et al., *Strategic Financial Analysis for Higher Education*.
    19. Mezzina et al., *Strategic Financial Analysis for Higher Education*
    20. Mezzina et al., *Strategic Financial Analysis for Higher Education*

Chapter 8
Grants and Contracts

Sponsored Research

Research costs money. In academe, this research money comes from sources either within the institution or external to the institution, such as federal and state governments, industry, and nonprofit foundations. Depending on the source of support, research is called university research or sponsored research, respectively. Together, they comprise organized research.

Sponsored research: What does that mean? When external sources pay for research, basic and applied, they "sponsor" the research by awarding the institution a grant or a contract. Research supported in this way is called sponsored research, and it is administered by the university's office of sponsored projects. In the *Uniform Guidance*, the federal government expands the definition of sponsored research to include "activities involving the training of individuals in research techniques (commonly called research training) where such activities utilize the same facilities as other research and development activities and where such activities are not included in the instruction function."[1] Notably, this expanded definition limits sponsored training to training in research techniques.

The *Uniform Guidance* uses other terms for more general nonresearch sponsored activities. It defines "sponsored instruction and training" as "specific instructional or training activity established by grant, contract, or cooperative agreement." For example, the federal government may sponsor a workshop on methods of controlling the spread of measles. In addition, the *Uniform Guidance* defines "other sponsored activities" as "programs and projects financed by Federal and non-Federal agencies and organizations which involve the performance of work other than instruction and organized research." Examples include health service projects and community service programs. However, when any of these activities are undertaken by the institution without outside support, they are classified as "other institutional activities."

Because the federal government funds the majority of sponsored research in universities, this chapter concentrates on federal grants and contracts. However, the underlying principles pertain to most nonfederal sponsoring agencies as well.

Legal Differences between Grants and Contracts

Although both grants and contracts provide money to support research, there are fundamental legal and accounting differences between the two award types.[2] And these differences have profound financial and administrative implications for the university.

A contract is a legally binding procurement relationship between the sponsor and the recipient. The results (service or product) of a contract benefit the contracting agency (the sponsor). The contract obligates the principal investigator to furnish a project outcome or service that is defined in detail in the written contract, and it binds the sponsor to pay for it. In contract jargon, the outcome—a service or a product—is known as "consideration." Thus, the sponsoring agency receives some form of consideration for its investment; the nature of this consideration (for example, a nozzle design, a computer-code encryption algorithm, a training workshop, and so forth) is documented in the written contract. Importantly, any changes in the consideration (such as the sponsor's desire for a modified nozzle design, an additional algorithm, or an additional workshop session) require a formal amendment to the contract. A contractual agreement is enforceable by law; the contractor may recover damages if the recipient (the university) fails to deliver the promised service or product.

Likewise, a grant is awarded to accomplish a specific goal. In the federal government's terms, "a grant is a form of assistance to a designated class of recipients authorized by statute to meet recognized needs, usually listed as 'specific aims' in the grant proposal. However, unlike contracts, grant needs—the consideration—are not needs for goods or services required by the federal government itself. The needs are those of a nonfederal entity, whether public or private, which the Congress has decided to assist as being in the public interest."[3] The usual purpose of a grant is to enhance knowledge about a topic or to provide services or training for the recipient's or public's benefit. Furthermore, unlike a contract, the outcome is usually not tangible consideration. The outcome generally consists of an annual report to the granting agency that documents progress toward achieving the specific aims. This report includes publications, patents, and copyrights arising from the research. In addition, the university provides the granting agency with periodic reports on how the grant money was spent.

Responsibility for the performance of the grant's project rests primarily with the principal investigator, with little or no involvement of the granting agency. If a federal-granting agency, such as the National Institutes of Health (NIH) or the National Science Foundation (NSF), intends to play a significant role in a grant's programmatic activities, the grant award is redefined as a cooperative agreement. Despite the redefinition, it is still administered as a grant.

For government agencies, grants provide greater funding flexibility than contracts. The amount of an award may be increased without additional consideration in the case of grants but not contracts. This might occur if a grant were awarded initially for less than the permissible ceiling (approved by a review panel or statute) because of limited funds. However, the agency may want to increase an award via a revised budget or administrative supplement in subsequent years when more funds become available. The Government Accountability Office (GAO) allows the agency to increase a grant award without additional consideration. In contrast, the agency cannot increase a contract award unless the government receives additional consideration, namely, a service or a product needed by the government. In the words of the GAO, "statutory authority exists for the payment of [grant] funds without consideration other than the benefits to accrue to the public and the United States."[4]

Interestingly, the GAO has ruled that a grantee may assign future grant proceeds to a bank in return for an interim loan, just as payments receivable under a contract may be assigned to a bank as collateral for a loan.[5] Consequently, a university can use future grant proceeds as security for a bank loan to alleviate cash-flow difficulties in the fulfillment of the grant's conditions. From a legal perspective, this is logical because the courts interpret the rights and obligations of the grant recipient in terms of contract law. Accordingly, the acceptance of a grant with conditions that must be met (for example, reports and so forth) creates a contract between the federal government and a grantee.[6] In the US Supreme Court's words, "federal grants create binding contracts between the United States and the recipient."[7] Thus, the federal government may sue a university to enforce compliance with grant conditions, just as if there were a written contract.

Subcontracts

A grant or contract may include a provision to hire an individual or business not affiliated with the university to perform part or all of the grant or contract's obligations. This provision is called a subaward (or subcontract). The grant or contract recipient, that is, the university, is called the primary contractor, and the hired individual or business is called a subrecipient, subawardee, or subcontractor (they all mean the same thing). In this context, federal jargon calls the university a pass-through entity: "pass-through entity means a non-Federal entity [the university] that provides a subaward to a subrecipient to carry out part of a Federal program [the federal grant or contract]."[8] Accordingly, the grant or contract budget provides funds to pay the subrecipient for its services, including both direct and indirect costs. And the university passes these funds through to the subrecipient.

Most commonly, subcontracts are on a cost-reimbursable basis. In these cases, the subcontractor submits invoices to the primary contractor, the university, after work is performed according to terms and schedules documented in the subcontract.

Less commonly, subcontracts pay a fixed amount, not exceeding $150,000, without regard to the actual costs incurred by the subrecipient. The OMB recommends that historic information about the work to be performed should be used as a guide when proposing and fixing the price of the work that will be performed. Once the price is established and the fixed-amount subaward is issued, payments are based on achievement of milestones (for example, per patient, per procedure, per assay, or per milestone) and not on the actual costs incurred. If the subrecipient can complete the work at less than the fixed price, it keeps the savings, and vice versa. However, this is not a "blank check" for the subrecipient, who remains accountable to the primary contractor for performance and results. At the end of the award, the university must certify to the federal government "that the [subaward] project or activity was completed or the level of effort was expended. If the required level of activity or effort was not carried out, the amount of the Federal award must be adjusted."[9]

On government projects, the subcontracting agreement is solely between the primary contractor (the university) and the subrecipient. In other words, the government has no direct contractual relationship with the subrecipient. Legally, this is called privity of contract. Therefore, all activities associated with subcontracts must go through the primary contractor. It follows that the use of a subcontractor does not allow the university a means of getting around any requirements of the grant or contract. Regardless of the existence of a subcontract, the primary contractor remains fully responsible for compliance with all federal regulations and full performance of all the duties and obligations under the original grant or contract.

The subcontract contains provisions to protect both the prime contractor and the subcontractor. In general, the subcontract binds the subrecipient to the same contractual requirements as the primary contractor. This provision is documented in so-called flow-down clauses that specify the contractual obligations, often using nearly the same wording used in the original grant or contract with the awarding agency. In the extreme, the entire prime contract is used for the subcontractor. These "blanket flow-down clauses" should be avoided, for they could obligate the subcontractor to fulfill requirements that don't apply to its work. And the granting agency may have certain rights with the respect to the prime contractor (such as the right to terminate the contract or to receive proprietary information) that the prime shouldn't share with the subcontractor. At minimum, as a matter of good business, well-written subcontract flow-down clauses should protect both the prime and the subcontractor in some way.

Federal Cost Principles

Federal grant and contract awards must adhere to administrative guidelines presented in the "*Uniform Guidance.*"[10] In this context, the guidelines for spending award money are called cost principles. Restated, universities must use the same cost principles in the *Uniform Guidance* for both grants and contracts.[11] On top of the *Uniform Guidance*, most contracts (but not grants) are subject to additional administrative stipulations of the Federal Acquisitions Regulation (FAR), which applies primarily to procurement.[12] Thus, when administering contracts, the institution must adhere to the cost principles and audit requirements stipulated in the *Uniform Guidance*, as well as all other acquisition-related matters governed by the FAR. Furthermore, any institution receiving a government-funded subcontract also must comply with these cost principles. *Caveat:* These cost principles do not apply to scholarships, fellowships, traineeships, other fixed amounts, and fixed-amount awards.

The *Uniform Guidance* cost principles address three major aspects of federal grant and contract administration:

- definition of direct and indirect costs
- allowability of costs
- allocation to specific cost pools

Adherence to these cost principles is fundamentally important for proper accounting of grants and contracts. Therefore, a primary responsibility of a university's office of sponsored projects is to ensure that all costs charged to the sponsored research award comply with these guidelines.

Modified Total Direct Costs

The federal cost principles define direct and indirect costs conventionally, as in chapter 4. Recapitulating those definitions in the context of grants and contracts, direct costs are expenses specifically incurred to achieve a contract's or grant's objectives. In the words of the *Uniform Guidance*, "Direct costs are those costs that can be identified specifically with a particular final cost objective, such as a Federal award, or other internally or externally funded activity, or that can be directly assigned to such activities relatively easily with a high degree of accuracy."[13] And indirect costs are expenses incurred by the institution on behalf of more than one specific project—or, in accounting terms, more than one specific cost objective. According to the OMB, they are "incurred for a common or joint purpose benefitting more than one cost objective, and not readily assignable to the cost objectives specifically benefitted, without effort disproportionate to the results achieved."[14]

The federal cost principles introduce an additional definition: modified total direct costs (MTDC). This definition arises because some direct-cost items don't benefit significantly from indirect-cost activities and services. Therefore, they are excluded from the direct costs in some federal cost accounting procedures. These exclusions *modify* the direct costs, thus creating the so-called *modified total direct costs*. In this context, the main exclusions are costs for:

- tuition remission
- student financial aid, including scholarships and fellowships
- patient care
- subcontracts in excess of $25,000
- equipment items costing more than $5,000 (capital equipment)
- capital expenditures

The rationale for these exclusions is fairly straightforward. Tuition remission, scholarships and fellowships, stipends, and dependent allowances to university students or postdoctoral scholars are not coupled directly to specific university activities and do not rely heavily on the overall infrastructure. Thus, they are excluded from the MTDC. In contrast to these financial-aid stipends, fellowships that pay salaries and wages or honoraria are not excluded. Furthermore, subcontracts, equipment purchases, and capital expenditures (such as constructing a building) can involve large expenditures, but they do not necessarily take advantage of a university's indirect services. So, they are also excluded from the MTDC. As will be shown in chapter 9, the MTDC plays a pivotal role when allocating indirect costs.

Allowability

All costs, direct and indirect, charged against a specific government-sponsored contract or grant must be allowable under federal guidelines. Restated, costs can be paid using federal funds only if they are allowed according to the *Uniform Guidance*. Conversely, unallowable costs cannot be paid using federal funds. Consequently, if a university erringly pays an unallowable cost with federal funds, it must refund that money to the funding agency.

To be allowable, costs charged to a federal sponsored research award must be necessary and reasonable for the performance of the award. That means that they must be required to perform the proposed work and that they must make sense. For example, a bottle of sodium chloride is a necessary and reasonable expense in a molecular biology project; in contrast, a pair of binoculars would seem unnecessary and hardly reasonable. In the context of a particular award, a cost's necessity and reasonableness must be able to withstand public scrutiny. Accordingly, objective individuals not affiliated with the institution would agree that costs are appropriate for a sponsored research award. Furthermore, allowability must conform to any federal limitations or exclusions on the types or amounts of cost items.

Apropos federal limitations and exclusions, the *Uniform Guidance* has an extensive list of what is and is not allowable. Stated simply, federal funds cannot be used to pay for certain expenses. Starting at the top, the long list of specific unallowable costs includes:

- advertising
- alcoholic beverages

- bad debt expenses
- donations
- entertainment
- fines and penalties
- fund-raising
- lobbying

As mentioned, any funds spent on an unallowable item (such as liquor) must be paid back to the funding agency. Consequently, if the item cannot be returned to the vendor for a full refund, its cost must be paid by some other fund where it is an allowable cost. This can cause difficulties if the investigator and the department don't have other sources of unrestricted money to cover this obligation. At that point, the dean and perhaps the chief research officer may be asked for help. As discussed in *Managing the Research University*, "in those cases, the chief research officer may lend the money with a pre-arranged payback agreement (over three years, for example). However, he or she seldom gives the money outright; that would be bad policy, for it rewards mismanagement."[15] At worst, the individual who authorized the unallowable expenditure may be personally liable for the cost; in agency-law terms, as a fraudulent agent of the university, that individual is liable for the expense.[16]

To be allowable, a cost must also be allocable. That means that the cost was incurred solely to support or advance the work of a specific sponsored research award. In the words of the federal government: "A cost is allocable to a particular Federal award or other cost objective if the goods or services involved are chargeable or assignable to that Federal award or cost objective in accordance with relative benefits received." To meet the test of allocability, costs must be identified specifically with a sponsored project with a high degree of accuracy. In different terms, allocability means that the cost benefited some defined activity of the research project; it wasn't just a capricious expense. For example, the cost of a pair of binoculars for bird watching could not be allocated to a molecular biology project. The cost would not be allocable and, therefore, not allowable for the molecular biology grant.

So, in the eyes of a prudent person, the expenditures must be necessary (reasonable) to conduct a specific project (allocable) and in compliance with university, sponsor, and federal guidelines (allowable). University accountants evaluate each financial transaction charged to a sponsored research award against these three concepts to ascertain its legitimacy. Although the *Uniform Guidance* elaborates on these cost principles, the US Department of Health and Human Services (DHHS) advises that "if there is any question concerning the allowability of a charge, the PI [principal investigator] and/or department administrator should consult the sponsored programs office. Once the charge has been made, then appropriate documentation must be maintained so as to justify the allocability of the expense."[17]

Allowability also requires institutional accounting consistency. If an institution designates an expense as a direct cost on one federal award, *ceteris paribus* it must designate that same expense as a direct cost on all other federal awards. In other words, expenses incurred for the same purpose in the same circumstances must be treated consistently as either direct or indirect costs. The *Uniform Guidance* states this more emphatically: "it is essential that each item of cost incurred for the same purpose be treated consistently in like circumstances either as a direct or an indirect (F&A) cost in order to avoid possible double-charging of Federal awards."[18] Furthermore, institutional policies in this matter must be the same for both federal and nonfederal sponsors, and they must be followed consistently.

Allocation to Specific Cost Pools

The third major aspect of federal cost principles involves allocation of direct and indirect costs into various categories called cost pools.

For direct costs, this is fairly straightforward; they are assigned to specific cost objectives. Each major cost objective is a cost pool. Within academic institutions, the three primary cost-objective pools are instruction, research, and public service. Some universities may have additional cost objectives, such as a hospital, major research facility, or extensive nonsponsored research program.

The *Uniform Guidance* defines a university's primary cost objectives a bit differently, referring to them as the institution's four major functions:

- instruction
- organized research
- other sponsored activities
- other institutional activities

Other sponsored activities include items such as health service projects and community service programs. Other institutional activities are generally auxiliary enterprises, such as "residence halls, dining halls, hospitals and clinics, student unions, intercollegiate athletics, bookstores, faculty housing, student apartments, guest houses, chapels, theaters, public museums, and other similar auxiliary enterprises." Regardless of how the major cost objectives are defined, all direct costs must be assigned to one of these cost-objective pools.

For indirect costs, the allocation process is much more demanding from an accounting perspective. Consequently, indirect cost allocations will be considered in a separate chapter (chapter 9).

Effort and Salary

In general at most universities, any personnel working on a sponsored project are expected to generate salary support for this work from the grant or contract. This support must be commensurate to the individual's effort on the project. So, faculty members that spend 20 percent of their full-time work effort on a particular project are expected to generate 20 percent of their salary (plus fringe benefits) from a grant supporting that project.

Ideally, the percentages of effort and salary support should be equal. Why? Charging more salary than effort to the grant constitutes theft; the university (the grantee) is taking unearned salary from the federal government. For example, if the university claims 15 percent effort but 20 percent salary for a researcher on a project, then, in the eyes of the federal government, the university is taking the extra 5 percent salary without giving anything in return. This kind of mismatch between effort and salary has resulted in serious legal difficulties and costly (in the millions of dollars) penalties for several prominent research universities.[19] Conversely, charging less salary than effort to the grant constitutes cost sharing by the university. For example, if the researcher claims 20 percent effort on the project but only 15 percent salary, some source other than the sponsor (usually the university) must be paying voluntarily the extra 5 percent salary to cover the effort. Voluntary cost sharing is bad policy, and most universities will not willingly cost-share on a federal grant. ("Why spend the money if you don't have to?") Furthermore, the NSF prohibits voluntary cost sharing for most of its grant programs.

Because effort and salary should be matched, charging a researcher's full salary to federal grants and contracts carries some risk.[20] If 100 percent effort is charged to sponsored projects, no time is left for advising students or even writing grant proposals. So, for example, to remain compliant with federal guidelines, writing a renewal grant proposal must be done on the researcher's own time, not during working hours. Of course, this is not a popular option. Fortunately, the *Uniform Guidance* allows some leeway in this regard: "It is recognized that teaching, research, service, and administration are often inextricably intermingled in an academic setting. When recording salaries and wages charged to Federal awards for IHEs [institutions of higher education], a precise assessment of factors that contribute to costs is therefore not always feasible, nor is it expected."[21] Nonetheless, to allow time for activities not associated with sponsored projects, some universities limit salary support from grants and contracts for senior personnel to less than 100 percent. For example, a university may not allow principal and co-principal investigators to charge more than 90 percent of their salary and effort to external sources. In return, the university agrees to pay the remaining 10 percent from some nonfederal source, which may include reimbursed indirect costs.

Expanded Authority

Technically, the federal granting agencies (the NIH, the NSF, etc.) require grant awardees (that is, the universities) to obtain prior approval for any significant modifications in the terms of the award spelled out in the official notice of grant award. These terms include the scope of work, the duration of the award, and, most importantly, the budget. Significant modification of an award's budget (rebudgeting) constitutes a change of scope, which requires prior agency approval. According to the NIH, significant rebudgeting occurs when expenditures in a single direct cost budget category change by an amount more than 25 percent of the total costs awarded.[22] For example, if the award budget for total costs is $200,000, any rebudgeting that exceeds $50,000 in a budget category (for example, salary) is considered significant rebudgeting. Other agencies' policies are more or less similar.

When any of these situations occurs, the principal investigator must inform the federal agency program director seeking approval for the change of scope. Because the grant is awarded to the institution, the sponsored projects office must co-sign the written request.

However, most federal agencies amended this prior-approval requirement for many grant types by giving so-called expanded authority to institutions.[23] Expanded authority waives the normally required sponsor prior approval for specific actions. For example, a researcher may wish to extend the time allotted for performing the work without requesting any additional funds (a "no-cost extension").

Technically, prior approval of the funding agency is required for this action, but under expanded authority, it can be done without this explicit approval. The institution simply has to request this expanded authority, and it will be granted if the institution agrees to abide by the spirit of federal grant management guidelines. Most eligible institutions readily agree to abide by this spirit because expanded authority is a boon to researchers. It greatly simplifies and speeds up administration of an award.

Each agency has a list of specific actions affected by expanded authority. Although they vary, the lists cover mostly the same actions. The NIH, for example, waives prior approval requirements for the following actions:

- incurring award costs up to 90 days prior to the effective start date of the award
- extending an award with no additional funds for up to 12 months (a no-cost extension)
- acquiring special purpose equipment costing less than $25,000
- re-budgeting funds up to 25 percent of the total budget (excluding trainee costs)
- approving domestic and foreign travel requests not included in the award budget
- carrying forward grant funds from one year to the next (except in the final year)
- transferring funds between direct and indirect cost categories of the grant budget

The expanded authority to expend grant funds up to 90 days before receiving the actual notice of grant award is particularly useful, for it allows an investigator to get started promptly after learning that the award is forthcoming. However, pre-award spending is at the university's own risk since the terms and conditions of the federal award are not yet known. A university is responsible for any costs that subsequently are not allowed by the awarding agency. As a result, most sponsored research directors insist on receiving written notification from the granting agency that the award letter will be arriving within the 90-day period. This caution is well justified because until the official notice of grant award has been received, the federal agency is under no obligation to make the award and, therefore, to reimburse any advance expenditures. Understandably, if an advance exceeds several hundred thousand dollars, the chief research officer must exercise particular caution.[24]

Award Payments to the Institution

How does the institution get the award money? For starters, to keep track of awards, the federal government imposes several specific identifiers to each grant and contract. Prior to issuing an award, the federal government assigns an agency-specific identifying number to each grant and contract for its accounting and record-keeping purposes. Furthermore, it requires each recipient institution to obtain two unique identifiers: a Data Universal Numbering System (DUNS) number and an employer identification number (EIN) that identifies it to the IRS.[25] Different units within a university, such as the Office of Sponsored Programs and the College of Agriculture, may have separate DUNS numbers, but the university has only one EIN that serves as the institutional account number. Universities add their own identifiers to each award when they are assigned a fund or account number.

After a federal grant or contract has been awarded, via a Notice of Grant Award (NoA) or formal contract, respectively, the institution enters the terms of the award into its accounting system. These terms include the amount awarded for each budget category, the duration of the award, plus any restrictions on the use of these funds. Beginning on the official start date, the institution (the official grantee) can begin to spend the award.

When does the institution actually get its money? Technically, advanced funding is permissible if it will be disbursed (that is, spent) promptly after receipt of the federal funds. The federal government allows the institution to estimate its grant-related expenditures in advance and to receive advance funding to pay them via a monthly letter of credit "draw down" from the federal Treasury. But, from an accounting perspective, the federal agencies want the institution to minimize cash on hand. Therefore, most agencies require advanced funds to be spent within three days or less. According to the law: "Advance payments to a non-Federal entity must be limited to the minimum amounts needed and be timed to be in accordance with the actual, immediate cash requirements of the non-Federal entity in carrying out the purpose of the approved program or project. The timing and amount of advance payments must be as close as is administratively feasible to the actual disbursements by the non-Federal entity for direct program or project costs and the proportionate share of any allowable indirect costs."[26] As a result, the NIH and the NSF require the funds to be spent by the end of the next business day and three days after receipt of the money, respectively.[27]

Advanced funding of the entire award is permissible only under limited circumstances. In other words, at the time of the award, in most cases the federal government does not necessarily provide full funding to the institution. So, if the first-year budget is for $100,000, the government does not promptly send the institution a check for that amount. An exception to this rule occurs if the award is for an expensive piece of equipment or a construction project that costs more than the recipient institution can afford without advanced funding. In those cases, the agency may provide cash on a working capital advance basis. But even then, the advance is limited to the estimated amount needed for an initial disbursement cycle, which is usually one month.[28] Beyond that initial period, cost recovery is by reimbursement only.

Federal law requires the institution to deposit any advance payments in an interest-bearing account. Since these funds must be spent within three or fewer business days, they are deposited in so-called demand deposit accounts, such as interest-bearing checking accounts or negotiable order of withdrawal (NOW) accounts. Checks may be drawn on these accounts without advance notice, which provides the liquidity needed to spend money quickly. The institution may keep up to $500 in interest earned on advanced payments. However, any additional interest must be paid to the sponsoring agency using either the Automated Clearing House (ACH) network or a Fedwire Funds Service payment.[29] This regulation applies to interest earned on advanced funding from all federal agencies. Thus, an institution cannot expect to generate significant income—no more than $500—from interest earned on grant or contract awards.

In principle, therefore, a university could request advanced funding of predictable payments such as payrolls. However, few institutions take advantage of advance funding opportunities, mainly because their accounting procedures cannot reasonably meet these short deadlines.

Far more commonly, the institution recovers expenses incurred by the research project strictly by reimbursement. They receive the award money after they have spent it. Indeed, at least 90 percent of the institutions receiving NSF funding request payment on a reimbursement basis.[30] Payments are made—salaries and invoices from vendors are paid—using institutional funds, and then the institution asks the sponsoring agencies for reimbursement. In effect, the institution sends a bill to the funding agencies for the expenses incurred on behalf of the sponsored project. During the lag between institutional payments and reimbursement, the institution bears the costs of conducting the sponsored research. The difference between institutional expenditures and reimbursements is known as the "float." Using its own cash, the institution "carries the float." Notably, indirect costs are charged to individual awards as direct costs are paid; a university does not recover reimbursement for indirect costs from sponsors until direct costs of the awards are incurred.

A reimbursement request is prepared for each agency, using OMB Form 270.[31] The request documents the institutional EIN, address, letter of credit number, and for each individual project the amounts of the expenses (outlays) to-date, the amount reimbursed to-date, and the amount requested currently. For each agency, these data for the individual projects are summed to yield a single pooled reimbursement request. The institutional grants management office submits these requests electronically to the various agencies' payment management systems.

The federal government has several independent systems for managing award payments. For research institutions, the most commonly used are Research.gov and the Payment Management System (PMS) administered by the NSF and the DHHS, respectively.[32] The PMS also is used by numerous federal agencies in addition to DHHS, such as the US Department of Agriculture (USDA) and the National Aeronautics and Space Administration (NASA); it covers payments for about 75 percent of all domestic grant programs. All US Department of Defense (DOD) grant and contract payments utilize the Wide Area Workflow (WAWF) system administered by the Defense Finance and Accounting Service (DFAS).[33] And several other agencies, including the US Department of Energy (DOE), use the Automated Standard Application for Payments (ASAP) administered by the US Department of the Treasury.[34] Although there are technical differences between these cash management services, in principle they operate in much the same way.

Using one of these payment systems, the federal government pays the award via a letter of credit issued by the funding agency, such as the NSF or the NIH, to the Federal Reserve Bank. The letter of credit authorizes the institution to request an electronic drawdown of the funds approved in the award documents. Funds are sent from the Federal Reserve Bank to the institution's local bank through an electronic funds transfer (for example, ACH). The institution's controller or treasurer can access the money in its local bank account and allocate the money to the appropriate project accounts, checking that the amount allocated to each grant or contract account equals the amount requested for drawdown.

Operationally in a typical case, the institutional grants accounting office periodically generates a report showing the cash balance of every research grant and contract account. The periodicity of these reports varies from daily to monthly, depending on the institution. Generally, the frequency depends on the amount of research expenditures; the largest research universities may generate a report daily, but most institutions generate reports less frequently. All accounts that have a negative cash balance in these reports are flagged because a negative cash balance occurs if more money has been spent than has been deposited in the account. Thus, the institution requests reimbursement to "zero-out" these negative balances. That is, the reimbursement will bring the amount deposited in the account to equal the amount spent.

Any accounts that have a positive cash balance also require special attention. A positive balance indicates that more money has been deposited into the project's account than has been spent. This usually occurs when the agency provides advance payments. The account has "cash on hand" that must be spent within the allowable time limits or returned promptly to the federal government.

Post-Award Financial Reports

Most agencies require the institution to file an annual report, the Federal Financial Report (FFR), that documents cash receipts, cash disbursements, cash on hand, award amounts, and related financial information for each project.[35] The FFR usually is submitted electronically on OMB Form SF-425. In this context, cash disbursements are the sum of actual cash disbursements for direct charges for goods and services, the amount of indirect expenses charged to the award, and the amount of cash advances and payments made to subcontractors and contractors. These reports are due usually within 90 days after the end of a budget period; budget periods are one year in most cases. Notably, some agencies that require reimbursement (or advance payment) requests on a project-by-project basis (instead of a summary basis), such as the NSF, do not require these FFRs because their payment management systems extract the same information from the reimbursement and advance payment requests (Form 270).

If there is an unobligated balance at the end of a budget period, the institution may ask to have it carried over to the next budget period. Or, if there is an unobligated balance but no further budget period because the award ended, the institution may ask for a one-year no-cost extension. Usually, they may be renewed for a second year. Carry-overs and no-cost extensions do not increase the total amount of the award. They simply extend the time period for spending the award. Agencies usually approve these requests. In fact, agency approval is implicit for institutions with expanded authority.

A final FFR, sometimes known as the Financial Status Report (FSR), must be submitted within 90 days after the end-date of the entire project (3 to 5 years for many federal grants). According to the NIH, for example, these final FFRs "must indicate the exact balance of unobligated funds and may not reflect any unliquidated obligations. [In this context, "unliquidated" means that an outstanding purchase order or invoice has not yet been paid.] There must be no discrepancies between the Federal share of expenditures reported on the final FFR and the net cash disbursements reported to PMS on the Transactions section on the FFR." Clearly, the drawdown amounts in the letter of credit must match the expenditures reported in the FFR. So, the grants management office diligently reconciles grant and contract accounts to ensure that authorized amounts, expenditures, and receipts as shown on the letter of credit report, the university accounting system, and the FFR are in agreement.

After the 90-day period, the accounts are closed. No further drawdowns of federal money are permitted using the agencies' cash management systems. And all unobligated funds must be returned to the funding agency. Fortunately, most agencies allow for adjustments (up or down) in the final FFR for up to 15 months after the award has closed. Thus, if the institution receives a late-arriving ("trailing") invoice after the 90-day closure deadline but before the 15-month deadline, it may submit a revised FFR requesting reimbursement for the invoiced expenditure. *Caveat:* There must have been sufficient unobligated funds to cover this reimbursement. Total reimbursements cannot exceed the amount awarded.

Single Audits

Historically, the federal government has required periodic audits of institutions receiving federal funds. To standardize the many different audits, Congress passed the Single Audit Act in 1984.[36] This established what is now known as the single audit; it is also known as the A-133 audit, named after the OMB Circular A-133 on grant administration that preceded the *Uniform Guidance*. Accordingly, the GAO mandates audits of institutions receiving and spending more than $750,000 in federal funds during a fiscal year. Because the $750,000 threshold includes research grants and student aid, all research universities and many smaller institutions exceed this spending threshold and, as a routine matter, have annual single audits. Often the same CPAs prepare the financial statements and perform the single audit.

The audits cover financial statements, compliance with federal regulations, and institutional internal controls to minimize risks of noncompliance. Audit guidelines are published in the so-called *Yellow Book*, a compendium of generally accepted government auditing standards (GAGAS).[37] Similarly, compliance and internal control guidelines are published and available online.[38] Thus, following *Yellow Book* procedures, the auditors examine the university's most recent financial statements, including a schedule of federal award expenditures, and perform checks on various transactions. Furthermore, they examine institutional compliance with all federal regulations and internal controls. In general, the auditors test a minimum percentage of an institution's total federal awards. This is referred to as the "percentage of coverage" rule. The coverage levels are 20 percent of total federal awards expended for "low-risk" institutions (they have relatively clean audits in the past year) and 40 percent for all others.

Certain transactions attract particular attention. For example, any cost transfers that shift costs from one program to another attract particular attention, especially those occurring close to the end of a project period. Other examples that attract particular attention include procedures for determining the allowability of certain costs and for matching an investigator's actual effort versus the approved effort in the award. And subcontracts often receive close scrutiny.

At the completion of the audit, the auditors prepare a report documenting the results. The OMB provides sample templates for preparing these reports.[39] The report documents any "findings," which are conclusions of noncompliance with audit evaluation criteria at the time of the audit. The report also includes an "opinion" expressing the auditor's evaluation of the soundness of the institution's financial statements, compliance with federal regulations, and internal controls to ensure compliance. Opinions fall into four categories:

- unqualified
- qualified
- adverse
- disclaimer

An *unqualified opinion* is the best outcome. There are no findings; the financial statements conform to GAAP, and everything was either perfect or under the threshold for reporting. If there are findings, the unqualified opinion will be modified, resulting in a modified opinion. There are three types of modifications, represented in the latter three categories. A *qualified opinion* is given when the financial statements conform to GAAP except in a few cases that don't necessarily misrepresent the institution's financial condition. It reflects the auditor's discomfort with an unqualified opinion. An *adverse opinion* arises if the audit reveals widespread noncompliance with GAAP, resulting in an unfair representation of financial data. In this case, the institution, working with the auditors, must try to correct the problems. Understandably, an adverse opinion may have serious consequences, especially if the audit reveals illegal practices. A *disclaimer of opinion* occurs if an auditor cannot complete an accurate audit report, perhaps due to limited access to financial data or doubts about the format of reported information. This indicates neither an unqualified nor a qualified opinion regarding the financial statements.

In addition to financial statements, auditors report on compliance with regulations and other requirements related to major federal programs. In an extensive supplement to the *Uniform Guidance*, the A-133 Compliance Supplement, the OMB lists the compliance requirements to be audited for each federal agency. They include items such as cost allowability, cash management, procurement, and real property management.[40] In this context, issues of noncompliance can result in a modified opinion.

When evaluating findings of noncompliance, the auditors must address questionable costs (called questioned costs in accounting jargon). The auditor must report known questionable costs when the likely questionable costs exceed $25,000. The reporting goes beyond just known questionable costs that were specifically identified during the audit. The auditors also must estimate likely questionable costs that were not detected. They are estimated by extrapolation of known questionable costs from the percent of coverage (20 or 40 percent) to the entire institution. For example, if the auditors detected one questioned cost in a 20 percent audit, they would infer that four additional questioned costs went undetected. In reporting questionable costs, the auditor must include information to provide proper perspective for judging the prevalence and consequences of the questionable costs.

Accordingly, auditors pay close attention to internal controls, that is, to institutional procedures designed to minimize the risk of noncompliance with federal regulations. After all, failures of compliance can result in costly disallowances and penalties, so it benefits the institution if these failures can be averted. Thus, auditors describe internal control findings according to their seriousness (from least to most) as a:

- deficiency
- significant deficiency
- material weakness

A *deficiency,* or more explicitly a control deficiency, exists when the design or operation of an internal control during routine tasks does not allow for the timely prevention or detection of noncompliance with a federal regulation. A *significant deficiency* is a control deficiency, or combination of control deficiencies, that adversely affects the institution's ability to administer a federal program in a way that results in "more than a remote likelihood that noncompliance" will not be prevented or detected. And a *material weakness* is a significant deficiency, or combination of significant deficiencies, that results in more than a remote likelihood that material noncompliance with a type of compliance requirement of a federal program will not be prevented or detected. Stated flippantly, it is a glaring significant deficiency.

The auditors submit a draft of their report to the institution. After reviewing the draft report, the institution must prepare a "corrective action plan" to address each audit finding. This plan must provide the name of the contact person responsible for corrective action, the corrective action planned, and the anticipated completion date. If the institution disagrees with the audit findings or believes corrective action is not required, then the plan must include an explanation and specific reasons. The corrective action plan is attached as a separate document to the auditor's findings, completing the final report.

Typically, the final report is submitted to the governing board. In addition to this report, the institution must file a summary of the audit results, including the corrective action plan, to the Federal Audit Clearinghouse (FAC), along with a data collection form, Form SF-SAC, within the earlier of 30 calendar days after receipt of the auditor's report or 9 months after the end of the audit period.[41] The FAC then distributes these materials to the federal agencies for any follow-up actions.

Federal agencies take audits seriously. Adverse opinions can trigger further scrutiny of grant management procedures and expenditures. Moreover, unconvincing corrective actions can result in delays or even stoppage of federal funding until problem issues are resolved. Indeed, in 1991, all federal funding to the University of Hawaii was stopped for three days until the university submitted an acceptable corrective action plan following an auditor's finding of, among other accounting transgressions, an unusually high number of journal vouchers switching a cost from one grant to another after the grants had terminated and, more importantly, two material weaknesses in internal controls.[42] Needless to say, this was a major disruption to university operations. And "heads rolled."

USDA Capacity Grants

Within the realm of federal grants and contracts, one category warrants special attention because of its formula-based allocation and administration methods, namely the USDA capacity grants. All states receive so-called capacity grants awarded annually by the USDA through its National Institute for Food and Agriculture (NIFA). These grants, designed to bring the latest and most relevant agricultural research to the public and into the classroom, are allocated according to specific formulas established by Congress. The three largest capacity grants were established in the following acts:

- Hatch Act of 1887
- Smith-Lever Act of 1914
- McIntire-Stennis Act of 1962

Because these grants are awarded by formula, the awards are known collectively as USDA "formula funds." Administratively, these funds are awarded to the state, which then appropriates them to their public institutions. This route bypasses the office of sponsored projects, so, by some logic, the capacity grants might not be considered sponsored projects. Nonetheless, these formula funds are awarded specifically to support research.

In their authorization statutes, the allocation formulas for these grants are described in simple terms. However, the interpretation of these formulas is not necessarily so simple. In fact, application of the formulas can sometimes become confusing. To alleviate possible confusion, the formula calculations will be presented.

In the Hatch and Smith-Lever Acts, the eligible institutions include the land-grant universities in the 50 states, the District of Columbia, Puerto Rico, and the so-called insular areas, namely, the territories of American Samoa, Guam, and the Virgin Islands, the commonwealth of the Northern Marianas, and the Federated States of Micronesia, under the terms of the Compact of Free Association with the United States.[43] Thus, there are 57 eligible institutions. *Note:* In this context, the term "state" refers to all 57 eligible participants. In addition, two states, namely, Connecticut and New York, have two designated land-grant institutions; they share the state's single allocation. In the McIntire-Stennis Act, the eligible participants are the 50 states plus Puerto Rico, the Virgin Islands, American Samoa, and Guam, for a total of 54. The 1890 and 1994 institutions receive comparable Hatch and Smith-Lever capacity grants via separate appropriations, namely, the Evans-Allen Act and Equity in Educational Land-Grant Status Act of 1994, respectively.[44] Furthermore, the 1890 and 1994 institutions receive McIntire-Stennis funding from the state's formula allocation.

The Agricultural Research, Extension, and Education Reform Act (AREERA) of 1998, which amended the Hatch and the Smith-Lever Acts, requires that all formula-funded research undergo scientific peer review. But the review is not at the federal level. This review requirement is the responsibility of the individual universities; that is, the reviews occur "in-house." This responsibility may be delegated to a regional association of universities for regional multistate activity.

Like other sponsored research funds, the formula funds are disbursed on a reimbursement basis to the university via letters of credit. Unobligated balances (within limits, that is) at the end of the federal fiscal year are available for expenditure in the subsequent year. Notably, indirect costs and tuition remission are not allowable formula-fund expenses; the recipient universities and, therefore, the states are expected to pay for these costs as their contribution to the land-grant mission.

Hatch Act

This act authorizes direct payments of federal funds to each state to establish and operate an agricultural experiment station in conjunction with the land-grant institution. The station is usually a component of the College of Agriculture. To coordinate multistate activities, the experimental stations are organized into four geographical regions: North Central, North East, Southern, and Western.

Agricultural experiment station allocations to individual land-grant universities are determined by a formula established in the Hatch Act.[45] Using the previous year's allocations as a baseline funding level, the act authorizes any additional appropriations to the individual universities according to the following formula:

- 3 percent is allotted to the secretary of agriculture "for administration of this Act."
- 25 percent is "allotted to the States [combined] for cooperative research in which two or more State agricultural experiment stations are cooperating to solve problems that concern the agriculture of more than one State"; this allocation is known as the "multistate research fund."
- 20 percent is "allotted equally to each State."
- 26 percent "bears the same ratio to the total amount allotted as the rural population of the State bears to the total rural population of all the States [combined] as determined by the last decennial census."
- 26 percent "bears the same ratio to the total amount to be allotted as the farm population of the State bears to the total farm population of all the States [combined] as determined by the last preceding decennial census."

Collectively, the latter three formula components are known as the "regular research fund." Thus, after subtracting 3 percent for administration and 25 percent for multistate research, the regular research components are 72 percent of the total appropriation.

The states must expend 25 percent of their total allocation (multistate plus regular research), or two times the level spent in fiscal year 1997 (whichever is less), on activities that integrate cooperative research and extension. The 1890, 1994, and insular land-grant universities are exempt from this requirement. However, they may participate voluntarily in these types of activities.

Also, according to law, the NIFA deducts additional amounts from the total appropriation to fund its Small Business Innovation Research (SBIR) program administration and Biotechnology Risk Assessment Research Grants program administration.[46] These deductions are agency-wide and are spread across all NIFA research programs. The approximate amounts deducted from the Hatch Act formula funds are about 3 percent and 0.35 percent of the total appropriation, respectively. However, the exact amounts vary slightly from year to year, depending on the overall NIFA budget details. Importantly, unlike the 3 percent deduction for federal administration, these deductions are not part of the formula, but like the federal administration deduction, they come "off the top" of the original appropriation.

Regular research fund. After these administrative deductions, the regular research fund is allocated in a straightforward way according to the formula. Noticeably, in all of the calculations, percentages are not always exact beyond the whole percent level due to rounding errors and minor administrative adjustments by the NIFA. Thus, for example, the formula may call for 3 percent, but the actual amount used in the calculations is 2.84 percent, which rounds up to 3 percent.

To illustrate the regular research fund allocation algorithm, calculation of the 2016 allocation for Montana's land-grant institution, Montana State University, is shown in table 8.1. In this example, the 2016 federal budget had not been passed by Congress at the time of the NIFA allocation announcement, so federal spending was based on a continuing resolution. Therefore, the 2016 allocations were based on the 2015 base appropriation, $243,701,000; the NIFA points out that adjustments to the 2016 allocations will be made after passage of a final budget.[47]

According to the formula, the regular research allocation for distribution to the states ($183,791,586) for both years comprises 75 percent of the total appropriation. The federal administration, small business administration, and biotech risk assessment must be deducted from this amount, reducing the regular research fund allocation available for distribution to the states to $172,525,323 and $172,423,744 in 2015 and 2016, respectively. At this point, it helps to remember that according to the formula, the FY 2016 allocation is added to (or subtracted from) the FY 2015 allocation. In this example, the FY 2016 allocation is $101,579 less than the FY 2015 base allocation. So, in FY 2016, this amount will be subtracted from the amount allocated in FY 2015. In other words, the states will get less money in FY 2016 than in FY 2015. Furthermore, according to the Hatch Act, each of the 6 insular states receives $100,000 in addition to its base, and the total amount ($600,000) is deducted from the regular research allocation, increasing the amount to be subtracted from the FY 2015 allocation to $701,579.

After these calculations, the net regular research fund allocation for FY 2016 is allocated to individual states according to weights for each component of the formula. Initially, the equal-share weights are calculated: 20 percent of the formula comprises 27.778 percent (20/72 percent) of the regular research fund for allocation to the states, and this percentage is divided among the 57 recipient institutions,

Table 8.1. Hatch Act regular research allocation for FY 2016 to Montana State University

	Parameters	FY 2015	FY 2016	Change
Total appropriation		243,701,000	243,701,000	
Allocation available for distribution to the states				
Regular research fund	75%	183,791,586	183,791,586	
Federal administration	3%	(5,532,538)	(5,537,891)	
Regular research fund for allocation to the states	72%	178,259,048	178,253,695	
Additional research support deductions				
Small business administration	3%	(5,018,793)	(5,191,855)	
Biotech risk assessment	0.35%	(714,932)	(638,096)	
Regular research fund allocation		172,525,323	172,423,744	(101,579)
Base to insular "states"				(600,000)
Net regular research fund allocation for FY 2016				(701,579)
Formula weights				
Equal shares				
Formula percentage	20%			
Formula weight (formula %/research fund %)	27.778%			
Number of recipients	57			
Equal share percentage of formula weight	0.487%			(3,419)
Rural population				
Formula percentage	26%			
Formula weight (formula %/research fund %)	36.111%			
US rural population	59,835,846			
Montana rural population	436,280			
Montana percent of rural population	0.729%			
Montana percent of formula weight	0.263%			(1,847)
Farm population				
Formula percentage	26%			
Formula weight (formula %/research fund %)	36.111%			
US farm population	2,507,993			
Montana farm population	35,030			
Montana percent of farm population	1.400%			
Montana percent of formula weight	0.504%			(3,539)
Montana allocation				
Total formula weight	1.255%			
Base allocation				(8,805)
Total regular research allocation		1,871,676	1,862,871	

yielding each state's equal percentage of the net regular research fund allocation, 0.487 percent. In equation form, for each state:

$$\text{state's equal share} = \frac{equal\ share\ formula\ percentage}{regular\ research\ fund\ percentage}$$
$$\times \frac{1}{number\ of\ recipients} \times net\ allocation$$
$$= \frac{20\%}{72\%} \times \frac{1}{57} \times (-\$701{,}579)$$
$$= 0.00487 \times (-\$701{,}579)$$
$$= -\$3{,}419$$

So, in 2017, each state's 2017 equal share allocation is reduced by $3,419.

The Montana rural- and farm-based allocation components are calculated similarly using rural and farm population data derived from the 2010 US census and 2012 USDA census, respectively.[48]

$$\text{Montana rural allocation} = \frac{rural\ formula\ percentage}{regular\ research\ fund\ percentage}$$
$$\times \frac{Montana\ rural\ population}{US\ rural\ population} \times net\ allocation$$
$$= \frac{26\%}{72\%} \times \frac{436{,}280}{59{,}835{,}846} \times (-\$701{,}580)$$
$$= 0.00263 \times (-\$701{,}580) = -\$1{,}847,$$

and

$$\text{Montana farm allocation} = \frac{farm\ formula\ percentage}{regular\ research\ fund\ percentage}$$
$$\times \frac{Montana\ farm\ population}{US\ farm\ population} \times net\ allocation$$
$$= \frac{26\%}{72\%} \times \frac{35{,}030}{2{,}507{,}993} \times (-\$701{,}580)$$
$$= 0.00504 \times (-\$701{,}580) = -\$3{,}539$$

Therefore, Montana's 2016 rural and farm allocations decreased by $1,847 and $3,539, respectively, compared to the 2015 allocations.

The equal-share, rural, and farm components are added together to get the total 2016 allocation, which is −$8,805. Because the amount is negative, this allocation amount is subtracted from last year's base ($1,871,676) to obtain the state's total regular research allocation for 2016, $1,862,871.

Multistate research fund. The multistate research allocation is calculated on a pro rata basis. Like the Hatch regular research funds, the current year's allocations are based on the previous year's allocations, going back to the 1955 base allocations. However, the NIFA retains the authority to adjust individual state allocations to support national—that is, interregional—and regional projects (thus the word "multistate"). In national and regional groups, the directors of the state agricultural extension stations decide which interregional and regional projects to support "off the top"—that is, in addition to projects funded in a state's base allocation. Accordingly, these allocations are called off-the-top allocations. Each year, only about 15 to 20 states benefit from these off-the-top allocations. To pay for these off-the-top costs, each state must contribute to a trust an amount proportional to its percentage of the total interregional and regional base allocations.

Multistate calculations for Montana's 2016 allocation are illustrated in table 8.2. Noticeably, the allocations are itemized for each of the four national regions: North Central, North East, Southern, and Western. Montana is in the Western region (table 8.2, *upper panel*). As in the regular research fund calculations, the administrative deductions are made first, yielding the net multistate research fund amounts for allocation to the states. The 2016 allocation ($56,263,470) is 99.94 percent of the 2015 allocation ($56,297,417). Montana's 2015 base allocation ($980,567) is multiplied by this percentage to obtain the 2016 base allocation ($979,976).

The interregional and regional off-the-top allocations are then itemized by region (table 8.2, *lower panels*). Notably, Montana did not receive any off-the-top allocations in either 2015 or 2016. Nonetheless, it must pay into the trust that covers the cost of these off-the-top allocations. Montana's share of the interregional and the regional trust costs is based on the percentage of its base allocation relative to the net multistate research fund allocation (1.7418 percent) and Western regional allocation (7.4519 percent), respectively.

Using these percentages, the state's 2016 trust costs to fund the off-the-top programs were then calculated:

$$Montana\ interregional\ cost = \frac{Montana\ base\ allocation}{net\ multistate\ allocation}$$
$$\times total\ interregional\ allocations$$
$$= \frac{\$979,976}{\$56,263,470} \times \$2,299,847$$
$$= 1.7418\% \times \$2,299,847 = \$40,058$$

Table 8.2. Hatch Act multistate research allocation for FY 2016 to Montana State University

	Parameters	FY 2015	FY 2016
Total appropriation		243,701,000	243,701,000
Allocation available for distribution to the states			
Multistate research fund	25%	59,909,414	59,909,414
Federal administration	3%	(1,748,745)	(1,750,491)
Subtotal available for allocation to the states	22%	58,160,669	58,158,923
Administrative research support deductions			
Small business administration	2.8%	(1,637,484)	(1,693,949)
Biotech risk assessment	0.35%	(225,768)	(201,504)
Net multistate research fund allocation		56,297,417	56,263,470
Allocation by region			
North Central		15,090,419	15,081,320
North East		11,157,446	11,150,718
Southern		16,890,918	16,880,733
Western		13,158,634	13,150,699
Montana base allocation			
2016/2015 net multistate ratio	0.9994		
Base allocation (previous year × net multistate ratio)		980,567	979,976

Interregional and regional off-the-top allocations

	Interregional	Regional
North Central	466,250	547,980
North East	562,432	295,696
Southern	569,750	465,564
Western	701,415	515,204
Totals	2,299,847	1,824,444
Montana	0	0

Interregional and regional trust costs

Montana		
Base allocation percent of net multistate allocation	1.7418%	
Base allocation percent of net Western regional allocation		7.4519%
Trust cost (base percent × total interregional off-the-top)	40,058	
Trust cost (base percent × Western regional off-the-top)		38,392
Montana allocation		
Base allocation		979,976
Off-the-top additions		
Interregional		0
Regional		0
Off-the-top trust costs		
Interregional		(40,058)
Regional		(38,392)
Montana total allocation		901,525

and

$$\begin{aligned} \textit{Montana regional cost} &= \frac{\textit{Montana base allocation}}{\textit{Western region base allocation}} \\ &\quad \times \textit{total Western regional allocations} \\ &= \frac{\$979,976}{\$13,150,699} \times \$515,204 \\ &= 7.4519\% \times \$515,204 = \$38,392 \end{aligned}$$

These trust costs were subtracted from Montana's base allocation to yield the state's total allocation for 2016 ($901,525).

Smith-Lever Act

To disseminate information generated from the experiment stations' research, the Smith-Lever Act created a Cooperative Extension Service associated with each land-grant institution (excluding the District of Columbia).[49] In return for this support, these institutions participate in extension programs to educate the public in improved agriculture methods, nutrition, and other areas. The typical extension agent is an employee of the land-grant institution but may have office facilities provided by the state or county. Historically, there has been one extension agent for every county (thus, the name "county agent"), although now there has been some consolidation.

The NIFA supports this extension service using a formula similar but not identical to that of the Hatch Act. According to the Smith-Lever formula, the appropriation is allocated as follows:

- 4 percent "shall be allotted to the Federal Extension Service for administrative, technical, and other services, and for coordinating the extension work of the department and the several States, Territories, and possessions."

Of the remainder:

- 20 percent "shall be paid to the several States in equal proportions."
- 40 percent "shall be paid to the several States in the proportion that the rural population of each bears to the total rural population of the several States as determined by the census."
- 40 percent "shall be paid to the several States in the proportion that the farm population of each bears to the total farm population of the several States as determined by the census."

The allocation calculations use about the same algorithm as used for the Hatch Act regular research funds. There are, however, two noticeable differences. First, in the Hatch Act regular research algorithm, the allocation available for distribution to the states is considered to be 72 percent of the appropriation (100 percent of the appropriation less 3 percent for the administrative component and 25 percent for the multistate component). Thus, the formula percentages are normalized to the 72 percent base; for example, the normalized 20 percent equal-share percentage becomes 27.778 percent (20/72 percent). And the calculations are based on these normalized percentages, called the weights. In contrast, the Smith-Lever Act algorithm considers the allocation available for distribution to the states to be 100 percent of the appropriation (not 72 percent); although the 4 percent administrative component comes out of the appropriation, it is considered separately. Second, according to the NIFA, the Smith-Lever funds are for extension, not research. Therefore, in the Smith-Lever Act algorithm, there are no deductions for the research-oriented small business administration and biotechnology risk assessment grants programs.

To illustrate the algorithm in this context, Montana State University's 2015 and 2016 Smith-Lever Act allocations are calculated in table 8.3. Again, as in the Hatch Act example, the total appropriation ($300,000,000) in 2015 is the same as in 2016 because of the federal budget continuing resolution. The federal administration deduction (nominally 4 percent, rounded up to the whole number) was $1,842,686 less in 2016 than in 2015. Therefore, the net appropriation in 2016 is $1,842,686. As in the Hatch Act allocations, each of the 6 insular states receives $100,000 annually, and the total amount ($600,000) is deducted from the allocation available for distribution. After these deductions, the net allocation available for distribution to the states according to the formula is $1,242,686.

The formula is then applied in a straightforward way. Initially, it allocates 20 percent of the appropriation in equal shares to the 56 eligible "states." Thus, each state receives 0.3571 percent (20 percent/56) of the net allocation, which equals $4,438. Then, the Montana rural and farm population components are calculated in the same way: (0.7291 percent × 40 percent × $1,242,686) = $3,624 and (1.3967 percent × 40 percent × $1,242,686) = $6,943, respectively. Adding together the 3 components, the 2016 Smith-Lever funds allocated to Montana State University increased by $15,005 relative to the FY 2015 allocation, for a total FY 2016 allocation of $2,742,508.

Table 8.3. Smith-Lever Act allocation for FY 2016 to Montana State University

	Parameters	FY 2015	FY 2016	Change
Total appropriation		300,000,000	300,000,000	
Federal administration	4%	(13,166,296)	(11,323,610)	
Net appropriation		286,833,704	288,676,390	1,842,686
Base to insular "states"				(600,000)
Net allocation available for distribution				1,242,686
Formula allocations				
Equal shares				
Formula percentage	20%			
Number of recipients	56			
Equal share percentage	0.3571%			
Montana equal share			4,438	
Rural population				
Formula percentage	40%			
US rural population	59,835,846			
Montana rural population	436,280			
Montana percent of rural population	0.7291%			
Montana rural population share			3,624	
Farm population				
Formula percentage	40%			
US farm population	2,507,993			
Montana farm population	35,030			
Montana percent of farm population	1.3967%			
Montana farm population share			6,943	
Montana total addition to base			15,005	
Montana total allocation		2,727,503	2,742,508	

McIntire-Stennis Act

This act authorized formula funding to increase forestry research on the production, utilization, and protection of forested land by schools of forestry, land-grant colleges, and the state agricultural experiment stations.[50] Funds are awarded by formula to 54 eligible institutions.

According to the formula, two allocations are made "off the top":

- 3 percent of the total appropriation "shall be made available to the Secretary for administration of this Act."
- $25,000 is allocated as a base amount to each state.

Significantly, the $25,000 base amount allocated to each state is different from the base allocated to each state in the Hatch and Smith-Lever Act formulas. In those cases, the state's previous year's allocation is the base. Thus, unlike the Hatch or Smith-Lever formulas, the McIntire-Stennis base is not the previous year's allocation; it is simply $25,000.

Some states have more than one eligible institution. In those cases, the state's allocation is distributed to the eligible institutions by the governor's office. Also, funds are expected to be expended in the fiscal year of appropriation, but the NIFA allows a one-year carryover into the next fiscal year of up to 5 percent of a fiscal year's allotment.

Because McIntire-Stennis Act funds support research, the NIFA deducts allocations for the small business administration and biotechnology risk assessment research programs. Like the Smith-Lever Act but unlike the Hatch Act allocation algorithms, the McIntire-Stennis algorithm considers these, the federal administration, and the equal-share base allocations to be separate from the amount available for distribution to the states. So, there are no normalizing adjustments to the formula percentages.

After these "off-the-top" deductions, the remainder of the appropriation is the net allocation available for distribution to the states. By the formula, it is allocated percentage-wise based on three factors calculated for each state:[51]

- 40 percent is based on the area of nonfederal commercial forest land.
- 40 percent is based on the volume of timber cut annually from stock.
- 20 percent is allocated based on the total expenditures for forestry research from nonfederal sources.

An individual state's proportionate share of each factor, called the factor-weighted ratio, is calculated for each of these three factors:

$$factor\ weighted\ ratio = \frac{state\ amount\ of\ factor}{total\ US\ amount\ of\ factor} \times factor\ percentage$$

From this point on, the McIntire-Stennis formula is based on a ranking method.[52] Each individual state's three factor-weighted ratios are summed, and the summed ratios for all states are rank ordered from smallest to largest. An individual state's rank relative to the sum of all of the other ranks (that is, $1+2+3+\ldots+54$) is then multiplied by the net allocation available for distribution to the states. The $25,000 equal-share base is added to yield the gross allocation. Finally, the small business administration and biotechnology risk assessment taxes are deducted to give the final, net allocation.

This allocation algorithm is illustrated in table 8.4, which calculates Montana's 2016 allocation for the University of Montana.[53]

Table 8.4. McIntire-Stennis Act research allocation for FY 2016 funding to the University of Montana

	Parameters	2016
Total appropriation		33,961,000
Allocation available for distribution to the states		
Federal administration	3%	(1,048,478)
Base amount per state	25,000	
Number of states	54	
Equal allocation to states		(1,350,000)
Subtotal allocation available for distribution		31,562,522
Administrative research support deductions		
Small business administration	3%	(958,617)
Biotech risk assessment	0.10%	(33,220)
Net allocation available for distribution		30,570,685
Formula allocations		
Nonfederal commercial forest land (acres × 1000)		
Total US	401,477	
Montana	6,942	
% weight	40%	
Rank component	0.0069	
Volume of timber cut annually from stock (cu. ft. × 1000)		
Total US	15,533,485	
Montana	197,903	
% weight	40%	
Rank component	0.0051	
Nonfederal expenditures for forestry research		
Total US	146,111,871	
Montana	4,691,455	
% weight	20%	
Rank component	0.0064	
Total rank component	0.0184	
Montana allocation		
Montana rank among all states' ranks	32	
Sum of ranks for all states (1 + 2 + 3 + . . . + 54, adjusted for ties)	1490	
Relative rank (Montana/sum)	0.0215	
Subtotal allocation (relative rank × net allocation)		656,672
Base amount		25,000
Montana total allocation		681,672

Noticeably, the previous year's allocations are not included; unlike the Hatch Act and Smith-Lever Act, the McIntire-Stennis allocations are not based on previous years' allocations, so they are not part of the calculation. For starters, the NIFA takes 3 percent of the total appropriation for administration of the fund. Then, it sets aside a base amount of $25,000 for each of the 54 recipient states for subsequent allocation. And it deducts allocations for the small business administration and biotechnology risk assessment research programs.

The remainder, the net allocation ($30,570,685), is allocated by the ranking process. For each factor, the factor-weighted ratio (also called the rank component) is calculated:

Montana nonfederal

$$\text{commercial forest land ratio} = \frac{6,942}{401,477} \times 40\% = 0.0069,$$

$$\text{Montana timber cut ratio} = \frac{197,903}{15,533,485} \times 40\% = 0.0051$$

and

Montana nonfederal forestry

$$\text{research expenditure ratio} = \frac{\$4,691,455}{\$146,111,871} \times 20\% = 0.0064$$

These 3 factor ratios (rank components) add up to 0.0184. When the total rank components of all 54 states are arranged in rank order, Montana ranks 32nd largest, which is 2.1477 percent of the sum of ranks (1 through 54, adjusted for ties). Thus Montana's gross allocation ($656,672) equals 2.1477 percent of the net allocation for distribution. Adding the state's $25,000 base allocation yields Montana's total allocation, $681,672.

Matching Requirements

The federal funds awarded by each of these three NIFA programs (Hatch, Smith-Lever, and McIntire-Stennis Acts) must be matched on a one-to-one basis by the recipient universities, using nonfederal funds. That is, for every federal dollar expended there must be a nonfederal dollar expended. Notably, for each program, the required match equals the awards' base allocations, not the total allocations. In each case, the institution must demonstrate that nonfederal dollar amounts are available and budgeted for expenditure before the NIFA will release the federal funds. The matching funds must be spent within the fiscal year for which the federal funds have been released.

Many states provide their land-grant universities with sufficient appropriations for agriculture research and extension activities to meet the NIFA matching requirements. The universities simply document the state funds in federal financial reports. Another way for universities to meet the matching requirement is by taking credit for salaries paid with state or other nonfederal money to personnel working on faculty members' approved Hatch, Smith-Lever, or McIntire-Stennis projects.

Table 8.5. Calculated matching contribution for one individual researcher based on faculty salary paid by the state or other nonfederal funds

	Matching funds
Full-time salary	$100,000
Fringe benefits (33%)	$33,000
Total salary + fringe benefits	$133,000
Imputed indirect cost (50%)	$66,500
Total salary cost	$199,500
Percent effort on Hatch project	40%
Matching amount	$79,800

A sample calculation of salary-based matching funds for one individual researcher is shown in table 8.5. Although the federal funds cannot be used to pay indirect expenses, the match includes indirect costs paid by the university; the indirect cost rate (50 percent of the total salary plus fringe benefits in this example) equals the institution's indirect rate for all government-sponsored research. As a control, on a monthly basis, the institution must certify that the time spent on the project was equal to the time shown on the project documentation (in this example, 40 percent).

By law, the NIFA may reduce or waive the matching requirements for the insular areas, including Puerto Rico and the District of Columbia. And they almost always do. The match for Hatch and Smith-Lever Act funds, for example, is reduced routinely by half for the insular areas; that is, the match is 50 percent of the formula allocation. Moreover, the match for McIntire-Stennis Act funds for the insular areas is waived completely.

Summary

When external sources pay for research, they "sponsor" the research by awarding the institution a grant or a contract. Contracts are legally binding procurement relationships between the sponsor and the university that obligate the university to furnish a project outcome or service defined in the contract. Grants are awarded to accomplish a specific goal, but, unlike contracts, the usual purpose of a grant is to enhance knowledge about a topic or to provide services for the recipient's or public's benefit. A grant or contract may include a subcontract to hire an individual or business not affiliated with the university to perform part or all of the grant or contract's obligations. Federal grant and contract awards must adhere to administrative guidelines, known as cost principles, presented in the so-called *Uniform Guidance*. Accordingly, all allowable costs charged against a federal contract or grant must be necessary and reasonable for the performance of the award. Also, they must be allocable— incurred solely to support or advance the work of a specific sponsored research award. The federal government pays grant and contract awards via a letter of credit on behalf of the institution to the Federal Reserve Bank. Commonly, the institution recovers expenses incurred by the research project strictly by reimbursement. Most agencies require the institution to file an annual report, the FFR, which documents financial information for each project. The federal government requires periodic audits (called A-133 audits) of institutions receiving federal funds, covering financial statements, compliance with federal regulations, and institutional internal controls to minimize risks of noncompliance. All land-grant institutions receive so-called USDA capacity grants, known as "formula funds," designed to bring relevant agricultural research to the public and into the classroom. These funds must be matched on a one-to-one basis by the recipient universities, using nonfederal funds.

Notes

1. 2 C.F.R. §200 App. III A.1.b.(1).

2. *Using Procurement Contracts and Grant and Cooperative Agreements*, 31 U.S.C. 6301-6308 (2014); US General Accountability Office, *Principles of Federal Appropriations Law*, 3rd ed., vol. 2 (2004), 10-9.

3. US General Accountability Office, *Principles of Federal Appropriations Law*, 3rd ed., vol. 2, 10-9.

4. 41 Comp. Gen. 134 (1961).

5. *Assignment of Claims Act*, 41 U.S.C. § 15.

6. *Principles of Federal Appropriations Law*, 3rd ed., vol. 2, 10-6–10-7.

7. *U.S. v. Miami University*, 94 F. Supp. 2d 1142 (2000).

8. 2 C.F.R. § 200.74.

9. 2 C.F.R. § 200.332.

10. Office of Management and Budget, "Uniform Administrative Requirements, Cost Principles, and Audit Requirements for Federal Awards, 2 C.F.R. §200," http://www.ecfr.gov/cgi-bin/text-idx?tpl=/ecfrbrowse/Title02/2cfr200_main _02.tpl (accessed June 19, 2017).

11. Federal Acquisition Regulations System,*Cost Accounting Standards for Educational Institutions*, 48 C.F.R. 9905.

12. *Federal Acquisition Regulation*, 48 C.F.R.

13. *Uniform Administrative Requirements, Cost Principles, and Audit Requirements for Federal Awards*, 2 C.F.R. § 200.413.

14. 2 C.F.R. § 200.56.

15. Dean O. Smith, *Managing the Research University* (New York: Oxford University Press, 2011), 51.

16. *Understanding Authority in Higher Education* (Lanham, MD: Rowman and Littlefield, 2015), 220.

17. US Department of Health and Human Services, "Allowable, Allocable, Reasonable Costs," https://ori.hhs.gov/education/products/rcradmin/topics/financial/tutorial_2.shtml (accessed January 26, 2015).

18. 2 C.F.R. § 200.412.

19. Smith, *Managing the Research University,* 139–143.

20. Council on Governmental Relations, "Policies and Practices: Compensation, Effort Commitments, and Certification" (2007), http://www.cogr.edu/sites/default/files/COMPENSATION_EFFORT_COMMITMENTS_AND_CERTIFICATION.pdf (accessed March 12, 2018).

21. 2 C.F.R. § 200.430 (h)(8)(i)(i)(x).

22. National Institutes of Health, "NIH Grants Policy Statement" (2015). § 8.1.

23. National Science Foundation, "Research Terms and Conditions Prior Approval and Other Requirements Matrix," https://www.nsf.gov/bfa/dias/policy/fedrtc/priorapproval_oct08.pdf (accessed January 6, 2017).

24. Smith, *Managing the Research University,* 134.

25. Internal Revenue Service, "Employer Identification Number," http://www.irs.gov/Charities-&-Non-Profits/Employer-Identification-Number (accessed April 26, 2015); Office of Management and Budget, "Use of Universal Identifier by Grant Applicants," *Federal Register* 68, no. 124 (2003).

26. 45 C.F.R. § 75.305(b)(1).

27. National Institutes of Health, "Payment," *NIH Grants Policy Statement* (2013), http://grants.nih.gov/grants/policy/nihgps_2013/nihgps_ch6.htm#smartlink_ach (accessed April 26, 2015); National Science Foundation, "Payment Policies," *Proposal and Award Policies and Procedures Guide Part II—Award and Administration Guide* (2014). § 3.C.2.

28. 45 C.F.R. §92.21(e).

29. 45 C.F.R. §75.305(b)(9).

30. National Science Foundation, "NSF's Financial Management Awards Survey Response to Users," https://www.nsf.gov/bfa/dfm/survey/surveysummary.pdf (accessed April 30, 2015).

31. Office of Management and Budget, "Grants Management Forms," https://www.whitehouse.gov/omb/grants_forms (accessed May 8, 2015).

32. US Department of Health and Human Services, "Payment Management Services," http://www.dpm.psc.gov/about_us/about_us.aspx?explorer.event=true (accessed April 22, 2015); National Science Foundation, "Award Cash Management Service," Research.gov, https://www.research.gov/research-portal/appmanager/base/desktop?_nfpb=true&_pageLabel=research_node_display&_nodePath=/researchGov/Service/Desktop/AwardCashManagementService.html (accessed April 22, 2015).

33. Department of Defense, "Wide Area Workflow (WAWF)," http://www.dfas.mil/ecommerce/wawf/info.html (accessed April 23, 2015).

34. Department of the Treasury, "Automated Standard Application for Payments (ASAP)," Bureau of the Fiscal Service, http://www.fiscal.treasury.gov/fsservices/gov/pmt/asap/asap_home.htm (accessed April 29, 2015).

35. Office of Management and Budget, "Grants Management Forms."

36. 2 C.F.R. § 200.

37. US Government Accountability Office, "Government Auditing Standards (the Yellow Book)" (2011), http://gao.gov/yellowbook/overview (accessed January 10, 2017).

38. US General Accountability Office, "Assessing Compliance with Applicable Laws and Regulations" (1989), http://www.gao.gov/products/OP-4.1.2 (accessed January 11, 2017); US Government Accountability Office, "Standards for Internal Control in the Federal Government: The Green Book" (2014), http://www.gao.gov/products/gao-14-704Ghttp://www.gao.gov/products/gao-14-704G (accessed January 11, 2017).

39. American Institute of Certified Public Accountants, *Government Auditing Standards and Single Audits—Audit Guide* (New York: Wiley, 2016), chapter 13, appendix.

40. Office of Management and Budget, "OMB Circular A-133 Compliance Supplement," https://www.whitehouse.gov/omb/circulars/a133_compliance_sup plement_2016 (accessed January 11, 2017).

41. Federal Audit Clearinghouse, "Form SF-SAC Worksheet & Single Audit Component Checklist," https://harvester.census.gov/facides/Files/2015_2018%20 Checklist%20Instructions%20and%20Form.pdf (accessed January 11, 2017). 2 C.F.R. §200.512 (a)(1).

42. David Yount, *Who Runs the University: The Politics of Higher Education in Hawaii, 1985–1992* (Honolulu: University of Hawaii Press, 1996), 208–211.

43. United States, "Compact of Free Association Act of 1985, Public Law 99-239," uscode.house.gov/statutes/pl/99/239.pdf (accessed November 18, 2016).

44. "7 U.S.C. § 3222—Agricultural Research at 1890 Land-Grant Colleges, Including Tuskegee University," https://www.law.cornell.edu/uscode/text/7/3222 (accessed November 27, 2016); "7 U.S.C. § 7601 Equity in Educational Land-Grant Status Act of 1994," https://www.law.cornell.edu/uscode/text/7/7601 (accessed November 27, 2016).

45. Association of American Universities and the Association of Public and Land-Grant Universities, "The Land-Grant Tradition," http://www.aplu.org /library/the-land-grant-tradition/file (accessed November 8, 2016), 18.

46. National Institute of Food and Agriculture, "2016 Explanatory Notes," www.obpa.usda.gov/19nifa2016notes.pdf (accessed November 27, 2016).

47. Association of Public and Land-Grant Universities, "Land-Grant.Org FY 2016 Documents," http://www.land-grant.org/FY2016Documents.html (accessed November 27, 2016).

48. US Census Bureau, "2010 Census Urban and Rural Classification and Urban Area Criteria," https://www.census.gov/geo/reference/ua/urban-rural-2010 .html (accessed November 9, 2016); US Department of Agriculture, "USDA Census of Agriculture, State Level Data," https://www.agcensus.usda.gov/Publi cations/2012/Full_Report/Volume_1,_Chapter_1_State_Level/Montana/ (accessed November 9, 2016); "USDA Census of Agriculture 2012 Census Highlights Farm Demographics—U.S. Farmers by Gender, Age, Race, Ethnicity, and More," https:// www.agcensus.usda.gov/Publications/2012/Online_Resources/Highlights/Farm _Demographics/ (accessed November 9, 2016).

49. Association of American Universities and the Association of Public and Land-Grant Universities, "The Land-Grant Tradition," 20.

50. Steven H. Bullard et al., "A 'Driving Force' in Developing the Nations' Forests: The McIntire-Stennis Cooperative Forestry Research Program," *Journal of*

Forestry (April–May 2011), scholarworks.sfasu.edu/cgi/viewcontent.cgi?article =1058&context=forestry (accessed November 15, 2016); United States, "McIntire-Stennis Act 16 U.S.C. § 582" (accessed November 18, 2016).

51. National Institute of Food and Agriculture, "Current Research Information System Reports Funding Summaries, Table B.," http://cris.nifa.usda.gov /fsummaries.html (accessed November 15, 2016); Sonja N. Oswalt et al., "Forest Resources of the United States, 2012: A Technical Document Supporting the Forest Service Update of the 2010 RPA Assessment" (2014), http://www.fia.fs.fed.us /program-features/rpa/index.php (accessed November 14, 2016). Tables 10 and 36.

52. D. H. Thompson and Stephen H. Bullard, "History and Evaluation of the McIntire-Stennis Cooperative Forestry Research Program," *Stephen F. Austin State University SFA ScholarWorks Faculty Publications Forestry* (2004), scholar-works.sfasu.edu/cgi/viewcontent.cgi?article=1036&context=forestry (accessed November 15, 2016). Appendix C.

53. National Institute of Food and Agriculture, "McIntire Stennis Capacity Grant FY 2017 McIntire Stennis (M-S) Cooperative Forestry Research Program—Capacity RFA—Modified 08 26 2016," https://nifa.usda.gov/program/mcintire -stennis-capacity-grant (accessed November 14, 2016).

Chapter 9
Indirect Costs

Indirect Cost Allocations

In several contexts, universities want to assign indirect costs to specific cost objectives. For example, responsibility center management budget models depend on assignment of each responsibility center's share of the institutional indirect costs. Or, reimbursement of indirect costs incurred by a project sponsored by a federal grant depends on assignment of the project's share of the institutional indirect costs. As the NACUBO emphasizes, to evaluate the costs and benefits of academic programs and to determine the price of many services, indirect costs need to be allocated to individual activities of the institution.[1] Despite inherent difficulties with indirect cost allocations, there are standard methods to allocate indirect costs with more or less accuracy.

Fixed-Cost Classification

Fixed-cost classification is the simplest way to allocate indirect costs. This method works with costs such as depreciation and labor that can be classified as fixed. They are allocated as a fixed charge to a specific cost objective. For example, in an imaging facility (the cost objective) that serves the entire university, equipment depreciation of a general-purpose electron microscope is allocated to the facility. Likewise, wages for employees working solely for the imaging facility that houses the microscope are allocated to the facility, as are expenses for routine supplies needed to operate the facility.

Despite their simplicity, however, fixed-cost allocations are not suitable for many indirect costs. Heating, telephone, water, sewage, electricity, and internet access are examples. Unless they are metered for every cost objective, these indirect costs cannot be assigned as fixed costs. Some other allocation method must be used.

Proportional Allocation

A commonly used allocation method is based on a cost objective's proportional benefit from the institutional indirect costs. In other words, proportional indirect cost allocation assigns a percentage of an indirect cost to each cost objective benefiting from the cost. The allocation basis depends on the nature of the cost. On the one hand, a university's heating bill might be allocated according to the number of square feet assigned to each cost objective. For example, if the chemistry department occupies 5 percent of the university's assignable space, then 5 percent of the heating bill would be assigned to that department. On the other hand, internet access might be allocated evenly between every cost objective. If there are 25 departments, then 4 percent of the internet cost would be allocated to each department, and so forth, using whatever base seems most appropriate and fair for the particular indirect cost.

Activity-Based Allocation

The accuracy of these allocations can be improved if the actual activities performed by the cost objective factor into the base. For example, the electricity cost of air-conditioning for a computer facility is more than for an office building. So, the activity basis (kilowatt hours) will be more accurate than a square-footage basis. This method is known as activity-based allocation. Or, another example, the cost of providing counseling services for freshmen is more than for graduate students. So, in this case, the indirect costs will be allocated on an activity basis (student FTE enrollment) to the appropriate cost objectives, with more allocated to the undergraduate than to the graduate-school student services. Despite the improved accuracy, however, the extra work needed for activity-based allocation is daunting, so this method is not used commonly in a university setting.

Sponsored Project Indirect Cost Allocation

In the *Uniform Guidance*, the federal government has well-established methods for allocating indirect costs incurred by a university in the performance of a grant or contract.[2] Because most universities receive and must account for federal funds, the government's allocation method has become the de facto standard in academic institutions. It can be used to allocate indirect costs to specific cost objectives within the institution (departments, colleges, centers, etc.) for budgeting purposes as well as for federal cost accounting. Because it is the de facto standard for all indirect cost allocations, the federal procedures for allocating indirect costs will be described in detail.

Note on terminology: The *Uniform Guidance* refers to indirect costs as facilities and administrative costs, or, more succinctly, "F&A costs." All three terms may be used interchangeably, but in the context of sponsored projects, the adjective "F&A" is used most frequently. For the most part, it will be used in the ensuing discussion.

Ideally, the F&A costs for each individual grant or contract would be reimbursed on a project-by-project basis. Unfortunately, the F&A costs for each specific grant or contract cannot be determined readily. Indeed, it would be most impractical to calculate the exact F&A costs incurred on a project-by-project basis because that would require estimates of utility costs, administrative support, and other services for each and every project. Repeating the example, a specific project's fraction of a laboratory building's air-conditioning, hot and cold water, and electricity costs could not be ascertained without extensive metering. And if the project is conducted in two or more buildings, the exact reckoning becomes even more complicated. Few academic institutions attempt to identify indirect costs of any sort with that level of specificity or scrutiny.

Given those practical complexities, how does the institution determine the indirect costs associated with individual sponsored projects? There is a clever answer to this question. Instead of calculating a project's exact F&A costs, the institution calculates an estimate of the project's share of the institution's total F&A costs based on the ratio of the project's MTDC to the institution's overall sponsored-activity MTDC. To simplify the arithmetic, institutions determine their so-called institutional F&A rate—the fraction of the institution's overall F&A costs relative to its overall sponsored-activity MTDC. This is a critical concept because knowing this rate, F&A costs assigned to an individual sponsored project can be calculated easily:

project F&A costs = institutional F&A rate × project MTDC

The institutional F&A rate lies at the core of indirect cost accounting, mainly because it reduces a complicated accounting process to something quite simple. Indeed, to understand university finances, it certainly helps to appreciate how the institutional F&A rate is determined.

The *Uniform Guidance* describes three methods to calculate institutional F&A rates: the long-form method, the simplified method, and the *de minimus* method. Each method is based on expenditures reported in the audited financial statements. By default, most research universities use the long method, but, as will be discussed in context, smaller institutions may use one of the other two alternatives. Regardless of which method is used, institutions must submit an *F&A rate proposal* to their cognizant agency, usually the NIH or the Office of Naval Research (ONR), documenting exactly how they derived their F&A rates. Ultimately, the government must approve the proposal before federal F&A reimbursements can be claimed.

The *Uniform Guidance* provides concise directions for calculating institutional F&A rates using these methods. In fact, they are so tersely concise that a nonexpert in government cost-accounting procedures may find them baffling. To resolve any apparent mystery to this process, the allocation of indirect costs in all three methods will be analyzed.

The Long-Form Method

Following the *Uniform Guidance* protocol, F&A rate calculations using the long-form method involve six steps:

1. Identify institutional cost objectives.
2. Reconcile financial statement data to a functional format.
3. Subtract excluded and unallowable costs.
4. Assign all indirect costs to pools.
5. Allocate indirect costs to cost objectives.
6. Calculate indirect cost rates.

Going down the list in order, the first four steps standardize indirect cost reporting and organize them into specific pools. The next step apportions the indirect costs to the cost objectives according to the benefit derived from them, and the last step calculates the indirect cost rates. Because "the devil is in the details," the process will be illustrated, using the financial statement expenditure data in table 4.3 as a base.

Identify Institutional Cost Objectives

Initially, the institutional cost objectives must be identified. If the goal is to allocate costs for university budgeting purposes, the cost objectives might be the individual schools and colleges, athletics, university press, and so forth. They may even include specific departments or degree programs. In these cases, the indirect costs of providing a particular degree can be estimated. If the goal is to seek reimbursement of F&A costs incurred while conducting government-sponsored research, the *Uniform Guidance* specifies four specific cost objectives:

- instruction
- organized research
- other sponsored activities
- other institutional activities

Expenditures associated with these cost objectives correspond to expenditures in the instruction, research, public service, and auxiliary enterprise categories in the NACUBO-recommended classifications (table 4.1). For clarity, the *Uniform Guidance* provides further detail about their four cost objectives.

Instruction refers to all instructional activities, "whether they are offered for credits toward a degree or certificate or on a noncredit basis, and whether they are offered through regular academic departments or separate divisions, such as a summer school division or an extension division." It also includes so-called departmental research, which is nonsponsored research that is not separately budgeted and accounted for as research. As an example, a department chair gives a faculty member $5,000 out of the department's operating budget for some research project. Costs of instruction include items such as professors' salaries, teaching assistant stipends, training supplies, and so forth. Uncommonly, sponsored instruction and training supported by an extraordinarily large or unique grant or contract may be placed into a separate cost-objective category as a major institutional function.

Organized research encompasses all research sponsored by federal and nonfederal agencies and organizations. Importantly, this also includes activities involving the training of individuals in research techniques (commonly called research training) "where such activities utilize the same facilities as other research and development activities and where such activities are not included in the instruction function."[3] Typically, NIH training grants fall in this category. In addition, the organized research function includes university research and development activities that are not sponsored but are budgeted and accounted for as research. This includes research supported by institutional funds, such as PI and postdoctoral fellow salaries, research assistant stipends, lab supplies, and so forth.

Other sponsored activities are programs and projects financed by federal and nonfederal agencies and organizations that involve the performance of work other than instruction and organized research. Most of these activities, such as sponsored health service projects, workshops, nonfederal drug studies, and community service programs, are classified functionally as public service. Accordingly, the other sponsored activities cost objective replaces the public service expenditure classification in the context of indirect cost allocation.

Other institutional activities constitute a "catch-all" for all activities apart from instruction, organized research, and other sponsored activities. Examples include operation of residence halls, dining halls, hospitals and clinics, student unions, intercollegiate athletics, bookstores, faculty housing, student apartments, guest houses, chapels, theaters, public museums, and other similar auxiliary enterprises. Any nonsponsored public service activities and unallowable costs are also included in the "other institutional activities" category.

Reconcile Financial Statement Data

The second step in the indirect cost allocation process is to classify all costs into functional categories. Another term for this reclassification is "reconciliation." Because the financial statements tabulate expenses in functional classifications (for example, table 4.3), this is a perfunctory step. For reference, the reconciled functional statement expenses to be used throughout these F&A rate calculations are shown in table 9.1.

Subtract Excluded and Unallowable Costs

In the third step, all excluded and unallowable costs are subtracted. These include all costs that are excluded in the MTDC (such as tuition remission and capital equipment) and that cannot be paid with federal funds (unallowable costs). Table 9.1 illustrates these subtractions. In this example, tuition remission is excluded with financial aid. Also, in this example, unallowable expenses included the costs for fund-raising and lobbying. After subtracting these expenses, the totals for each category (that is, each row) still include both direct and indirect costs; they are the total costs. But these total costs have been modified through the exclusions, so the totals are now called modified total costs (MTC).

Table 9.1. Reconciled financial statement expenses with subtraction of excluded and unallowable costs

Functional activity	Reconciled expenses	Financial aid	Subcontracts	Capital equipment	Unallowable costs	Modified total costs (MTC)
Instruction	52,052,721	(8,435,856)		(188,924)		43,427,941
Research	74,757,309	(10,808,386)	(1,467,968)	(1,499,895)		60,981,060
Public service	5,638,106					5,638,106
Academic support	10,830,804					10,830,804
Student administration	14,590,093					14,590,093
Institutional support	19,218,556				(191,563)	19,026,993
O&M	13,267,827					13,267,827
Scholarships	1,101,624	(1,101,624)				
Auxiliary services	4,407,374					4,407,374
Depreciation	13,058,315					13,058,315
Total	208,922,729	(20,345,866)	(1,467,968)	(1,688,819)	(191,563)	185,228,513

Many accounting systems have built-in routines, sometimes called edits, which identify excluded and unallowable costs, thus simplifying these subtractions. Nonetheless, humans must often examine numerous transactions for unallowable costs that evaded these filters for some reason. In the jargon, they "scrub" the accounts.

Assign All Indirect Costs to Pools

After reconciliation of the financial statement data to functional categories and subtraction of unallowable and excluded costs, the indirect costs embedded in the modified total costs of each functional expense category are re-categorized into eight indirect cost pools specified by the *Uniform Guidance*. They are:

1. *depreciation* of buildings and equipment (building shell, improvements, elevators, heating and air-conditioning systems, casework, construction and design, etc.)
2. *interest* on debt (buildings, equipment, capital improvements, etc.)
3. *operations and maintenance* expenses (utilities, janitorial, repairs, security services, etc.)
4. *general administration* expenses (president's office, controller, human resources, general counsel, etc.)
5. *departmental administration* expenses (deans, department chairs, administrative and clerical staff, office supplies, etc.)
6. *sponsored projects* administration (vice president for research and staff salaries, etc.)
7. *student services* administration (admissions, registrar, counseling, student health services, catalogs, etc.)
8. *library* expenses (purchase of books, journal subscriptions, librarian salaries, etc.)

These pools sort further into two basic categories: facilities (F) and administrative (A), as shown in table 9.2.

To minimize ambiguity, the *Uniform Guidance* provides specific instructions about what indirect costs are included in each pool. In

Table 9.2. Facilities and administrative indirect cost categories

Facilities (F)	Administrative (A)
Depreciation (building and equipment)	General administration
Interest costs	Departmental administration
Operations and maintenance	Sponsored projects administration
Library	Student services

many accounting software systems, indirect costs are assigned codes that identify their pool assignments. Therefore, the reclassification of indirect costs from the major functional category to the appropriate indirect cost pool is fairly straightforward.

Reclassification is illustrated in table 9.3. Pedagogically, it helps to look at the table from two different perspectives: horizontal (rows) and vertical (columns). *Rows*: indirect costs for each of the 10 functional activities from the financial statements (listed in table 9.1) are tabulated in rows above the dashed line. These include three of the four cost objectives (remember, other sponsored activities replaced public service) and three of the eight indirect cost categories from the *Uniform Guidance* list (table 9.2): student services, operations and maintenance (O&M), and depreciation. The remaining five indirect cost categories (plus the "other institutional activities" category) are tabulated in rows below the dashed line. *Columns*: indirect costs in seven of the eight categories from the *Uniform Guidance* (plus the other institutional activities category) are tabulated in columns.

The goal of the reclassification is to move all indirect costs into the eight *Uniform Guidance* pools. So, for starters, look at the table from a horizontal perspective. All of the indirect costs in instruction, which are for departmental administration and interest, are moved into the departmental administration and interest indirect cost pools. Furthermore, all of the indirect costs in academic support and institutional support activity pools are moved into the *Uniform Guidance*-designated indirect cost pools. Specifically:

- *academic support* to departmental administration, general administration, library, and student services
- *institutional support* to sponsored projects administration and general administration
- *auxiliary services* to other institutional activities
- *O&M charged directly* to other institutional activities to the O&M total cost pool, thus consolidating the O&M costs

After these reclassifications, three functional-activity pools (academic support, institutional support, and auxiliary services) are empty. Their indirect costs have been moved (reclassified) into the *Uniform Guidance* indirect-cost pools. (The scholarships and fellowships pool is also empty because those costs were excluded; table 9.1.)

Also, after these reclassifications, the total costs in the four institutional cost objectives no longer contain any indirect cost compo-

Table 9.3. Reclassification of indirect costs to *Uniform Guidance* indirect cost groupings

Functional activity and indirect cost pools		Cost pools								
	MTC	Dept. admin.	Sponsored projects admin.	Direct charged O&M	General admin.	Library	Student services	Other institutional activities	Interest	Adjusted MTC MTDC
Instruction	43,427,941	(4,217,075)							(3,454,765)	35,756,101
Organized research	60,981,060									60,981,060
Other spons. activities	5,638,106									5,638,106
Academic support	10,830,804	(2,032,861)			(1,694,996)	(3,041,161)	(4,061,786)			
Student services	14,590,093						4,061,786			18,651,879
Institutional support	19,026,993		(4,757,468)		(14,269,525)					
O&M	13,267,827			676,569						13,944,396
Auxiliary services	4,407,374							(4,407,374)		
Depreciation	13,058,315									13,058,315
Interest									3,454,765	3,454,765
General admin.					15,964,521					15,964,521
Departmental admin.		6,249,936								6,249,936
Spons. projects admin.			4,757,468							4,757,468
Library						3,041,161				3,041,161
Other inst'l. activities				(676,569)				4,407,374		3,730,805
Total	185,228,513									185,228,513

nents; they contain only modified direct costs. Thus, the adjusted totals in these categories (right-hand column) represent modified total
direct costs—the MTDC. Significantly, the indirect costs and the direct costs have now been segregated; the indirect costs are in their
eight pools, and the direct costs are in the four institutional cost
objective pools.

Allocate Indirect Costs to Cost Objectives

After the indirect costs have been moved into their cost pools,
they are all then reassigned (that is, allocated) from those indirect
cost pools into the four institutional cost objective pools. Metaphor-
ically, all indirect costs in the eight indirect cost pools are "drained"
into the four institutional cost objective pools. The actual amount
drained into each cost objective pool depends on how much benefit
the cost objective derived from the indirect cost. In this way, the indirect costs are aligned with each cost objective function.

A critical, initial step when making these allocations is to account
for any indirect costs in one pool that benefit activities in other indirect cost pools. To state this differently, some indirect costs in one
pool benefit activities in other indirect cost pools. In cost accounting terms, the indirect costs in one pool are "cross allocated" to other
indirect cost pools. Importantly, the appropriate costs are subtracted
from one indirect pool and added to another, so there is no net
change in the total indirect cost amount. For example, a building
may house office space for sponsored projects administration, general administration, and student services. Therefore, indirect costs
associated with the building's depreciation may be cross allocated
to each of these other indirect cost pools. Procedurally, the fraction
of indirect costs in one pool to be assigned to other indirect cost
pools is usually based on some measurable criterion, such as ANSF,
MTC, FTE employees, or salaries and wages. Ultimately, after
making the cross allocations, the indirect costs (including the cross
allocations) are allocated to the institutional cost objectives.

Overall, cross allocations and allocations to the cost objectives use
a "step-down" accounting method. This procedure allocates sequentially the indirect costs in one pool to other indirect cost pools and
the cost objectives. In general, the indirect cost pool that contributes the most to the other pools but derives the least from the others
is the first to be allocated. For example, depreciation is distributed
across all other indirect cost categories but does not receive benefit
from them. (Student administration expenses, for example, could
not provide any benefit to depreciation.) Therefore, the depreciation

expenses are the first to be allocated into the other pools. Then, the pool that contributes the second most is allocated, and, in stepwise fashion, the remaining pools are allocated in descending order of contribution to the other pools.

Procedurally, once a pool has been fully allocated in this fashion, it is considered "closed"; it is empty, and no costs can be cross allocated back into it from the other indirect cost pools lower in the step-down order. Thus, the indirect cost pools are sequentially closed as their contents are allocated to the remaining pools. Ultimately, all indirect cost pools are allocated in this stepwise sequence to the four cost objectives.

Inherently, the order of this step-down distribution method affects the amount allocated to the four cost objectives. Consequently, the *Uniform Guidance* standardizes accounting procedures by stipulating the step-down order. "Depreciation, interest expenses, operation and maintenance expenses, and general administrative and general expenses should be allocated in that order to the remaining F&A cost categories as well as to the major functions and specialized service facilities of the institution. Other cost categories may be allocated in the order determined to be most appropriate by the institutions."[4]

Accordingly, a typical allocation sequence order is:

1. depreciation (building and equipment)
2. interest
3. operations and maintenance
4. general administration
5. departmental administration
6. sponsored projects administration
7. library
8. student services
9. instruction
10. organized research
11. other sponsored activities
12. other institutional activities

Thus, in sequence, the allowable building and equipment depreciation would be allocated to the remaining 11 pools. Then, the interest expenses would be allocated to the remaining 10 pools. The operations and maintenance would be allocated to the remaining 9 pools, and so on.

To illustrate this accounting procedure, the development and allocation of each indirect cost pool will be examined in the step-down order. A NACUBO case analysis presents this procedure in more detail.[5]

Depreciation. Depreciation of capital assets is considered an indirect cost according to the *Uniform Guidance.* Therefore, universities may be reimbursed for the depreciation expenses associated with the use of their capitalized assets such as buildings, capital improvements, and equipment in the performance of a grant or contract provided that they can be allocated properly to federal awards.[6] The depreciation method must be the same one used in the financial statements, usually the straight-line method over the useful lifetime (see chapter 5). If any federal funds contributed to the cost of the building or equipment, they must be subtracted from the depreciation schedule. (Otherwise, the federal government would end up paying twice for the equipment—in the original purchase and again in the depreciation.) Of course, no depreciation may be allowed on any asset that has outlived its useful life. And depreciation on any asset acquired solely for the performance of a nonfederal award is unallowable.

Incidentally, although the *Uniform Guidance* lumps building and equipment depreciation into a single "depreciation" pool, some institutions account for them separately in the F&A calculations. They will be calculated separately here and then combined in the final step.

For *buildings*, depreciation is allocated on the basis of ANSF. The square feet assigned to each cost pool are determined manually by conducting an institutional space utilization study of each building that must be reviewed periodically. This important and time-consuming study measures the percentage of space in the buildings that benefits each indirect cost pool. Each building's total depreciation is then allocated to the indirect cost pools according to these space percentages. This allocation procedure is illustrated in table 9.4. For example, the engineering building's depreciation in 2015 is $1,747,764. Within the building, the department administration (deans, department chairs, and their staff) occupies 6,944 square feet, which is 4.66 percent of the building's total ANSF (148,925 square feet). Therefore, 4.66 percent of the building's depreciation cost ($1,747,764) is cross allocated to the department administration indirect cost pool ($81,494). The remainder of the building's depreciation cost is allocated similarly to the instruction, organized research, and other sponsored activities cost pools. The allocations for each building are summed to obtain the total depreciation allocation for each of the indirect cost pools and the four cost objectives. So, for example, the total depreciation for all buildings allocated to instruction is $2,702,737.

Like buildings, *equipment* is depreciated over its useful life span, usually using the straight-line method. Fixed equipment within a building (for example, sterilizers, casework, fume hoods, cold rooms, and glassware washers) is usually included in a building's depreciation. However, other equipment, such as laboratory equipment, is depreciated separately over its useful life span. The useful life span varies between different equipment categories and between different universities. The University of California system provides a fairly typical schedule.[7] General laboratory equipment has a useful lifespan of 8 to 15 years. Computers usually have a lifespan of three to four years.

A sample equipment depreciation schedule for a faculty member's research laboratory is shown in table 9.5. This example was prepared on the last day of FY 2015, June 30, 2015. So, the equipment age is calculated relative to that date. For example, the age of the top item, the centrifuge, is the number of months (158) between the acquisition date (May 6, 2002) and June 30, 2015. The centrifuge and the computer server are both older than their useful life, meaning that they cannot be depreciated further. The microscope's age is 83 percent of its useful life (150 months/180 months). Therefore, $182.73 ($32,891/180) in depreciation can be claimed for each month in this fiscal year, for a total of $2,193. Comparable depreciation schedules are collected from each administrative unit, such as laboratories, colleges, libraries, and physical plants, to obtain the overall university equipment depreciation for the fiscal year. The university's equipment value and depreciation usually are reported in the notes to the financial statements (table 7.9).

The total university equipment depreciation is then allocated to the various F&A and cost objective pools, as shown in table 9.6. In this example, these are based on the actual usage of the equipment. However, depreciation allowances for equipment shared between university functions (for example, instruction and research) are allocated by either square footage or user numbers, whichever provides the most accurate and fair allocation.

Finally, the total university depreciation costs are calculated by summing the building and equipment components. For this example, the summed results (from tables 9.4 and 9.6) are shown in table 9.7.

Interest. Interest expenses, incurred from debt used to finance acquisition, construction, or remodeling of capital assets, are allocated

Table 9.4. Building depreciation cost allocation in FY 2015

Building name	Annual building depreciation	Assigned net square feet (ANSF)	O&M	General admin.	Dept. admin.	Sponsored projects admin.	Library	Student services	Instruction	Organized research	Other sponsored activities	Other institutional activities
Administration												
Square feet		108,617		48,647	4,836	16,201		26,681			10,549	1,703
% of ANSF				44.79	4.45	14.92		24.56			9.71	1.57
Depreciation	1,101,396			493,290	49,038	164,281		270,550			106,969	17,269
Engineering												
Square feet		148,925			6,944				38,955	90,492	12,534	
% of ANSF					4.66				26.16	60.76	8.42	
Depreciation	1,747,764				81,494				457,171	1,062,002	147,097	
Humanities												
Square feet		164,737			10,399		67,987		60,077	16,153	10,122	
% of ANSF					6.31		41.27		36.47	9.81	6.14	
Depreciation	1,534,584				96,832		633,323		559,663	150,543	94,223	
Life sciences												
Square feet		120,000			16,811				29,594	67,244	6,351	
% of ANSF					14.01				24.66	56.04	5.29	
Depreciation	2,975,425				416,832				733,789	1,667,329	157,474	

Physical plant											
Square feet	51,234	51,234									
% of ANSF		100.00									
Depreciation	505,126	505,126									
Physical sciences											
Square feet	165,132		12,699					45,967	103,147	3,319	
% of ANSF			7.69					27.84	62.46	2.01	
Depreciation	1,916,603		145,133					546,088	1,185,115	40,267	
Social sciences											
Square feet	128,141		8,495					29,689	67,274	22,683	
% of ANSF			6.63					23.17	52.50	17.70	
Depreciation	1,752,454		116,177					406,026	920,038	310,212	
Student union											
Square feet	55,011										55,011
% of ANSF											100.00
Depreciation	1,091,434										1,091,434
Totals											
Square Feet	941,797	51,234	48,647	60,184	16,201	67,987	26,681	204,282	344,310	65,558	56,714
Depreciation	12,624,787	505,126	493,290	905,506	164,281	633,323	270,550	2,702,737	4,985,027	856,243	1,108,703

Table 9.5. Individual laboratory equipment depreciation schedule (calculated on June 30, 2015)

Acquisition date	Description	Acquisition cost	Federal funds	Net cost	Useful life (mos.)	Age (mos.)	Depreciation
May 6, 2002	Centrifuge	18,608		18,608	132	158	
Dec. 27, 2002	Microscope	32,891		32,891	180	150	2,193
Dec. 22, 2003	Incubator	5,099		5,099	168	138	364
Aug. 5, 2006	Freezer	6,923		6,923	108	107	769
June 21, 2008	Electronic balance	5,895		5,895	168	84	421
Apr. 26, 2009	Spectrophotometer	6,777		6,777	168	74	484
May 6, 2009	Biosafety cabinet	7,386		7,386	84	74	1,055
Oct. 21, 2009	Stereo microscope	22,589	(22,589)		180	68	
May 9, 2010	PCR system	30,460	(30,460)		84	62	
Nov. 21, 2010	Microscope camera	16,165		16,165	84	55	2,309
May 18, 2011	Computer server	5,448		5,448	48	49	
June 16, 2012	Vibration-free table	6,493		6,493	120	36	649
Totals		164,734	(53,049)	111,685			8,245

Table 9.6. Equipment depreciation cost allocations

Administrative unit	Cost pools											Totals
	Depreciation	O&M	General admin.	Dept. admin.	Sponsored projects admin.	Student services	Library	Instruction	Organized research	Other sponsored activities	Other institutional activities	
Administration	15,040		9,809		5,231							15,040
Agriculture	67,152			5,244				26,861	23,503	11,544		67,152
Arts and sciences	39,030			7,806				15,612	13,661	1,951		39,030
Athletics	53,491										53,491	53,491
Business	8,128			4,598				3,530				8,128
Education	3,347			3,347								3,347
Engineering	107,588			6,959				32,276	53,794	14,559		107,588
Housing and food	3,228										3,228	3,228
Library	80,460						80,460					80,460
Outreach	2,750			2,750								2,750
Physical plant	53,314	53,314										53,314
Total	433,528	53,314	9,809	30,705	5,231		80,460	78,279	90,958	28,053	56,718	433,528

Table 9.7. Total depreciation costs

Cost pools	Depreciation		
	Building	Equipment	Total
O&M	505,126	53,314	558,441
General administration	493,290	9,809	503,099
Department administration	905,506	30,705	936,211
Sponsored project administration	164,281	5,231	169,512
Library	633,323	80,460	713,783
Student services	270,550		270,550
Instruction	2,702,737	78,279	2,781,016
Organized research	4,985,027	90,958	5,075,985
Other sponsored activities	856,243	28,053	884,296
Other institutional activities	1,108,703	56,718	1,165,421
Totals	12,624,787	433,528	13,058,314

in a manner similar to building depreciation expenses. Their allocations are based on the same square footage data. Or, in the words of the *Uniform Guidance*, "These costs must be allocated in the same manner as the depreciation on the buildings, equipment and capital improvements to which the interest relates."[8] Thus, allocation spreadsheets similar to those used in the building depreciation calculations (for example, table 9.4) are prepared using the same square footage data.

Sample interest calculations are presented in table 9.8. The interest payments for each building were based on the debt-financing terms summarized in table 7.11. The campus utilities upgrade benefited the entire campus, so, like depreciation, the interest was allocated based on ANSF (table 9.4). The physical sciences building interest benefited four activities, and the interest allocations were based on ANSF for those activities. The other buildings are part of the auxiliary enterprise, so their interest payments were allocated totally to other institutional activities.

The *Uniform Guidance* adds several conditions to these otherwise straightforward interest calculations. Of course, the institution must use the capital assets (building and equipment) in support of federal awards. To protect the federal government from interest claims that exceed "fair market value," the cost and the financing terms of any facilities or equipment must be determined by an unrelated third party—that is, via an "arm's length" transaction. Furthermore, incurring debt to purchase a building or piece of equipment must be the least costly alternative. For example, "a capital lease may be determined less costly than purchasing through debt financing, in which case reimbursement must be limited to the amount of inter-

Table 9.8. Allocation of interest payments in FY 2015

Building	Total interest	O&M	General admin.	Dept. admin.	Sponsored projects admin.	Library	Student services	Instruction	Organized research	Other sponsored activities	Other institutional activities
Dormitory A	15,327										15,327
Dormitory B	21,323										21,323
Student housing A	298,985										298,985
Student housing B	43,339										43,339
Dining hall	221,231										221,231
Campus utilities upgrade	195,348	10,627	10,090	12,483	3,360	14,102	5,534	42,372	71,417	13,598	11,763
Student housing C	772,108										772,108
Refinance dormitory C	413,861										413,861
Refinance dormitory D	404,990										404,990
Student union	107,495										107,495
Physical sciences building	960,759			61,396				299,151	504,208	96,003	
Totals	3,454,765	10,627	10,090	73,879	3,360	14,102	5,534	341,523	575,625	109,601	2,310,421

est determined if leasing had been used."[9] And, understandably, interest attributable to a fully depreciated asset is unallowable.

One further condition limits an institution's ability to earn interest by investing borrowed money before actually paying for a capital asset. That might occur, for example, if the institution were granted a loan and received the money but didn't make payment on a new asset (for example, a building) until a month later. During that month, the institution could invest the borrowed money, thus earning interest on the loan. That constitutes arbitrage, which is limited by federal policy. The limitations on arbitrage are strictest when the debt arrangements exceed $1 million. In those cases, the institution must calculate the monthly cash flow from federal reimbursements: inflows from federal reimbursements and so forth minus outflows from debt principal and interest payments and so forth. According to the *Uniform Guidance*, "for any month in which cumulative cash inflows exceed cumulative outflows, interest must be calculated on the excess inflows for that month and be treated as a reduction to allowable interest cost. The rate of interest to be used must be the three-month Treasury bill closing rate as of the last business day of that month." Thus, the institution "must reduce claims for reimbursement of interest cost by an amount equal to imputed interest earnings on excess cash flow attributable to the portion of the facility used for federal awards."[10] This reduces F&A reimbursement for interest because any investment income earned by arbitrage must be deducted from a claim for federal reimbursement of interest expenses.

But there is a noteworthy loophole in this condition. If the institution contributes at least 25 percent toward the acquisition cost of the facility, these arbitrage limitations do not apply. Therefore, by this "25 percent equity contribution rule," it is advantageous for an institution to contribute at least 25 percent toward the cost of any facility. Or, stated differently, the institution should not borrow more than 75 percent of the acquisition cost. This initial equity contribution is similar to a down payment toward the cost of a facility.

Operations and maintenance. The O&M costs of institutional facilities involved in federally sponsored activities are reimbursable. According to the *Uniform Guidance*, they include "expenses incurred for administration, supervision, operation, maintenance, preservation and protection of the institution's physical plant."[11] Numerous fairly recognizable O&M activities fall into this broad category: janitorial and housekeeping, utilities, grounds maintenance, landscaping, security and public safety, environmental safety, hazard waste disposal, refuse disposal, central receiving, and ordinary or normal repair and maintenance. Less obvious activities include space and capital leasing, facility planning and management, physical plant administration, noncapitalized expenditures in the plant fund, and property and liability insurance. All in all, this is a large indirect cost pool, often the largest. Moreover, the O&M F&A rate is not capped. So, the more an institution spends on O&M, the more it recovers.

Ideally, the O&M costs for utilities such as electricity, natural gas, water, and sewage are determined by metering. Where space is devoted to a single function and metering allows unambiguous measurement of usage related to that space, this is usually feasible, and costs must be assigned to the function located in that space. This would normally include buildings and space associated with student housing, general administrative activities, auditoriums, classrooms, and other institutional activities. However, where space is allocated to different functions and metering does not allow unambiguous measurement of usage by function, utility costs should be allocated by square footage of a site, building, floor, or room.

Normally, O&M expenses are allocated to the other indirect cost pools and the institutional cost objectives in the same way as depreciation and interest expenses. Expenses associated with only a single function are assigned 100 percent to that function. These include most nonacademic administrative offices such as purchasing, payroll, accounting, and human resources; the physical plant; residence halls; and libraries. Multiple function space—that is, space used in support of more than one function—"shall be allocated to the individual functions performed in each building on the basis of useable square feet," usually determined by the institutional space utilization survey (as in table 9.4). And, like depreciation allocations, if individual rooms are used jointly by more than one function, O&M expenses are allocated further based on either the number of FTEs or salaries and wages of the benefiting function.

The allocation procedure must account for any O&M expenses paid directly. Typically, auxiliary activities such as hospitals, bookstores, housing and food services, and athletic facilities pay O&M costs directly through a recharge system. These O&M costs are incurred at an administrative unit level (hospitals, etc.), rather than as part of a central facilities organization. They may be a result of chargebacks to the departments from the central facilities department for maintenance items or other O&M services. The federal government recognizes that these are allowable O&M costs but is concerned that some institutions may be treating them inconsistently. Thus, to ensure transparency, the direct-charged costs are identified clearly throughout the allocation process.

In this context, some O&M costs can be treated legitimately as direct and indirect where unlike circumstances exist. As the Council on Government Relations (COGR) points out, "Equipment maintenance on a piece of equipment purchased and used solely on one project is a justifiable direct cost to the project, whereas equipment maintenance contract costs related to a piece of equipment shared by all of the researchers in a department normally would be considered indirect. Similarly, rent for an off-campus facility for the sole use of one project can be charged directly, whereas rent for a facility that houses multiple functions and projects normally would be considered indirect and included in the O&M pool."[12]

When developing the O&M cost pool, the expenses for each O&M component (physical plant maintenance, utilities, security, etc.) are grouped into three categories. The first two depend on whether they serve all functions, including other institutional activities (OIA) or all functions except OIA; the sum of these two categories represents the O&M costs in the reconciled financial statement (table 9.1). The third category contains O&M costs that were paid directly.

Sample O&M cost pool development is illustrated in table 9.9. O&M costs reported in the financial statement ($13,267,827; table 9.1) were sorted into two categories, depending on whether they benefited all functions (that is, the entire university) or all functions except other institutional activities (*upper panel*). In this example, the physical plant costs benefited the entire university (including auxiliary enterprises), but utilities and security did not benefit the other institutional activities; presumably, the auxiliary enterprises paid for those costs separately. Then, O&M costs paid directly by housing, food service, and athletics ($676,569, *middle panel*) were added to the O&M expenses listed in the financial statements to yield a subtotal of the O&M expenses ($13,944,396). Cross allocations to O&M from the depreciation and interest pools were added subsequently to obtain the total allocable O&M pool amount ($14,513,464).

This total amount was allocated to the other indirect cost pools based on the same square footage measurements used for depreciation and interest allocations, as shown in table 9.10. For example, components of the general administration cost pool for all functions occupy 48,647 ANSF (table 9.4), which constitutes 5.46 percent of the total ANSF for all functions. (*Note:* This total does not include the O&M ANSF because the O&M indirect costs are fully allocated

Table 9.9. Operations and maintenance (O&M) cost pool

	Total expenses	All functions	All functions except OIA	Directly paid O&M
O&M from financial statement				
Physical plant	5,779,464	5,779,464		
Utilities	5,993,518		5,993,518	
Security	1,494,845		1,494,845	
Financial statement O&M	13,267,827	5,779,464	7,488,363	
Directly paid O&M				
Housing and food service	600,877			600,877
Athletics	75,692			75,692
Directly paid O&M	676,569			676,569
Subtotal O&M	13,944,396	5,779,464	7,488,363	676,569
Cross allocations				
Depreciation	558,441	558,441		
Interest	10,627		10,627	
Total	14,513,464	6,337,905	7,498,990	676,569

to the other pools.) Consequently, the general administration allocation for all functions ($346,208) is 5.46 percent of the total O&M costs for all functions ($6,337,905).

Recognizing that research laboratories consume more energy than nonlaboratory space, the *Uniform Guidance* allows the addition of a utility cost adjustment (UCA) to the calculated F&A rate for organized research.[13] Specifically, a utility cost adjustment of up to 1.3 percentage points may be included in the F&A cost rate for organized research. The other cost objectives are not eligible for a UCA—just organized research. Arithmetically, the adjustment is based on the relative energy utilization index (REUI), which is the ratio of laboratory energy use to the corresponding index for overall average college or university space. Currently, the REUI is 2.0, which means that the laboratory space utility costs are double the costs of nonlaboratory space. The ratio is recalculated every one to five years and is posted on the OMB website.

As usual in these allocations, the utility costs for all laboratory space ideally would be metered separately, thus measuring the exact costs. Accordingly, the *Uniform Guidance* states that "where space is devoted to a single function and metering allows unambiguous measurement of usage related to that space, the adjusted [utility] costs must be assigned to the function located in that space." But, in many if not most cases, space is allocated to more than one

Table 9.10. O&M pool allocations

Pool/cost objective	Total ANSF	All functions		All functions except OIA		Directly paid O&M		Total allocation
		% of ANSF	Amount	% of ANFS	Amount	% of ANSF	Amount	
General admin.	48,647	5.46	346,208	5.83	437,493			783,700
Dept. admin.	60,184	6.76	428,313	7.22	541,247			969,561
Spons. proj. admin.	16,201	1.82	115,298	1.94	145,699			260,997
Library	67,987	7.63	483,845	8.15	611,422			1,095,267
Student services	26,681	3.00	189,882	3.20	239,948			429,829
Instruction	204,282	22.94	1,453,820	24.50	1,837,151			3,290,971
Organized research	344,310	38.66	2,450,362	41.29	3,096,453			5,546,815
Other spons. activities	65,558	7.36	466,559	7.86	589,577			1,056,136
Subtotals	833,850	93.63	5,934,286	100.00	7,498,990			13,433,276
OIA	56,714	6.37	403,618			100.00	676,569	1,080,187
Totals	890,564	100.00	6,337,905		7,498,990	100.00	676,569	14,513,464

function (for example, classrooms and research laboratories), and, therefore, metering does not allow unambiguous measurement of usage by function. In those cases, the adjusted utility costs must be allocated on a square-footage basis weighted for the increased laboratory costs.

These weighted calculations are illustrated in table 9.11. Initially, unweighted utility costs are calculated, prorated on assigned square footage. To calculate the UCA, the square footage of laboratory space is multiplied by the REUI, yielding the weighted "effective square footage." With an REUI factor of 2, this increases the laboratory square footage by a factor of 2 in subsequent utility cost calculations. In a sense, laboratories gain "virtual" space. The utility costs for laboratory and nonlaboratory space for each building are then recalculated using the weighted square footage. The differences between the weighted and unweighted utility costs for laboratory space equal the utility cost adjustments for each building. The overall adjustment ($1,010,697) is then divided by the MTDC for organized research ($60,981,060, from table 9.3) to determine the percentage increase that can be added directly to the organized research F&A rate.

In this example, the calculated UCA is 1.66 percent of the research MTDC. However, the allowable UCA amount may not exceed 1.30 percent. Where did this number come from? Historically, this adjustment evolved from special cost studies submitted by 50 universities documenting the increased utility costs of some research facilities. The weighted average of these adjusted costs resulted in a 1.30 percent increase in the F&A rate calculated using square footage and FTEs.[14] Therefore, the OMB now limits the UCA to 1.30 percent. If the calculated adjustment exceeds 1.30 percent, then the capped adjustment is set at 1.30 percent.

Importantly, if an institution claims a UCA, it may not meter utility costs at a resolution greater than the whole building level. With multiple meters per building, there is the potential of research receiving an excessive allocation of utility costs. Furthermore, it is unacceptable for a university to meter for a selected period of time (for example, in August when air-conditioning costs are particularly high) and project the costs for the year.

General administration expenses. General administration (GA) expenses are those that have been incurred for the institution-wide executive and administrative offices and other expenses of a general character that do not relate solely to any major function of the institution (instruction, organized research, other sponsored

Table 9.11. Utility cost adjustment calculation

Building name	ANSF			Unweighted utility cost		
	Laboratory	Non-laboratory	Total	Laboratory	Non-laboratory	Total
Administration		108,617	108,617		691,229	691,229
Engineering	119,140	29,785	148,925	758,196	189,549	947,745
Humanities		164,737	164,737		1,048,371	1,048,371
Life sciences	86,400	33,600	120,000	549,842	213,827	763,669
Physical plant		51,234	51,234		326,049	326,049
Physical sciences	116,773	48,360	165,133	743,133	307,759	1,050,892
Social sciences	8,422	119,719	128,141	53,597	761,881	815,478
Student center		55,011	55,011		350,085	350,085
Total	330,735	611,063	941,798	2,104,768	3,888,750	5,993,518

Note: REUI factor = 2.
Utility cost adjustment percentage of organized research MTDC = 1.66%; percentage allowable = 1.30%.

activities, or other institutional activities). The financial statement usually includes them in the "institutional support" category. Examples include expenses incurred by administrative offices that serve the entire university system (if the university is, in fact, part of a system); central offices of the institution such as the president's or chancellor's office, the offices for institution-wide financial management, business services, budget and planning, personnel management, and safety and risk management; the office of the general counsel; and the operations of the central administrative management information systems. In contrast, GA expenses must not include expenses incurred within nonuniversity-wide deans' offices, academic departments, organized research units, or similar organizational units; these costs are usually allocated to the departmental administration pool. Likewise, they must not include expenses incurred for the development office, alumni relations, public relations, or investment counsel; these costs are usually allocated to the other institutional activities function.

The GA cost pool includes the base amount from the institutional financial statement plus additional cross-allocations from the depreciation, interest, and O&M pools. The total cost pool expenses then should be allocated to the remaining indirect cost pools and institutional functions on an MTC basis. That is, allocations of the total GA indirect costs are based on the relative percentage of the benefiting pools' MTC.

The development and allocation of the total GA cost pool, illustrated in table 9.12, is straightforward. The basic cost pool ($15,964,521) is derived from the reclassified indirect costs (table 9.3). And the cross allocations are simply added to yield the total

Effective sq. ft.	Weighted total ANSF	Weighted utility cost			Utility cost adjustment
		Laboratory	Non-laboratory	Total	
	108,617		511,576	511,576	
238,280	268,065	1,122,278	140,285	1,262,562	364,081
	164,737		775,897	775,897	
172,800	206,400	813,873	158,253	972,126	264,031
	51,234		241,308	241,308	
233,546	281,906	1,099,981	227,771	1,327,752	356,848
16,844	136,563	79,334	563,866	643,200	25,737
	55,011		259,097	259,097	
661,470	1,272,533	3,115,465	2,878,053	5,993,518	1,010,697

Table 9.12. General administration pool development and allocation

Cost pool	Amount
General administration	15,964,521

Cross allocations	
Depreciation	503,099
Interest	10,090
Operations and maintenance	783,700
Total cross allocations	1,296,889
Total general administration allocation	17,261,410

Pool allocation

Cost pool	MTC		Allocation
	Amount	Percent	
Departmental administration	6,249,936	4.50	776,763
Sponsored projects administration	4,757,468	3.43	592,066
Library	3,041,161	2.19	378,025
Student services	18,651,879	13.44	2,319,934
Instruction	35,756,101	25.76	4,446,539
Organized research	60,981,060	43.93	7,582,938
Other sponsored activities	5,638,106	4.06	700,813
Other institutional activities	3,730,805	2.69	464,332
Total	138,806,516	100.00	17,261,410

allocation pool (*top panel*). The total pool is then allocated to the remaining pools proportional to their MTC base (*bottom panel*). For example, the departmental administration MTC ($6,249,936) is 4.50 percent of the total MTC ($138,806,516). So, the departmental administration cost pool allocation ($776,763) is 4.50 percent of the total GA cost pool ($17,261,410).

Departmental administration expenses. Departmental administration (DA) expenses include the expenses of "administrative and supporting services that benefit common or joint departmental activities or objectives in academic deans' offices, academic departments and divisions, and organized research units . . . such as institutes, study centers, and research centers."[15] Thus, in the deans' offices, salaries and operating expenses attributable to administrative functions are included in this pool. Likewise, departmental expenses such as the salaries of secretarial and clerical staffs, the salaries of administrative officers and assistants, travel, office supplies, stockrooms, as well as an appropriate share of general administration and general expenses, operation and maintenance expenses, and depreciation are included in this pool.

The DA pool contains several components, some of them unique. For starters, each academic department becomes a subpool of the overall DA pool. That is, the expenses are allocated on a department-by-department basis; thus, an allocation schedule is prepared for each department. Accordingly, the administrative expenses of the dean's office of each college and school (including the graduate school) must be allocated to the academic departments within that college or school. This is done on the basis of a department's MTC, which can be obtained from its budget, for example.[16] Importantly, each departmental DA subpool contains only administrative costs; it does not contain costs associated with the performance of instruction, research, other institutional activities, or any other non-administrative functions or activities.

The allocation of the deans' administrative indirect costs to the departments is illustrated in table 9.13. Because a university usually has many departments, the allocation details can result in a massive spreadsheet that cannot be accommodated easily in a standard book format. Consequently, a scaled-down sample of several departments in three colleges (Arts and Sciences, Engineering, and Business) within a university is shown here. The college and departmental MTC amounts were obtained from their financial records, such as their operating budgets. The college deans' DA allocations were based on the colleges' proportion of the total academic MTC, which is allocated to instruction, organized research, and other sponsored activities (table 9.3). For example, the College of Arts and Sciences' MTC ($25,939,904) is 23.57 percent of the total academic MTC ($110,047,107); so, the college's DA allocation ($994,034) is 23.57 percent of the total institutional DA allocation ($4,217,075). Simi-

Table 9.13. Allocation of deans' departmental administration indirect costs to the departments

| College departments | MTC | | Dept. admin. allocation |
	Amount	% of college MTC	
Arts and sciences			
Dean's office	25,939,904	100.00	994,034
Biology	4,305,387	16.60	164,985
Chemistry	4,732,214	18.24	181,341
History	2,711,934	10.45	103,923
Mathematics	5,909,130	22.78	226,442
Physics	6,137,882	23.66	235,208
Psychology	2,143,356	8.26	82,135
Engineering			
Dean's office	73,596,324	100.00	2,820,258
Chemical	18,175,472	24.70	696,496
Civil	24,326,553	33.05	932,209
Electrical	21,198,829	28.80	812,353
Mechanical	9,895,470	13.45	379,201
Business			
Dean's office	10,510,880	100.00	402,784
Accounting	3,362,500	31.99	128,853
Finance	1,726,592	16.43	66,164
Management	2,944,954	28.02	112,853
Marketing	2,476,833	23.56	94,914
Total institutional	110,047,107		4,217,075

larly, the departments' DA allocations were based on the departments' proportion of the colleges' MTC. For example, biology's MTC ($4,305,387) is 16.60 percent of the College of Arts and Science's total MTC ($25,939,904); so, biology's allocation of the dean's DA indirect costs ($164,985) is 16.60 percent of the college's total DA allocation ($994,034).

The *Uniform Guidance* allows compensation for salaries and fringe benefits attributable to the administrative work (including bid and proposal preparation, filing effort reports, etc.) of faculty members (including department heads) and other professional personnel who normally conduct research and instruction. Inherently, however, these costs are difficult to develop because they are not identified specifically in most university accounting systems. They are usually embedded in the instruction and academic support functions. Thus, accurate allocation of personnel salaries and benefits as indirect costs to instruction or sponsored research would require extensive, burdensome reporting. These inherent accounting difficulties are compounded because the *Uniform Guidance* allows an institution to treat some DA costs as direct costs and others as indirect costs.

Recognizing these inherent difficulties, the *Uniform Guidance* eases the accounting burden by using several formulaic procedures in development of the DA cost pool. To simplify the effort reporting needed to document the administrative indirect costs for each individual faculty member or dean, the departments may claim an allowance equal to 3.6 percent of their MTDC. This unique allowance, the so-called faculty administrative allowance, is calculated separately for each function (for example, instruction, organized research, and other sponsored activities) of the department. In addition, by formula, the salaries and fringe benefits of professional administrators and business officers within the department are 100 percent allowable. Effort reports are not required to substantiate these two components of the DA pool.

Development of the pool becomes more complicated if the department has charged some sponsored projects directly for department administrative and clerical salaries and other administrative personnel. This occurs to a varying extent at most large research universities, usually in departments that have received large awards supporting a specialized center with dedicated administrative support needs, such as an NSF engineering research center. In those cases, the *Uniform Guidance* cautions that "special care should be exercised to ensure that costs incurred for the same purpose in like circumstances are treated consistently as either direct or indirect (F&A) costs."[17] And that's where things become more complicated.

According to the DHHS, "Inconsistent costing exists when a university charges support costs directly to sponsored activities and then assigns similar support costs attributable to nonsponsored activities to the DA cost pool."[18] For example, if a particularly large research project directly charges several administrative and clerical staff members' salaries (either the entire salary or a fraction of their salary), it would be inconsistent *not* to directly charge comparable salaries of administrative and clerical staff supporting nonsponsored departmental activities such as instruction. In the words of the DHHS, "Universities generally do not treat academic department support costs (e.g., the salaries of administrative and clerical staff, office supplies, postage, local telephone etc.) consistently. For example, administrative and clerical salaries are often charged directly to sponsored projects but not to instruction. The balances of administrative and clerical salaries that are not charged directly to sponsored projects are included in DA. This is a classic example of inconsistent costing and is not in compliance with the [*Uniform Guidance*]."

To compensate for this inconsistent costing, so-called direct charge equivalents (DCEs) are calculated for each department that includes departmental administrative support as direct costs in a grant or contract budget. The DCE makes a correction for the inconsistency by calculating a reduction to the DA indirect cost pool that represents the imputed value of departmental support costs related directly to nonsponsored activities. Stated differently, if a fraction of the salaries paid to clerical staff supporting sponsored research is direct charged to a research grant, then, to be consistent, a comparable fraction of the salaries paid to clerical staff supporting nonsponsored activities, such as instruction, should be direct charged as well. Even if there is no actual sponsored account (that is, grant or contract) to charge the instructional salary to, the imputed salary amounts—the direct charge equivalents—must be subtracted from the DA indirect cost pool. The federal government will not reimburse these DCEs.

For a department, the DCE is derived from the ratio of the salaries and wages (S&W) of general support staff members charged directly to sponsored accounts (that is, charged as direct costs) divided by faculty and professional S&W charged to sponsored accounts.

$$DCE_{S\&W} \; ratio = \frac{sponsored\ direct\ charged\ general\ support\ S\&W}{sponsored\ faculty\ and\ professional\ S\&W}$$

To be consistent, the corresponding ratio of nonsponsored general support S&W must equal this DCE ratio. Or, put another way, equivalence (consistency) occurs when

$$\frac{sponsored\ direct\ charged\ general\ support\ S\&W}{sponsored\ faculty\ and\ professional\ S\&W} = \frac{nonsponsored\ general\ support\ S\&W}{nonsponsored\ faculty\ and\ professional\ S\&W}$$

In this context, the nonsponsored general support S&W constitutes the DCE, the imputed amount equivalent to the direct charged general support.

Upon rearranging the equation, the amount of the nonsponsored general support S&W that must be treated as direct charged, the $DCE_{S\&W,}$ can be calculated:

$$DCE_{S\&W} = \frac{\begin{array}{c}(sponsored\ direct\ charged\ general\ support\ S\&W\,)\times\\(nonsponsored\ faculty\ and\ professional\ S\&W\,)\end{array}}{sponsored\ faculty\ and\ professional\ S\&W}$$

$$= DCE_{S\&W}\ ratio \times nonsponsored\ faculty\ and\ professional\ S\&W$$

But that's not all. The *Uniform Guidance* extends this logic one step further. If departmental nonlabor costs, such as office supplies, local telephone costs, postage, and so forth, are direct charged to a sponsor, then to achieve consistency, similar DCE adjustments must be made to departmental nonlabor costs that are not direct charged to a sponsor. Accordingly:

$$DCE_{nonlabor}\ ratio = \frac{sponsored\ nonlabor\ costs}{sponsored\ research\ nonlabor\ costs}$$

and

$$DCE_{nonlabor} = DCE_{nonlabor}\ ratio \times nonsponsored\ nonlabor\ costs$$

The total DCE adjustment is the sum of the DCE adjustments for salaries and wages and nonlabor costs.

These DCE calculations are illustrated for one department, chemical engineering, in table 9.14. Plugging the data into the DCE equations:

$$DCE_{S\&W} = \frac{184{,}670 \times 1{,}119{,}196}{1{,}593{,}805} = 138{,}948$$

and

$$DCE_{nonlabor} = \frac{32{,}598 \times 245{,}618}{560{,}227} = 14{,}292$$

Thus, the total DCE for S&W and nonlabor costs equals $153,240, which is the amount of departmental general support that cannot be added to the DA indirect cost pool. Accordingly, this amount is subtracted from the pool. *Note:* The same DCE amount will have been added to the instruction MTDC base.

Of course, if no departmental general support salaries and wages are budgeted as direct costs, then the DCE ratio is zero. Accordingly, the DCE equals zero, and all of the nonsponsored general support can be included in the DA indirect cost pool. This is the case in most departments.

Table 9.14. Department of Chemical Engineering DCE determination

Salaries and wages (S&W)	Costs
Sponsored research S&W	
Total sponsored research S&W	1,778,475
Direct-charged departmental support S&W	184,670
Net faculty and professional S&W	1,593,805
$DCE_{S\&W}$ ratio	11.59%
Nonsponsored faculty and professional S&W	1,199,196
$DCE_{S\&W}$	138,948
Nonlabor	
Total sponsored research nonlabor costs	592,825
Nonlabor costs direct charged to research	32,598
Net sponsored research nonlabor costs	560,227
$DCE_{nonlabor}$ ratio	5.82%
Nonsponsored nonlabor costs	245,618
$DCE_{nonlabor}$	14,292
Total DCE adjustment	153,240

Table 9.15. Cross allocations to the departmental administration pool

Indirect cost pool	Amount
Depreciation	936,211
Interest	73,879
Operations and maintenance	969,561
General administration	776,763
Total	2,756,415

Incidentally, the consistency principle applies to all pools, not just the DA pool. For example, if O&M indirect costs are direct charged to a grant, then a corresponding DCE for nonsponsored O&M costs must be calculated. The same holds for the other indirect cost pools, although directly charging costs in pools other than the DA pool seldom occurs.

The final component of the DA pool are the cross allocations from other indirect cost pools. They are tabulated in table 9.15.

The DA pools for each department can now be derived by combining the various pool components. This is illustrated in table 9.16, which should be read from left to right. Procedurally, the MTDC for each department is entered from departmental financial records. The total MTDC matches the total for the three functional activities in table 9.3 (instruction, research, and other sponsored activities).

Table 9.16. Departmental administration pool components

College Departments	MTDC			Totals	Faculty 3.6% DA allowance	Non-3.6% support	Deans office allocation	DCE adjustment	Cross-allocations	Total DA pool
	Instruction	Research	Other sponsored activities							
Arts and sciences										
Biology	1,444,814	2,371,300	186,134	4,002,248	144,081	303,139	164,985		107,759	719,964
Chemistry	1,451,932	2,755,932	179,013	4,386,877	157,928	345,337	181,341		118,115	802,721
History	962,083	1,542,638		2,504,722	90,170	207,213	103,923		67,439	468,744
Mathematics	1,813,031	3,414,664	255,468	5,483,163	197,394	425,967	226,442		147,632	997,434
Physics	2,118,619	3,436,012	132,679	5,687,310	204,743	450,573	235,208		153,129	1,043,652
Psychology	739,824	1,165,992	86,872	1,992,688	71,737	150,667	82,135		53,652	358,191
College total	8,530,304	14,686,538	840,166	24,057,008	866,052	1,882,895	994,034		647,726	4,390,707
Engineering										
Chemical	5,925,110	9,436,218	1,669,774	17,031,102	613,120	1,144,370	696,496	(153,240)	458,556	2,759,301
Civil	7,358,880	14,167,222	1,038,558	22,564,661	812,328	1,761,892	932,209		607,545	4,113,974
Electrical	7,317,221	12,250,005		19,567,226	704,420	1,631,603	812,353		526,840	3,675,216
Mechanical	2,873,872	5,396,569	995,724	9,266,166	333,582	629,303	379,201		249,488	1,591,574
College total	23,475,084	41,250,015	3,704,057	68,429,155	2,463,450	5,167,168	2,820,258	(153,240)	1,842,428	12,140,064
Business										
Accounting	1,241,237	1,457,297	490,624	3,189,158	114,810	173,342	128,853		85,867	502,871
Finance	629,079	809,878	187,546	1,626,504	58,554	100,088	66,164		43,793	268,600
Management	960,040	1,595,417	190,978	2,746,435	98,872	198,520	112,853		73,947	484,190
Marketing	920,357	1,181,915	224,735	2,327,007	83,772	149,827	94,914		62,654	391,166
College total	3,750,713	5,044,507	1,093,884	9,889,103	356,008	621,776	402,784		266,260	1,646,828
Totals	35,756,101	60,981,060	5,638,106	102,375,267	3,685,510	7,671,840	4,217,075	(153,240)	2,756,415	18,177,600

Using these MTDC amounts, the faculty 3.6 percent administrative allowance for each department is then calculated. For example, 3.6 percent of biology's total MTDC ($4,002,248) equals its faculty administrative allowance, $144,081. The next entry is the departments' base indirect costs, which equals the MTC minus the MTDC. For example, biology's MTC ($4,305,387, table 9.13) minus MTDC ($4,002,248) yields its base indirect costs ($303,139). The last three entries are the deans' office allocation (table 9.13), DCE adjustments (table 9.14), if any, and cross allocations, which are proportionate to the departments' share of the total MTDC. For example, the biology department's MTDC is 3.91 percent of the total MTDC ($102,375,267), so its cross allocation is 3.91 percent of the total cross allocation ($2,756,415). In the last column, all five indirect cost components are combined to yield the total DA pool for each department.

Finally, after developing the total DA pools, the DA allocations of each department must be allocated to the institutional cost objectives. These allocations are proportionate to each cost objective's share of the total departmental MTDC. This allocation is illustrated in table 9.17. For example, the biology instruction MTDC ($1,444,814) is 36 percent of the department's total MTDC ($4,002,248), and, accordingly, its instruction DA allocation is 36 percent of its total DA allocation ($719,964). In the last step, going vertically, the departmental allocations are summed to yield the institution's total DA allocations for each cost objective (for example, $6,308,438 for instruction, etc.).

Sponsored projects administration. Expenses incurred by a separate organization established primarily to administer sponsored projects are allocated to the sponsored projects administration (SPA) pool. The organization may be either an institutional unit, such as an Office of Sponsored Projects, or a separate entity contracted to administer the institution's sponsored portfolios, such as the Research Corporation of the University of Hawaii. The indirect cost pool usually includes salaries and expenses of pre- and post-award offices. In addition, it includes ancillary sponsored-project services such as purchasing, maintaining a stock room, and editing and publishing of research reports. Also, it can include research committees, special audits, human subjects reviews (institutional review boards), et cetera. Of course, care must be taken to eliminate any duplicate charges when this category includes activities similar or identical to those included in the general administration category or other indirect (F&A) cost items, such as accounting, procurement, or personnel administration.

Table 9.17. Departmental administration pool allocation to cost objectives

Department	Total departmental		Instruction			Organized research			Other sponsored activities		
	MTDC	DA allocation	MTDC	Percent	DA allocation	MTDC	Percent	DA allocation	MTDC	Percent	DA allocation
Arts and sciences											
Biology	4,002,248	719,964	1,444,814	36.00	259,187	2,371,300	59.00	424,779	186,134	5.00	35,998
Chemistry	4,386,877	802,721	1,451,932	33.00	264,898	2,755,932	63.00	505,714	179,013	4.00	32,109
History	2,504,722	468,744	962,083	39.00	182,810	1,542,638	61.00	285,934			
Mathematics	5,483,163	997,434	1,813,031	33.00	329,153	3,414,664	62.00	618,409	255,468	5.00	49,872
Physics	5,687,310	1,043,652	2,118,619	38.00	396,588	3,436,012	60.00	626,191	132,679	2.00	20,873
Psychology	1,992,688	358,191	739,824	38.00	136,113	1,165,992	58.00	207,751	86,872	4.00	14,328
College totals	24,057,008	4,390,707	8,530,304	36.00	1,568,749	14,686,539	61.00	2,668,778	840,166	3.00	153,180
Engineering											
Chemical	17,031,102	2,759,301	5,925,110	34.00	938,162	9,436,218	56.00	1,545,209	1,669,774	10.00	275,930
Civil	22,564,661	4,113,974	7,358,880	32.00	1,316,472	14,167,222	63.00	2,591,803	1,038,558	5.00	205,699
Electrical	19,567,226	3,675,216	7,317,221	37.00	1,359,830	12,250,005	63.00	2,315,386			
Mechanical	9,266,166	1,591,574	2,873,872	31.00	493,388	5,396,569	58.00	923,113	995,724	11.00	175,073
College totals	68,429,155	12,140,064	23,475,084	34.00	4,107,853	41,250,015	61.00	7,375,511	3,704,057	5.00	656,702
Business											
Accounting	3,189,158	502,871	1,241,237	40.00	201,149	1,457,297	44.00	221,263	490,624	16.00	80,459
Finance	1,626,504	268,600	629,079	39.00	104,754	809,878	49.00	131,614	187,546	12.00	32,232
Management	2,746,435	484,190	960,040	35.00	169,467	1,595,417	58.00	280,830	190,978	7.00	33,893
Marketing	2,327,007	391,166	920,357	40.00	156,467	1,181,915	50.00	195,583	224,735	10.00	39,117
College totals	9,889,103	1,646,828	3,750,713	38.00	631,837	5,044,507	51.00	829,290	1,093,884	11.00	185,701
Institution totals	102,375,267	18,177,600	35,756,101		6,308,438	60,981,060		10,873,579	5,638,106		995,583

Table 9.18. Sponsored projects administration pool development and allocation

Cost pool:	Amount
Sponsored projects administration	4,757,468

Cross allocations	
Depreciation	169,512
Interest	3,360
Operations and maintenance	260,997
General administration	592,066
Total cross allocations	1,025,936
Total sponsored projects administration allocation	5,783,404

Pool allocation:

Cost objective	MTDC Amount	Percent	Allocation
Sponsored instruction	2,944,767	4.23	244,822
Organized research	60,981,060	87.66	5,069,842
Other sponsored activities	5,638,106	8.10	468,741
Totals	69,563,933	100.00	5,783,404

The expenses included in the SPA pool usually are available readily from institutional financial records. Once in hand, they are allocated to the major cost objectives of the institution proportionate to each cost objective's share of the institutional MTDC. This straightforward, relatively simple procedure is illustrated in table 9.18. In this context, only the costs of sponsored instruction such as training grants and the like are included in the instruction cost objective. This amount is obtained from the sponsored projects office. Otherwise, the entire MTDC for sponsored research and other sponsored activities is included (see table 9.3). For simplicity, in this example, all organized research is considered sponsored research. The sponsored (organized) research MTDC ($60,981,060) comprises 87.66 percent of the total sponsored-project MTDC ($69,563,933). So, the sponsored research SPA allocation ($5,069,842) is 87.66 percent of the total SPA allocation ($5,783,404).

Library expenses. The library cost pool includes expenses incurred in operating the library and the acquisition of books, site licenses, and other library materials. Any applicable credits (for example, fines, copy center revenues, and so forth) are subtracted from the pool. Generally, the library is not a large component of the F&A rate. Nonetheless, it can be important because it is in the facilities category and, therefore, is not subject to an administrative cap.

Table 9.19. Library pool development, allocation basis, and pool allocation

Cost pool

	Amount
Library	3,041,161

Cross allocations	
Depreciation	713,783
Interest	14,102
Operations and maintenance	1,095,267
General administration	378,025
Total cross allocations	2,201,177
Total library allocation	5,242,338

Allocation basis

	FTE		
Category	Number	Percent	Allocation
Faculty and staff	347	5.70	298,898
Students	5,739	94.30	4,943,440
Totals	6,086	100.00	5,242,338

Pool allocation

			Allocation		
Cost objective	Salaries and wages	Percent of total	Faculty and staff	Students	Total
Instruction	52,052,721	38.03	113,685	4,943,440	5,057,125
Organized research	74,757,309	54.62	163,273		163,273
Other sponsored activities	5,638,106	4.12	12,314		12,314
Other institutional activities	4,407,374	3.22	9,626		9,626
Totals	136,855,510	100.00	298,898	4,943,440	5,242,338

Note: Salaries and wages include fringe benefits.

As usual, the cost pool is developed by adding the cross allocations to the library indirect cost allowance (see table 9.3). This is illustrated in table 9.19 (*top panel*). Library indirect costs then are allocated on the basis of library user FTEs (*middle panel*). This requires separating users into two categories, the faculty and staff and the students, based on the relative number of FTEs in each category. This separation is required because all costs incurred by students must be allocated to the instruction function. Procedurally, these allocations require an institutional library utilization study that analyzes usage by FTE head-count and also function (for example, instruction or research). The final step (*lower panel*) allocates the faculty and staff costs to the four institutional cost objectives, based on the relative salaries and wages, including fringe benefits.

In the example, 94.30 percent of the users were students, so 94.30 percent of the total library indirect cost allocation ($5,242,338) is assigned to the student category ($4,943,440). And that entire student allocation must be allocated to the instruction cost pool. The faculty and staff allocation ($298,898) is allocated proportionate to the salaries and wages of all faculty members and other professional employees associated with each cost objective. The salaries and wages (including fringe benefits) of faculty and staff members associated with instruction ($52,052,721) comprise 38.03 percent of the total institutional salaries and wages of faculty and staff members ($136,855,510); so, the library faculty and staff indirect costs allocated to instruction ($113,685) are 38.03 percent of the total faculty and staff allocation ($298,898). The amounts allocated to faculty and staff and to students are added to obtain the total allocation to the instruction cost objective ($5,057,125).

Student administration and services. The student administration and services (SAS) cost pool includes expenses incurred for the administration of student affairs and for services to students. Typically, these are activities such as the dean of students, admissions, registrar, counseling and placement services, student advisers, student health and infirmary services, catalogs, and commencements and convocations. These expenses are usually allocated to the instruction cost objective; indeed, according to the *Uniform Guidance*, "the expenses in this category must be allocated to the instruction function." The rare exception might be a student employment office that benefits sponsored research, for example. This straightforward allocation is illustrated in table 9.20, which allocates the entire amount to instruction. (This pool is also called *student services* for short.)

Step-down reconciliation schedule. Now that each indirect cost pool has been allocated in sequence to the four institutional cost objectives, all of the allocation data are entered into a so-called step-down reconciliation schedule. This schedule provides an easily visible recapitulation of the allocations described above, as the indirect cost pools "drain" in stepwise fashion into the four cost objective pools. After each indirect cost pool is drained, it is empty, with a balance of zero. In contrast, the four cost objective pools now contain all of the indirect costs.

The step-wise reconciliation schedule is illustrated in table 9.21. Pedagogically, the table should be read from top left to bottom right. At the outset, shown in the left-hand column, the total allowable indirect costs for each of the four cost objectives (functions) are initially zero; all of the indirect costs are in their indirect cost pools.

But then, going column by column from left to right, the indirect costs for each pool are allocated to the remaining pools, as shown in tables 9.3 through 9.20. Thus, in the first step, the depreciation pool is "drained" into the other 11 pools (table 9.7): $558,441 to O&M, $503,099 to general administration, et cetera. Then, the interest pool is drained into the other 10 pools: $10,627 to O&M, $10,090 to general administration, et cetera. Working to the right, each indirect cost pool is drained into the remaining pools. At the

Table 9.20. Student administration and services pool development and allocation

Cost pool	
	Amount
Student administration and services	18,651,879

Cross allocations	
Depreciation	270,550
Interest	5,534
Operations and maintenance	429,829
General administration	2,319,934
Total cross allocations	3,025,847
Total student administration and services allocation	21,677,726

Pool allocation

Cost objective	Percent	Allocated
Instruction	100.00	21,677,726
Totals	100.00	21,677,726

Table 9.21. Step-down allocation of indirect costs

Cost pools	Total allowable cost	Depreciation	Interest	O&M	General administration
Depreciation	13,058,315	(13,058,315)			
Interest	3,454,765		(3,454,765)		
O&M	13,944,396	558,441	10,627	(14,513,464)	
General administration	15,964,521	503,099	10,090	783,700	(17,261,410)
Departmental admin.	15,421,185	936,211	73,879	969,561	776,763
Sponsored projects admin.	4,757,468	169,512	3,360	260,997	592,066
Library	3,041,161	713,783	14,102	1,095,267	378,025
Student admin. services	18,651,879	270,550	5,534	429,829	2,319,934
Instruction		2,781,016	341,523	3,290,971	4,446,539
Research		5,075,985	575,625	5,546,815	7,582,938
Other sponsored activities		884,296	109,601	1,056,136	700,813
Other institutional activities		1,165,421	2,310,422	1,080,187	464,332
Totals	88,293,690				

conclusion of this process, all indirect costs have been allocated to one of the four major functions. That is, all of the indirect costs ($88,293,690) have been moved from the indirect cost pools into the four cost objective pools (*far right-hand column*).

Technically, this step-down procedure recognizes that some indirect cost pools contribute to other indirect cost pools by cross allocation. But, by closing a pool after its costs have been allocated, further allocations back into the closed pool from any of the remaining pools are excluded. So, the accuracy of this method is limited inherently. This technical limitation can be overcome by using a reciprocal method of allocation. In this procedure, all indirect costs in each pool are allocated simultaneously to the other pools and cost objectives, thus accounting completely for the indirect cost allocations. However, this method requires solving a system of simultaneous equations. Before the advent of modern computers, this was a daunting task. Consequently, the far simpler step-down method was adopted. Despite the computing power now generally available, the traditional step-down method is still preferred by government agencies.

Calculate Indirect Cost Rate

Using the data in the step-down schedule, the institutional indirect cost rates (that is, the F&A rates) for each indirect cost pool can be calculated easily. (For transparency, the *Uniform Guidance* requires calculation of a rate for each pool.) These calculations are illustrated in table 9.22. Initially, the indirect cost pools are sorted into facilities and administrative categories for each cost objective.

Departmental administration	Sponsored projects admin.	Library	Student admin. services	Total cost allocated
(18,177,600)				
	(5,783,404)			
		(5,242,338)		
			(21,677,726)	
6,308,438	244,822	5,057,125	21,677,726	44,148,162
10,873,579	5,069,842	163,273		34,888,055
995,583	468,741	12,314		4,227,484
		9,626		5,029,988
				88,293,690

Table 9.22. F&A rate calculation

Cost pool	Instruction			Organized research			Other sponsored activities		
	F&A cost allocation	MTDC	Rate (%)	F&A cost allocation	MTDC	Rate (%)	F&A cost allocation	MTDC	Rate (%)
Facilities (F)									
Depreciation	2,781,016	35,756,101	7.78	5,075,985	54,882,954	9.25	884,296	5,638,106	15.68
Interest	341,523	35,756,101	0.96	575,625	54,882,954	1.05	109,601	5,638,106	1.94
O&M	3,290,971	35,756,101	9.20	5,546,815	54,882,954	10.11	1,056,136	5,638,106	18.73
Library	5,057,125	35,756,101	14.14	163,273	54,882,954	0.30	12,314	5,638,106	0.22
F rate subtotals			32.08			20.71			36.57
REUI utility adjustment						1.30			
F rate totals			32.08			22.01			36.57
Administrative (A)									
General administration	4,446,539	35,756,101	12.44	7,582,938	60,981,060	12.43	700,813	5,638,106	12.43
Departmental admin.	6,308,438	35,756,101	17.64	10,873,579	60,981,060	17.83	995,583	5,638,106	17.64
Sponsored projects admin.	244,822	2,944,767	8.31	5,069,842	60,981,060	8.31	468,741	5,638,106	8.31
Student services	21,677,726	35,756,101	60.63		60,981,060			5,638,106	
Calculated A rates			99.02			38.58			38.40
Capped A rates			26.00			26.00			26.00
F&A rates									
On-campus			58.08			48.01			62.57
Off-campus			26.00			26.00			26.00

Note: Sponsored training grants are included in Instruction MTDC. Research facilities MTDC excludes off-campus projects.

(The federal government does not reimburse indirect costs for other institutional activities, so they are omitted from these rate calculations.) The costs in each pool are then expressed relative to some measure of institutional performance, called the base. For federal reimbursement, the most frequently used base is the MTDC. Notably, in these F&A rate calculations, the research facilities MTDC ($54,882,954) does not include costs incurred at off-campus facilities, so this MTDC value is less than the total organized research MTDC ($60,981,060, table 9.3).

The F&A rates for each indirect cost pool are calculated:

$$F\&A \ rate = \frac{F\&A \ cost \ allocation}{MTDC}$$

The rates for each indirect cost pool in the facilities and administrative categories are summed to yield the F and the A rates, respectively. And, together, addition of the F and the A rates yields the bottom line, the overall F&A rates.

The federal government imposes a significant limitation on F&A rates used for reimbursement calculations. For higher education institutions (but not other nonprofit organizations), the federal government caps the A rate at 26 percent of the MTDC. Regardless of the calculated A rate, only 26 percent may be used for federal reimbursement. So, in table 9.22, the bottom line for each cost objective equals the F rate plus the capped 26 percent A rate. For example, the applicable F&A rate for reimbursement of indirect costs incurred for on-campus sponsored research is 48.01 percent of MTDC: 22.01 (F) plus 26.00 (A) percent, although the calculated F&A rate is 60.59 percent of MTDC, 22.01 (F) plus 38.58 percent (A). Furthermore, off-campus projects are assumed to benefit from institutional administrative services but not campus facilities. Consequently, the off-campus F&A rate for reimbursement is only the A rate, 26 percent, for each cost objective.

Incidentally, the 26 percent administrative cap applies only to federal indirect cost reimbursement. From a mercenary point of view, it could, and does, get worse. Some nonfederal sponsors and even some federal agencies may impose lower caps. However, for internal budgeting, the calculated A rate may be used. For example, when allocating indirect costs of administrative support for instruction according to an RCM budget model, an institution most probably would use the calculated A rate for instruction, 99.02 percent.

At some institutions, separate rates may be calculated for specialized facilities that incur unusual indirect costs, such as hospitals, synchrotrons, high-energy laser facilities, experimental farms, primate centers, and so forth. These facilities are treated as additional, separate cost objectives (that is, institutional functions) throughout the calculation process, with their own separate F&A rates.

Arithmetically, factors that increase only the numerator (the F&A costs) also increase the F&A rate and, therefore, the amount of F&A costs recovered. Factors that increase only the denominator (MTDC) lower the F&A rate. Consequently, institutions usually try to maximize the numerator and minimize the denominator to increase their F&A rate. Common strategies to maximize the numerator include placing organized research activity and equipment in high-cost space; limiting student instructional activities in organized research space; and constructing new buildings or remodeling existing buildings to increase depreciation allowances. Common strategies to minimize the denominator include classifying organized research conservatively, subcontracting whenever possible, and minimizing cost sharing.

Preparing a long-form F&A rate proposal can be costly and time-consuming. In the best of circumstances, most institutions plan on about six months to prepare the necessary data and documentation plus an additional six months of negotiation. Thus, they begin the process one year in advance. There are several commercial vendors that prepare institutional F&A cost calculations; Huron and Maximus are two examples.[19] They charge about $200,000 to $250,000 and more, depending on the extent of their services, the size of the university, and other factors.

The Simplified Method

Fortunately for smaller institutions, the federal government provides a simpler method for calculating an F&A rate, appropriately called the simplified method. It is called the short form also, contrasting it to the long form. According to the *Uniform Guidance*, this method is available for institutions where the total direct costs do not exceed $10 million in a fiscal year.[20] These institutions are not required to use the simplified method, but there are several advantages to using it. Primarily, with the short form, it is relatively easy to prepare and calculate F&A rates.

The key features of the simplified method are that it:

- uses only one institutional cost objective and one indirect cost pool
- may not require a space utilization study for depreciation calculations
- does not require a library utilization study
- is not subject to the 26 percent cap on administrative costs

Thus, unlike the long-form method, the simplified method does not distinguish between the instruction, organized research, and other sponsored activities cost objectives. So, there is no need to allocate indirect costs into separate institutional functions because only a single F&A rate for all sponsored activities is calculated. On the one hand, this simplifies the cost-proposal development. On the other hand, it precludes on- and off-campus rates and special rates that might be appropriate.

Also, unlike the long form, indirect costs are assigned to a single indirect cost pool. However, this simplicity is modified by the need to classify them into four categories when developing the single indirect cost pool. They are:

- general administration and general expenses
- O&M of the physical plant and depreciation
- library
- departmental administration expenses

Significantly, there is no need to cross allocate indirect costs from one category to another because all indirect costs in these categories are in the single pool.

The simplified method of F&A rate calculation follows four sequential steps:[21]

1. Establish the total base costs (salaries and wages or MTDC).
2. Establish the indirect cost pool.
3. Subtract excluded and unallowable costs.
4. Calculate the F&A rate.

These steps will be illustrated using data from the private university financial statement of activities (table 7.3). Sample calculations are also illustrated in tutorials by the DHHS and Maximus, a commercial vendor.[22]

Total Base Costs

The base costs, either salaries and wages or MTDC, derive from the income statement. For pedagogical purposes, both base costs

Table 9.23. Expenses from the financial statement (in table 7.3)

Function	Salaries and wages	Natural Other operating expenses	Depreciation	Totals
Instruction	19,596,524	9,691,585	2,329,386	31,617,495
Research	1,177,900	582,538	140,014	1,900,451
Public service	762,923	377,309	90,687	1,230,919
Academic support	4,933,053	2,439,673	586,379	7,959,105
Student services	4,715,059	2,331,862	560,466	7,607,388
Institutional support	8,110,336	4,011,018	964,054	13,085,408
Auxiliary enterprises	12,413,064	6,138,959	1,475,507	20,027,530
Totals	51,708,860	25,572,944	6,146,493	83,428,296

will be developed. For that reason, expenses reported by functional classification (table 7.3) are shown also by natural classification in matrix form in table 9.23.

Regardless of which base will be used, the next step is to reconcile the functional costs from the financial statement to the expanded cost classifications recommended by the NACUBO (table 4.1). This involves the addition of four categories, scholarships, depreciation, interest, O&M, and the transfer of costs into them. This is illustrated in table 9.24. Expense classifications from the financial statement (table 9.23) are listed above the dotted line, with the four additional indirect categories below the dotted line. In the reconciliation, costs are transferred from the financial statement categories into these four additional categories. For example, scholarship costs ($966,474) are transferred from instruction to the added scholarship category.

Indirect Cost Pool

Conforming to the *Uniform Guidance*, the reconciled expenses are reclassified into the four categories of the indirect cost pool. Three indirect cost categories, general administration, library, and departmental administration (the O&M indirect cost category is included in the reconciled expenses), and a general catch-all "other direct cost category" have been added (below the dashed line). This catch-all category has been added to accommodate costs that cannot reasonably be assigned to any of the other categories. Then, indirect costs in the reconciled expense categories are transferred (reclassified) into the indirect cost categories.

This reclassification is illustrated in table 9.25. Cost categories from the reconciled financial statement (table 9.24) are shown above the dashed line. Furthermore, in this example, the expenditures are

Table 9.24. Reconciled expenses from the financial statement

Function	Financial statement totals		Reconciliation			Totals
		Scholarships	Depreciation	Interest	O&M	
Instruction	31,617,495	(966,474)	(2,329,386)	(243,039)	(1,060,725)	27,017,872
Research	1,900,451		(140,014)		(63,758)	1,696,680
Public service	1,230,919		(90,687)		(41,296)	1,098,936
Academic support	7,959,105		(586,379)		(267,017)	7,105,709
Student services	7,607,388		(560,466)		(255,218)	6,791,703
Institutional support	13,085,408		(964,054)		(438,998)	11,682,356
Auxiliary services	20,027,530		(1,475,507)		(671,897)	17,880,127
Scholarships		966,474				966,474
Depreciation			6,146,493			6,146,493
Interest				243,039		243,039
O&M					2,798,909	2,798,909
Total	83,428,296					83,428,296

Note: Financial statement cost categories are above the dashed line.

Table 9.25. Reclassification of financial statement expenses

Cost category	Reconciled expenses			Reclassifications			Reclassified expenses		
	Salaries and wages	Other	Total	Salaries and wages	Other	Total	Salaries and wages	Other	Total
Instruction	16,745,677	10,272,194	27,017,872	(559,193)	(275,422)	(834,616)	16,186,484	9,996,772	26,183,256
Research	1,051,602	645,078	1,696,680				1,051,602	645,078	1,696,680
Public service	681,121	417,816	1,098,936				681,121	417,816	1,098,936
Academic support	4,404,119	2,701,590	7,105,709	(4,404,119)	(2,701,590)	(7,105,709)			
Student services	4,209,498	2,582,205	6,791,703				4,209,498	2,582,205	6,791,703
Institutional support	7,240,724	4,441,631	11,682,356	(7,240,724)	(4,441,631)	(11,682,356)			
Auxiliary services	11,082,103	6,798,024	17,880,127	(100,458)		(100,458)	10,981,645	6,798,024	17,779,669
Scholarships	599,020	367,453	966,474				599,020	367,453	966,474
Depreciation		6,146,493	6,146,493					6,146,493	6,146,493
Interest		243,039	243,039					243,039	243,039
O&M	1,734,764	1,064,145	2,798,909	306,514	41,650	348,164	2,041,277	1,105,795	3,147,072
General administration				7,378,218	3,707,973	11,086,191	7,378,218	3,707,973	11,086,191
Library				2,168,436	876,458	3,044,894	2,168,436	876,458	3,044,894
Departmental administration				585,298	249,318	834,616	585,298	249,318	834,616
Other direct costs				1,866,027	2,543,246	4,409,273	1,866,027	2,543,246	4,409,273
Totals	47,748,628	35,679,668	83,428,296				47,748,628	35,679,668	83,428,296

Note: Reconciled financial statement cost categories are above the dashed line.

Table 9.26. Expense reclassification details

From	To	Cost item	Amount
Instruction	Departmental administration	20% of salaries and expenses of department heads	834,616
Academic support	Library Other direct costs	Library expenses Other academic support costs	3,044,894 4,060,814
Institutional support	General administration O&M Other direct costs Other direct costs	Other institutional support costs Campus security Unallowable activities Catalogues, commencements, etc.	10,985,734 348,164 123,798 224,661
Auxiliary services	General administration	Auxiliary services salaries	100,458

broken down into "salaries and wages" and "other" costs. This distinction is not mandated, but as will be shown below, total salaries and wages may be the base for the F&A rate calculation. So, it is handy to sort the data at this stage.

The reclassification details (table 9.25) are summarized in table 9.26. To make calculations easy, the *Uniform Guidance* allows an allocation of 20 percent of the expenses for department heads (salaries and wages of deans, department chairs and heads, clerical staff, office supplies, etc.) in the instruction category to departmental administration. In this example, that total amount is $834,616. Academic support and institutional support are not among the *Uniform Guidance*-recognized indirect cost categories. So, academic support costs are drained completely into the library and other direct cost categories. And institutional support costs are drained into the general administration, O&M (campus security is reclassified), and other direct cost categories. Finally, in this example, several employees' salaries ($100,458) are reclassified from auxiliary services to general administration.

Subtract Excluded and Unallowable Costs

In the third step of the simplified method, any unallowable or excluded costs are subtracted from these reclassified data. The unallowable costs are the same as for the long-form rate calculation, namely, those expenses that cannot be paid with federal funds, such as scholarships and depreciation of auxiliary facilities. The excluded costs are those removed to obtain the MTDC: equipment capitalized at more than $5,000, and so forth. Notably, when making depreciation and O&M adjustments, there is no need for a space utilization study since all of the adjusted depreciation and O&M expenses are allocated to only one pool.

Exclusions and adjustments are illustrated in table 9.27 and itemized in table 9.28. In this example, the federal contributions to work study programs are excluded from the instruction and research salaries and wages; otherwise, the federal government would be paying twice for these items. The depreciation and O&M categories exclude costs applicable to auxiliary services facilities; in the words of the *Uniform Guidance*, the expenses in the depreciation O&M and categories are "adjusted" for the costs of residence halls, dining halls, and other auxiliary services. Also, in another adjustment, O&M salaries and wages direct charged to auxiliary services ($16,380) are transferred from auxiliary services to the O&M category. The general administration category excludes costs of entertainment, alumni activities, and fund-raising. However, general administration costs related to other institutional activities such as residence halls, dining halls, student unions, athletics, et cetera, may be included.

After subtracting the unallowable and excluded expenses, the costs can be further segregated into direct and indirect costs, based on their accounting codes in the institutional financial system. This straightforward procedure is shown in table 9.29. Significantly, in this tabulation the total direct costs have been modified by the exclusions, so the total direct costs represent the MTDC.

Overall, the relative simplicity of this method should now be apparent. Unlike the long-form method, there is no need to cross allocate indirect costs, conduct space or library utilization studies, or allocate costs into the four major institutional cost objectives. And this simplified method doesn't require the step-down reconciliation process.

Calculate F&A Rates

The cost data are now ready for the F&A rate calculation. According to the *Uniform Guidance*, either total salaries and wages or MTDC may be used as the base for the F&A rate calculations. So, the rate equals the amount in the indirect cost pool divided by the salaries and wages in the direct cost pool or the MTDC. Using the data in table 9.29, the rates for both bases can be calculated for comparison.

Salaries and wages base:

$$F\&A\ rate = \frac{total\ indirect\ costs}{direct\ salaries\ and\ wages} = \frac{\$21,284,080}{\$34,618,833} = 61.48\%$$

Table 9.27. Exclusions and adjustments to reclassified expenses

Expense classification	Reclassified expenses			Exclusions and adjustments			Expenses after exclusions and adjustments		
	Salaries and wages	Other	Total	Salaries and wages	Other	Total	Salaries and wages	Other	Total
Instruction	16,186,484	9,996,772	26,183,256	(335,693)		(335,693)	15,850,790	9,996,772	25,847,562
Research	1,051,602	645,078	1,696,680	(21,852)		(21,852)	1,029,751	645,078	1,674,828
Public service	681,121	417,816	1,098,936				681,121	417,816	1,098,936
Academic support									
Student services	4,209,498	2,582,205	6,791,703				4,209,498	2,582,205	6,791,703
Institutional support	10,981,645	6,798,024	17,779,669		(16,380)	(16,380)	10,981,645	6,781,644	17,763,289
Auxiliary services	599,020	367,453	966,474	(599,020)	(367,453)	(966,474)			
Scholarships		6,146,493	6,146,493		(1,475,507)	(1,475,507)		4,670,985	4,670,985
Depreciation		243,039	243,039					243,039	243,039
Interest	2,041,277	1,105,795	3,147,072	(247,551)	(787,123)	(1,034,674)	1,793,726	318,672	2,112,398
O&M	7,378,218	3,707,973	11,086,191	(611,718)	(72,414)	(684,132)	6,766,500	3,635,559	10,402,059
General administration	2,168,436	876,458	3,044,894		(23,911)	(23,911)	2,168,436	852,547	3,020,983
Library	585,298	249,318	834,616				585,298	249,318	834,615
Departmental administration									
Other direct costs	1,866,027	2,543,246	4,409,273				1,866,027	2,543,246	4,409,273
Totals	47,748,628	35,679,668	83,428,296	(1,815,834)	(2,742,788)	(4,558,623)	45,932,794	32,936,879	78,869,673

Table 9.28. Exclusions and adjustments to the reclassified expenditures

Expense classification	Exclusions and adjustments	Total amount
Instruction	Federal share of Federal Work Study Program wages	(335,693)
Research	Federal share of Federal Work Study Program wages	(21,852)
Auxiliary services	O&M direct charged to auxiliary services	(16,380)
Depreciation	Auxiliary services facilities	(1,475,507)
Scholarships	Unallowable student aid	(966,474)
O&M	Capital expenditures	(247,551)
	Fines and penalties	(131,606)
	Auxiliary services facilities	(671,897)
	O&M direct charged to auxiliary services	16,380
General administration	Entertainment expenses	(134,618)
	Alumni activities	(166,475)
	Fund raising and investment costs	(383,039)
Library	Rare book purchases	(23,911)

MTDC base:

$$F\&A\ rate = \frac{total\ indirect\ costs}{MTDC} = \frac{\$21,284,080}{\$57,585,594} = 36.96\%$$

As in this example, the salaries and wages base always yields a larger F&A rate because S&W is a component of the overall MTDC; that is, the denominator is necessarily smaller when S&W is the base. Looking forward until the next rate calculation, institutions may prefer the MTDC base if they anticipate receiving grants and contracts in future years with particularly large MTDC.

Because the simplified method is not designed to optimize F&A recovery, a long-form proposal might be expected to result in a higher F&A rate. When would it pay to change from the short- to the long-form proposal preparation? The answer depends on the added expense of preparing the long-form proposal, which may approach $200,000. If the long-form proposal increased the F&A rate by 1 percent, then an additional 1 percent of the MTDC will be recovered in future years. For example, if the MTDC were $5,000,000, then a 1 percent increase in the rate would result in a $50,000 increase in F&A recovery. So, if the cost of preparing the long-form proposal were $200,000, it would take 4 years to break even. In that case, it hardly pays to use the long form. But a 4 percent increase in the F&A rate would shorten the break-even time to only one year. In that case, it would clearly pay to prepare the long-form proposal.

Table 9.29. Direct and indirect costs after exclusions and adjustments

| | Costs after exclusions and adjustments | | | | | |
| | Direct (MTDC) | | | Indirect | | |
Expense classification	Salaries and wages	Other	Total	Salaries and wages	Other	Total
Instruction	15,850,790	9,996,772	25,847,562			
Research	1,029,751	645,078	1,674,828			
Public service	681,121	417,816	1,098,936			
Academic support						
Student services	4,209,498	2,582,205	6,791,703			
Institutional support						
Auxiliary services	10,981,645	6,781,644	17,763,289			
Scholarships					4,670,985	4,670,985
Depreciation					243,039	243,039
Interest				1,793,726	318,672	2,112,398
O&M				6,766,500	3,635,559	10,402,059
General administration				2,168,436	852,547	3,020,983
Library				585,298	249,318	834,615
Departmental administration						
Other direct costs	1,866,027	2,543,246	4,409,273			
Totals	34,618,833	22,966,760	57,585,594	11,313,961	9,970,119	21,284,080

The *De Minimus* Method

Institutions that have never received or currently do not have a negotiated F&A rate may use a *de minimis* rate equal to 10 percent of the MTDC.[23] It may be used indefinitely. This rate is a convenient default for subcontractors who do not have a negotiated rate. However, negotiated rates typically exceed 10 percent of MTDC. So, the recovered indirect costs may be substantially less when using the *de minimis* rate.

Comparative calculations illustrate the different yields using the *de minimis* and the long-form method. Using the long-form data in table 9.22, the organized research MTDC is $60,981,060 (assuming no off-campus research activities), and the on-campus F&A rate is 48.01 percent. Therefore:

$$long\ form\ F\&A\ recovery = 48.01\% \times \$60,981,060 = \$29,277,007$$
$$de\ minimis\ F\&A\ recovery = 10\% \times \$60,981,060 = \$6,098,106$$

The difference is $23,178,901, which is a sizable amount. But this must be balanced against the costs of preparing the long-form rate. The "break-even" point can be calculated:

$$break\ even\ MTDC = \frac{long\ form\ proposal\ cost}{negotiated\ F\&A\ rate - 10\%}$$

So, if the long-form proposal preparation (either in-house or using a commercial vendor) cost is $200,000, and the anticipated negotiated F&A rate is 48.01 percent, then the MTDC must exceed $526,177 for the increased F&A recovery to offset the proposal cost. That is, in this example, if the MTDC amount is less than $526,177, it pays to use the *de minimis* rate. Both lower negotiated F&A rates and higher proposal preparation costs will increase the break-even value.

Rate Approval

After completing the F&A rate proposal, it is submitted to the federal government for negotiation and approval. After reviewing an institution's F&A rate calculations, the cognizant federal agency almost always amends the proposal—downward. The reasons vary: a cost is disputed, an allocation is questioned, and so forth. The institution may protest the adjustment, and this is followed by negotiations until acceptable rates are approved by the cognizant agency.

Usually, a rate is approved for a period of two to four years. Because of the exhaustive time and effort involved in preparing an indirect cost proposal, most institutions choose a four-year period.

For educational institutions, the rate is "predetermined," which means that the institution calculates project-specific F&A costs using this rate for the entire two- to four-year period until the next F&A rate negotiation. Whenever a new rate is calculated, the financial statement data used in the calculations are derived from the preceding year, called the base year. So, reimbursements for the following four years depend on F&A costs incurred during the preceding base year. In practice, the use of predetermined rates means that the university benefits financially if the institutional MTDC increase relative to those of the base year. This puts subtle pressure on faculty members to generate grants: increase the MTDC, bring in more F&A reimbursement.

Some institutions schedule major indirect cost items for the base years to maximize reimbursement. Technically, of course, they will be reimbursed sooner or later regardless of when the costs are incurred. But there are financial advantages to getting reimbursed sooner, before inflation erodes the monetary value of the reimbursement.

Project-Specific Indirect Cost Reimbursement

With an approved F&A rate in hand, an institution can easily calculate the F&A costs attributable to a specific project. For most federal grants and contracts, the amount of the total institutional F&A applied to a specific project depends on the amount of the project's MTDC relative to the institution's total MTDC. Thus, if a project's MTDC is 10 percent of the institution's overall MTDC, then the project's F&A costs are 10 percent of the overall institutional F&A costs.

This relationship can be expressed algebraically:

$$\frac{project\ F\&A}{institutional\ F\&A} = \frac{project\ MTDC}{institutional\ MTDC}$$

Therefore, rearranging algebraically:

$$project\ F\&A = \frac{project\ MTDC}{institutional\ MTDC} \times institutional\ F\&A$$

and

$$project\ F\&A = project\ MTDC \times \frac{institutional\ F\&A}{institutional\ MTDC}$$

The latter term expressing the ratio of institutional F&A to overall institutional MTDC is the institutional F&A rate (as calculated above), or stated simply, the F&A rate. That is,

$$F\&A\ rate = \frac{insitutional\ F\&A}{institutional\ MTDC}$$

And this yields the fundamental working formula for calculating an individual project's F&A:

$$project\ F\&A = project\ MTDC \times F\&A\ rate$$

The individual project's F&A costs equal the project's MTDC times the institutional F&A rate. Consequently, knowing the institutional F&A rate, an experienced research officer or principal investigator can look at a grant budget and quickly calculate the expected F&A costs in a grant proposal or award.

Project F&A calculation is illustrated using the grant budget in table 9.30. Assuming that the F&A rate is 50 percent of the institutional MTDC,

$$project\ F\&A = \$183,000 \times 50\% = \$91,500$$

Consequently, the total project budget equals the total direct costs plus the F&A: $339,500.

Note on the numbers: The project F&A ($91,500) equals 50 percent of the MTDC ($183,000) but only 27 percent of the total budget ($339,500). Note also that the F&A costs associated with the subaward, a subcontract to another institution or vendor, are included in the direct cost category, not the project's F&A category. And the amount is based on the subcontractor's institutional F&A rate. If the subcontractor does not have a negotiated F&A rate, the institution

Table 9.30. Sample grant budget for F&A cost calculation

Budget category	Direct costs	Exclusions	Modified direct costs
Personnel salary and fringe benefits	120,000		120,000
Consultant costs	10,000		10,000
Equipment			
Spectrophotometer	20,000	20,000	
Microscope	4,000		4,000
Supplies	15,000		15,000
Travel	4,000		4,000
Inpatient care costs	10,000	10,000	
Subawards	60,000	35,000	25,000
Subawards F&A costs	5,000		5,000
Total direct costs	248,000	65,000	183,000
F&A costs	91,500		
Total costs	339,500		

may negotiate a rate with the subcontractor, subject to *Uniform Guidance* regulations, or simply use a *de minimis* default rate equal to 10 percent of the subaward MTDC amount, as in this example.

Because the F&A rate is derived from the institution's overall research activity and is thus an average value, any given project's actual F&A costs may differ from the estimated amounts calculated in this way. For example, the actual F&A costs of a sponsored history project might be far less than the estimated value, whereas those of a high-energy physics project may be far more than the estimated value. However, the estimates represent average indirect costs. When summed, the calculated F&A costs of all individual projects equal the overall institutional F&A costs.

In this example, the MTDC is the base. Some funding agencies use a base different from the MTDC, such as total salaries and wages or modified total costs. In those cases, the project-specific F&A is calculated from the ratio of the project base to the institutional base. Regardless of which base is used, it must be used consistently throughout the calculations.

Summary

In several contexts, universities want to assign indirect costs to specific cost objectives. A commonly used method is based on a cost objective's proportional benefit from the indirect costs. In other words, proportional indirect cost allocation assigns a percentage of an indirect cost to each cost objective benefiting from the cost. In the *Uniform Guidance*, the federal government has well-established methods for allocating indirect costs (F&A costs) incurred by a university in the performance of a grant or contract. Because most universities receive and must account for federal funds, the government's method has become the de facto standard in academic institutions. The first step in the indirect-cost allocation process is to identify the institutional cost objectives. If the goal is to seek reimbursement of indirect costs incurred while conducting government-sponsored research, the cost objectives are the university's four major functions: instruction, research, other sponsored activities (for example, public service), and other institutional activities (for example, auxiliary services). After arranging costs itemized in the financial statements into functional categories, all federally excluded and unallowable costs are subtracted, yielding the MTDC. Indirect costs are then assigned to eight cost pools specified in the *Uniform Guidance*. The indirect costs in all eight pools are allocated proportionally to the four institutional cost objective pools using a step-down method. Lastly, institutional indirect cost rates are calculated by dividing each cost objective's indirect costs into its MTDC base. The *Uniform Guidance* caps administrative indirect cost rates at 26 percent. Institutions with less than $10 million in direct costs may use a simplified method, with only one cost objective and indirect cost pool, for determining indirect cost rates. And there is a very simple *de minimus* default method. Project-specific indirect costs are calculated by multiplying the project's MTDC by the institutional indirect cost rate.

Notes

1. National Association of College and University Business Officers, "College and University Cost Identification and Allocation" (1997), http://www.nacubo .org/documents/business_topics/Shipley%20cost%20allocation%20paper -FINAL.pdf (accessed April 3, 2017).

2. 2 C.F.R. § 200 App. III

3. 2 C.F.R. § 200 App. III A.1.b(1).

4. 2 C.F.R. § 200 App. III A.2.e(2).

5. National Association of College and University Business Officers, "F&A Cost Rate Proposal" (2002), http://www.nacubo.org/Documents/NACUBO%20 -%20University%20of%20Cost%20Analysis%20Case%20FYxx.pdf (accessed February 6, 2015).

6. 2 C.F.R. § 200.436.

7. University of California, "Useful Life Indices for Equipment Depreciation," http://eulid.ucop.edu/ (accessed June 8, 2015).

8. 2 C.F.R. § 200 App. III B.3.

9. 2 C.F.R. § 200.449 (c)(4).

10. 2 C.F.R. § 200.449 (b)(7).

11. 2 C.F.R. § 200 App. III B.4.

12. David Kennedy, "DCA Best Practices Manual—COGR Interpretations, December 2007" (2011), http://www.cogr.edu/Pubs_Financial.cfm (accessed August 3, 2015).

13. 2 C.F.R. § 200 App. III B.4.c.

14. Office of Management and Budget, "Cost Principles for Educational Institutions," https://www.whitehouse.gov/omb/fedreg_a21060198/ (accessed August 19, 2015).

15. 2 C.F.R. § 200 App. III B.6.a.

16. 2 C.F.R. § 200 App. III B.6.b(2)c(1-2).

17. 2 C.F.R. § 200 App. III B.6.b(2)

18. Department of Health and Human Services, "DCA Best Practices Manual for Reviewing College and University Long-Form Facilities and Administrative Cost Rate Proposals" (Division of Cost Allocation, 2006), 87.

19. Huron Consulting Group, "Facilities & Administration (F&A) Cost Recovery Services," http://www.huronconsultinggroup.com/Expertise/Education/Research _Enterprise_Solutions/Facilities_and_Administration_Cost_Recovery_Services (accessed February 17, 2015); Maximus, "Cost Allocation Plans," http://www .maximus.com/financial-services/cost-allocation (accessed February 17, 2015).

20. 2 C.F.R. § 200 App. III D.

21. 2 C.F.R. § 200 App. III D (1).

22. Department of Health and Human Services, "Sample Indirect Cost Proposal Format—Simplified Method," Program Support Center, https://rates.psc.gov/fms/dca/shortform1.pdf (accessed September 14, 2015); Jason Guilbeault, "Simplified Method for Preparing the Facilities and Administrative Cost Rate Proposal," Maximus, http://ncuraregioni.org/uploads/3/3/6/2/3362892/52.simplified_method_idc.pdf (accessed February 18, 2015).

23. 2 C.F.R. § 200.414(c)(4)(f).

Chapter 10
Institutional Financial Strategies

Variable Financial Strategies

Each institution has its own financial strategies for raising, investing, and spending money. As shown in the preceding chapters, some financial strategies are standard because they must adhere to GAAP or federal guidelines. Or, there is really only one practical way of doing them. But other strategies can vary, depending on institutional history, culture, and preferences. This variability distinguishes one university from another. Indeed, two universities may appear quite similar from a statistical perspective—comparable mission, enrollment, research expenditures, and so forth. But, internally, they may be quite dissimilar due to different approaches to financial management. For example, despite their outward similarities, Stanford University and the University of Southern California are quite dissimilar internally due, in part, to different financial practices.

Regardless of approach, the ultimate goal of most financial strategies is to increase the institution's capacity to accomplish its mission. More succinctly, the goal is to build capacity: to increase faculty members' productivity, improve the physical plant, provide helpful support services, and develop a sound overall academic infrastructure. Funds are raised, invested, and spent in ways designed to increase capacity, either implicitly or explicitly.

Variations in key strategies can have an impact on university finances. It would be impractical to survey the impact of all potentially variable strategies; there are too many of them. Suffice it to say that the impact doesn't always involve a lot of money. In fact, sometimes, very little money is involved. But, within the university, even a small pool of discretionary cash can make a significant improvement in morale. Conversely, sometimes the impact involves a lot of money. And this can create subtle tensions that can modulate morale. These concepts will be developed by examining different approaches to several financial strategies common to many universities.

But first, the core of many, if not most, institutional financial strategies will be introduced: the return on investment.

Return on Investment

Like most businesses, universities seek financial gain from the investment of their resources. Universities spend money on faculty members or facilities with the expectation of monetary return. Stated differently, the university invests its own money and expects a return on that investment. The return on investment (ROI) may derive directly or indirectly from myriad sources such as tuition income generated by the faculty members' teaching endeavors; state appropriations for agricultural extension activities; grant and contract awards; royalties and licensing income.

A prime example occurs when a new faculty member in the sciences and engineering is given start-up funds to establish an independent research program. Implicitly, the faculty member is expected to generate income for the university from grant funds within several years. For the university, reimbursed indirect costs yield the best ROI, mainly because they are unrestricted, unlike the direct costs. Therefore, the faculty member is expected more specifically to generate indirect cost reimbursement from federal grants within several years. This expectation may not be written explicitly in an employment contract, but it is usually made quite clear by the dean or department chair.

Politically, this ROI concept within the university is unpalatable to many faculty members. It adds a mercenary pall on the academic profession. But, among deans and higher-level administrators, ROI is widely accepted as a financial metric in the decision-making process when hiring new faculty members and, for that matter, retaining more senior faculty members.

In quantitative terms, the relationship between the investment and the return, the ROI, is expressed as a percentage:

$$ROI = \frac{(return - investment)}{investment} \times 100\%$$

So, if a faculty member receives $500,000 in institutional start-up funds (the investment) and, within 5 years, $1,500,000 in indirect costs from federal grant funds (the return),

$$ROI = \frac{(1,500,000-500,000)}{500,000} \times 100\% = 200\%$$

In this case, the university doubled its money in 5 years. It invested $500,000 and earned a net $1,000,000 (that is, $1,500,000–$500,000). This is a fairly typical benchmark return in many science and engineering fields. Indeed, as a rule of thumb at some universities, newly hired engineering faculty members are expected to generate indirect cost reimbursement from external sources exceeding at least three times the amount of their start-up package within five years, which corresponds to an ROI of 200 percent.

Understandably, the ROI may not always be positive. In this example, if the faculty member generates less than the $500,000 investment, the ROI would be negative, and the university would have lost money on the investment. Naturally, that is not desirable. If the faculty member generates $500,000, the return equals the investment, and the ROI would be zero. At least, the university would break even. Of course, the expected ROI will depend on the faculty member's research topic, federal funding priorities, and various other factors. But few universities expect an ROI less than zero percent in well-funded areas of engineering and the natural sciences. They expect at least to break even.

Indeed, a positive ROI is the goal of most strategic investments. In a nonresearch environment, a newly hired faculty member may be expected to teach several undergraduate courses each year. The salary constitutes the investment, and tuition income constitutes the return. If the target ROI is not met because of insufficient enrollment in one or more courses, the faculty member may be assigned additional responsibilities. A football coach is expected to win games. The coaching staff salaries, player scholarships, equipment, and stadium facilities constitute the investment, and ticket sales, broadcast revenue, and donations constitute the return. If the ROI is not met, the coach is fired. And likewise for investments throughout the campus.

With this core in the background, several examples of variable strategies for managing university resources will now be looked at through a financial lens.

Institutional Insurance

As an introductory example, strategies for managing risk will be examined. The traditional risk management strategy has been to carry insurance programs for liability and property. Like most individuals, universities take the position that they can afford the cost of insurance but not the cost of a catastrophic casualty, which would probably come out of the operating budget. The managed risk is an acceptable return on the insurance costs from both the administrators' and the faculty members' perspective.

Typically, universities will carry at least four different kinds of insurance:

- liability
- automobile
- medical malpractice
- property

Liability insurance covers all employees acting in the course and scope of their university employment, paying for losses incurred by outside parties resulting from the negligent performance of university operations. In addition to general liability insurance, automobile insurance covers liability and physical damage for university-owned and -leased vehicles. And it usually covers rental vehicles, as well. Similarly, medical malpractice insurance covers liability for medical professionals acting in the course and scope of their university employment. Of course, this is particularly important coverage for university-affiliated medical schools and hospitals. But it is important also for employees at campus health-care facilities, such as student health centers. Property insurance covers university-owned property, generally including privately owned property in the university's custody. Typical programs cover a long list of perils, including theft, vandalism, water damage, and fire. For businesses, property claims are the most common type of claims.[1]

In some cases, the insurance is bought from commercial vendors. In those cases, the university is fully insured. However, since the cost of insurance premiums has escalated over the past several decades, more and more universities have established in-house, self-financed insurance programs backed up by commercial policies for extraordinarily expensive losses. These programs adhere closely to commercial insurance guidelines on coverages and exclusions.

To fund these self-insured programs, the institutions set up one or more reserve accounts to pay for property losses, third-party claim payments, and premiums for excess insurance. Depending on the university's budget model, departments may be charged annual premiums to pay for their coverage. For example, each fiscal year,

Harvard University charges departments a premium, allocated per building, to maintain the property and liability insurance reserve. Likewise, departments with university vehicles are charged an annual premium per vehicle to maintain the automobile insurance reserve.[2]

Commercial insurance policies may supplement these self-insurance programs to cover specific liability and property programs, especially if they are potentially very costly. Examples might include student events and athletic events. The cost of these supplementary policies is generally borne by the sponsoring organization.

Normally, universities pay for claims to replace or repair losses out of their various self-insurance reserve funds. For most perils, there is a deductible amount ranging from $1,000 to $5,000. Water damage, which can be particularly costly, is the major exception, with coverage limited to a small percentage, for example, 10 percent, of any loss over $50,000. Importantly, money in these reserve funds derives from the operating fund. As claims are paid, the reserve fund balance is replenished by transfers from the operating fund. Therefore, insurance payments reduce money available for other academic priorities. From an ROI vantage point, a university's risk management office must balance the generosity of insurance payments against other potential uses of the money. Sometimes, to faculty members' chagrin, other academic priorities outweigh generous or speedy insurance coverage.

Faculty Salaries

A priori, procedures for paying faculty salaries might seem straightforward: set a base salary and issue a paycheck once or twice per month. There might not appear to be much room for variation in this routine task. However, subtle differences in even the simplest aspects of these procedures arise at various universities. And less subtle variations arise in summer-salary and soft-money appointments. These variations have financial implications for both the faculty members and the university.

Nine-Month Appointments

In the various schools and colleges of most universities, generic tenure-track and tenured faculty appointments extend through the academic year. Traditionally, this has been from September through May. The actual dates and number of working days may vary, but these faculty members are paid only for work during the academic year—not the summer. Depending on the academic calendar, this translates into a 9- or 10-month appointment. Commonly, however, they are called nine-month appointments, regardless of the exact length of the academic year, and that term will be used for simplicity.

Often, the faculty members may choose whether to receive their pay only during the academic year (with 9 or 10 monthly payments) or spread out into 12 monthly payments. Some universities pay twice monthly, thus doubling the number of paychecks. Regardless, the percentages of withheld taxes and fringe benefits remain the same either way.

There are slight financial consequences of payment frequency. On the one hand, if salary is paid in nine installments, a faculty member can earn interest on the amount set aside for the unpaid summer months. On the other hand, if salaries are paid in 12-month installments, the university can earn interest on the difference between the monthly payments on a 9- and 12-month basis.

In either case, the amount of interest earned is small because of the short term of the investment. Nonetheless, over time and with many employees, the amounts add up. To illustrate how much is at stake, the interest earned by an individual faculty member and the university is calculated in table 10.1. Monthly payments, including fringe benefits (table 4.8), of a $100,000 academic-year salary are shown for 9- and 12-month pay periods. In each case, the total academic-year compensation (salary plus fringe benefits) is $129,480.

Looking at the 9-month payment examples, for a faculty member, 9-month gross salary payments of $11,111/month decrease to $7,778 net salary payment per month after taxes et cetera (estimated at 30 percent of the gross salary) are withheld. This is $1,945 more than the corresponding 12-month net salary payments ($5,833 per month). Over 9 months, the monthly differences add up to $17,509, assuming that none of it is invested. If the monthly difference ($1,945) is invested regularly at 2 percent annual interest, the forward value after 9 months is $17,617 ($17,509 in principal and $117 in interest). That is, the faculty member earns $117 annually by receiving payments over the 9-month period rather than the 12-month period.

For the university, extending payments (salary plus fringe benefits) from 9 to 12 months reduces the monthly payout to the faculty member by $3,597. Over 12 months, the monthly differences add up to $43,160. If the monthly difference ($3,597) is invested at 2 percent annual interest, the forward value after 12 months is $43,558 ($43,160 in principal and $398 in interest). Therefore, the university

Table 10.1. Interest earned when an academic-year salary is paid over a 9- or 12-month period

	Salary	
Academic year		
Salary	100,000	
Fringe benefit rate	29.48%	
Fringe benefits	29,480	
Total salary plus fringe benefits	129,480	
Monthly		
Number of monthly payments	9	12
Number of payments/month	1	1
Amount per payment (paid at end of month)	11,111	8,333
Fringe benefits paid per month by the university	3,276	2,457
Total monthly cost to the university	14,387	10,790
Taxes etc. withheld from monthly paycheck	30.00%	30.00%
Net monthly paycheck to the individual	7,778	5,833
Investment earnings per year		
Investment interest rate	2.00%	2.00%
Faculty		
Difference in monthly payment relative to 12 months	1,945	
Difference over all monthly payments relative to 12 months	17,509	
Forward value (over number of monthly payments)	17,626	
Net interest earned	117	
University		
Difference in monthly payment relative to 9 months		3,597
Difference over all monthly payments relative to 9 months		43,160
Forward value (over number of monthly payments)		43,558
Net interest earned		398
Number of faculty		1,000
Total interest earned		397,840

earns $398 annually for this individual faculty member by paying the annual salary over 12 instead of 9 months. That is not much money. But, if there are 1,000 faculty members with an average annual salary of $100,000, the university earns a total of $397,840 (which rounds up to $398,000). So, the interest earned in this case is quite small for each faculty member, but for the university as a whole, the total amount earned becomes more substantial as the number of faculty members increases. And the money is unrestricted and can be used for academic priorities. As a practical matter, the actual earned interest income available for academic uses must be adjusted for any additional costs to the university of issuing 12 instead of 9 paychecks.

12-Month Appointments

The appointments in several schools and colleges within a university extend through the entire year. Most notably, schools in the health sciences (medicine, nursing, allied health sciences, veterinary medicine, etc.) often have annual appointments. The rationale is that medical patients need treatment any time during the year; therefore, the faculty must be available for clinical instruction and service throughout the year. Similarly, colleges in agricultural sciences (agriculture, forestry, natural resources, etc.) have annual appointments. The rationale is that the growing season for most crops is in the summer; therefore, the faculty must be available for instruction and extension service during that time. In both cases, the appointments are for 12 months (with no vacation) or 11 months with 1 month of vacation (48 work weeks). For brevity, both appointments will be called 12-month appointments.

With some exceptions, faculty members with 12-month appointments are paid roughly 33 percent more than those with 9-month appointments. This corresponds to 3 additional months of salary at the 9-month rate. Therefore, the 12-month appointment does not necessarily increase the monthly pay, but it increases the number of months paid per year. So, if a 9-month appointment pays $100,000 annually ($11,111 monthly for 9 months), the corresponding 12-month appointment pays $133,333 annually ($11,111 monthly for 12 months). For the most part, fringe benefits rates are the same for 9- and 12-month appointments. Despite the added income, 12-month appointments aren't always desirable. The primary disadvantage is that the faculty member is expected to work for the university during the summer months. For some individuals, this is undesirable because it limits opportunities to undertake more lucrative or enjoyable projects during the summer months.

Summer Appointments

Faculty members with nine-month appointments may supplement their academic-year salaries via a university appointment during the summer. (Of course, they are free to work outside the university, as well.) The university appointment may be to teach a class, participate in a research project, or serve in some administrative role. In the simplest situations, the summer appointment extends the academic-year appointment into the summer. Accordingly, the summer salary is based on the academic year salary rate and is derived from the university operating budget. Alternatively, the appointment may be through some auxiliary enterprise, such as teaching a course offered by a university outreach program or summer school. In those cases, the summer-salary income is derived from the auxiliary enterprise budget, which obtains its revenue from user fees (which include course tuition and fees). Therefore, the salary amount may depend on market factors such as number of credit hours taught, student enrollment, and course production costs. For any university appointment, however, the summer-salary rate (that is, dollars per month) cannot exceed the academic-year rate, unless the summer workload exceeds academic-year workload standards. As an example, short, intensive courses offered between academic terms or during the summer commonly exceed academic-year workload standards and can be quite lucrative for the faculty members teaching the courses.

In the simplest scenario, summer salaries paid from grant or contract awards also extend the academic year appointment into the summer. The primary accounting difference is a change in funding source, from an academic-year to a summer-salary account code. In more complicated scenarios, summer salaries from grants and contracts may be considered "overload" or "supplemental" pay, which may require separate summer appointments.

The amount of summer salary that can be earned depends on the institution's definition of an academic year. Fewer weeks in the academic year means more weeks in the summer, and that means more pay periods in the summer and potentially more expense to the university but more income for the faculty member. This is illustrated in table 10.2, which presents 2 alternative definitions of an academic year: 39 weeks (the standard 9-month appointment) and 37 weeks. They correspond to 13 and 15 weeks in the summer, reckoned as 33.33 and 40.54 percent of the total weeks in the academic year, respectively. Noticeably, the $100,000 base salary translates into a higher weekly salary for the shorter (37-week) academic year. Moreover, although the base salaries are the same ($100,000), during the summer, the 15-week appointee can earn up to $7,207 ($40,541 − $33,333) more than the 13-week appointee because of higher pay over more pay periods. For the faculty member, that is good, of course. For the university, it is more costly, but only if the summer salary isn't paid by an externally funded source (such as a federal research grant).

Universities may limit how much can be paid to faculty members employed during the summer in terms of months instead of dollars.

Table 10.2. Summer salary calculations for two alternative academic-year lengths

	Academic year	
Number of weeks	39	37
Weekly salary	2,564	2,703
Monthly salary	11,111	11,712
Total salary	100,000	100,000
	Summer	
Number of weeks	13	15
% of academic year	33.33	40.54
Number of months	3.00	3.46
Weekly salary	2,564	2,703
Total summer salary	33,333	40,541
Base + summer salary	133,333	140,541

Note: Base salary = 100,000.

At maximum, a faculty member on a 9-month (39-week) appointment can receive 3 months of summer salary, with no formal vacation time. Reckoning that faculty members will take one month of vacation, some universities limit summer-salary support to two months. And, in some institutions, even more elaborate formulas determine how many months can be claimed. At the University of Wisconsin–Madison, for example, "faculty, academic staff, or limited appointee on an academic year (9-month) appointment may not exceed eight months (8/9ths) of summer salary over any consecutive three-year period."[3] Seemingly, the university expects faculty members to take at least one month of vacation every three years.

Soft-Money Appointments

A soft-money appointment refers to a university appointment supported by salary derived in part or entirely from an external source, such as a federal grant or contract. In this context, "soft" means that the salary money is no longer available when the external source, such as a grant, expires. This is in contrast to "hard," which means that the salary source is not dependent on some source external to the university; the salary is in the university's budget. The soft-money component of an appointment can be for an entire year or a specific bloc of time.

Like universities, some federal agencies also limit the number of months of salary support that can be paid from grants and contracts. The NSF, for example, limits "senior personnel" such as the principal investigator and faculty members to two months of salary per year from all NSF sources unless specifically budgeted and approved by the NSF.[4] *Note:* This means that if a PI has three active NSF awards, the total number of months for which support may be received cannot exceed a total of two months from all three awards, not two months from each of the three awards. This regulation effectively limits NSF soft salary support to two months.

The NSF two-month policy does not apply to "soft-funded" employees such as research scientists and similar individuals who are normally supported only through sponsored funding. Their positions are not supported by permanent operating-budget dollars. Nor does it apply to postdoctoral fellows.

More importantly, the federal government limits the number of salary dollars that can be earned from a federal award. Salary paid from federal sources cannot be at a rate higher than the recipient's institutional base salary (IBS). In this context, the IBS is defined as the annual compensation (not counting fringe benefits) paid by the university for an individual's appointment, whether that individual's time is spent on research, instruction, administration, or other activities. It excludes any income that an individual earns outside of duties performed for the university. According to the *Uniform Guidance*, "charges for work performed on Federal awards by faculty members during the academic year are allowable at the IBS rate . . . in no event will charges to Federal awards, irrespective of the basis of computation, exceed the proportionate share of the IBS for that period. This principle applies to all members of faculty at an institution."[5] Thus, faculty members cannot incorporate higher salaries into their grant budgets without formal pay raises authorized by the university.

In addition to this general limitation on salary rates, the NIH limits the dollar amount of salary that an individual may receive annually from an NIH grant. The maximum amount changes occasionally; in 2017, the cap was $187,000. Therefore, regardless of an individual's IBS, she may not receive more than $187,000 in salary support from the NIH. Incidentally, the NSF does not have this cap.

When institutional base salaries are less than the NIH cap, salaries up to the cap can be awarded. But, when they exceed the cap, the NIH adjusts the actual amount that can be awarded based on the cap and the effort. These adjustments for a $200,000 12-month salary, which exceeds the cap, are illustrated in table 10.3. Three appointment types are shown: full-time 12-month, full-time 9-month, and half-time 12-month. The calculation algorithms are the same for each appointment type, so, for pedagogical simplicity, attention

Table 10.3. Salary adjustments made by the NIH when institutional base salaries exceed the current salary limitation (restriction)

	Appointment type		
	Fulltime 12-month	Fulltime 9-month	Halftime 12-month
Institutional base salary	200,000	150,000	100,000
Effort to be expended on project	50.00%	30.00%	30.00%
Requested			
Direct salary requested	100,000	45,000	30,000
Fringe benefits rate	29.48%	29.48%	29.48%
Fringe benefits requested	29,480	13,266	8,844
Subtotal requested	129,480	58,266	38,844
F&A rate	48.01%	48.01%	48.01%
F&A requested	62,166	27,974	18,650
Total requested	191,646	86,240	57,494
Awarded			
Direct salary annual restriction	187,000	140,250	93,500
Direct salary restriction based on effort	93,500	42,075	28,050
Fringe benefits	27,564	12,404	8,269
Subtotal restricted	121,064	54,480	36,319
F&A	58,125	26,157	17,437
Total restricted award	179,189	80,635	53,757
Reduction due to restriction	12,457	5,605	3,737

will focus on the full-time 12-month appointment. With 50 percent effort on the project, the investigator requests 50 percent salary support from the NIH: $100,000 annually (50 percent of $200,000). After adding fringe benefits and F&A costs (table 9.22), the total salary request becomes $191,646. But the NIH adjusts the award to keep within the cap. In this case, at 50 percent effort, the maximum salary award is $93,500 (50 percent of $187,000). Adding fringe benefits and F&A costs to this amount results in a total award amount of $179,189, which is $12,457 less than the request.

As shown implicitly in this example, an individual's base salary per se is not constrained by the federal salary limitations. The rate limitation simply limits the amount that may be awarded and charged to federal grants and contracts. The university may pay a salary amount that exceeds the salary cap with nonfederal funds. So, in this example, to bring the salary up to $200,000, the university must pay $6,500 ($100,000 − $93,500) with nonfederal funds. Notably, if the investigator has more than one NIH grant award, the total salary that can be funded from all awards is $187,000; the $12,457 reduction in this award cannot be paid from another NIH award.

Some schools, primarily elite medical schools, require most faculty members to generate a fraction of their salary from external sources: grants, contracts, clinical revenue, endowments, and so forth. In addition, some institutions hire soft-money researchers. They must generate a fraction—if not all—of their salary from external sources; usually, their salary comes from grants and contracts. In return, they are not required to teach and perform pubic service. In these cases, the institution sets a base salary but contractually provides funding for less than 100 percent of this base; the faculty member must obtain the remaining fraction (up to 100 percent) from other sources. The university may guarantee a job (with tenure) but not a salary.

To mitigate the stress imposed by these soft-money requirements, the university usually provides bridge funding for a year or so if grant income is insufficient to provide full salary. In addition, start-up packages for these faculty members usually provide enough funding to cover up to a year or two of salary support. Furthermore, to allow new researchers time to generate sufficient grant income to pay their full salary, the institution may begin by paying the full salary but then gradually decrease its contribution over a several-year period. This is illustrated in figure 10.1, where the institution paid the full salary during the first year but reduced its contribution by 25 percent per year after that. By year five, it no longer contributed to the salary; the researcher must obtain full salary from grants or other external sources.

Outside Employment

Universities may allow faculty members a specific amount of time for outside employment. The amount of time varies between institutions. For example, the University of California system allows 39 days per academic year (one day per week) and the California State University system allows 40 days per academic year.[6] Faculty members may use this time for any purpose, such as consulting, working on a start-up company, or other enterprise. And there are no limitations on how much money can be earned during this time. Other institutions may not specify time allowed for outside employment, requiring institutional approval on a case-by-case basis. Furthermore, as at Colorado College, they may insist that the outside employment "should contribute to the faculty member's professional development and, when possible, enhance the public reputation of the College."[7]

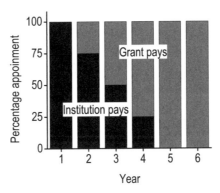

Figure 10.1. Transition from institutional salary support to externally generated salary support. The institutional base salary is 100 percent of the salary.

Despite the leniency of these outside-employment policies, there are two fundamental caveats pertaining to ethics. First, the university must always remain the primary work commitment. Otherwise, the faculty member has a conflict of commitment, and that can be cause for dismissal. Second, by law, faculty members receiving federal grant funds must disclose to the institution any financial interests exceeding $5,000, and the institution must develop a plan to manage any significant financial conflicts of interest.[8] Within these ethical boundaries, many faculty members benefit financially from the opportunity to work part-time outside the university. Indeed, this opportunity is an expected perquisite at many institutions.

Incidentally, a university's outside employment policy provides an interesting measure of a faculty member's hourly worth. This requires explanation. Normally, faculty members are required to work as many hours as necessary to do their job (teaching, research, and service). Consequently, faculty members' salaries are not based on a specific number of hours or days worked per week, so the value of a day's work is not defined. However, this value can be imputed by dividing the annual salary by the number of days worked per year. This is illustrated in table 10.4. According to the US Office of Personnel Management, the standard work year consists of 260 days (2,087 hours.)[9] But if a faculty member is allowed 1 day per week for outside employment, the workweek consists of 4 and not 5 days, or 208 days per year. So, by this logic, the salary per day for a 4-day workweek is 25 percent more than for a 5-day workweek. In other words, the faculty members' hourly worth increases as the number of days allowable for outside employment increases. Of course, these calculations have no impact on the faculty member's IBS, but they can serve as benchmark remuneration for outside employment.

Table 10.4. Calculated salary per day for different allowances for outside employment, based on 100,000 annual salary

Days per week allowable for outside employment	0	0.5	1
Number of work days per week	5	4.5	4
Number of working days per year	260	234	208
Salary per day	384.62	427.35	480.77
Salary per hour	48.08	53.42	60.10

F&A Costs Reimbursement

Like faculty salaries, a priori the administration of reimbursed F&A costs might not seem to be terribly complex. The university incurs research-related indirect cost expenses, claims reimbursement from the federal government, and spends the money according to its own priorities. However, subtle differences in the administrative approach to reimbursed F&A costs can have a significant impact on university finances.

F&A Rate Comparisons

As an introductory example, the financial implications of varying institutional strategies for calculating F&A rates will be examined. Although the calculation algorithms must adhere to the *Uniform Guidance*, universities differ in how aggressively they account for indirect costs. Less aggressive universities risk "leaving money on the table," while more aggressive universities risk costly and embarrassing disallowances. Indeed, in 1990–1991, Stanford University was the subject of a federal audit, congressional hearings, and numerous media reports because of questionable items (such as a $1,200 early nineteenth-century Italian fruitwood commode) included in the F&A general administration indirect cost pool.[10]

As shown in chapter 9, F&A rates depend on the amount of indirect costs incurred for each cost objective. The negotiated F&A rates for on-campus organized research vary considerably, ranging between about 40 and 70 percent of MTDC. To demonstrate the range of values, the F&A rates of the top 50 research universities ranked according to research during 2014–2015 were analyzed statistically.[11] The average value for all of these institutions is 56 percent of MTDC. As shown in figure 10.2 (*left panel*), the average values for the 22 public and the 28 private institutions are 54 and 59 percent of MTDC, respectively; this difference is significant statistically ($t_{39} = 4.02$, $P_{2\text{-tailed}} = 0.0003$). The gap between public and private institutions appears to be narrowing, however. Using data from the late 1980s, Charles A. Goldman and T. Williams reported that the

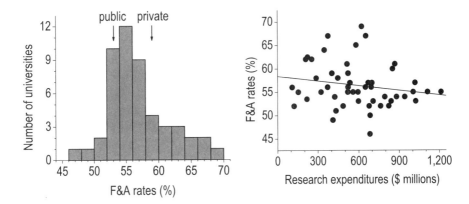

average F&A rates for public and private universities were 47 and 60 percent, respectively.[12]

These differences raise an intriguing question: Why do private universities have higher average F&A rates than public universities? There are no definitive answers to this question. However, there is a reasonable speculative answer based on differences in financial strategies: private universities have greater incentives to maximize F&A cost recovery. As William F. Massey and Jeffrey E. Olson put it, the disparity is because "private universities have different sources of financing and benefit more from cost recovery."[13] In their analysis of F&A rates, Martha Lair Sale and R. Samuel Sale conclude: "Because private universities obtain a much smaller percentage of their support from public sources than do public universities, private universities may have an institutional incentive to be more aggressive in pursuing higher F&A cost recovery rates. Public universities often have less incentive to identify and recover indirect costs because of their relations to state funding sources that require certain recovered costs be forfeited."[14] Thus, differences in the incentive to claim F&A reimbursement translate to differences in the financial strategies for supporting sponsored research.

Because the administrative rate is capped at 26 percent, which applies to most universities, difference between F&A rates must be in the facilities rate component. And a major expense in that component is building depreciation. Unlike private universities, public universities often benefit from the state's payment of building and other infrastructure costs. Some public institutions may not always include all of these costs, which can be substantial, in their F&A rate calculations—although the *Uniform Guidance* allows reimbursement of state-incurred expenses such as depreciation. Private universities don't receive this state support; they must pay these costs

Figure 10.2. F&A rates for on-campus organized research of 50 major research universities in 2014-2015, with the average values (arrows) for public and private universities (*left panel*), and their relationship with research expenditures (*right panel*)

themselves. Consequently, they charge the federal government for these infrastructural costs through F&A reimbursement, and this raises their F&A rate. As the level of state support for public universities declines, their incentive to recover F&A costs increases; thus, public institutions may become more like their private counterparts in developing their F&A rates. Indeed, increasing incentives for public universities to recover F&A costs may explain the decreasing gap between the average rates of public and private universities.

Importantly, institutions with lower F&A rates don't necessarily have inferior research infrastructures. Nor do they necessarily have less research activity, as shown in figure 10.2 (*right panel*); F&A rates and research expenditures are not correlated ($r = -0.185$, $t_{48} = -1.304$, $P = 0.199$). Of course, institutions with newer, highly sophisticated research buildings may have higher F&A rates. However, several unrelated factors lower the F&A rate. Subcontracts lower the F&A rate because the institution can recover indirect costs on only the first $25,000 of the subcontract. Therefore, institutions with numerous subcontracts tend to have lower F&A rates. Likewise, institutions with numerous grants from government agencies (such as the USDA), nonprofit foundations, or industries that pay low or no indirect costs tend to have lower F&A rates. This occurs because all of the research funds received from any source go into the F&A base, the denominator of the rate calculation. Unless there is a corresponding increase in F&A costs, which is unlikely, this has the effect of lowering the final F&A rate and actually reducing the total reimbursement from the federal government.

F&A Reimbursement Allocation

As manifest in the different F&A rates, a key element of many financial strategies is incentive. Within the university, this includes incentives to develop innovative teaching materials, offer interesting courses, generate intellectual property, and so forth. Some universities offer a particularly powerful incentive to apply for research grants by distributing reimbursed F&A funds to the faculty members for investment in their research programs. To understand this incentive, it helps first to answer the question: What happens to F&A money when it is reimbursed? The answer depends on state and institutional policies.

In all cases, the F&A reimbursement funds are no longer considered federal money from an accounting perspective. Although the money comes from the federal government, it reimburses expendi-

tures paid from myriad sources of institutional money. Thus, reimbursed F&A funds have relatively few spending constraints; indeed,
from an accounting perspective, generally they are considered unrestricted funds. In that sense, they are quite valuable to the university. Moreover, because they are unrestricted, F&A reimbursement funds usually can be carried forward from one fiscal year to
the next, with no time limit on spending them, which further am-
plifies their usefulness and attractiveness to public universities.

Although the money is deposited into a university account, some
states do not allow public institutions to spend it—or at least not all
of it. In most cases, a public university can spend only what the legislature allows it to spend via an appropriation, regardless of the
money's source. For example, if the university collects $100 million
in F&A costs but the legislature authorizes only $70 million in ex-
penditures from this source, the remaining $30 million cannot be
spent until the state increases the spending limit. And usually that
requires legislation. (The CFO must accurately predict future F&A
cost recovery to avert this situation.) Or, the legislature uses F&A
costs to cover part of the university's state general-funds budget. Understandably, this is not considered a desirable situation by university administrators because they have little or no control over how
these F&A funds can be spent; the legislature does. In states where
this occurs, the president and the CFO probably will be trying regularly to convince state legislators to allow the university to have full
control of the F&A cost return.

On the premise that F&A reimbursement funds should be reinvested in research, governing board policies at some institutions or
state laws may designate use of reimbursed F&A funds to support
research. The support may not be apparent to most faculty members. For example, F&A reimbursement funds may be used to pay
for the costs of running the chief research officer's operations such
as sponsored projects administration, animal care, institutional review board, and so forth. In contrast, the support may be visible
explicitly. For example, the F&A reimbursement funds may be allocated transparently to deans and directors as a component of their
units' operating budget. A fraction also may be set aside for the provost's or the chief research officer's discretionary use, such as providing start-up funding and so forth. Regardless of the details, the
use of F&A reimbursement to support research constitutes university subsidization of the research effort if the university paid for
those reimbursed indirect costs using funds from other resources.

Many researchers consider themselves entitled to reimbursed F&A funds. In their opinion, "I wrote the grant that generated this money; the university wouldn't have gotten these funds if it weren't for me. So, that money belongs to me." Of course, this claim is fallacious because the F&A funds constitute reimbursement of expenses paid by the university. The individual researcher had negligible influence on how these expenses were incurred or how they were reimbursed. In a sense, the institution might claim that "we wouldn't have had these expenses if it weren't for you." Nonetheless, most institutions recognize that returning some of the recovered F&A to the researcher either directly or via a dean or director provides a goodwill incentive to submit more grant proposals. Again, any return of F&A recovery to the researcher constitutes subsidization of the sponsored research mission, and that subsidy must come from some other institutional source.

Incidentally, the institution is required to perform the specific aims of a research grant regardless of the disposition of reimbursed F&A funds—even if the university were to receive no reimbursed F&A funds. Within the institution, this obligation extends to the principal investigator. Moreover, the principal investigator's obligation remains unchanged if the institution were to reduce its level of indirect cost support, such as discontinuing janitorial service. This is because the F&A rate agreements address costs and not services. As the University of California, Berkeley puts it, the rate agreements "do not specify in any way levels of service to be provided to research projects."[15]

Research Expenditure Recording

The allocation of F&A costs within the university depends on the way an institution records research awards and expenditures. To put this in context: research institutions usually have academic departments and organized research centers and institutes. Typically, faculty members belong to home departments, where they teach and conduct research; and, accordingly, the home department administers the faculty members' appointments, paychecks, et cetera. However, some faculty members also conduct research in university research centers and institutes or in collaboration with members of another home department. And they may submit grant proposals through these other units instead of their home department.

These multiple affiliations introduce complications into the institution's recording of grant revenue. Which unit gets credit for a faculty member's grant expenditures: the home department or the unit where the research was actually performed? To resolve this issue, most institutions require principal investigators to document how expenditures (and revenue) will be recorded before the grant application is submitted. This is an important a priori step because there are significant financial implications.

The implications are illustrated in figure 10.3, where sample research expenditure data are recorded by either the principal investigators' home departments (black bars) or performance units (gray bars) where the research was conducted. Most principal investigators' home departments are in the schools and colleges where they teach. However, some of their research is conducted in one of the research centers. For example, faculty members in the College of Natural Science's Department of Biology and the Department of Physics conduct research in the stem cell and the applied physics research centers, respectively. If research expenditures are credited to the home units (*left panels*), the College of Natural Science is credited with nearly $29 million in expenditures. However, if expenditures are credited to the research centers where the research was performed, the performance units (*right panels*), the college is credited with less than $2 million in expenditures. Conversely, the two research centers are credited with significantly more expenditures.

Financially, these differences in recorded research expenditures have further implications. The differences in the F&A cost allocations between expenditures recorded by home department versus performing unit (figure 10.3) are shown in figure 10.4. A positive difference means that the unit received a greater allocation when the F&A costs were attributed to the home units. And vice versa; a negative difference means that the unit received a smaller allocation when the F&A costs were attributed to the home unit. So, for example, when the home department (black bars) receives the expenditure credit, the College of Natural Science F&A cost allocation is nearly $14 million more than if the performing unit (gray bars) had received the credit. And the stem cell and applied physics research centers' allocations are about $7 million less. Understandably, if reimbursed F&A funds are distributed to the schools, colleges, and research centers proportionate to the amount they generated, the method for recording research expenditures can be a contentious topic on campus.

Recovering New Building Costs

Financial strategies for funding campus infrastructure also vary between institutions. Most rely heavily on debt financing, but

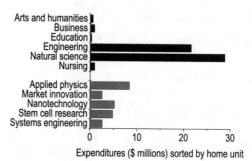

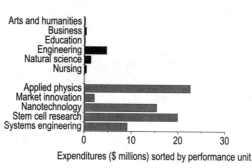

Figure 10.3. Research expenditures sorted by investigators' home departments (*top panel*) and units where the research was performed (*bottom panel*). Home departments and performance units are indicated by the black and the gray bars, respectively.

a few rely mostly on cash payment. And, in some cases, universities sell campus assets, such as buildings and utility grids, to private investors and then lease them back. Always, there is a sharp eye on the ROI.

In the context of research capacity, there is another source of revenue that may reduce the financial burden of acquiring and maintaining new buildings, specifically F&A reimbursement. Theoretically, depreciation, interest paid on long-term debt, and O&M are allowable costs for reimbursement by the federal government. The amount allowable for reimbursement of depreciation, interest, and O&M depends on one primary variable: the percentage of the building's space used for research. Stated slightly differently, the amount allowable for reimbursement is proportional to the percentage of the building used solely for research. For example, if only 75 percent of the building is used for research, then only 75 percent of the additional indirect costs are allowable for reimbursement. Thus, to recover the full costs of depreciation, interest, and additional O&M, the entire building must be used for research. But that is impractical because hallways, common areas, classrooms, and other areas not specifically for research must be deducted from the building's allowable research space. Significantly, the presence of students working on anything but a sponsored research project reduces the research space. Thus, more research and less instruction yield more reimbursement. And this trade-off sets the stage for fur-

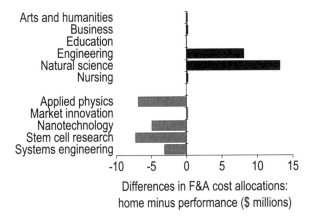

Figure 10.4. Difference in F&A cost allocations between recording expenditures by home departments (black bars) versus performing units (gray bars). Home departments are in the schools and colleges.

ther variability in financial strategies for maximizing F&A reimbursement in this context.

The actual amount of allowable reimbursement generated depends on the amount of additional MTDC from grant awards generated by the building's occupants. Theoretically, if F&A rates were recalculated continuously, this would not be the case, for every change in MTDC would cause the inverse change in F&A rates, thus keeping reimbursement constant. But university F&A rates are not recalculated continuously. They are predetermined and are recalculated every two to four years. Consequently, changes in MTDC during the period between base years result in changes in the amount reimbursed because they are not countered by an inverse change in the F&A rate.

A simple example illustrates this point. The financial parameters of a hypothetical $50 million building are shown in table 10.5. It was financed with a $25 million gift (equity) and a $25 million bond issue, maturing in 30 years (*upper left panel*). The new building means new operating costs. At 5 percent interest paid twice annually, the university pays $1,617,670 per year in bond interest costs. The new building also incurs additional O&M costs. It comprises 10.82 percent of the campus ANSF (*upper right panel*). Therefore, the incremental O&M costs ($600,000) are 10.82 percent of the campus allowable O&M costs ($5,546,815). And depreciation expenses increase. Assuming that the building's useful life is 50 years, depreciation is $1,000,000 per year. Altogether, the additional facilities costs of the new building (excluding the library) are $3,217,670. However, because only 75 percent of the building is used for research, the additional facilities costs allowable for reimbursement (F) are $2,413,253 (*lower panel*).

Table 10.5. Hypothetical new building financing and allowable F cost parameters

New building financing		O&M costs	
Cost	50,000,000	Campus ANSF	941,797
Equity	25,000,000	New building ANSF	101,875
Bond issue	25,000,000	New building % ANSF	10.82%
Bond payments		Campus allowable O&M	5,546,815
Rate	5.00%	New building O&M	600,000
No. of years	30		
No. of payments per year	2		
Interest per year	1,617,670		
Percent for research	75.00%		

Indirect cost	Additional building costs	Allowable F costs	F rates (%)
Depreciation	1,000,000	750,000	9.25
Interest	1,617,670	1,213,253	1.05
O&M	600,000	450,000	10.11
Total	3,217,670	2,413,253	20.41

The amount of additional MTDC that must be generated to recover the additional indirect facilities costs is shown in figure 10.5,
which derives from the parameters in table 10.5 and the F rates for
depreciation (9.25 percent), interest (1.05 percent), and O&M (10.11
percent) in table 9.22. If the building's occupants fail to generate any
additional MTDC, the total F&A reimbursement is the same as before the new building was constructed; there will be no additional
reimbursement. But, as the additional MTDC increases, more F&A
is recovered. The additional MTDC required to equal the allowable
F reimbursement (the break-even MTDC) can be calculated:

$$\text{break-even } MTDC = \frac{\text{allowable incremental costs}}{F \text{ rate}}$$

$$= \frac{\$2,413,253}{20.41\%} = \$11,823,873$$

Therefore, the new building's occupants must generate an additional
$11,823,873 in MTDC just to recover the allowable incremental costs
of depreciation, interest, and O&M. The need to bring in nearly $12
million in MTDC "to pay the bills" exerts implicit pressure on the
building's researchers. The impact of this pressure on faculty morale depends on the university's financial strategy: How important
is the need to recover these additional indirect costs? Or, asked differently: How important is a positive ROI in this situation?

In this context, there are several practical strategies for maximizing the facilities reimbursement. Buildings should be occupied to
the greatest extent possible with research projects that generate full

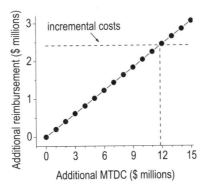

Figure 10.5. Additional facilities indirect cost reimbursement generated by additional MTDC. The allowable incremental costs of the new building ($2,413,253) and the break-even additional MTDC ($11,823,873) are shown by the horizontal and vertical dashed lines, respectively.

F&A costs. The University of California, Berkeley advises placing research activities in the "most expensive spaces including things like the stadium and the art museum."[16] Of course, indirect cost waivers and voluntary cost sharing should be eschewed. As a corollary, sponsored research that generates less than the full F&A reimbursement should be housed in rental space. Furthermore, administrative space should occupy the cheapest space on campus since the administrative rate is capped. In fact, it should be moved off campus if possible. And, as the University of California, Berkeley recommends, "keep faculty offices to one per faculty member regardless of multiple appointments."[17]

More general strategies for optimizing university resources may result in less F&A reimbursement but more net income. For example, if the option is available, administrative indirect costs should be direct charged. In that way the award pays the full costs, in contrast to the reduced amounts recovered through F&A cost reimbursement. Although interest on long-term debt is a reimbursable F&A cost, usually it is advantageous to keep that debt as low as possible because some grants may not pay the full F&A costs. Interest can be reduced by increasing institutional equity in a capital asset. Sources of equity include state funding, donor gifts, corporate partnerships, and the like.

Under-Recovery of Indirect Costs

As shown in the rate-proposal calculations (table 9.22), universities do not necessarily recoup the full indirect costs incurred by sponsored research. The under-recovery of indirect costs has significant ramifications for university finances in general and capacity building in particular. These ramifications will be examined in detail, but first, some relevant background information.

Shortly after World War II, the US government decided to conduct much of its research in universities. In his 1945 report to President Harry Truman, *Science, the Endless Frontier*, Vannevar Bush established the basis for that decision.[18] Arising from the report was the principle that universities "should be neither unduly taxed nor rewarded" in the conduct of government-sponsored research.[19] In other words, they were to be fully reimbursed for the total costs of government-related business expenses, as documented in their annual financial statement; they should break even. This practice was known as "cost-based reimbursement."

At the time, the ONR was the dominant sponsor of government research. It was accustomed to cost-based reimbursement from its dealings with commercial military vendors. Continuing this custom, the ONR treated universities in the same way, allowing them to recover the full costs of government-related business. But the ONR's dominance was to change, for the report also recommended the creation of a "national research foundation" to oversee this transition to university-based research. Accordingly, in 1950, Congress passed legislation establishing the NSF, which became the primary sponsor and, therefore, source of funding for the government's basic research. Moreover, not long after the creation of the NSF, the DHHS (mainly via the NIH) began to expand its research funding, and during its "golden years" from 1955 to 1968, it became the largest sponsor of university-based research.

The ascendance of the NSF and the NIH brought changes to the cost-reimbursement paradigm. Unlike the ONR, which viewed university-based research as a procurement, these agencies viewed their funding as a social-service subsidy to the universities. As Robert Rosenzweig notes, the NIH management culture "could hardly have been more different from that of the military. It was a granting rather than a contracting culture. Unlike the military, in which research was seen as a product that had to be bought in the interests of national defense, the social services tradition was that of the grant-in-aid, to enable the recipient to do something that the recipient would be doing even without the grant, though perhaps at a slower rate or a lower level."[20] This change in approach would have a profound impact on university finances, for it meant that the universities were expected to cover some of the costs incurred when conducting the government's research. They could no longer break even.

Ideally, under the principle of cost-based reimbursement, the federal government reimburses universities for all indirect costs of federally sponsored research. Therefore, a university should recover the costs of hiring new staff members to administer its sponsored grants and contracts, giving them pay raises, contracting preparation of F&A cost proposals to private vendors, subscribing to more academic journals, and so forth. Or, at least it should recover these additional indirect cost expenses as of the next base year, when the institutional F&A rate is renegotiated to reflect those additional costs.

Realistically, however, the federal government restricts the actual reimbursement. The full indirect costs are not recovered. As noted in the F&A rate calculations (chapter 9), the federally imposed 26 percent cap on administrative indirect cost reimbursement precludes full recovery for many academic institutions. Thus, if the calculated administrative (A) rate is 39 percent of MTDC, the university will not recover indirect costs equaling 13 percent of its MTDC (39 percent − 26 percent). Any expenses exceeding the 26 percent cap, regardless of necessity, must be borne by the institution. Furthermore, most federal agencies limit F&A rates on some kinds of awards.[21] For example, the USDA limits indirect costs to no more than 30 percent of total awarded funds on numerous grants and does not allow any indirect costs on others.[22] Similarly, the NIH limits indirect costs on research training grants to 8 percent of MTDC.[23] And, of course, the institution cannot claim reimbursement for any waived indirect costs on a federal award.

Most nongovernment foundations also limit indirect cost reimbursement. For example, both the American Heart Association and the Alzheimer's Association cap indirect cost recovery at 10 percent of MTDC. As pointed out by the Association of American Universities (AAU) and the Association of Public and Land-Grant Universities (APLU), "Historically, most foundations view their grants as supporting an activity or a scientist currently doing research in an area of science that falls within the mission of the foundation, therefore *supplementing* existing support the researcher or university has from other sources."[24]

Nonetheless, universities accept these nonfederal foundation grants, knowing that they (not the federal government) will be subsidizing the research funded by the award. Furthermore, these grants usually lower the federally-approved F&A rate. Their administrative overhead is relatively minor, so these grants don't appreciably affect the F&A rate numerator; besides, the administrative rate is usually capped at 26 percent. However, because all the funds received from any source go into the F&A base, the additional funding from foundations (or industry) goes into the denominator of the rate calculation. This has the effect of *lowering* the final F&A rate and,

Table 10.6. Indirect cost recovery in 2013

Institution type	Total research expenditures	Total indirect costs	Recovered indirect costs	Unrecovered indirect costs	% of indirect costs unrecovered
Public	44,870,141	9,860,725	6,540,926	3,319,799	33.66
Private	22,171,013	6,083,750	4,680,450	1,403,300	23.07
Totals	67,041,154	15,944,475	11,221,376	4,723,099	29.62

Note: Costs are in $ thousands.

therefore, reducing the total reimbursement from the federal government. The institution must subsidize the remaining indirect costs from other sources.

How much money is at stake due to under-recovery of indirect costs? According to the NSF, only about 70 percent of total indirect costs are reimbursed nationally. Stated the other way around, about 30 percent of indirect costs are not recovered by the universities. This is shown in table 10.6.[25] The percentage of unrecovered F&A costs is less for private universities than for public universities (23.07 versus 33.66 percent, respectively), due primarily to the private universities' more aggressive strategy for claiming reimbursement of facility costs. Procedurally, the NSF derives these percentages by calculating the expected recovery from all federal awards using institutional F&A rates and MTDC, which are available from federal databases. These data are compared to actual institutional F&A recovery, and the differences between expected and actual F&A recovery are considered to be under-recovered F&A costs. In a separate report, the RAND Science and Technology Policy Institute estimates that the federal government reimburses between 70 and 90 percent of the negotiated indirect costs.[26]

In 2013, the loss due to unrecovered F&A among all US research universities was about $4.7 billion (table 10.6). The amount unrecovered varies between institutions, of course. As an example, the University of California "estimates that the true costs of its research exceed direct and indirect cost recovery by as much as $600 million annually, and it must make up for this deficit from other sources."[27] Even for more modest research institutions, this loss can be in the millions of dollars annually. For example, the University of Alabama in Huntsville recovered 93 percent of its F&A costs—a very high recovery—but the unrecovered 7 percent still amounted to $1.3 million. Clearly, F&A reimbursement is not a "money maker" for universities.

Correlates of Increased Research Expenditures

Ironically, therefore, because of indirect cost under-recovery, the institution loses money on every research grant or contract, federal and nonfederal. These are real losses, not accounting artifacts; the F&A costs derive from actual expenditures (money out the door to pay utility bills, staff salaries, and so forth).

These losses incurred by sponsored research efforts must be covered by institutional funds, such as tuition, endowment income, state appropriations, and patent-generated revenue. As a consequence, there may be corresponding decreases in institutional expenditures available for instruction, public service, or student aid. The losses also may be covered by deferring scheduled maintenance of existing facilities, including buildings, laboratories, and classrooms. In other words, the institution may be forced to delay investments in maintaining and improving the facilities, equipment, and other infrastructure necessary for carrying out the institution's missions, including instruction and research, in order to pay for the unrecovered F&A costs of organized research.

With these losses, why would a university want to increase its research expenditures? Does income from some other source increase commensurately? Or is there some commensurate nonmonetary factor that yields a positive ROI? To answer these questions, the relationship between research expenditures and 12 sources of institutional revenue and prestige were analyzed statistically for 50 top universities ranked by research expenditures. Except when noted otherwise, data were collected from the 2015 *Carnegie Classification of Institutions of Higher Education*.[28] In each analysis, Pearson correlation coefficients (r) were calculated and tested for statistical significance at the 0.05 level. In other words, the correlations were considered significant statistically when $P \leq 0.05$. The data for each analysis were also plotted graphically (for example, figure 10.2, *right panel*) and examined for anomalies that might influence the correlation coefficients; none were found.

The results are summarized in figure 10.6. Three of the 12 sources of prestige and revenue (black bars) were correlated significantly with institutional research expenditures: faculty awards, annual giving, and the number of start-up companies. The other nine sources (gray bars) were not correlated significantly with research expenditures. Before drawing final conclusions, these results for each source will be placed in a rational context.

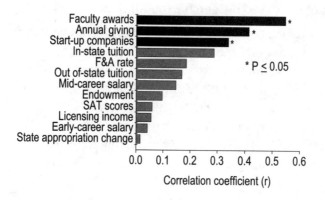

Correlation coefficient (r)

Figure 10.6. Correlations between research expenditures and 12 sources of prestige and revenue. The black bars (and asterisks) indicate that the correlation coefficient is significant statistically at the 0.05 level (P ≤ 0.05); the gray bars indicate that the correlation coefficient is not significant statistically at the 0.05 level (P > 0.05).

Institutional Prestige

From an idealistic point of view, increased research expenditures manifest expansion of the university's mission to generate new knowledge. In that sense, a prominent research enterprise is a source of institutional pride and prestige. Reflecting human nature, there are numerous rankings of institutional prestige using various measurements as the means of comparison, such as the number of faculty awards, SAT scores of the incoming freshman class, et cetera. Given the monetary burden of the research mission, the question arises whether research expenditures correlate with these measures of institutional prestige.

Faculty awards constitute a major source of institutional prestige. And there is a strong relationship between research expenditures and the number of faculty awards, as shown in figure 10.6; the correlation is quite significant ($r=0.546$, $t_{48}=4.520$, $P<0.001$). However, the causal relationship is unclear: does research prominence attract highly lauded faculty members, or do highly lauded faculty members generate more research grants? Either way, this source of institutional prestige goes up with increased research expenditures. Unfortunately, however, faculty awards do not normally generate significant revenue for the university, certainly not enough to offset the unrecovered F&A costs.

The SAT test scores of incoming students are another source of institutional prestige. But there is no apparent relationship between research expenditures and the median SAT scores of incoming students; certainly, the correlation between them is not significant statistically ($r=0.060$, $t_{48}=-0.413$, $P=0.681$). Thus, increased research expenditures (and the correspondingly increased number of faculty awards) do not necessarily attract undergraduate students with significantly higher SAT scores.

Abstractly, increased prestige raises the value of all degrees awarded by the institution and, therefore, the earning power of the degrees. Thus, the salaries earned by alumnae might be expected to correlate with research expenditures. But this is not necessarily the case. Neither early-career (entry-level) nor mid-career salaries of alumnae are correlated with a university's research expenditures ($r = 0.042$, $t_{48} = -0.293$, $P = 0.771$; $r = 0.147$, $t_{48} = -1.029$, $P = 0.309$, respectively).[29] Quite clearly, salary levels depend on factors other than the institution's research reputation.

From a marketing point of view, the prestige of research prominence might justify charging higher tuition and fees. But, as shown in figure 10.6, neither out-of-state nor in-state tuition is correlated with research expenditures ($r = 0.168$, $t_{48} = -1.184$, $P = 0.242$; $r = 0.287$, $t_{26} = 1.527$, $P = 0.139$, respectively).[30] In this analysis, tuition at private universities was considered out-of-state tuition. Like salary levels, tuition levels depend on factors other than the institution's research reputation, especially at public institutions.

Furthermore, in public institutions, state legislatures do not respond significantly to a university's research stature; "states rarely recognize research in their funding formulas."[31] Indeed, in all of 28 public institutions analyzed, state appropriations decreased between 2008 and 2014.[32] The magnitude of this change is not correlated with research expenditures ($r = 0.016$, $t_{26} = 0.080$, $P = 0.937$). Thus, public policy decisions about state funding for higher education, like tuition, depend on far more complex variables than research expenditures.

Fund-Raising

Does the cachet of enhanced research expenditures enhance a university's fund-raising appeal? More specifically, does increased prominence in research tend to attract increased funding from private donors? Apparently yes. As shown in figure 10.6, annual giving is correlated significantly with research expenditures ($r = 0.413$, $t_{48} = 3.142$, $P = 0.003$).[33] Presumably, private donors are enticed by an institution's research prowess; they prefer to invest in high-profile research universities. However, the overall endowment amount is not related significantly to research expenditures ($r = 0.097$, $t_{48} = 0.672$, $P = 0.505$), most probably because the assets for many institutions have been accumulating long before the explosive growth in government-sponsored research.[34]

Nonetheless, nationally, private donations *in toto* fall far short of the amount required to make up for unrecovered F&A. The 50 institutions in this analysis account for 45 percent of the overall national research expenditures and, by inference, 45 percent of the national unrecovered F&A, which would be $2.1 billion. The total annual giving by private donors equals $12.4 million, only 0.6 percent of the unrecovered F&A. Adding a 4 percent payout from their endowments to the annual giving brings this amount to $21.8 million, which is still vastly insufficient to offset the unrecovered F&A.

Licensing Income

Hypothetically, increased research expenditures might correlate with increased generation of intellectual property. And this would translate into more licensing income: more research, more patents, more licensing income. However, research expenditures are not correlated significantly with licensing income from intellectual property ($r = 0.056$, $t_{48} = -0.383$, $P = 0.704$), as shown in figure 10.7 (*left panel*).[35]

The total licensing revenue among all universities, $3.1 billion, would certainly offset the unrecovered F&A. However, as shown in figure 10.7 (*right panel*), the bulk of this revenue is concentrated in only a few institutions; indeed, 10 institutions account for more than 80 percent of the licensing income. Furthermore, most universities distribute about one-third of this income to the inventor, reducing the amount available for institutional purposes. Thus, "the vast majority of licensing deals yield little or no money, and for most universities the royalty returns are low."[36]

Economic Development

Although state and local governments seldom reward universities monetarily for increasing research expenditures, they generally support—indeed, expect—growth of their universities' research enterprise. The reason is economic; universities generate about $2.50 in economic activity for every $1 in research expenditures.[37]

Moreover, research universities spawn start-up companies that invigorate local economies. The number of startups correlates significantly with research expenditures, as shown in figure 10.6 ($r = 0.338$, $t_{48} = 2.443$, $P = 0.018$).[38] This positive correlation is amplified in the public's perception by the notable successes of start-up companies associated with particularly entrepreneurial universities

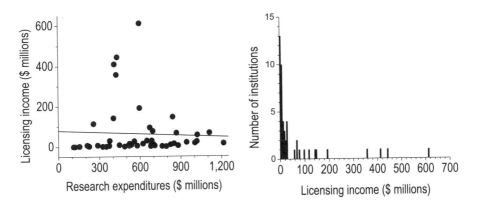

such as Stanford and the Massachusetts Institute of Technology (MIT). However, like licensing income (figure 10.7, *right panel*), start-up companies generate significant financial return for only a few universities. Of course, there is always the hope that the owner of a successful start-up company will someday make a generous donation to the institution.

Two technical comments about the statistical analysis warrant mentioning. First, the parametric correlation coefficients, r, assume that the data are from normal populations. As a control, the corresponding nonparametric Spearman correlation coefficients, rho, were also calculated. The results were not notably different. Second, all of the correlation coefficients were positive; none was negative. Although many of them were not significant at the 0.05 level, at least they did not indicate that increased research expenditures had a depressing impact on any of the 12 variables.

In conclusion, the financial strategies of many institutions reflect ambitions to increase research expenditures—that is, to generate more grants and contracts. The choice of these strategies comes at a cost. From a mercenary point of view, ultimately, most universities must rely on operating revenue from tuition, endowment income, and state appropriations to help cover the indirect costs of sponsored research. Except for annual giving, increased research expenditures do not correlate with any other substantial increase in revenue from other sources. Nonetheless, despite the financial ramifications of increasing research capacity, universities revel in one important consequence of lofty research expenditures: prestige. And, for members of the broad university community, that can be an invaluable return on investment.

Figure 10.7. Licensing income versus research expenditures (*left panel*) and the licensing income per university (*right panel*).

Summary

The potential return on investment (ROI) lies at the core of many financial strategies. Indeed, a positive ROI is the goal of most strategic investments. Managed risk is an acceptable return on the cost of insurance. To counter rising premiums, many universities have established self-financed insurance programs. From an ROI perspective, the generosity of an insurance payment must be weighed against other potential uses of the money. Faculty members with nine-month appointments may supplement their academic-year salaries via a university appointment during the summer. Universities usually limit how much can be paid to faculty members employed during the summer in terms of months instead of dollars. Some universities rely heavily on soft-money appointments supported by salary derived from an external source, such as a federal grant. Salary paid from federal sources cannot be at a rate higher than the recipient's institutional base salary. To mitigate the stress imposed by these soft-money requirements, the university usually provides bridge funding for a year or so if grant income is insufficient to provide full salary. Private institutions generally have higher F&A rates than public institutions, which may have less incentive to maximize F&A cost recovery. At some institutions, a fraction of F&A cost reimbursement is distributed to the faculty members as an incentive to compete for sponsored research grants. Universities can recover a fraction of the depreciation and interest expenses of a research building through F&A reimbursement. The amount reimbursed is proportionate to the amount of space within the building specifically for research. Universities do not recoup the full indirect costs incurred by sponsored research. So, why would a university want to increase its research portfolio? The answer is prestige; except for annual giving, increased research expenditures do not correlate with a substantial increase in revenue from any other sources.

Notes

1. Marianne Bonner, "10 Most Common Types of Claims," https://www.thebalance.com/common-insurance-claims-462673 (accessed March 14, 2018).
2. Harvard University, "How Does the University's Self-Insurance Programs Work?" https://rmas.fad.harvard.edu/faq/how-does-universitys-self-insurance-programs-work (accessed May 8, 2017).
3. University of Wisconsin–Madison, "Summer Appointments for Faculty, Academic Staff, and Limited Appointees on C-Basis," https://kb.wisc.edu/page.php?id=53006 (accessed October 6, 2017).

4. National Science Foundation, "Proposal & Award Policies & Procedures Guide" (2017), https://www.nsf.gov/publications/pub_summ.jsp?ods_key=gpg (accessed July 10, 2017). Ch. II C.2.g(i)(a).

5. 2 C.F.R. § 200.430 (a)(2).

6. California Faculty Association, "Collective Bargaining Agreement Article 35.3 (a), Outside Employment," https://www.calfac.org/resource/collective-bargaining-agreement-contract-2014-2017#additional-employment (accessed January 5, 2018); University of California, "General University Policy Regarding Academic Appointees, APM-025: Conflict of Commitment and Outside Activities of Faculty Members," www.ucop.edu/academic-personnel-programs/_files/apm/apm-025-07-01.pdf (accessed January 4, 2018).

7. Colorado College, "Faculty Handbook, XI. Employment Outside the College," https://www.coloradocollege.edu/search/?search=faculty+outside+employment (accessed January 6, 2018).

8. 45 C.F.R. § 50, subpart F.

9. Office of Personnel Management, "Pay & Leave Pay Administration Fact Sheet: Computing Hourly Rates of Pay Using the 2,087-Hour Divisor," https://www.opm.gov/policy-data-oversight/pay-leave/pay-administration/fact-sheets/computing-hourly-rates-of-pay-using-the-2087-hour-divisor/ (accessed January 5, 2018).

10. Donald Kennedy, *Academic Duty* (Cambridge, MA: Harvard University Press, 1997), 168–177.

11. National Science Foundation, "Higher Education R&D Expenditures, Ranked by FY 2015 R&D Expenditures: FYs 2006–15," https://ncsesdata.nsf.gov/herd/2015/html/HERD2015_DST_16.html (accessed January 4, 2018).

12. Charles A. Goldman and T. Williams, *Paying for University Research Facilities and Administration* (RAND Science and Technology Policy Institute, 2000), 39.

13. William F. Massy and Jeffery E. Olson, "Indirect Cost Rate Variation for University Research: Several Conventional Explanations Do Not Work," *Research in Higher Education* 35, no. 4 (1994).

14. Martha Lair Sale and R. Samuel Sale, "Indirect Cost Rate Variation Determinants in University Research, an Empirical Investigation," *Research in Higher Education Journal* 6 (2010).

15. University of California, Berkeley, "Facilities and Administrative Costs Overview," http://cfo.berkeley.edu/sites/default/files/facilities_and_administrative_costs_overview_mar2016.pdf (accessed May 2, 2017).

16. University of California, Berkeley, "Facilities and Administrative Costs Overview."

17. University of California, Berkeley, "Facilities and Administrative Costs Overview."

18. Vannevar Bush, "Science, the Endless Frontier" (1945), https://www.nsf.gov/od/lpa/nsf50/vbush1945.htm#ch3.9 (accessed December 24, 2014).

19. Robert Rosenzweig, "Politics of Indirect Cost," in *A Continuing Evolution—Responding to Federal Requirements* (Washington, DC: Council on Government Relations, 1998).

20. Rosenzweig, "Politics of Indirect Cost," 3.

21. Council on Governmental Relations, "Federal Funding Agency Limitations on Cost Reimbursement" (2010), http://cogr.edu/Pubs_Financial.cfm (accessed February 27, 2015).

22. National Institute of Food and Agriculture, "Indirect Costs Chart," US Department of Agriculture, http://www.csrees.usda.gov/business/awards/indirect _cost.html (accessed February 26, 2015).

23. National Institutes of Health, "Reimbursement of Facilities and Administrative Costs," http://grants.nih.gov/grants/policy/nihgps_2012/nihgps_ch7 .htm (accessed February 27, 2015).

24. Association of American Universities and the Association of Public and Land-Grant Universities, "Frequently Asked Questions (FAQs) About the Indirect Costs of Federally Sponsored Research," https://www.aau.edu/sites/default /files/AAU%20Files/Key%20Issues/Intellectual%20Property/Indirect-Cost-FAQ _2017.pdf?id=18472 (accessed May 19, 2015).

25. National Science Foundation, "Higher Education R&D Expenditures, by Type of Cost, Highest Degree Awarded, and Institutional Control: FYs 2012–13," http://ncsesdata.nsf.gov/datatables/herd/2013/html/HERD2013_DST_13.html (accessed March 27, 2015).

26. Goldman and Williams, *Paying for University Research Facilities and Administration*, 23.

27. University of California, "Annual Accountability Report" (2013) (accessed March 31, 2015), 115.

28. Carnegie Classification of Institutions of Higher Education, "2015 Update Public File," http://carnegieclassifications.iu.edu/downloads.php (accessed November 2, 2017).

29. PayScale, "College Salary Report 2014–2015," http://www.payscale.com /college-salary-report/all-bachelors (accessed April 16, 2015).

30. National Center for Education Statistics, "College Navigator," http://nces .ed.gov/collegenavigator/?q=tufts&s=all&l=93&ct=1+2&ic=1&id=168148#expenses (accessed April 1, 2015).

31. Nate Johnson and Takeshi Yanagiura, "How Did Revenue and Spending Per Student Change at Four-Year Colleges and Universities between 2006–07 and 2012–13?" (2015), http://www.aplu.org/library/public-university-spending -per-student-between-2006-07-and-2012-13 (accessed September 25, 2015); Research Universities Futures Consortium, "The Current Health and Future Well-Being of the American Research University" (2012), www.researchuniversities futures.org (accessed March 31, 2015).

32. Michael Mitchell, Vincent Palacios, and Michael Leachman, "States Are Still Funding Higher Education Below Pre-Recession Levels" (2014), http://www .cbpp.org/cms/?fa=view&id=4135 (accessed April 7, 2015).

33. Betty Capaldi Phillips et al., "The Top American Research Universities 2013 Annual Report" (2013), http://mup.asu.edu/2013-Report.html (accessed April 1, 2015).

34. Phillips et al., "The Top American Research Universities 2013 Annual Report."

35. Association of University Technology Managers, *AUTM U.S. Licensing Activity Survey FY 2011* (Deerfield, IL, 2012).

36. Richard Pérez-Peña, "Patenting Their Discoveries Does Not Pay Off for Most Universities, a Study Says," *The New York Times* (2013), http://www.nytimes .com/2013/11/21/education/patenting-their-discoveries-does-not-pay-off-for -most-universities-a-study-says.html?_r=1 (accessed March 31, 2015); Walter D.

Valdivia, "University Start-Ups: Critical for Improving Technology Transfer" (2013), http://www.brookings.edu/research/papers/2013/11/university-start-ups-technology-transfer-valdivia (accessed March 31, 2015).

37. Dean O. Smith, *Managing the Research University* (New York: Oxford University Press, 2011), 278–280.

38. Association of University Technology Managers, *AUTM U.S. Licensing Activity Survey FY 2011,* Deerfield, IL. Appendix B.

INDEX